MACMILLAN SOCIAL STUDIES

School Friends
Family life and the school as a community

Places Near and Far
The local community and the world beyond

Communities Today and Yesterday
Comparison of communities within the United States

The Earth and Its People
Communities in grassland, mountain, desert, polar, tropical , and island regions

The United States and the Other Americas
History and geography of the United States, and of
Canada and Latin America

Nations of the World
History and geography of Europe, Asia, Africa, and Australia

Macmillan Social Studies

The United States
and the Other Americas

Allen Y. King
Ida Dennis
Florence Potter

GENERAL EDITORS
Prudence Cutright
John Jarolimek

GEOGRAPHY CONSULTANT
Loyal Durand, Jr.

Macmillan Publishing Co., Inc.
New York
Collier Macmillan Publishers
London

Printed in the United States of America
ISBN 0-02-148040-0
9 8 7 6 5 4 3 2 1

Macmillan Publishing Co., Inc.
866 Third Avenue
New York, NY 10022
Collier Macmillan Canada, Ltd.

Contents

11

Diagrams, Charts, and Graphs

1 American Beginnings

Unit Preview

In very early times there were no people living in the area now known as North and South America. The northwestern tip of North America was separated from Asia by a narrow channel of the ocean. When the level of the oceans became lower, the strip of land between Asia and North America could be seen. People and animals could then walk between the two continents.

The people who made the crossing came to be known as Indians by the Europeans. Groups settled in different parts of the continent. They learned to use the resources of their environment. Some of them stayed in North America. Other Indians traveled south and created empires in Central and South America.

Except for the Vikings, Europeans discovered the Americas while trying to reach Asia by sea. This is what Christopher Columbus was doing when he reached the islands off the southeastern shore of North America. Many Europeans came to the Americas after Columbus. They soon realized that these lands were not Asia but a new land.

Columbus sailed under the flag of Spain. So did many of the explorers who followed him. Spain gained much territory in the Americas. England claimed land in North America because John Cabot sailed there. The French sent Cartier, Champlain, and La Salle. Henry Hudson explored the Americas for the Dutch.

Things to Discover

If you look carefully at the picture, map, and time line, you can answer these questions.
1. The arrows on the map show the routes taken by people who came to North America. To what part of the continent did most people come? What ocean did they cross?
2. The picture shows what people might have seen when they first landed on the northeastern coast of North America. What resources would settlers have looked for before starting a colony?
3. Did Cabot explore North America before or after Columbus sailed to America?
4. What did Champlain do in 1608?
5. How many years after De Soto reached the Mississippi did La Salle explore it?

Words to Learn

You will meet these words in this unit. As you read, you will learn what they mean and how to pronounce them. The Word List will help you.

altitude	natural resource
climate	navigator
colony	polar region
conservation	source
ecology	temperate region
glacier	tributary
immigrant	tropic
irrigation	tundra
latitude	vegetation
mouth	Viking

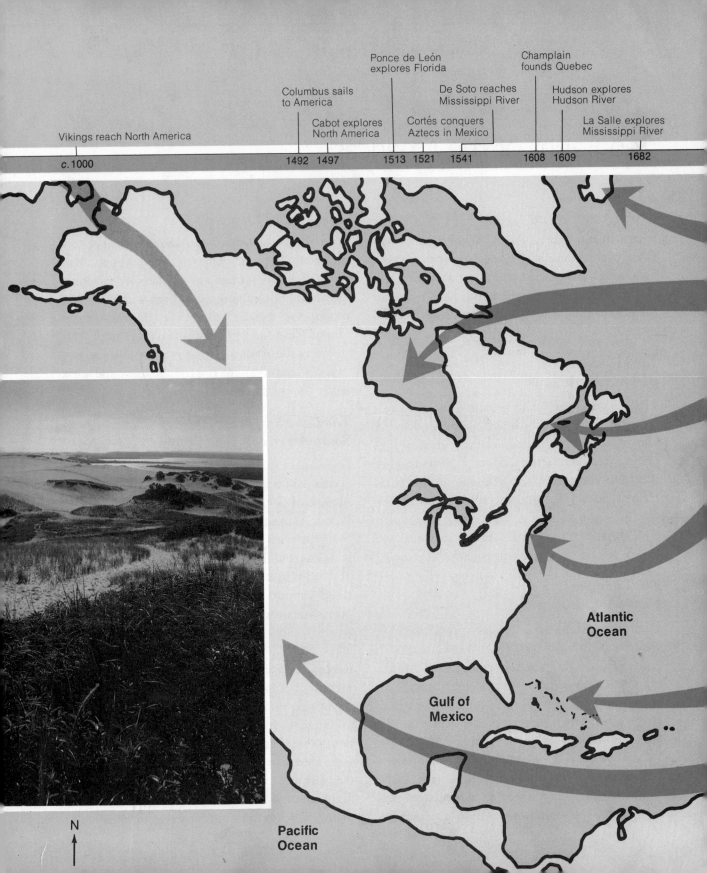

Vikings reach North America

Columbus sails
to America

Cabot explores
North America

Ponce de León
explores Florida

De Soto reaches
Mississippi River

Cortés conquers
Aztecs in Mexico

Champlain
founds Quebec

Hudson explores
Hudson River

La Salle explores
Mississippi River

c. 1000   1492 1497   1513 1521 1541   1608 1609   1682

Atlantic
Ocean

Gulf of
Mexico

Pacific
Ocean

N

1

Geography of the Americas

Most of you who study this book live somewhere in the United States. What kind of surface does the land have where you live? Does it have hills? Is it a level region, or a plain? Or is it a plateau (pla tō′), where the land is higher than the land around it and almost level?

Land Features of the Americas

The map on page 13 shows the different kinds of land surfaces of North and South America. A map which shows plains, hills, mountains, and plateaus is called a physical map. Your teacher will help you find where you live on this map. How is the surface where you live shown? The map key will help you. Find other places that have the same kind of land surface as where you live. What do the other colors in the key show?

The Land Surface of North America

High rugged mountain ranges extend through western North America from Alaska to South America. The sharp peaks of the Rocky Mountains rise high in the sky. Find the Rockies on the physical map on page 13. West of the Rockies is a wide plateau region. You can see this high, almost level, land on the map.

Near the Pacific Ocean are other high mountain ranges. In many places the mountains slope to the Pacific Ocean. Deep valleys separate the ranges. East of the Rockies is a great plains region. Find it on the map.

In the eastern part of our country is a low mountain region. This is the Appalachian (ap′ə lā′chē ən) Highland. The Appalachian ranges are not so steep or so high as the western mountains. Fertile valleys lie between their ranges. Find the Appalachians on the map.

Along the Atlantic Coast is a low level region called a coastal plain. It extends south and west along the eastern coast.

The Land Surface of South America

Look again at the physical map of North and South America on page 13. As you can see, the surface of South America is much like that of North America.

In the west the high Andes (an′dēz) Mountains extend from the Caribbean (kar′ə bē′ən) Sea to the southern tip of South America. Find these mountains on the map. Their highest peaks are always capped with snow, even on the equator. High valleys and narrow plateaus, blue lakes and rushing streams lie between these mountain ranges. The Andes are the second highest mountains in the world. The world's highest mountains are in Asia.

Ranges of low mountains are found in eastern South America. These are the Guiana (gē ä′nə) and Brazilian (brə zil′yən) highlands. Wide plateaus and plains stretch between the eastern highlands and the Andes. Find these highlands, plains, plateaus, and mountains on the map.

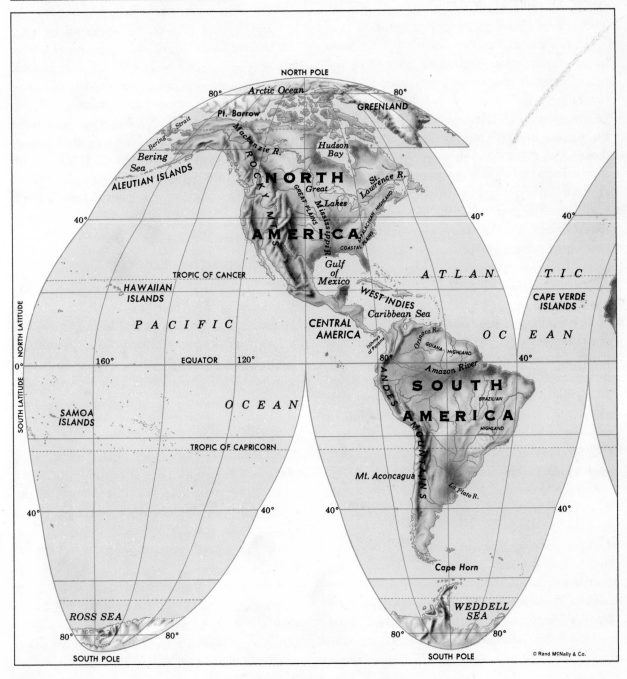

NORTH AND SOUTH AMERICA

0   400   800   1600 Miles
0   644   1287   2576 Kilometers

Mountains
Plateaus
Hills
Plains

NORTH POLE

80°   *Arctic Ocean*   80°
GREENLAND

Bering Strait
Pt. Barrow
Mackenzie R.
Hudson
Bay
Bering Sea
ALEUTIAN ISLANDS
R O C K Y   M T S.
N O R T H
Great
Great Lakes
St. Lawrence R.
GREAT PLAINS
Mississippi R.
APPALACHIAN HIGHLAND

40°   A M E R I C A   40°   40°

TROPIC OF CANCER
COASTAL PLAINS
Gulf
of
Mexico
A T L A N   T I C

HAWAIIAN
ISLANDS
WEST INDIES
CAPE VERDE
ISLANDS

P A C I F I C
CENTRAL
AMERICA
Caribbean Sea
O C   E A N

NORTH LATITUDE
0°
SOUTH LATITUDE

160°   EQUATOR   120°
Isthmus of Panama
80°   *Orinoco R.*
GUIANA   HIGHLAND
40°

Amazon River
O C E A N
S O U T H
BRAZILIAN

SAMOA
ISLANDS
A M E R I C A
HIGHLAND

A N D E S   M O U N T A I N S

TROPIC OF CAPRICORN

Mt. Aconcagua
La Plata R.

40°   40°   40°   40°

Cape Horn

ROSS SEA
WEDDELL
SEA

80°   80°   80°   80°
SOUTH POLE   SOUTH POLE

© Rand McNally & Co.

River Systems of the Americas

The map of North and South America on page 13 shows that the continents are alike in ways besides land surface. Both have great river systems. A river system is a river and all its branches.

The Mississippi (mis'ə sip'ē) River system is the longest river system in North America. It drains the great central plain of the United States. Far to the north, in Canada, the Mackenzie (mə ken'zē) River with its branches flows north into the Arctic Ocean. The St. Lawrence River flows into the Atlantic Ocean. The St. Lawrence system, which connects with the Great Lakes, forms a waterway that extends almost halfway across North America. Find these river systems on the physical map on page 13.

South America also has three great river systems. In the north is the Orinoco (ôr'ə nō'kō) River system. The Orinoco flows into the Caribbean Sea. To the south are the La Plata River and its branches. The greatest of all is the Amazon River system. The Amazon rises high in the Andes and flows eastward to the Atlantic Ocean. Turn to the map of the Americas on page 13. Find the three great river systems.

Comparing the Americas

The Americas are alike in other ways besides in their land surfaces and river systems. Both North and South America are shaped like triangles. They are joined by a narrow neck of land, or isthmus (is'məs). This neck of land is called the Isthmus of Panama. North and South America also share the Western Hemisphere (hem'is fēr), or western half of the earth.

The physical map of the Americas on page 13 shows that the two continents differ in several ways. Notice that the equator (i kwā'tər) crosses the northern part of South America. The equator does not cross any part of North America. We shall find out later some ways in which this makes North America different from parts of South America. Unlike South America, North America has a plain along much of its eastern coast. In South America the mountains often slope to the coast.

Climate of the Americas

The most important physical difference between North and South America is in *climate* (klī'mit). The kind of weather a place has year after year is called its climate. Climate means how much rain a place receives, how hot or cold it gets, and how long or short its summers and winters are.

Latitude and Climate

The *latitude* (lat'ə tōōd) of a place helps to explain its climate. Latitude is the distance north or south from the equator. Places north of the equator are in the northern latitudes. Places south of the equator are in the southern latitudes. Places on the equator are at zero latitude, or 0°.

The places farthest from the equator are called the poles. The North Pole and the South Pole are at either end of the earth's axis. The axis is the imaginary line through the earth on which the earth rotates. At each pole the lati-

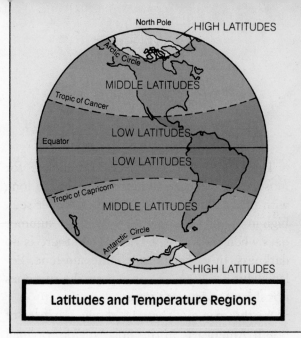

Latitudes and Temperature Regions

This map shows the *latitudes* of North and South America. If the map were large enough for you to see the land, where would you expect to see the following: icebergs, tropical forests, oak trees?

tude is 90°. Find the North Pole and the South Pole on the map on this page.

Also notice on this map the east-west lines located between the equator and the poles. These lines, parallels of latitude, are necessary in order to tell how far a place is north or south of the equator. They are imaginary lines used to help us understand maps better. There are five special parallels. The equator is one. Find the Tropic of Cancer and the Tropic of Capricorn (kap′rə kôrn′) on the map. Now find the Arctic (ärk′tik) Circle and the Antarctic (ant ark′tik) Circle.

If you know the latitude of a place, you can always tell something about its climate. Usually, the farther a place is from the equator, or the higher its degrees of latitude, the colder it is.

Notice on the map that the Tropic of Cancer is north of the equator and that the Tropic of Capricorn is south of the equator. Places on both sides of the equator between these two parallels of latitude are in the low latitudes. The direct rays of the sun never strike the earth north of the Tropic of Cancer or south of the Tropic of Capricorn.

In the low latitudes the sun at noontime is high in the sky. The earth receives the direct rays of the sun. Temperatures there are much the same day after day the year round. Almost all places in the low latitudes are hot. They never have cold weather except in very high mountain regions. It is summer all year round. Plants grow in these low latitudes which could not grow where it is cold. Places in these latitudes do not have winter, spring, or fall. Instead they have only two seasons. Part of the year is

the rainy season, part is the dry season.

You can easily remember that the low latitudes are nearest the equator. Because they are nearest the equator, their parallels of latitude have the lowest numbers. Low latitudes are called the *tropics* (trop′iks).

Look at the map again. Notice how much of South America lies between the Tropic of Cancer and the Tropic of Capicorn. How different North America is! Only its narrowest part lies in the low latitudes. This should tell you one way in which the climate of the two continents is different.

Find the Arctic Circle and the Antarctic Circle on the map above. Places between the Arctic Circle and the North Pole are in the high latitudes. Places between the Antarctic Circle and the South Pole are also in the high latitudes. These areas near the poles are far from the equator. The high latitudes are called the *polar regions* (pō′lər rē′jənz).

15

The polar regions have a cold climate for most of the year. In summer the days are long with much sunshine. Yet the sun is never seen high in the sky. In some parts there are summer days when the sun never sets. Then there is no darkness. In winter there is little sunshine. Polar nights are long. In some parts the sun does not shine for days at a time.

As the map on page 15 shows, no part of South America is in the polar region, or high latitudes. What part of North America is in the high latitudes?

The middle latitudes are between the low latitudes and the high latitudes. North of the equator the middle latitudes are between the Tropic of Cancer and the Arctic Circle. South of the equator they are between the Tropic of Capricorn and the Antarctic Circle. Find the middle latitudes on the map on page 15. If you live in the parts of the United States or Canada south of the Arctic Circle, you live in the middle latitudes.

The middle latitudes are also called the *temperate regions* (tem′pər it rē′jənz). These regions have four seasons—winter, summer, spring, and autumn. Northern parts of the middle latitudes have cold winters. Lakes and streams freeze. Snow falls. People enjoy skiing and skating during winter in the temperate regions.

In areas near the low latitudes the winters are cool but not very cold. People go there to enjoy mild winters. The middle latitudes have great differences in climate because they stretch from the tropics to the polar regions.

According to the map, which of the Americas has more land in the temperate region?

Altitude and Climate

The height of land, or its *altitude* (al′tə tood′), also affects climate. Altitude is measured from the level of the ocean or sea. Places high above sea level are cooler than places near sea level. The higher you go above sea level, the cooler it becomes.

On the physical map of North and South America on page 13 find the Andes Mountains in South America. North of the Tropic of Capricorn the Andes are in the tropics. But places in these mountains do not have a tropical climate because they are high above sea level. In the low latitudes, many people like to live in the highlands where the climate is cool.

The Seasons

Places south of the equator are in the Southern Hemisphere, or southern half of the earth. Places north of the equator are in the Northern Hemisphere. The seasons north of the equator are the opposite of those south of the equator.

While we are having winter in the Northern Hemisphere, people in the Southern Hemisphere are having summer. In the Southern Hemisphere the shortest day comes in June. The longest day comes in December. When the Northern Hemisphere is having spring, the Southern Hemisphere is having autumn. What season is it now in the Southern Hemisphere?

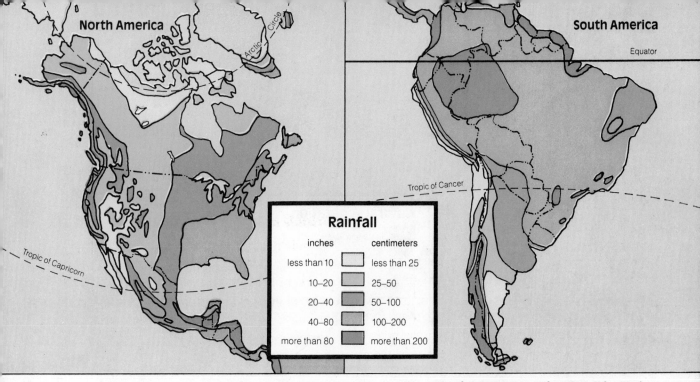

North America

South America

Arctic Circle

Equator

Tropic of Cancer

Tropic of Capricorn

Rainfall

inches		centimeters
less than 10		less than 25
10–20		25–50
20–40		50–100
40–80		100–200
more than 80		more than 200

Rainfall is necessary for plant life. Find where you live on the map. How much yearly rainfall does your area have? What parts of South America have the most rainfall?

Rainfall and Climate

Rainfall is an important part of the climate. The amount of rain or snow that falls in a place during a year is called its rainfall. Rainfall is measured in inches or centimeters. Snow is a form of rain. It takes 6 inches (15 cm) of snow to make about 1 inch (2.5 cm) of rain. The maps on this page show how much rainfall the Americas get in a year.

Look at the key for the rainfall map of North America above. Places that are colored red get the most rain. The rain that falls there in a year measures more than 80 inches (203 cm). Where there is such heavy rain, there are thick forests of large, tall trees and other plants.

Find places on the map having more than 20 to 40 inches (51 to 102 cm) of rain a year. The best farming regions in the Americas have

20 to 80 inches (51 to 203 cm) of rain yearly. Trees also grow well in these regions. How are these areas shown on the rainfall maps?

Less than 20 inches (51 cm) of rain is not enough for many kinds of crops. Some places do not get even 10 inches (25 cm) of rain. These are dry lands or deserts (dez′ərtz). They usually need *irrigation* (ir′ə gā′shən), a way of bringing water to dry land through pipes or sprinklers. When these dry lands are irrigated, they produce abundant crops of different kinds.

Vegetation and Climate

The plant life in a region is called its *vegetation* (vej′ə tā′shən). Trees, grass, and other plants which people have not planted are called natural vegetation. Regions that have little rainfall or much cold weather may have little

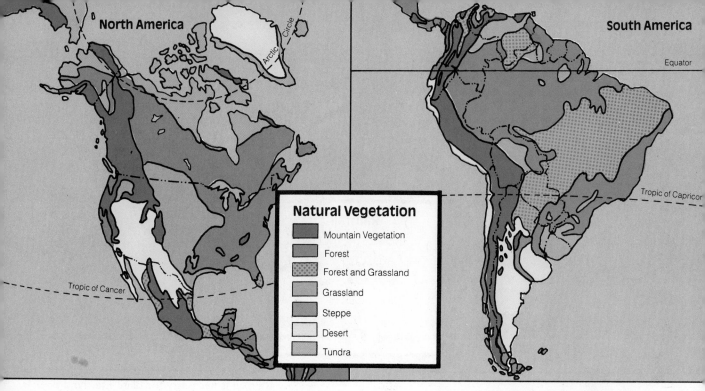

North America

South America

Arctic Circle

Equator

Tropic of Capricorn

Tropic of Cancer

Natural Vegetation

- Mountain Vegetation
- Forest
- Forest and Grassland
- Grassland
- Steppe
- Desert
- Tundra

Amounts of rainfall help determine the natural *vegetation* of an area. What kind of vegetation covers most of North America?

natural vegetation. Few plants may grow there. Where the rainfall is heavy and the weather is warm, the natural vegetation is dense. Thick forests and many other plants grow well in warm, rainy climates.

The maps on this page show the natural vegetation in the Americas. The keys on each map show where the different kinds of vegetation grow. By comparing the vegetation maps with the rainfall maps, you can tell how important rainfall is to plants. How much rain falls in forest lands?

Notice the many forest lands on the natural vegetation map of North America. In these forests are evergreen trees such as pine, fir, spruce, and hemlock. Trees such as maple, elm, and oak also grow there. In South America the tropical forests, or rain forests, have still other kinds of trees. The hot, moist

climate makes them grow tall and close together.

Both of the Americas have desert lands. Wherever there is enough moisture in these lands, plants grow. Because of the small amount of rainfall, desert plants and grasses usually grow in clumps with bare ground between them.

In the northern part of North America is a *tundra* (tun'drə), a large, treeless plain. It is so cold that the soil below the surface of the earth is always frozen.

Grasslands receive more rain than deserts, but less than forest areas. In these lands grasses and other plants cover the ground. There are few trees. A very large grassland is called a steppe. Find some grasslands on the natural vegetation maps on this page. Where is the grasslands area of the United States?

18

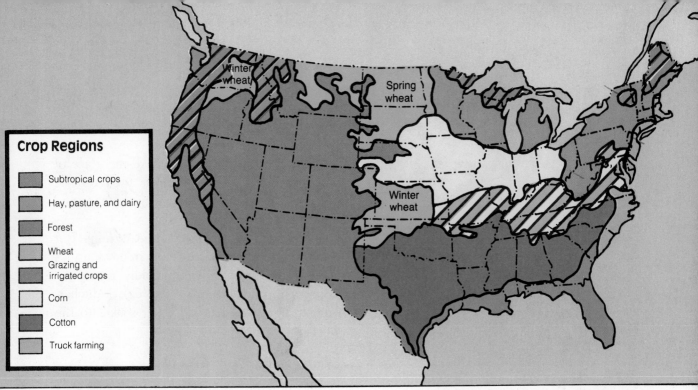

Crop Regions

- Subtropical crops
- Hay, pasture, and dairy
- Forest
- Wheat
- Grazing and irrigated crops
- Corn
- Cotton
- Truck farming

Winter wheat

Spring wheat

Winter wheat

This map shows the areas, or belts, in which different farm products are raised in the United States. No large areas are left unused.

Resources of the Americas

Both North and South America have many of nature's riches. These riches are called *natural resources* (nach′ər əl rē′sôrs′əz), or materials found in nature that are useful or necessary for human life. Natural resources become valuable when people learn how to use them. Millions of people in the Americas make their living from the resources of these lands. People are also resources of the Americas. They are its human resources.

Natural Resources

Both North and South America have fertile grasslands and great plains. Because of the favorable rainfall, temperature, and soils, many different kinds of crops can be grown. Forests furnish lumber and hold the soil in place. Iron, copper, tin, lead, silver, nickel, gold, and other useful minerals are found in the earth. Coal and oil are used for heating homes and running factories. Many kinds of birds and other wildlife live in the Americas. The lakes, streams, and oceans contain many fish. People who live in America are fortunate to have these riches. We should use our resources, but we should not waste them.

The Waste of Our Resources

When people from Europe first came to America, they found the land much as it had been for thousands of years. The American Indians had lived close to the land, but they had carefully used its riches. The European settlers soon began to make changes in the land. They cut down forests for lumber. They cleared land for farming. Cattle and sheep were turned out to graze on the grasslands. Minerals

One way to practice *conservation* is to plant more trees. Here a pine seedling, or young pine tree less than three feet (.9 meters) high, is being planted.

were dug from the earth. Cities, factories, and railroads were built as the population grew. More food and more raw materials were needed from the farms, the forests, and the mines. Sometimes waste minerals were dumped into rivers. Nature's gifts seemed endless. People became careless. They did not think that these resources might someday be used up.

Saving Our Natural Resources

Many people now realize we must practice *conservation* (kon′sər vā′shən). Conservation is the wise use of our natural resources. Some natural resources are destroyed by use. Coal, oil, iron, and other minerals, once used, can never be replaced. When we use our minerals and other natural resources wisely, we are practicing conservation.

We can practice conservation in many ways.

New trees can be planted to take the place of those used for lumber. Forest fires can be prevented if we are careful with matches and campfires.

Soil is often washed away in heavy rains. But planting grass or bushes on steep hillsides keeps water from flowing rapidly down the slopes. This prevents gullies (gul′ēz), or ditches, from forming and lets the water soak into the ground.

Living as Partners with Nature

People now are beginning to learn that they must live as partners with nature. To do this better, people study *ecology* (ē kol′ə jē). Ecology is the study of the ways in which living things relate to one another and to their natural surroundings. Ecology teaches us how we can make wise use of natural resources. It also shows how other resources, such as energy from the sun, might be developed. Because they used their surroundings wisely, the American Indians were our first ecologists.

Do You Know?

1. Name three ways in which North and South America are alike.
2. Name two ways in which these two continents are different.
3. What is latitude? How does latitude affect climate?
4. How does altitude affect climate?
5. How should our natural resources be used?

20

Before You Go On

Using New Words

tropic   conservation
climate   vegetation
altitude   natural resource
tundra   latitude
ecology   temperate region
irrigation   polar region

The phrases below explain the words or terms listed above. Number a paper from 1 through 12. After each number write the word or term which matches the definition.

1. A place in the middle latitudes
2. The study of how living things relate to their natural surroundings
3. A place in the low latitudes
4. Bringing water to dry land through pipes or sprinklers
5. The kind of weather a place has
6. A place in the high latitudes
7. The plant life in a region
8. The height of land above sea level
9. The imaginary lines which tell the distance north or south of the equator
10. The wise use of natural resources
11. A large, treeless plain
12. Material found in nature that is useful or necessary for human life

Finding the Facts

1. What different kinds of land surfaces does a physical map show?
2. What is a river system? What is the longest river system in North America? What is the greatest river system in South America?
3. What is the latitude of the equator?
4. What places are in the low latitudes? What places are in the high latitudes? What places are in the middle latitudes?
5. From what point is altitude measured?
6. What happens to the climate as you move to higher altitudes?
7. What is rainfall? How is rainfall measured?
8. What type of vegetation grows where heavy rainfall occurs?
9. What part of the American continents is a tundra?
10. What are some kinds of natural resources?
11. What are some ways in which we can practice conservation?
12. What can ecology teach us?
13. What and where are the second highest mountains in the world?
14. What river system goes almost halfway across North America?

2

The First People in the Americas

Scientists disagree on the exact time when the first people arrived in the Western Hemisphere. But many think it was between 20,000 and 40,000 years ago. Scientists do agree that people had spread throughout the Americas by 12,000 years ago. How did these early travelers enter the Americas, and why? To find the answer to these questions we must look at North America when it was in the grip of the great ice sheets.

The map shows what North America looked like in the Ice Age. In what ways has the coastline changed?

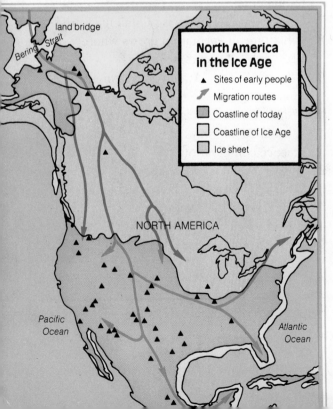

An Age of Ice

Eighteen thousand years ago, the climate of the Americas was much colder than it is now. Great sheets of ice, called *glaciers* (glā′shərz), covered most of what is now Canada and northern parts of the United States. Some glaciers were more than a mile thick. The glaciers moved slowly across the land, changing the shape of the earth's surface. During this time the level of the sea dropped. A strip of land, or isthmus, appeared between Asia and the Americas. This isthmus, which is now under water, is called the land bridge. It was located in the Bering Strait. Asia and North America are only 60 miles (96 km) apart across the Bering Strait. Find the Bering Strait on the map of the Ice Age on this page. The land bridge was covered with grasses which animals fed upon. Huge bison, deer, and other animals roamed from Asia into North America.

Early peoples depended on animals for food, clothing, shelter, and weapons. People hunted animals together. They followed the herds eastward across northern Asia into North America. As time went on, the glaciers began to melt. Both animals and hunters could move southward to warmer lands. After a time they reached all parts of both Americas. They learned to use the resources they found.

Today, the descendants of these people are called American Indians. They were the first *immigrants* (im′ə grənts) to America. Immigrants are people who move from one land to another to make their homes.

Wooly mammoths had thick hair to protect them from the Ice Age cold. These huge animals came to North America from Asia. They died out many thousands of years ago.

Indian Ways of Living in North America

About 5,000 years ago, people of the Americas discovered that plants grow from seeds. They learned to grow beans, squash, tomatoes, peppers, and potatoes. Tobacco and peanuts were other crops. From the seeds of the cacao (kə kā'o) tree they made a drink. We make chocolate from the seeds of the cacao tree today. Maize (māz), or corn, was another important crop. When Europeans came to America, they learned about all these crops. Today, millions of the world's people live on foods developed by American Indians.

Indian groups learned many skills besides hunting and farming. Some became potters and weavers. Others learned to make ornaments from gold, silver, and copper. Making baskets and working with leather were other crafts. Each group had its own language and customs.

Some Indians lived in much the same way as their parents, grandparents, and ancestors had lived. Others learned different ways of getting food, clothing, and shelter. They stopped moving from place to place, built homes, and began farming. They lived and worked together in groups or tribes. They developed governments and built large, fine cities.

ESKIMOS

Athabaska River

Nelson River

CREE

ESKIMOS

Saskatchewan River

BLACKFOOT

NEZ PERCE

Missouri River

CHIPPEWAS

OTTAWAS

CHINOOKS

Columbia River

CHEYENNES

CROWS

DAKOTAS

HURON

IROQUOIS

EASTERN
WOODLAND INDIANS

WALLA WALLAS

SAULK AND FOX

DELAWARE

POMO

PLAINS INDIANS

ILLINOIS

Ohio River

SHOSHONES

UTES

ARAPAHOS

Arkansas River

SHAWNEES

CHEROKEES

Atlantic Ocean

NAVAJOS

SOUTHWEST INDIANS

CREEKS

Mississippi River

COMANCHES

MOJAVES

(PUEBLO INDIANS)

ZUNI   HOPI

APACHES

Rio Grande

SEMINOLE

Pacific Ocean

AZTECS

Tenochtitlán

Chichén Itzá

MAYAS

CARIBS

CHIBCHAS

**Indian Tribes
of North America
(about 1500)**

Different Tribes in North America

Each tribe of people in North America had its own ways of living. There were hundreds of different languages spoken in North America. But all tribes used their natural surroundings to supply their basic needs. The next sections describe a few of the many tribes that lived here before the Europeans came.

The Plains Indians

The Cheyenne (shī en′) people were one of the tribes of Plains Indians. They lived on the rolling, grassy plains west of the Missouri River. As people who depended on hunting to survive, they were always on the move. Supplies were dragged on poles. They had to transport their tepees, or skin tents, from one camp to another.

It took many buffalo hides to make a tepee. It was a Cheyenne custom to ask friends to help. First, the hides were stretched out on the ground with the hairy side down. Then they were fastened to the ground with stakes. Next, the flesh was scraped off. After working on one side, the Indians turned the hides over and removed the hair with elk bone. After that, skins were made into leather by rubbing them and letting them dry in the sun. Then the skins were softened by being pulled back and forth through a hole in a buffalo shoulder bone.

Indian groups were living throughout the Americas when the first Europeans arrived. Over the years some tribes developed into great nations. Did any of these Indians live where you now live?

Long ago some Indians used dogs to pull their supplies on poles tied together. There were no horses in the Americas then.

After the buffalo skins were prepared, they were spread out on the ground to be cut. Holes were made in the skins with sharp-pointed bones. Then they were sewed together by putting pieces of dried sinew (sin′yo͞o) through the holes. Sinew is the strong cord in the buffalo which fastens muscles to bones.

While the work was being done in camp, braves would set out to hunt buffaloes on the grassy plains. The buffalo was the most important resource for the Plains Indians. Its meat was their food. Its skin was made into leather for tepee covers, clothing, robes, and cooking vessels. Arrow points, knives, and axes were made from its horns. The Indians made spoons, bowls, and cups from buffalo bones. They used buffalo sinew for sewing and for bone strings.

The returning buffalo hunters arrived with hides and meat at the end of a successful day. The camp would be lit by the glow of many campfires. Some meat was roasted over the fires. Part of the meat would be dried and made into pemmican (pem′i ᶄ ən). Pemmican would be eaten later when food was not plentiful. After supper the hunters told of the day's hunt. Each hunter had to stick to the actual facts. The Cheyenne, like other American Indians, put great value on telling the truth.

Iroquois women collected the sap from maple trees to make maple sugar. The Indians drank the first sap of the spring to help prevent illness.

Indians of the Eastern Woodlands

East of the Mississippi River lived the Eastern Woodland Indians. One of these groups was the Iroquois (ir′ə kwoi). The Iroquois lived in houses made of poles and bark. These were called "longhouses." The roof was curved. From the front, a longhouse looked like an upside-down letter "U". It was about 60 feet (18 m) long and 18 feet (5.4 m) wide. It was divided into eight or more family compartments.

Like the Cheyenne, the Iroquois were hunters. But they hunted deer instead of buffaloes. They raised corn, beans, and squash. They gathered nuts and wild strawberries. In spring they made maple sugar by boiling the sap of maple trees.

The Iroquois were a powerful tribe. They were really a group of five tribes who had joined together and formed a union called "The Five Nations." Later, a sixth tribe joined the Iroquois. By uniting, the Iroquois kept peace among themselves. At times, leaders of the tribes held meetings called councils. Rules for the tribes and other agreements were made at these councils. The women picked the council members. The women could remove council members if they did not do a good job.

The union of the Iroquois people came to be called the "Great Council Fire." It was a way of government that was admired by the Europeans who came later. The rule of the Great Council Fire lasted until about 100 years ago.

Pueblo Indians have lived in these adobe houses in Taos, New Mexico, for thousands of years. Eskimos in Alaska still use reindeer to pull heavy loads across the snow-covered ground.

Indians of the Southwest

Some American Indians lived in the desert region of the Southwest in early times. The states of Arizona and New Mexico are located there today.

One important group which settled in the Southwest was the Pueblo (pweb′lō) Indians. To protect themselves, these Indians built their houses close together on hills and cliffs. These houses were built of dried clay, called adobe (ə dō′bē). Some of these Pueblo houses were four or five stories high. Each story was set back like a step from the story below. The roof of one house formed the balcony, or porch, of the house above. Ladders could be pulled up in time of danger. Many families lived in these houses.

The Pueblo Indians were farmers. Because there was little rain, they lived near rivers. They dug ditches to carry water from the rivers to their fields. This irrigation made it possible for the Pueblos to raise corn and pumpkins in the desert lands.

The Pueblos wove blankets from the cotton they raised. They learned how to make pottery from clay.

Long after the Pueblos settled in the Southwest, the Navajos (nav′ə hōz′) came from the north. The Navajos were hunters and knew little of living in other ways. At first, they raided the Pueblos and took corn. Gradually, however, they learned from the Pueblos how to grow corn and to weave cotton. Today the Navajos are the largest Indian tribe in the United States.

Eskimos of the Far North

The Eskimos lived along the northern coasts of North America. Eskimo life followed the seasons.

In spring the Eskimos moved inland to fish in fresh-water lakes, to pick berries, and to hunt caribou.

Tourists can enjoy a boat ride among floating gardens near Mexico City. Planted years ago, the gardens are now islands of trees and flowers.

Winter days were the time for ice hunting. Eskimo families usually made winter homes of stone, earth, and driftwood. They built their homes along the coast near good seal-hunting grounds. The seal was important to the Eskimo. Seal meat was often the only winter food. Oil for fuel came from seal blubber. Seal hides were made into boots, coats, and tents. The hides were also used to cover long, narrow boats called kayaks (kī′aks). During the long winter nights, Eskimos enjoyed telling stories and carving stone figures.

The Aztecs of Mexico

The rich and powerful Aztec (az′tec) Indians were one of many tribes in the great valley of central Mexico. Gradually, they conquered other tribes. Their city, Tenochtitlán (tä nôch′ tē tlän′), was founded in 1325. At first, the city was only a small island village in the middle of a lake. As the power of the Aztecs grew, Tenochtitlán became a splendid city of great white buildings and green gardens. It was criss-crossed by canals instead of streets. Houses were connected by bridges over the canals. On the northern edge of Tenochtitlán was a great marketplace. Goods from all over Mexico were traded there. Mexico City now stands in place of the old Aztec city. Wide avenues have replaced the canals.

Tenochtitlán was a city of islands. Many of these islands were "floating gardens." The Aztecs made them by scooping mud from the lake bottom. The mud was piled on reeds that had been woven together. Trees and crops were planted on this mud base. Their roots held the mud more firmly in place. Some floating gardens exist today near modern Mexico City.

The Mayas of Central America and Mexico

Farther south, in parts of what are now Mexico and Central America, lived the Maya (mī′yə) Indians. These people studied the sun, the moon, and the stars. They invented a calendar and marked off the days, months, and years. The Mayas developed a system of mathematics, picture-writing, and record-keeping. Their beautiful buildings were made of stone. The Mayas had productive farms. They could feed all the people of their cities by raising corn.

Ruins of Mayan temples can be seen in Mexico and Central America today. Descendants of the Maya Indians still live and raise corn in the land of their ancestors.

Early Polynesians sailed across the Pacific Ocean and settled many islands. They knew the ocean currents and could travel for long distances. From islands in the South Pacific, some Polynesians journeyed to Hawaii.

Sailors of the Western Ocean

The islands that form the state of Hawaii are in the Pacific Ocean just south of the Tropic of Cancer. These islands were visited 2,000 years ago by Polynesians (pol'i nē'zhənz) who came in large canoes. They came from the islands of the South Pacific known as Polynesia.

The Polynesian sailors used special maps in their island-to-island voyages. Branches were bent to represent directions of ocean currents. Sea shells or pebbles were placed to locate islands. In the hands of skilled Polynesian sailors, the maps guided them across their water world. Polynesians may even have voyaged to and from the west coast of South America.

The Polynesians lived pleasantly on the tropical islands and surrounding seas. Their ways of life changed little until the coming of Europeans. Today, descendants of these people are citizens of Hawaii.

Do You Know?

1. How did the first people reach America?
2. Why was the buffalo so valuable to the Plains Indians?
3. Who were the Mayas? What were some of their accomplishments?
4. What is adobe? What was it used for?
5. How and where did Eskimos get oil for fuel?

3
Exploring the Americas

People of Norway were the first Europeans to find the continent of North America. Other Europeans knew nothing of this discovery. They were more interested in finding a way to get to Asia by sea. They wanted spices, precious stones, and other goods. Later, explorers from many nations sailed across the ocean and began settling in the Americas.

The Vikings Sail Westward

In a castle in Norway some people are listening to a story of adventure.

"Eric the Red," the storyteller says, "was one of the *Vikings* (vī′kingz), or sea rovers, who left Norway many years ago. He went to live in Iceland, an island in the western ocean. But he had troubles with his neighbors and left.

"Eric sailed west. He found a larger island. Eric saw a few green plants growing along the coast, so he named it Greenland. He went back to Iceland for his family and other settlers.

The Vinland Voyage

"Eric never left Greenland, but his son Leif did. In about the year 1,000 Leif set out on a long voyage. He sailed south and west of Greenland. Leif finally reached a low coast covered with

The *Vikings* were daring explorers. They sailed in long, open ships, using oars and one sail. Leif Ericson's ship probably looked like this one.

trees. Grapes grew everywhere. Because grapes are used to make wine, Leif called the country Wineland, or Vinland.

"Leif Ericson built a house and stayed until winter came. Then he decided to return to Greenland.

"Later, Leif's brother led a group of Vikings to Vinland. They traded with the skrellings. Then trouble broke out between the Vikings and the skrellings. Leif's brother was killed. The Vikings left Vinland never to return."

If you guessed that Vinland was in North America, you were right. If you guessed that the skrellings were American Indians, you were right again. Leif Ericson had sailed along the eastern coast of North America. The Vikings did not write of their travels. But they told sagas (sä′gəz), or stories of their adventures. More than 200 years later the sagas were put into writing.

Finding New Routes to the East

In the years after the Vikings' visit to North America the people of Europe did little traveling. Most of them were too poor to travel. Their lives were spent living and working on lands belonging to rich, powerful landowners called lords.

Gradually people of Europe began to travel more. Some went to towns or fairs to trade. Others journeyed to holy places to worship. These people were called pilgrims (pil′grəmz).

At first, pilgrims visited the holy places near their homes. Then they began to visit the Holy Land where Jesus had lived. The Holy Land was Palestine, a country in western Asia. The Arab people of Palestine welcomed the pilgrims.

Then Turks from Asia conquered the Arabs. Like the Arabs, the Turks were Muslims (muz′limz). Muslims followed the teachings of Mohammad (mō ham′id). The Turks did not welcome Christian pilgrims. The angered Christians wanted to drive the Turks from the Holy Land. So they raised armies and traveled to the country of Palestine.

Wars between the Christians and the Muslims followed. These wars were called Crusades (kroo sādz′). Christians who fought in the wars were called Crusaders.

The Beginning of Trade

The Crusades went on for about 200 years. When they ended, the Turks still controlled the Holy Land. But something had changed. Like the pilgrims, the Crusaders had seen new lands and great cities.

Home again in Europe, the Crusaders told of fine cloth, jewels, and spices. Europeans wanted to enjoy these things for themselves. Trade soon started between European cities and cities near the Holy Land.

Europeans knew that products were carried to Palestine from eastern Asia by caravans, or groups of pack camels. The caravans traveled overland from China and India. So some European traders began to send caravans to India and China. The Polos, a family of Italian traders, traveled by caravan across Asia to China in 1271. Marco Polo wrote a book about his travels in the Far East.

Europe's trade with the Far East grew rapidly between 1300 and 1500. Western European merchants brought coarse woolen goods, iron goods, and leather to the markets on the eastern Mediterranean. They traded these for the spices, jewels, and silks from the Far East.

Traders began to follow regular routes, or roads, to the Far East. There were three trade routes that were most used. All three routes were partly by land and partly by sea. After the Turks conquered the Holy Land, traders were no longer allowed to go through Palestine on their way across Asia to China. Then the Turks blocked the northern route across Asia. Trade between Europe and the Far East almost came to an end.

An All-Water Route to the Far East

"We must have the products of the Far East," said Europeans. "Without spices our food will spoil."

"Unless we find a new route to the East we are ruined," groaned the merchants. "We will lose our customers who buy fine silks.

"An all-water route would be best," they agreed. "It costs less and is safer than a land route. We would earn more money."

Prince Henry the Navigator

Prince Henry was the son of the king of Portugal. He was sure that an all-water route to the Far East could be found. Portugal, on the Atlantic Ocean, is well located for trade. Prince Henry started a school for sailors. They made and studied maps. The best *navigators* (nav′ i gā′tərz), who guide ships, taught sailors how to plan voyages. Prince Henry became known as "Henry the Navigator."

By this time stronger, faster sailing ships were being built. New sailing instruments had been invented. The compass helped sailors know in which direction they were sailing. Another instrument helped them know how far from the equator they were. Now they could know which latitude they were in.

"We must find a sea route around Africa to India," said the prince. He sent one ship after another to sail south along the west coast of Africa. But Prince Henry died without finding a water route to India.

Portuguese sailors continued searching for an all-water route to Asia. "Sail as far south as you dare," ordered the new King, John II. "Then build a tower on the shore to show where you turned back." Each year towers were built farther and farther south along the western coast of Africa.

In 1488 a Portuguese captain, Bartholomeu Dias, (bär′too loo mā′oo dē′əs) ran into a storm. "We are east of Africa and sailing north!" shouted Dias when the storm was over. "On to India!" But the fearful crew refused to sail on. Dias had to return to Portugal.

"We sailed around the southern tip of Africa," Dias told the king. "I called it the Cape of Storms." "No," said the king, "we will call it the Cape of Good Hope."

In 1498 Captain Vasco da Gama (väs′kō də gä′mə) sailed around Africa. His ships reached India and the Spice Islands. The crews brought back spices and other products. An all-water route to the East had been found!

32

The sailors of Portugal became famous. They used the route around Africa to trade for the products of the East. In 1500 a ship bound for India was blown off its course. It reached a land far to the west. The captain, Pedro Cabral (pā′ drō kə bräl′), claimed this land for Portugal. In this way a part of South America became a Portuguese possession.

The Story of Columbus

The search for a sea route to the Far East was exciting. Remember, when Europeans spoke of the "East" or "Far East," they meant the distant lands of Asia. Sometimes they used the word "Indies" for these places. To reach these lands, some explorers tried sailing south and east around Africa. One captain decided to sail west into the Atlantic Ocean. His name was Christopher Columbus.

Christopher Columbus grew up in the seaport city of Genoa, Italy. Genoa was a great trading center on the Mediterranean Sea.

When Columbus was about 19, he became a sailor. While attending a school for sailors, he began to think about sailing west to reach the East. He believed that, if the earth was round, a person could reach Asia by sailing west. Others did not agree with Columbus. A voyage to the Far East by sailing west would be too long, they thought.

Columbus wanted to prove he was right, but he needed money and ships. He asked the king of Portugal to help him. The king did not believe that the Indies could be reached by sailing west. He refused to help Columbus.

Columbus did not give up. He traveled to Spain. But the Spanish were fighting a war and had no money to spare. The kings of England and France were not interested in Columbus's ideas either.

Then the fighting in Spain ended. But Spain was poor. Queen Isabella saw Columbus's idea as a way for Spain to get riches from the Indies. She sent word to Columbus that Spain would give him ships, crews, and supplies to sail west.

The inscription of this early sixteenth-century painting of Christopher Columbus identifies him as the first to enter by ship the opposite side of the world.

33

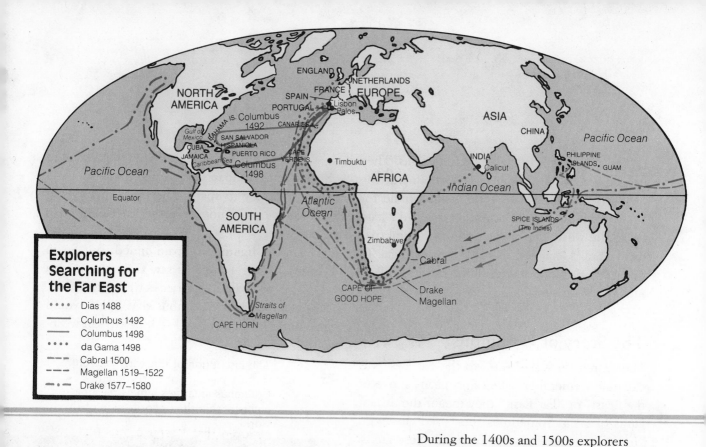

Explorers Searching for the Far East

····	Dias 1488
———	Columbus 1492
———	Columbus 1498
····	da Gama 1498
– – –	Cabral 1500
– – –	Magellan 1519–1522
–·–·–	Drake 1577–1580

During the 1400s and 1500s explorers traveled thousands of miles in their search for an all-water route to the Far East. Trace the voyages of the explorers on the map. Did any of them ever reach the Far East?

The First Voyage of Columbus

It was Friday, August 3, 1492, when Columbus and the crew of 90 sailors sailed from Palos, Spain. They had three ships—the *Santa Maria,* the *Niña,* and the *Pinta.* Most of the crew were Spanish. Others came from Portugal and Italy.

Ever westward sailed the three ships. Days passed without sight of land. The crew became afraid. Columbus tried to cheer them up. But the crew was ready to turn back. Then they agreed to sail west for three more days. If land was not found by then, they would turn back.

Luckily things began to change. Signs of land appeared. Land birds flew overhead. Weeds drifted by the ships. Two days passed. Then on

October 12, 1492, the lookout shouted "Tierra!" Tierra (tyer′ə) is the Spanish word for land. It was land at last!

At dawn Columbus and the crew rowed to shore. Columbus carried the flag of Spain and gifts for the ruler of the country. The people who lived on the island called themselves Arawaks (är′ə wäks). They called their island Guanahani (gwä′nə hä nē). Because Columbus believed he had reached the Indies, he called the people "Indians." He named the island San Salvador.

Since then, these people have been called Indians. The islands in this area have been called the West Indies.

Columbus explored parts of other islands such as Cuba and Hispaniola (his′pən yō′lə). The crew found some gold on Hispaniola.

The *Santa María* ran aground on Hispaniola and was wrecked. Indians helped Columbus save some of the supplies. Columbus used timbers from the wreckage to build a fort. Some of the crew stayed near the fort and looked for more gold. Columbus returned to Spain with six Indians and some gold.

What a welcome Columbus received in Spain! Queen Isabella and King Ferdinand gave him many honors. Everyone believed Columbus had reached India by sailing west.

Later Voyages

Columbus made three more voyages. On the second voyage he returned to Hispaniola. But no Spaniards were there. They had treated the Indians badly and had been killed.

A new settlement was built on Hispaniola. It was called "Isabella." It was the first Spanish settlement in the Americas. Columbus sailed among the islands of the West Indies seeking a passage to India. He found no passage but did find other islands such as Jamaica (jə mā′kə).

On the third voyage Columbus went ashore on the continent of South America. Then he returned to Hispaniola. He was arrested by the new governor of Hispaniola for mistreating the settlers. When Columbus went back to Spain, he was a prisoner.

Queen Isabella and King Ferdinand set Columbus free and helped him make a fourth voyage. On this, his last voyage, Columbus failed once more to find a passage to Asia.

Today we know that Columbus had come to the continents of North and South America. But he did not know this. To the end of his life he believed he had reached islands near Asia.

Not Columbia, But America

The land Columbus discovered is not named for him. In 1497, Amerigo Vespucci (ä′mə rē′gō ve spoō′chē), another Italian sailor, sailed along the eastern coast of South America. He wrote letters about his trips. In one he said, "This is a new continent. A whole new world lies between Europe and Asia."

Some of Amerigo's letters were read by a geographer in Europe who was making a world map. He believed that Vespucci was right. On the map he called the continent "America," after Vespucci's first name.

Other Spanish Explorations of the Americas

After Columbus's voyages, more people came to the Americas under the flag of Spain. One was a Spaniard named Vasco de Balboa (väs′kō dā bal bō′ə).

Balboa Sees the Pacific

In Panama Balboa met Central American Indians who told him of a great sea beyond the mountains. Balboa decided to look for this sea.

In 1513 Balboa gathered a group of Spaniards. They crossed the isthmus that connects North America and South America. The distance was about 50 miles (80 km). But their route led across steep mountains and hot,

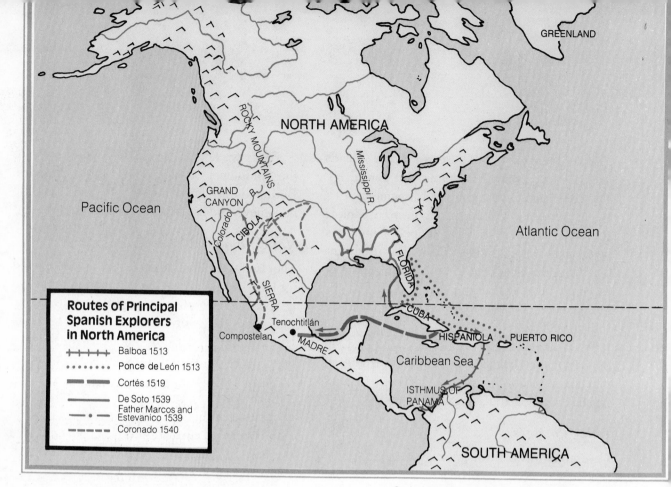

Routes of Principal Spanish Explorers in North America

+++++	Balboa 1513
•••••	Ponce de León 1513
▬▬▬	Cortés 1519
———	De Soto 1539
—•—•—	Father Marcos and Estevanico 1539
– – –	Coronado 1540

GREENLAND

NORTH AMERICA

Pacific Ocean

ROCKY MOUNTAINS

GRAND CANYON

Colorado R.

CIBOLA

SIERRA

MADRE

Mississippi R.

FLORIDA

Atlantic Ocean

CUBA

Compostelan

Tenochtitlán

HISPANIOLA

PUERTO RICO

Caribbean Sea

ISTHMUS OF PANAMA

SOUTH AMERICA

Some European nations waited for many years before settling in the Americas. But Spain was quick to start its *colonies*. What cities were founded by the Spanish?

steaming rain forests. Balboa drove the group on. Near the top of the last mountain, he ordered them to wait. He wanted to be the first to see the body of water that lay beyond.

Balboa stood on the mountain top. He looked down on quiet, blue waters. He had no idea how far west the ocean went, nor what lands it touched. He was the first European to reach the eastern shore of the Pacific. He named it the South Sea.

Ponce de León in Florida

In 1513 another Spaniard looked for another body of water. His name was Juan Ponce de León (hwän pōns′ dā lā′ōn). He was looking for the waters of the fountain of youth. Of course, he never found such a fountain. But he did explore Florida looking for it. Ponce de León was the first Spaniard to explore a part of North America. His explorations gave Spain a claim to the southeastern part of North America.

Magellan's Great Voyage

In 1519 Ferdinand Magellan sailed across the Atlantic and along the coast of South America. Magellan was a Portuguese, but he sailed for the King of Spain. Like Columbus, Magellan believed he could reach the East by sailing west.

Europeans still wanted the products of the Spice Islands. Find these islands on the map of explorers searching for the Far East on page 34.

Magellan's five ships sailed southward along the coast of South America, looking for a passage through the land. The crew spent the winter in the southern part of the continent. The weather was cold and some sailors wanted to go home.

When spring came, Magellan persuaded them to sail on. They kept looking for a passage to the Pacific. One ship was lost, but the crew was saved. Finally, near the southern end of South America, they found a strait. One of the ships slipped away and returned to Spain. But the other three ships entered the strait. After several weeks they reached the Pacific Ocean.

Week after week they sailed. Many of the crew became ill and died. Months went by. Then Magellan and the crew, starved and ill, reached Guam (gwäm), an island in the western Pacific. Magellan continued westward. He came to a group of islands near Asia. These islands were later named the Philippines for King Philip of Spain. Magellan led an attack against the people on one island and was killed. The crew left one ship behind and sailed on to the Spice Islands. Here they had to leave another ship behind.

One September day in 1522 Magellan's last ship, the *Victoria,* returned to Spain laden with spices. Three years had passed since its departure. Only eighteen thin and ragged crew members returned on the ship. They had sailed around the earth. This journey proved that the Far East could be reached by sailing west. Trace the voyage of Magellan's ship on the map of explorers searching for the Far East on page 34.

Traders knew Magellan's route to the Spice Islands was too long and costly. Soon Spaniards stopped looking for a water route to the East.

Cortés and the Aztecs

In America another Spaniard had discovered a very rich land. His name was Hernando Cortés (er nän′dō kôr tes′).

Cortés was in Cuba when he heard about a land with much gold in the southern part of North America. We know this land as Mexico. Cortés was eager for riches. In 1519 he formed an army and sailed to the eastern coast of Mexico. There he founded Veracruz—the first Spanish settlement on the mainland of the Americas. Find Veracruz on the map of Spanish explorers in the Americas on page 36.

The Indians on the coast told Cortés about the Aztecs. The Aztecs, as you have read, were a great tribe who lived in the central part of Mexico. After long, hard marches Cortés and an army of Spaniards reached the Aztec city of Tenochtitlán. The Spaniards were stunned. Few cities in Europe were as large or as beautiful.

Montezuma (mon′tə zoo′mə), the Aztec ruler, had heard that fair-skinned people were coming. He went to meet Cortés. He took gifts of gold, silver, and fine cloth to the Spaniards. He hoped they would take the gifts and leave. But the treasures only made the Spaniards eager for more.

Montezuma then invited the Spaniards to the city and gave them lavish gifts. Cortés took the Aztec ruler prisoner. Fighting broke out. But

Tenochtitlan.

This is an early drawing of the meeting of Montezuma and Hernando Cortés at Tenochtitlán. Some of the many gifts the Aztec gave the Spaniard are pictured.

Aztec weapons were no match for those of the Europeans. In 1521 Cortés conquered the Aztec people.

Cortés sent shiploads of gold and silver from Mexico to the Spanish king. Spain no longer needed to trade with the East to get rich.

De Soto and the Mississippi

Hernando de Soto (er nän′dō də sō′tō), the rich governor of Cuba, went to Florida to look for gold in 1539. For more than 4 years his party of Spaniards and blacks explored the southern part of what is now the United States. Mosquitoes and fever in the swamps of Florida made life miserable. There was fighting with the American Indians with loss of life on both sides. The group pushed westward. In 1541 De Soto and his followers were the first Europeans to see the Mississippi River.

Then De Soto became ill and died. He was buried in the Mississippi River. The survivors built boats and drifted down the river. Later they reached Mexico. The land drained by the Mississippi River had been claimed for Spain.

Spanish Explorers of the Southwest

In 1539 Estevanico (es′tā vä nē′kō), a black African who explored for Spain, entered the region that is now New Mexico. He and Father Marcos, a Catholic priest, were seeking the fabled Seven Cities of Cibola (sē′bə lə). Cibola was said to be a place rich with gold and other treasure. Estevanico did not find Cibola. What he found was a Pueblo Indian village. Trouble broke out there and Estevanico was killed.

Spurred on by the hope of finding treasure, Francisco Coronado (kôr′ə nä′dō), another

Spanish explorer, entered the same region. He too failed to find cities of gold. However, part of Coronado's group became the first Europeans to see the Grand Canyon. Coronado went on exploring throughout the Southwest. Because of his explorations, all lands west of the Mississippi River were claimed for Spain.

English Explorers in America

When news of Columbus's voyage reached England, King Henry VII was unhappy. "England should have a chance to get rich as well as Spain," he thought.

John Cabot was an Italian navigator who had moved to England. He wanted to find a northwest passage to Asia. King Henry VII gave him permission. In 1497 Cabot sailed westward into the Atlantic. He had one ship and a crew of 18.

Cabot's Voyages

Cabot sailed almost straight west across the Atlantic Ocean. There he found land. Like Columbus, Cabot thought he had reached Asia. But he had reached an island off the coast of North America. Cabot and the crew were the first Europeans to see this part of North America since the Vikings.

In the shallow waters near Newfoundland, Cabot and the crew found millions of fish. These fishing grounds, called the Grand Banks, are one of the richest fishing grounds in the world. Find the Grand Banks on the map of French, English, and Dutch explorers on page 42.

Cabot sailed southward along the coast of North America for many miles. But he found no cities, no spices, no gold.

King Henry was disappointed. But the English soon found out how important the Grand Banks were. They sent ships there to fish. For many years these fishing banks were a great source of wealth to England. Later, England claimed North America because of John Cabot's voyages.

Sir Francis Drake

About 60 years after John Cabot's voyages, a new ruler came to the throne of England. During Queen Elizabeth's rule, England began to challenge Spain on the high seas. English sailors became good navigators. Their ships were well designed for faster and easier sailing. Some English sailors captured Spanish ships and took their treasure to England.

The best known of the English sailors was Francis Drake. Time and again, Drake robbed the Spanish ships. But he was not satisfied with robbing ships on the Atlantic coast only. He sailed through the Strait of Magellan to the Pacific Ocean. Then he sailed north along the west coast of South America. He kept sailing until he came to the coast of what is now California. Drake crossed the Pacific and followed Magellan's route back to Europe. Trace Drake's route on the map of explorers searching for the Far East on page 34.

Drake was the second person to sail around the world. Queen Elizabeth rewarded Drake by making him a knight. After that he was called "Sir Francis Drake."

Sir Walter Raleigh was one of the most interesting figures in English history. This soldier, explorer, writer, and businessman helped start *colonies* in North America.

Raleigh's Colonies

An English noble decided to settle the land in North America claimed by England. Sir Walter Raleigh (rô′lē) spent much money trying to start a *colony* (kol′ə nē) in North America. A colony is a group of settlers living in an area apart from, but under the control of, the country from which they come. Starting a colony was a good way to help a country hold the land it claimed.

Raleigh's colony was on Roanoke (rō′ə nōk′) Island, off the coast of what is now North Carolina. But the settlers spent their time looking for gold instead of growing food. Soon the food they had brought with them was gone. Luckily, Raleigh's friend Francis Drake arrived to see how they were getting along. The starving settlers begged him to take them home. They all returned to England.

Although his first colony failed, Sir Walter Raleigh did not give up. In 1587 he sent another group of colonists to Roanoke Island. However, crops did not grow well on the poor soil of the island. The governor, John White, went back to England for more food and supplies. He had to leave behind his daughter. His granddaughter, Virginia Dare, was the first English baby born in America.

At this time England was at war with Spain. There were no ships sailing to America. It was 3 years before White could return to Roanoke Island. When he returned, he found all the colonists gone! The only trace left behind was the strange word "Croatoan" (krō ə tō′ən) carved on a tree trunk. No one has ever found out the meaning of this word. This settlement came to be called the "Lost Colony". No further settlements were attempted by Raleigh.

French Explorers in America

Late in the summer of 1534 Jacques Cartier (zhäk′ kär tē ā′) was exploring the waters of a gulf near Newfoundland. The King of France had sent Cartier to look for a westward passage

An Age of Exploration

Explorer	Date of Exploration	Country Represented	Purpose	Results
Christopher Columbus	1492-1502	Spain (Columbus was Italian)	Find trade route to the East by sailing west	First European since the Vikings to arrive at the Americas
Amerigo Vespucci	1497	Spain (Vespucci was Italian)	Find all-water trade route to Asia	Explored the coastline of South America; person for whom Americas are named
John Cabot	1497	England (Cabot was Italian)	Find northwest passage around North America to Asia	Claimed the northeastern part of North America for England
Pedro Cabral	1509	Portugal	Find trade route to India by sailing around Africa	Claimed what is now Brazil for Portugal
Sebastian Cabot	1509	England, then Spain (Cabot was Italian)	Find northwest passage around North America to Asia	Explored the coast of South America for Spain
Juan Ponce de León	1513	Spain	Find the fountain of youth	Explored the coast of Florida and claimed the lands for Spain
Vasco de Balboa	1513	Spain	Find gold, riches, and an ocean	First European to see the Pacific Ocean
Ferdinand Magellan	1519-1522	Spain (Magellan was Portuguese but became a Spaniard before his voyage)	Find southwest passage to the Far East	First explorer to sail around the earth
Hernando Cortés	1519-1522	Spain	Find gold and riches; conquest	Conquered the Aztecs of Mexico; founded Veracruz, first European settlement on the mainland of of the Americas
Giovanni da Verrazano	1524	France (da Verrazano was Italian)	Find northwest passage to the Indies	Explored the east coast of North America
Juan Cabeza de Vaca	1528	Spain	Explore the American Southwest	First European to explore the American Southwest
Francisco Pizarro	1531	Spain	Find gold and riches; conquest	Conquered the Incan Empire in South America
Jacques Cartier	1534, 1535	France	Find northwest passage to Asia around North America	Claimed the region of the St. Lawrence River for France
Estevanico	1539	Spain (Estevanico was African)	Find the "Seven Cities of Cibola"	Explored parts of what is now southwestern United States
Francisco Coronado	1540-1542	Spain	Find the "Seven Cities of Cibola"	Claimed all lands west of the Mississippi for Spain
Hernando De Soto	1541	Spain	Find gold and other riches	First European to see the Mississippi River
Jean Rodriquez Cabrillo	1542	Spain (Cabrillo was Portuguese)	Find gold, riches, and land for Spain	Claimed the coast of California for Spain
Martin Frobisher	1576-1578	England	Find northwest passage around North America to Asia	Unsuccessful in finding a northwest passage
Sir Francis Drake	1577-1580	England	Capture Spanish treasure ships	Second to sail around the earth
Sir Walter Raleigh	1584-1587	England	Find places to colonize for trade	Failed to establish lasting colonies
Samuel de Champlain	1608-1616	France	Find places to establish a fur trade in North America	Established the first French colonies along the St. Lawrence River
Henry Hudson	1609-1610	Netherlands and the Dutch East India Company	Find northwest passage to the Far East	Claimed the Hudson River area for the Netherlands; explored Hudson Bay for England
Louis Joliet and Father Jacques Marquette	1673	France	Explore the Mississippi River to its mouth	Traveled the river to what is now Arkansas
La Salle	1682	France	Explore the entire length of the Mississippi	Explored the entire length of the Mississippi; named the Mississippi Valley Louisiana; claimed it for France

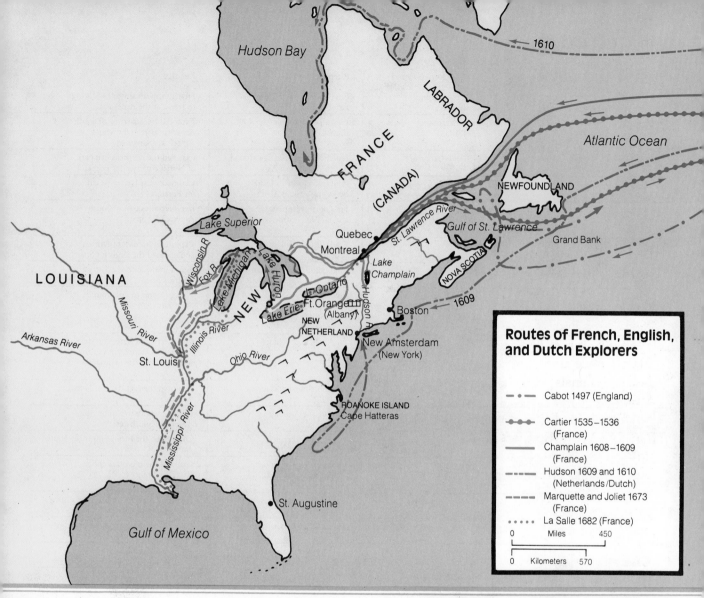

Map labels: Hudson Bay, LABRADOR, Atlantic Ocean, FRANCE (CANADA), NEWFOUNDLAND, St. Lawrence River, Gulf of St. Lawrence, Grand Bank, Lake Superior, Quebec, Montreal, Wisconsin R., Fox R., Lake Michigan, Lake Huron, Lake Champlain, NOVA SCOTIA, LOUISIANA, L. Ontario, NEW, Lake Erie, Ft. Orange, (Albany), NETHERLAND, NEW, Boston, 1609, Missouri River, Illinois River, Ohio River, NEW AMSTERDAM (New York), Arkansas River, St. Louis, Mississippi River, ROANOKE ISLAND, Cape Hatteras, St. Augustine, Gulf of Mexico

Routes of French, English, and Dutch Explorers

- —·— Cabot 1497 (England)
- —●— Cartier 1535–1536 (France)
- ——— Champlain 1608–1609 (France)
- —··— Hudson 1609 and 1610 (Netherlands/Dutch)
- — — — Marquette and Joliet 1673 (France)
- ····· La Salle 1682 (France)

0 Miles 450
0 Kilometers 570

Jacques Cartier was France's first explorer in North America. Trace the route he followed. Who was another French explorer? Who gave England a claim to North America? Trace the route followed by Henry Hudson.

Cartier and the St. Lawrence River

The next year Cartier came back to the Gulf of St. Lawrence. He sailed westward feeling sure that he would reach the Pacific Ocean. The waterway grew narrow at the place where Mon-

through America. Cartier sailed in and out among the islands until he found what he thought was a water passage. But winter prevented him from exploring it. Cartier had to sail home. What Cartier thought was a water passage to Asia was really the Gulf of St. Lawrence.

treal (mon'trē ôl') now stands. Cartier knew he was not following a passage to Asia. He named the waterway the St. Lawrence River. Find this river on the map of French, English, and Dutch explorers on page 42.

The Great Lakes, the St. Lawrence River, and the rivers that flow into them drain a large area. Cartier claimed all this land for France. It was called New France.

French fur traders were not interested in New France until fox, beaver, and other fur-bearing animals were discovered in its forests. Such furs would sell for a good price in France. So French trading companies sent traders to New France to get furs. These traders spent years in the forests trading with the Indian trappers for furs. They shipped the furs to France. But in time the traders went home. Many years passed after Cartier's voyage before the French built homes there.

Champlain and Quebec

One morning in 1608 a ship flying a French flag lay in the St. Lawrence River. Indian canoes were beached on the shore near the Indian village of Quebec (kwi bek'). The French were getting ready to build a fort and a storehouse to hold supplies.

"We will build our fort on this cliff high above the river," said the French leader. "We can come here in case of attack. Our homes will be at the foot of the cliff near the river, where we can trade with the Indians for furs. Ships from France can easily reach us."

Samuel de Champlain (sham plān'), the French leader, had brought 27 people to make a settlement in the land France claimed. It was named Quebec and became the first lasting French settlement in North America.

Champlain set out to find a northwest passage through America. With Huron (hyoor'ən), Indians he went south. Champlain found a large lake in what is now New York State. It is called Lake Champlain in his honor. He helped the Hurons defeat their enemy, the Iroquois.

By 1615 Champlain had reached Lake Huron, named for his Indian friends. He sent out other explorers. By the time he died, in 1635, France controlled the Great Lakes region. Find these lakes on the map on page 42.

Joliet and Marquette

In 1673 two French explorers had reached the Mississippi River. They were Louis Joliet (loo'ē jō'lē et') and Father Jacques Marquette (zhäk' mär ket'), a priest. They were searching for the *mouth* (mouth), or the end, of the river. Other French explorers had found the *source* (sôrs), or beginning, of the river.

Joliet and Marquette went south down the Mississippi past the *tributaries* (trib'yə ter'ēz) of the Ohio and Arkansas rivers. A tributary is a river which flows into a larger river. They turned back when Indians told them the river did not flow west to the Pacific or east to the Atlantic. The Indians said that the great river continued south.

La Salle

One of the great French explorers was La Salle (lə sal'). His ship was the first ever to sail on the Great Lakes.

In 1682 La Salle set out to find the mouth of the Mississippi River. In spite of many misfortunes he followed the river to its mouth at the Gulf of Mexico. He named the Mississippi Valley Louisiana in honor of King Louis XIV. He claimed the area for France.

La Salle sailed to France to get colonists. He wanted to build a settlement at the mouth of the Mississippi. In this way he hoped to hold the land for France. Sailing back to Louisiana, the captain of La Salle's ship failed to find the river's mouth. When the colonists landed they were on Spanish territory and in great danger. Some of La Salle's followers turned on La Salle and killed him. Then Comanche (kə man'chē) Indians killed his followers.

La Salle's dream of a colony failed, but he added the great Mississippi Valley to the French claims. The map of European claims in North America on page 45 shows that the French claimed the land drained by the St. Lawrence and the Mississippi rivers. They controlled the great waterways which were the only roads into North America.

The Dutch in America

The Dutch, as the people of the Netherlands are called, began late in the race to claim new lands. The Netherlands is a small country in northern Europe. A group of Dutch merchants, called the Dutch East India Company, wanted to increase their trade with the Far East. These traders sought a northeast passage around northern Europe. They thought such a route would be shorter than the route around

Africa. In 1609 the traders hired Henry Hudson, an English navigator, to find this passage to Asia. With a crew of 20 Dutch and English sailors, Hudson set out.

Hudson's Voyages

Hudson and the crew of 20 soon found the northern seas to be stormy and full of icebergs. Rather than risk the lives of the crew, Hudson changed course. He hoped to find a northwest passage to Asia around North America. Once across the Atlantic Ocean, Hudson sailed into a large harbor, or protected body of water. The *Half Moon,* Hudson's ship, sailed up the river which flowed into the harbor. For a while, Hudson thought it might be the northwest passage. The river is now called the Hudson River after Henry Hudson. He claimed the surrounding land for the Netherlands. Later, the English claimed this land.

The Dutch East India Company was disappointed that Hudson had failed to find a short route to the Far East. But they were pleased with the valuable furs Hudson and the crew brought back. They named the lands Hudson had explored New Netherland. The Dutch East India Company established settlements to protect their land claims and the fur trade. They built Fort Orange, located at what is now Albany, New York. They built another fort on the island where New York City is today.

The Dutch chose their locations well. They controlled the finest harbor on the east coast of North America. Study the map of early settlements in the Northeast on page 57. Find New Amsterdam, now New York. It is at the mouth

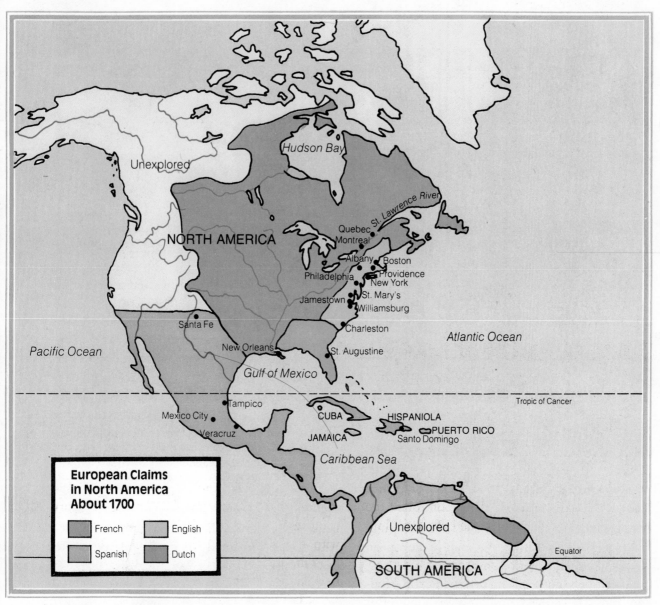

European Claims
in North America
About 1700

French		English
Spanish		Dutch

Hudson Bay

Unexplored

NORTH AMERICA

St. Lawrence River

Quebec
Montreal
Albany   Boston
Philadelphia   Providence
New York
Jamestown   St. Mary's
Williamsburg

Santa Fe

Charleston

Pacific Ocean

New Orleans   St. Augustine

Gulf of Mexico

Atlantic Ocean

Tropic of Cancer

Tampico
Mexico City   CUBA   HISPANIOLA
Veracruz   JAMAICA   PUERTO RICO
Santo Domingo

Caribbean Sea

Unexplored

Equator

SOUTH AMERICA

This map shows how much land was claimed in the Americas by four European nations about 200 years after Columbus's voyages.

of the Hudson River on New York Bay. Notice that the large island and the mainland almost surround the bay.

Trading companies were still interested in finding short routes to Asia. An English trading company hired Henry Hudson to sail for them. They wanted to locate a northwest passage to Asia. In 1610, Hudson again crossed the Atlantic. This time he sailed into a bay in northern North America. A bay is an arm of the sea that

Henry Hudson sails his ship, the *Half Moon,* up the river later named for him. Besides exploring the Hudson River, this English sea captain also sailed along the Atlantic Coast as far as what is now South Carolina.

extends into the land. This bay is now known as Hudson Bay. Find it on the map of European claims in North America on page 45.

After spending a bitter, cold winter in Hudson Bay, the crew wanted to go home. But Hudson wanted to continue to explore for a northwest passage. The crew took control of the ship. They set Henry Hudson, his son, and his loyal crew members adrift in a tiny boat. The crew returned to England and told of the huge bay in the heart of North America. Hudson Bay was claimed for England. But Henry Hudson had disappeared without a trace.

Explorers gave Spain, Portugal, France, England, and the Netherlands claims to North America. It remained for groups of settlers to back up these claims.

Do You Know?

1. What kind of land did Leif Eriscon find?
2. Why did European merchants want to trade with the Far East?
3. How did America get its name?
4. How did Raleigh try to help England hold the land it claimed?

To Help You Learn

Using New Words

tributary	colony
immigrant	mouth
glacier	ecology
navigator	source
irrigation	Viking

The phrases below explain the words listed above. Number a paper from 1 through 10. After each number write the word that matches the definition.

1. The beginning of a river
2. The end of a river
3. The study of how living things relate to their surroundings
4. One of the sea rovers, often from Norway, who were among the first Europeans to find North America
5. A great sheet of ice
6. A group of settlers living in an area apart from, but under the control of, the country from which they came
7. A river which flows into a larger river
8. A person who moves from one land to another to make a home
9. Bringing water to dry land through pipes or sprinklers
10. A person who guides ships

Finding the Facts

1. How does the latitude of a place help to explain its climate?
2. What does conservation mean?
3. Why did early peoples cross northern Asia into North America?
4. In what way were American Indian tribes alike?
5. Why did Europeans need an all-water trade route to the Far East?
6. Why was Magellan's voyage important?
7. What part of our country did Ponce de León, De Soto, Estevanico, and Coronado each explore for Spain?
8. What explorer gave England a claim to land in the Americas? How did England try to hold its claims?
9. What English explorer gave the Netherlands a claim to land in North America?
10. What did each of the following French explorers do in North America: Cartier, Champlain, Joliet and Marquette, and La Salle?

Learning from Maps

1. Look at the physical map of North and South America on page 13. What two oceans does the Bering Strait connect? What three oceans border North America? What isthmus joins North America and South America? Through which continent does the equator pass?
2. Look at the maps of natural vegetation on page 18. Which continent has a tundra? A steppe? A desert? Which part of each continent has mountain vegetation?

3. Turn to the map of explorers on page 34. Which explorer traveled from Portugal to India? Who traveled from Spain to San Salvador? In what year did Dias travel around the Cape of Good Hope? From which country did Drake leave? Who went around the world first, Drake or Magellan? Trace the voyages of Drake and Magellan on a globe.

4. Look at the map showing routes of the principal Spanish explorers in the Americas on page 36. Which explorer traveled from Hispaniola to Panama? Who went to the area of Cibola? What river did De Soto cross? From which island did Ponce de León begin his travels?

5. Turn to the map showing routes of French, English, and Dutch explorers on page 42. Who was the first explorer to travel to the Gulf of St. Lawrence? What area did Hudson explore in 1609? What did Hudson explore in 1610? Which explorer, Champlain or Cartier, traveled down the St. Lawrence River first? Which explorers traveled on the Mississippi River? Which explorers reached the Gulf of Mexico?

6. On the map on page 45 find the land in North America claimed by European nations in 1700. Which nation claimed the largest area? Which claimed the land where Jamestown is located? Which claimed the lands where Santa Fe and St. Augustine are located? What region was unexplored?

Using Study Skills

1. **Time Line:** The following events are not in the order in which they happened. Write them in the correct order. Check with your book for the dates.
   a. Jacques Cartier explores the Gulf of St. Lawrence.
   b. Joliet and Marquette explore part of the Mississippi River.
   c. Pedro Cabral reaches a part of South America.
   d. Estevanico and Father Marcos search for Seven Cities of Cibola.
   e. Henry Hudson explores Hudson Bay for England.
   f. Balboa sees the Pacific Ocean.

2. **Chart:** Look carefully at the age-of-exploration chart on page 41. Make a list of the explorers who were looking for new trade routes or passages to Asia. List those who were looking for gold or riches in the Americas. List the explorers who were looking for a place to establish a colony in the Americas.

   Which explorers found what they were seeking?

   Which explorer was not a European? Which three European countries did most of the exploring of North America?

   How many years passed between the voyage of Columbus and La Salle's exploration of the Mississippi River?

Thinking it Through

1. A weather report in an Argentine newspaper for July 31 said: "Today the temperature in Buenos Aires will go down to freezing." Could this report be true? Explain.
2. Long ago, five and later six, Iroquois tribes joined together to form a nation. They promised to help each other if attacked. Today many countries have united to form the United Nations to maintain world peace. Compare the purposes of the two groups.
3. There were no European voyages to the Americas for almost 500 years after the Vikings. Why do you think there were so many voyages of exploration after the voyage of Columbus?
4. Someone once said that Columbus's voyage to America was "a lucky accident." Do you agree? Explain.
5. The Americas were not named for Columbus. Do you think they should have been? What other possible names could have been given to the Americas?

Projects

1. Write a story about the "Lost Colony" of Roanoke. Try to explain what "Croatoan" meant and what really happened to the settlers.
2. Your class might like to have a social studies club. If so, have a class meeting to discuss how it would be set up.

Every club has committees to do its work. A committee is made up of several members who do one kind of work or project. Each committee should have a leader or chairperson for a project.

One group of students might like to belong to the Explorers' Committee. The members of this committee will find out more about faraway places.

The Explorers' Committee might find out about Henry Hudson's last voyage. Hudson, his son, and seven sailors were put adrift in a small boat and were never heard from again. Why did this happen? What do people think became of Hudson?

Some students might like to start a Research Committee. They will learn more about people and events in the past.

The Research Committee might choose to study Indian names. More than half of the 50 states in the United States have Indian names. How many of these do you know? What Indian groups lived in your state before the arrival of the Europeans? Use an encyclopedia to find out how they lived. Are their descendants still living in your state today?

Other students might form a Reading Committee. They will find interesting books to read and share with the class.

The Reading Committee might look for books about Aztec legends. The stories of the Plumed Serpent and the Smoking Mirror could be retold to the class.

2 Becoming a Nation

Unit Preview

Five European countries—Spain, England, France, Portugal, and the Netherlands—claimed land in the Americas in the early 1600s. Some people came to the Americas to find religious freedom. Others came for adventure or to find riches.

The first permanent British settlement in North America was made in the Southeast in 1607. The second was made in the Northeast in 1620. British people kept coming to North America long after these settlements. Georgia was the last of the original thirteen colonies to be settled. More and more people came to settle colonies on the Atlantic coast of North America.

By 1763 there were thirteen British colonies along the Atlantic coast. After a war with the French, the British became the major power in North America. The British began to place demands on the colonists. They put taxes on products like paper and tea. British troops were stationed in cities.

The colonists wrote to the king about these problems. He never sent a reply. The colonists then decided to break away from the British government. On July 4, 1776, the colonies declared their independence. But to gain independence they had to fight a long war. Fighting began at Lexington in 1775, and ended when the British surrendered at Yorktown in 1781.

Things to Discover

If you look carefully at the picture, map, and time line, you can answer these questions.

1. The map shows the thirteen British colonies in North America. What ocean borders these colonies?
2. The picture shows a marching band dressed as Virginia colonists. When was the colony of Jamestown, in Virginia, founded?
3. When did the Pilgrims come to Plymouth? How many years was this after the founding of Jamestown?
4. What document was adopted in 1776?
5. How many years passed between the battles of Lexington and Concord and the British surrender at Yorktown?

Words to Learn

You will meet these words in this unit. As you read, you will learn what they mean, and how to pronounce them. The Word List will help you.

act	money crop
assembly	piedmont
boycott	plantation
charter	representative
constitution	surrender
indentured servant	tax
independence	tidewater region
indigo	treaty

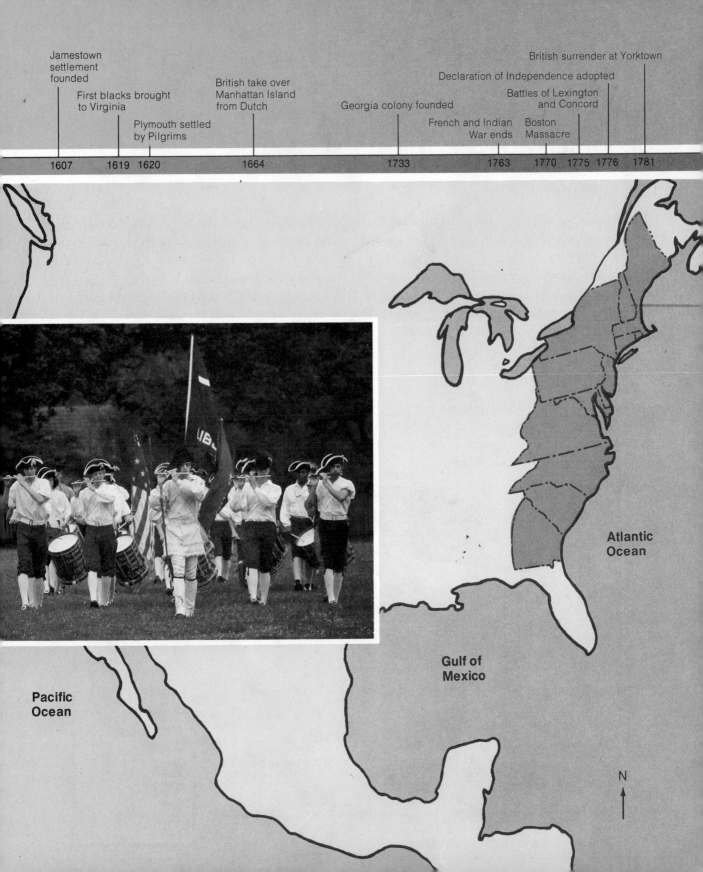

Jamestown
settlement
founded

First blacks brought
to Virginia

Plymouth settled
by Pilgrims

British take over
Manhattan Island
from Dutch

Georgia colony founded

French and Indian
War ends

Boston
Massacre

British surrender at Yorktown

Declaration of Independence adopted

Battles of Lexington
and Concord

1607   1619 1620   1664   1733   1763   1770 1775 1776 1781

Atlantic
Ocean

Gulf of
Mexico

Pacific
Ocean

N

1
Geography of the Thirteen Colonies

The landforms of the eastern United States were important to the Europeans who set up colonies here more than 300 years ago. The map below shows how the East Coast would look if we could fly high enough to see it all at one time. This region has many different land and water forms.

The Atlantic Coastal Plain

The Atlantic Coastal Plain extends from Cape Cod, in Massachusetts, south to Florida. This coastal plain rises only a little above sea level and borders on the Atlantic Ocean.

The soil of the Atlantic Coastal Plain is deep and sandy. It is suited to raising vegetables and fruits. American Indians and early settlers could raise the food they needed.

The Atlantic Coastal Plain has many bays and harbors. A coastline with many bays and harbors is called an irregular coastline. Many fish live in the coastal waters. With fishing grounds and protected harbors, many colonists turned to the sea for their living.

Early settlers established a foothold in the Atlantic Coastal Plain. What cities on the Coastal Plain became important harbors? Why was it a good place for people to live?

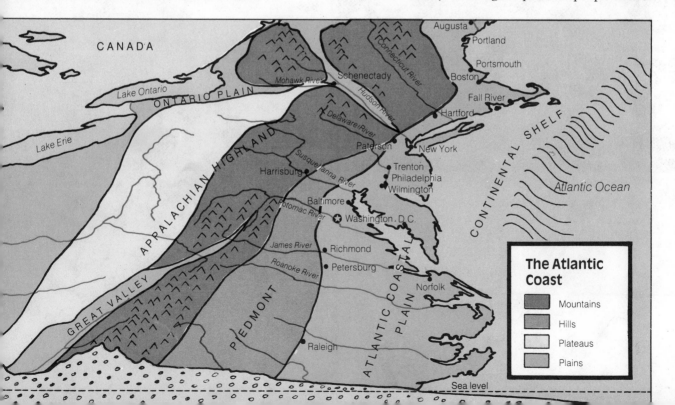

The Atlantic Coast

- Mountains
- Hills
- Plateaus
- Plains

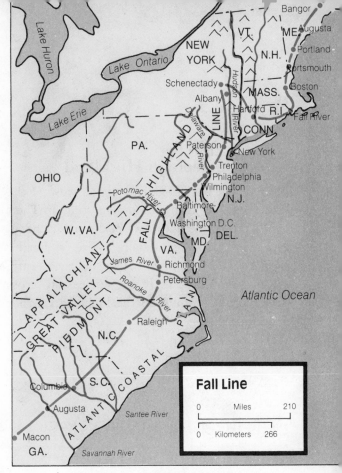

In the area of Virginia, Maryland, and Delaware, rivers flow across land that is near sea level. Ocean tides flow upstream for many miles. These tides cause the rivers to flood their banks for some distance inland. Therefore, this section of the coastal plain is called the *tidewater region* (tīd′wô′tər rē′jən). Many colonists had farms along these rivers. Ships from Europe could stop at the farms to load or unload products.

The Fall Line

The map on this page shows that the rivers of the Atlantic Coastal Plain have their sources in the Appalachian Highland. The rivers flow across the *Piedmont* (pēd′mont) with its foundation of hard rock. A piedmont is an upland region lying along or near the foot of a mountain range. The place where the Piedmont and the Atlantic Coastal Plain meet is known as the fall line. The eastern edge of the Piedmont forms a rocky ledge, and the rivers tumble over it to the lower coastal plain. Waterfalls are found at the edge of the Piedmont in these rivers.

Below the fall line the rivers are slow and wide. Colonial ships sailed up some rivers as far as the falls.

These waterfalls were used to power water wheels. Grain and lumber mills were built at the falls by the early settlers. Soon towns grew up along the fall line. Some towns became the busy manufacturing cities of today. Baltimore in Maryland, Trenton in New Jersey, and Richmond in Virginia are some of these manufacturing cities.

Nineteen major cities eventually developed along the fall line, a narrow area between the Piedmont and the Coastal Plain.

The Piedmont

As coastal lands became crowded, colonists moved inland to the Piedmont region. The Piedmont lies between the Atlantic Coastal Plain and the Appalachian Highland. It extends from the Hudson River south to central Alabama. Find the Piedmont on the map of the fall line on this page.

The Piedmont is a region of rolling hills, green valleys, and slopes covered with trees. Its foundation is hard rock, but the soil is deep and fertile. Settlers could raise crops and livestock on the Piedmont. They could also use wood from the Piedmont forests to build and repair their wooden ships.

The Appalachian Highland

The Appalachian Highland to the west of the Piedmont has many mountain ranges. Their slopes are gentle and their peaks are rounded. However, these mountains were a barrier to the early colonists. They did not settle in the region at first. It was not easy to cross over the mountains, and the highland was not good for farming.

Do You Know?

1. Why did American Indians and early colonists find it easy to raise food in the Atlantic Coastal Plain?
2. What is the fall line?
3. How was the Piedmont region useful to the colonists?

2
Settling the Colonies

Spaniards were the first settlers from Europe in the Americas. Soon after Columbus's voyage, Spaniards began to settle in South America and the southern part of North America. Today, Spanish is the chief language spoken in much of this area.

Later, settlers came to the rest of North America. These settlers were from Spain, Great Britain, France, Germany, and the Netherlands. These settlers established thirteen colonies that became the foundation of the United States.

The Founding of Virginia

As you know, Sir Walter Raleigh twice failed to found a British colony in Virginia. About 20 years later, some people in England decided to form a company to found a colony in Virginia.

King James I gave the company a *charter* (chär′tər). The charter was a paper that granted them the right to form a company, carry on trade, and make settlements in Virginia. The company was named the London Company.

The London Company offered to pay the costs of travel and settlement for all people who would go to Virginia to live. In return, the settlers promised to send the company all the gold and silver they found for 7 years. After that, the land and its products would belong to the colonists.

The Building of Jamestown

In the spring of 1607 a group of colonists sailed up Chesapeake (ches′ə pēk) Bay. See the map of early settlements on page 57. At the mouth of a broad river they built their settlement. In

54

honor of their king, they named the river the James and their settlement, Jamestown.

These first settlers of Jamestown were mainly interested in looking for gold and silver. The important job of clearing the land and planting crops did not seem important to them. They did not worry about using up their food.

Captain John Smith became the leader of the colony. He brought a sense of purpose to Jamestown. He locked up the food supplies in the common storehouse. "Only those who work shall eat," he said. How the settlers grumbled! But they went to work.

However, the settlers had started working too late. Winter came, and their homes were not finished. They had not raised enough food. Their ship had returned to England for more supplies. Luckily for the colonists, the Powhatan (pou′ə tan′) Indians agreed to supply Jamestown with food. Later on, Pocahontas (pō′kə hon′təs), daughter of an Indian chief, and other Indians taught the colonists how to grow corn and potatoes.

The colony was barely surviving. Then John Smith was badly burned in a gunpowder explosion. He returned to England for treatment. The following winter many settlers died from lack of food. That winter became known as the "starving time."

The members of the London Company were worried about their colony. They knew a strong leader was needed. They decided to send three ships to Jamestown. The ships brought a governor, 500 settlers, and a year's supply of food. England had its first permanent, or lasting, settlement in North America.

This likeness of Captain John Smith is in his book *The Generall Historie of Virginia, New England and the Summer Isles*, published in England in 1624.

Virginia in 1619

Two important events occurred in Virginia in 1619. One was the arrival of 90 women. Until then few women had come to Jamestown.

Another important event in 1619 was the arrival of the first blacks from Africa. Landowners were unwilling to work the land themselves. They wanted a source of cheap labor. The American Indians would not work for the settlers. When a Dutch ship brought 20 blacks, the Virginians traded goods for them.

At first many of the blacks were treated as *indentured servants* (in den′chərd sur′vənts). Indentured servants would work a few years for the person who had paid the cost of their passage to America. Although there were some free blacks, most blacks came to be treated as slaves, the permanent property of their owners. Slavery became an institution throughout many colonies. It was an institution that benefited only slave owners. Slaves had no rights and no protection under the law.

John Rolfe, one of the colonists, discovered that money could be made by raising tobacco and shipping it to Europe. So the colonists began to grow tobacco. Black slaves provided the cheap labor that was needed for working in tobacco fields.

Soon colonists had *plantations* (plan tā′shənz) on which they raised only tobacco. A plantation is a large farm on which one crop is raised. Tobacco became the first *money crop* (mun′ē crop), or crop that is grown to be sold rather than to be used directly by the farmer.

Self-Government in Virginia

The members of the London Company decided to allow the colonists to make their own laws. The colonists could organize an *assembly* (ə sem′blē) to govern themselves. An assembly was a group of leaders who made laws for the colony.

The colonists were glad to take part in their government. But there was not room for all the colonists from the 11 settlements or towns to attend the assembly. So each town voted for 2 *representatives* (rep′ri zen′tə tivz), or people to

act for the town at assembly meetings. Only white males who owned land could vote.

The representatives who attended the assembly were called burgesses (bur′jis əz). The burgesses met with the governor and other officers of the company in Jamestown. The Virginia House of Burgesses held its first meeting on July 30, 1619. This lawmaking assembly was the beginning of representative government in our country.

The Settlement of Massachusetts

The earliest settlements in the northern part of the Atlantic Coastal Plain were made in Massachusetts (mas′ə choo′sits). These colonists came primarily for religious reasons.

King James I wanted all the people to belong to the Church of England. But some groups of British people thought that no king had the right to order people to attend a certain church. One group who refused to attend the king's church wanted to separate from the Church of England. They were called Separatists (sep′ər ə tists).

One group of Separatists decided to go to the Netherlands, a nearby country in Europe. There they could go to any church. They had freedom of religion. For a while the Separatists were happy in their new homes. Then they became homesick for England.

"Let us go to America," someone suggested.

Why do you think most early settlements in North America were near the ocean? Which early settlements were inland? How do you explain their location?

56

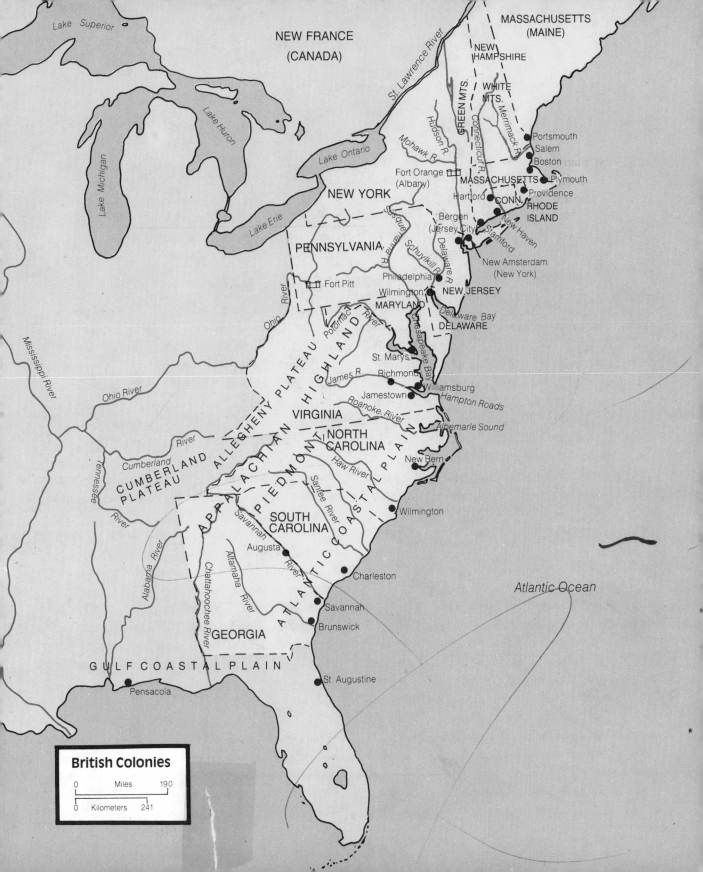

"There our children could be raised as English people on English soil." They received permission from the king and the London Company to go to America to build a colony. Because the Separatists had traveled from place to place looking for religious freedom, they came to be called Pilgrims.

The Voyage to America

In September of 1620, the Pilgrims set sail in a ship called the *Mayflower*. More than 2 months later, they reached Cape Cod in Massachusetts. The Pilgrims decided not to sail south to the land the London Company had given them. Instead, they looked for a better spot along the coast. They agreed to choose their own leaders and to make laws that would benefit everyone. They chose John Carver as their governor. They signed an agreement, the *Mayflower Compact,* that stated that they would be ruled by laws that they would make.

The Plymouth Settlement

Late in December 1620, the settlers found a place where a river flowed into a bay. The settlement they founded was named Plymouth. Only a few buildings and the stockade were finished that winter. A stockade is a high fence built for protection.

All this time the Pilgrims lived on the *Mayflower*. They did not have enough food. Almost half of the group died, including Governor Carver. William Bradford was chosen to be the new governor.

Two things helped to save the colonists from dying. They were given corn by the Indians, and they were able to catch many fish from Cape Cod Bay.

When at last spring came, the Pilgrims cut trees, hunted, trapped, and fished. The lumber, fish, and furs were loaded onto the *Mayflower* and sent to England.

Pilgrims and Indians

Samoset was a Pemaquid (pem'ə kwid) Indian. He had learned English from some British sailors who had come to fish. Samoset visited the Pilgrims with Squanto (skwän'tō), a Pawtuxet (päw tuk'set) who also spoke English.

Squanto taught the Pilgrims how to plant corn. He put fish into the ground with the seed to fertilize, or make the soil richer. When the soil was fertilized, a better corn crop could be grown. Squanto also taught the Pilgrims how to hunt and how to spear fish. The Pilgrims and Indians lived in peace for many years.

In the winter of 1621, the Pilgrims set aside a day of thanks for their good fortune. They invited Chief Massasoit (mas'ə soit) of the Wampanoags (wäm'pə nō'əgz) and other Indians who had helped them. The feast held by the Pilgrims was the first New England Thanksgiving. Earlier, in 1619, settlers at Berkeley Plantation on the James River in Virginia had observed a religious celebration of thanksgiving.

The Puritans

Other people in England also wanted to leave the country because they could not worship as they wished. These people were members of a group known as Puritans. Puritans did not want to separate from the Church of England. They

Before landing in North America, the Pilgrims aboard the *Mayflower* signed the Mayflower Compact. It was the first plan for self-government in America.

wanted instead to purify it. By "purify" they meant that they wanted plainer buildings and simpler religious services.

These Puritans belonged to the Massachusetts Bay Company, which had been formed to build colonies and to trade with North America. The king had given the company a charter granting the right to settle on Massachusetts Bay north of Plymouth. A Puritan settlement had already been started at Salem, Massachusetts, in 1628. See the map of early settlements on page 57.

About 1,000 Puritans left Great Britain for Massachusetts in 1630. Among them was Anne Bradstreet. She became America's first woman poet. Before the Puritans sailed, they chose John Winthrop as the governor of their colony.

Starting Massachusetts Bay Colony

The Puritans found most of the people in Salem ill. The leaders decided to find a more healthful place in which to settle.

Governor Winthrop's colonists followed the coastline south. They found a brook of clear water flowing into Massachusetts Bay. There the Puritans built a town which they called Boston.

Each year more Puritans arrived. By 1640 there were 22 towns in the Massachusetts Bay Colony. All were on uplands along the coast and usually beside streams or rivers.

Town Meetings

Each Massachusetts town had a meeting house. It was used as a church. It was also the place where the people carried out the business of the town. Later the Puritans built town halls in which to hold meetings. At the town meetings laws were made and officers chosen. Only those in good standing with the church could vote.

The Town Hall in Boston was the most important meeting house in the colony. There the

Life in the early Plymouth colony is re-created at Plimoth Plantation, near the site of the Pilgrims' landing. Visitors can see buildings, the stockade, people in Pilgrim dress, and a reconstruction of the *Mayflower* called *Mayflower II*.

assembly, which made laws for the colony, met several times a year. Each town sent one or two representatives to the assembly. It was the duty of the representatives to choose a governor and other officers. The representatives voted on problems that had to do with the whole colony. Through the town meetings and the assembly the colonists ruled themselves.

Education

The Puritans wanted their children to be able to read. At first children were taught at home or went in groups to a neighbor's house. Soon a law was passed requiring each town of 50 or more families to support a school. Towns with 100 families had to have "grammar schools." Six years after Boston was settled, Harvard College was started. Harvard was the first college in North America.

The Pequot Indians

Many Puritans did not get along well with the Indians. The Pequot (pē′kwät) Indians had lived in the Connecticut River Valley for a long time. In 1636 colonists accused a Pequot of killing a Massachusetts settler. The colonists burned a Pequot village. They attacked another Pequot village and killed hundreds of Indians. Most of the remaining Pequots were captured and sold as slaves.

The Settling of Rhode Island

The Puritans had come to America for freedom to worship in their own way. People of other religions came to Massachusetts for the same

Indians from the Narragansett tribe cared for Roger Williams after he left the Massachusetts Bay Colony. Why do you think the Indians helped Roger Williams?

reason. The Puritans were very strict. They wanted other colonists to worship as they did.

Not all Puritans, however, believed that everyone should have to follow Puritan ways. Roger Williams, a Puritan minister, believed in religious freedom. He was disappointed when he saw how Puritan leaders treated people who worshipped differently. Williams told the Puritans that they had been unfair to the Indians. He declared that the land in the Americas belonged to the Indians. He said the colonists should have paid the Indians for it.

The Puritan leaders wanted to send Williams to England to be punished for speaking out against them. But Roger Williams slipped away from the colony one cold, winter evening. He wandered alone until some Indians found him. They fed and cared for him. An Indian chief sold Roger Williams a large area of land near Narragansett Bay.

Religious Freedom in Rhode Island

Other persons who were unhappy in Massachusetts joined Roger Williams. At the mouth of a river flowing into Narragansett Bay they built a settlement in 1636. They called it Providence. Roger Williams went to England to get a charter from the king for the new colony. The colony was named Rhode Island.

Anne Hutchinson was another person who was driven from Puritan Boston. Anne and her husband William were forced from the Puritan church because she disagreed with the ministers' teachings. She held discussion groups for people in her home and led them to question the Puritan teachings. Anne was arrested, but she outsmarted the judges at her trial. Because they feared her questions, the leaders drove her from the colony. Anne Hutchinson went to Rhode Island where she founded the settlement of Portsmouth.

Anyone who wanted religious freedom was welcome in Rhode Island. It was the first colony in America where people of any religion were able to settle.

The Settling of Connecticut

Thomas Hooker was another Puritan minister who did not like the strict laws of Massachusetts. He led a group of men, women, and children westward. They built a town on the banks of the Connecticut River where Hartford now stands. Other towns were built along the river and the coast. These towns later joined to form the colony of Connecticut.

Connecticut was also started by people from other colonies. It had no charter from the king. Because every group needs laws, the leaders wrote a *constitution* (kon'stə too'shən), or group of laws, to govern the colony. Connecticut had the first written constitution in modern times that actually worked.

New Hampshire and Maine Pioneers

Before the Pilgrims and Puritans arrived, people had come to North America to fish. They had made settlements along the coast north of Massachusetts. For a while these people were under Massachusetts rule. They were unhappy with the harsh Puritan laws. In time the area that is now New Hampshire became a separate colony under control of the king. The area that is now Maine remained part of Massachusetts long after the United States became an independent nation.

Building New Netherland

New Netherland, claimed by the Dutch, included the Hudson River Valley and part of the Atlantic Coastal Plain.

The Dutch first came to America looking for furs. The fur traders, sent by the Dutch West India Company, did not build towns. But they did build trading posts. One of these was at Fort Orange on the Hudson River. The city of Albany now stands there.

The Dutch government wanted to start colonies in North America to hold the land it claimed. In 1624 a group of Dutch families arrived in New Netherland. Some of them sailed up the Hudson River to Fort Orange. The rest built New Amsterdam near a trading post on Manhattan Island.

Three years after the colony had been set up, Peter Minuit paid the Algonquian (al gong′kē ən) Indians about $24 worth of goods for Manhattan Island. Today New York City stands where New Amsterdam stood, at the mouth of the Hudson River.

Peter Stuyvesant (stī′ve sənt) was one governor who really wanted the colony of New Amsterdam to succeed. He was a strict governor, but he tried to make life in the colony safer. He had the fort made stronger and became friends with the Indians. The colony grew.

Under the British Flag

nerd

The British had been watching New Amsterdam with envy because it had the best harbor on the Atlantic coast. One day in 1664, four British warships sailed boldly into the harbor. Their commander sent a message to Governor Stuyvesant. It demanded that he *surrender* (sə ren′dər), or give up control of, the fort.

Governor Stuyvesant did not want to surrender. But the colonists refused to support him. The British took the Dutch fort without a struggle.

New Netherland became the property of the Duke of York. The British duke changed the name of the colony to New York. Later the colony was divided into three colonies, New York, New Jersey, and Delaware. The Duke of York kept New York. The two other colonies changed ownership several times.

Peter Stuyvesant was angry when the English demanded that the Dutch surrender New Netherland. New Netherland then became New York.

The Settling of New Jersey and Delaware

New Jersey was first settled by people from Sweden, a country in Europe, then by the Dutch. After the British gained control of it, people from Great Britain and from the other colonies came to New Jersey. This colony changed ownership until it became a royal colony in 1702. As a royal colony it belonged to the king instead of to a company.

The first settlement in Delaware was made by people from Sweden. Then Delaware became part of New Netherland. After the British took New Netherland, Delaware belonged to the Duke of York. Later, he sold Delaware to William Penn, who owned the nearby English colony of Pennsylvania.

The Delaware colonists were not pleased. They were used to making their own laws. They did not want to lose their rights of self-government. William Penn decided to allow Delaware to have its own assembly. But it continued to be ruled by the governor of Pennsylvania for years.

The Founding of Pennsylvania

The colony of Pennsylvania was settled by Quakers, a religious group also called the Society of Friends. Quakers were treated harshly in England because of their religious beliefs. These beliefs included not killing people. Therefore, Quakers would not serve as soldiers. They also believed in equality and would not show certain signs of respect to their leaders. Their leader, William Penn, believed that in America Quakers would be free to practice their beliefs. In 1681 a charter for land west of the Delaware River was given to William Penn. The land was named Pennsylvania, which means "Penn's Woods." William Penn became owner of a tract of land larger than all of England.

William Penn and other Quakers arrived in Pennsylvania in 1682. They built a town between the Delaware and the Schuylkill (skool′kil) rivers. It was named Philadelphia, the "City of Brotherly Love."

Penn had a charter for the colony. But he still felt he should pay the real owners. So Penn and Chief Tamanend (tam′ə nend) of the Delaware Indians arranged a *treaty* (trē′tē), or an agreement between groups of people or nations. Penn paid the Delaware Indians for the land

just as he would have paid European landowners. He made an agreement to live at peace with the Indians. As long as Penn lived, the agreement was kept.

Government in Pennsylvania

Governor Penn tried to run Pennsylvania for the good of the people. To help build a fair government, Penn wrote a constitution. In it, he provided for religious freedom.

Rapid Growth of Pennsylvania

Pennsylvania had little coastland. Because the people needed seaports, William Penn bought Delaware from the Duke of York. Penn tried to get more settlers from Europe to come to Pennsylvania. He promised them cheap land and free passage to America. Many pioneers were attracted by Penn's offer. As more Europeans came, Pennsylvania grew rapidly.

Earning a Living

More and more colonists came to the northeastern part of America. They settled in river valleys, on plains, and in the highlands.

Farming, Hunting, and Fishing

The colonists in North America soon began to farm the land. Farming was an important way of getting food. Farming was easy on the Atlantic Coastal Plain of the middle colonies of New York, Pennsylvania, New Jersey, and Delaware.

The colonies of Massachusetts, New Hampshire, Connecticut, and Rhode Island made up the New England colonies. Colonists in New Eng-

William Penn arranged a *treaty* with Chief Tamanend of the Delaware Indian tribe. Penn treated the Indians so fairly that they never attacked his colony.

land found it much harder to raise enough food on their rocky uplands. They had to hunt and fish to add to their food supply. Luckily these colonists could catch codfish in great quantities. Soon they were sending shiploads of dried cod to England each year.

As time passed, skilled workers began to work at their own trades. They traded their extra goods for other goods they needed. Sometimes it would be hard to make a trade. A shoemaker might need clothes at a time when a tailor did not need shoes. So the colonists began to use money to buy what they needed.

More and more New Englanders became skilled workers. Other colonists bought what these workers made. In this way New England became a manufacturing region.

Machines, Factories, and Towns

New England has many swift rivers and falls. Early settlers used the water power to turn mill wheels to grind grain. When new machines were invented the water power was used to turn these also.

The new machines were too large to go into houses or shops. Buildings called factories were built to hold them. Many workers were needed to tend the factory machines. People from New England and workers from all parts of Europe came to work in the factories.

Factory workers were busy at their jobs all day. They depended on others for things they needed. People who could provide these things set up shops. In time, towns grew around the factories.

The Founding of Maryland

You have read about the Pilgrims, the Puritans, and the Quakers. All of these people came to America to find freedom of religion. English Catholics, too, were unhappy under their king.

George Calvert, the first Lord Baltimore, was a Catholic. King Charles I granted George Calvert a charter and 10 million acres (4 million ha) of land north of Virginia. This colony was to be called Maryland in honor of Queen Mary, who

Salisbury, Connecticut, was one of many colonial towns in New England that had factories powered by swift-flowing water. This factory made objects from iron.

was married to Charles I. The charter made Calvert the owner of Maryland. But he could make no laws without the consent of the colonists.

George Calvert died before his plans for the colony were ready. The king gave the charter to Calvert's son Cecil. Cecil Calvert sent his brother as Maryland's first governor, to insure the colony's success.

Settling St. Marys

Leonard Calvert and the colonists reached Maryland in the spring of 1634. They explored the Potomac River (pə tō′mək) and Chesapeake (ches′ə pēk′) Bay. They built the town of St. Marys at the mouth of the Potomac River. See the map of early settlements on page 57.

Lord Baltimore's colonists had chosen their site well. Most of Maryland lies on the Atlantic Coastal Plain. Fertile soil, broad rivers, good harbors, and a mild climate made life pleasant. There were plenty of oysters and fish in Chesapeake Bay for eating.

The Settlers and the Algonquian Indians

Maryland's climate and soil were excellent for tobacco. The Algonquian Indians showed them how to plant corn and tobacco. There was no fighting with the Indians over land. The Indians thought this part of the Tidewater was unhealthy. They were willing to sell the land to the settlers.

The settlers took large sections along the rivers which flowed into Chesapeake Bay. They raised tobacco to be shipped back to Europe. Ships could sail right up to their plantation docks. Maryland became a colony of tobacco plantations.

Extending Religious Freedom in Maryland

Protestants as well as Catholics had settled in Maryland. Governor Calvert allowed the settlers to worship as they wished. Maryland had an assembly like Virginia's House of Burgesses to advise the governor. The assembly passed a law stating that all people who were Christians were welcome in Maryland. But Puritans who had been driven from Virginia gained control of Maryland. Their rule lasted only a few years before Lord Baltimore regained control.

Margaret Brent

Margaret Brent was a Maryland colonist. At a time when women had few rights, she became an important person. She helped the governor put down a rebellion. She demanded and got a voice and vote in the assembly. When Governor Calvert died, she served as governor of the colony.

Colonies in the Carolinas

England and Spain claimed the land between Virginia and Florida. Both countries knew that it would belong to the country that settled it first. In 1663 eight English nobles asked the king for land in America. He granted them the region from Virginia south to Florida. This region was given the name Carolina by King Charles II.

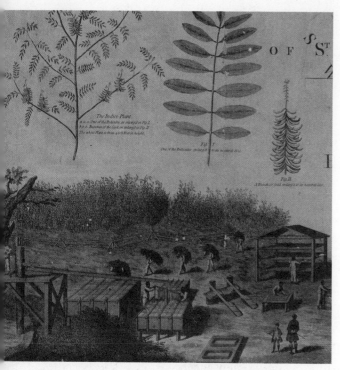
Many people worked as slaves on South Carolina *indigo* plantations. Slaves worked in all stages of indigo processing.

Settling Northern Carolina

West of the swampy coastlands between Virginia and northern Carolina, settlers found the forest of the Atlantic Coastal Plain. Tall, straight masts for ships could be made from the pines that grew there. Turpentine could also be made from the pine trees. These Carolina pioneers organized a colony of small farms. Some cleared land to grow corn, wheat, and vegetables for their families. A few raised tobacco and sold it in Virginia. Many hunted and trapped.

People from other colonies and from Europe joined these early settlers. They, too, built cabins in small clearings. There were few schools and churches and little money in this land. Because of the small farms there was little slavery.

Settling Southern Carolina

The first colonists in southern Carolina built Charles Town on the best harbor south of Virginia. Later it was called Charleston.

The settlement in southern Carolina grew. People from Great Britain, the West Indies, and other countries settled near Charleston. Several Protestant families who had been driven out of Catholic France arrived.

The English and French settlers began to plant rice which grew well in the hot, wet lowlands. The settlers brought in black slaves to work in the rice fields. By the end of the colonial period there were three black slaves to every white person in South Carolina.

Eliza Lucas had seen *indigo* (in′di gō′) plants growing in the West Indies. Indigo was used to make a blue dye to color cloth. She thought the plants would grow well in the hot, damp climate of southern Carolina. Eliza was right. Indigo became the second most important crop in southern Carolina.

A Struggle for Control

Many American Indians lived in southern Carolina. The Catawbas (kə taw′bəz), Cherokees (cher′ə kēz), and Yamasees (yam′ə sēz) were the most important groups. These Indians lived in towns. They built log and thatched-roof houses. Most were farmers as well as hunters.

The people of Carolina and the Yamasee Indians did not get along. Time and again the Yamasees tried to stop settlers from taking over their lands. Finally, the Yamasees attacked settlements in both northern and southern Carolina. The colonists united and the Yamasees were defeated.

Dividing Carolina

The nobles who owned the colony made a plan of government for Carolina. It gave the people so few rights that they objected.

The owners became discouraged and sold their land back to King Charles. So in 1721 Carolina became a royal colony.

Up to this time Carolina had been considered one colony. It had been ruled by one governor. But the land and the people of the north were different from those of the south. Between the northern settlements and those of the south were great forests. So when Carolina became a royal colony, the region was divided into North Carolina and South Carolina.

The Founding of Georgia

By the early 1700s there were still no British colonies south of South Carolina. Spaniards were moving into the region from Florida. The king of England wanted British people to settle there.

James Oglethorpe (ō′gəl thôrp′), a British lawmaker, knew this. He asked King George for permission to found a haven for the poor and unemployed people in England. Then King George gave Oglethorpe money to help start

the colony. Oglethorpe called the colony Georgia in honor of King George II.

The Settlement of Savannah

Oglethorpe and the settlers sailed for Georgia in 1733. A number of the settlers were debtors released from British prisons. A debtor is a person who owes money. The debtors went to America to work off their debts. Several miles up the Savannah River a settlement was built. Oglethorpe named it Savannah. Some settlers went farther up the river. There they built Augusta. Georgia was the last of the thirteen original colonies to be established.

Farms and Plantations

Governor Oglethorpe wanted to make friends of the American Indians. He paid them for their land and dealt fairly with them.

Each settler in Georgia received land for a house in town and for a farm outside of town. The farms were small. But the settlers soon learned that rice and indigo grew well in their hot, damp climate. They wanted to have large plantations like those in South Carolina. In 1749 slaves were brought into the colony to grow the rice and indigo. Later cotton began to be grown. There were still small farms. But Georgia had also become a colony of plantations.

Trouble with the Spaniards

The Spaniards in Florida were angry when the British settled in Georgia. Then war broke out between Spain and Great Britain. The Spaniards tried to get the Indians to fight the colonists in Georgia. Governor Oglethorpe had

Williamsburg
A Colonial Town

Williamsburg became the center of Virginia government in 1699 after Jamestown was burned. Today Williamsburg is a restored town. The large buildings and houses were rebuilt to look as they did in colonial times.

About 250 years after its founding, a group of Americans decided to restore Williamsburg. In tearing down modern buildings in Williamsburg, the builders reached the earliest foundations. Then it was easy to put up buildings the size and shape of the first ones. Government buildings, shops, taverns, inns, and even the jail were rebuilt. Streets were given their old names. In a short time the town looked just like a town of the 1700s. Fine horse-drawn carriages with drivers in colonial costume still appear. People dressed in colonial costumes are there to show visitors the many interesting sights of the old colonial town. As in colonial times, skilled workers make everything by hand. ■

Savannah was built on a steep bank of the Savannah River. Heavy goods were brought from boats to the town with a crane.

always treated the Indians fairly, so they refused to take sides. The British and the Spanish fought but neither side won.

The Government of Georgia

James Oglethorpe was judge, ruler, and army leader in Georgia for 12 years. At first, soldiers were used to help govern and protect the colony. The settlers helped make laws. In 1754 Georgia became a royal colony.

The British Colonies

England now had thirteen colonies along the Atlantic Coast of North America. To the north was land claimed by France. Spain claimed the land to the south. Little was known about the land to the west.

For many years the colonists lived near the coast facing England across the Atlantic. But only about half of the colonists came from England. The rest came from Scotland, Ireland, Africa, Germany, the Netherlands, France, Sweden, Finland, Poland, and other countries.

Do You Know?

1. What was the first permanent British settlement in North America?
2. What two groups made early settlements in Massachusetts? Why?
3. Who founded Pennsylvania? Why?
4. Which was the last of the thirteen colonies to be established?

Before You Go On

Using New Words

money crop   plantation
representative   treaty
indentured servant assembly
tidewater region   indigo
constitution   charter
piedmont   surrender

The phrases below explain the words or terms listed above. Number a paper from 1 through 12. After each number write the word or term that matches the definition.

1. A group of leaders who made laws for a colony
2. To give up control of
3. A section of the coastal plain where rivers rise and fall with the ocean tide
4. A written group of laws governing an area
5. A plant from which a blue dye is made
6. A crop that is grown to be sold
7. An upland region between a plain and mountains
8. An agreement between groups of people or nations
9. A large farm on which one crop is raised
10. A person who acts for a group
11. A paper granting certain rights, such as permission to make settlements
12. A person who works a certain length of time for the person who has paid the cost of his or her passage to America

Finding the Facts

1. Why did colonists have farms on the rivers of the tidewater region?
2. How did the early colonists use the waterfalls of the fall line?
3. What landform prevented the early colonists from moving inland?
4. What was the House of Burgesses? Who attended the meetings?
5. What was the Mayflower Compact?
6. What colony did each of the following help found: Roger Williams, Anne Hutchinson, Thomas Hooker, Peter Stuyvesant, William Penn, Lord Baltimore, and James Oglethorpe?
7. What colonies were settled by the Dutch, by people from Sweden, or by both groups?
8. What was life like in northern Carolina? What was it like in southern Carolina?

3
Independence from England

For almost 150 years the English colonists lived along the Atlantic coast. Then small numbers of colonists began to move across the Appalachian Mountains into the Ohio Valley.

The French and Indian War

In the 1750s English colonists who crossed the mountains were met by French settlers already in the Ohio Valley. The English thought the land belonged to Great Britain. The French said it was French land. They said La Salle had claimed the land for France.

A struggle began for the Ohio Valley. Both Great Britain and France wanted to control North America and the rich fur trade. This struggle, which began in 1756, was called the French and Indian War because many American Indians helped the French. The Iroquois Indians helped the British.

Great Britain sent General Braddock with an army to drive the French from the Ohio country. But the French and Indians defeated Braddock's army. Braddock was wounded and later died. George Washington became the head of the Virginia and British forces.

More British troops arrived to fight the French. They captured French forts on Lake Ontario and Lake Champlain. The most important French fort was at Quebec (kwi bek') in Canada. This fort was the key to North America. It was built on a high bluff, and allowed the French to control the St. Lawrence River, which led to the interior of North America. After 2 months of failure, General Wolfe, the British leader, sent British troops up a narrow pathway to the top of the bluff. A short but costly battle followed. The French were defeated.

A few months later the war was over. In 1763 Great Britain and France signed a treaty. France gave all the lands east of the Mississippi River to Great Britain. France also gave Louisiana, the region west of the Mississippi River, to Spain. The map of European claims on page 74 shows how the treaty changed the map of North America. As a result of the treaty, Great Britain became the leading power in North America.

Events Leading to War with the British

The year 1763 was an eventful one for the colonies. The new king, George III, wanted to control the American colonies more closely. So he announced the Proclamation (prok'lə mā'shən) Line which prevented colonists from settling west of the Appalachian Mountains. King George did not want colonists moving west and taking Indian lands. He wanted this region preserved for the fur trade. The colonists thought the British had no right to stop them from moving west. After all, they had just helped drive France from these very lands.

The French and Indian War had been costly. England needed money to pay its war debt. The government thought the colonists should pay part

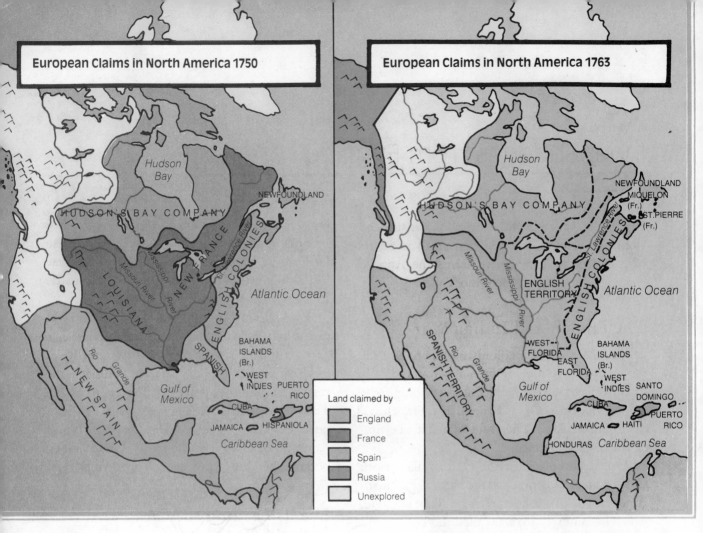

European Claims in North America 1750

Hudson Bay

HUDSON'S BAY COMPANY

NEWFOUNDLAND

NEW FRANCE

Missouri River

Mississippi River

LOUISIANA

ENGLISH COLONIES

Atlantic Ocean

Rio Grande

NEW SPAIN

SPANISH

BAHAMA ISLANDS (Br.)

WEST INDIES

PUERTO RICO

Gulf of Mexico

CUBA

JAMAICA HISPANIOLA

Caribbean Sea

European Claims in North America 1763

Hudson Bay

HUDSON'S BAY COMPANY

NEWFOUNDLAND
MIQUELON (Fr.)
ST. PIERRE (Fr.)

Missouri River

Mississippi River

ENGLISH TERRITORY

St. Lawrence River

ENGLISH COLONIES

Atlantic Ocean

SPANISH TERRITORY

Rio Grande

WEST FLORIDA

EAST FLORIDA

Gulf of Mexico

BAHAMA ISLANDS (Br.)

WEST INDIES

CUBA

JAMAICA HAITI

SANTO DOMINGO

PUERTO RICO

HONDURAS Caribbean Sea

Land claimed by

England
France
Spain
Russia
Unexplored

England, France, and Spain had claimed land in North America by 1750. Which country claimed the largest area? In 1763, four countries claimed land. Name them.

of the cost of the war. So the government passed a number of *tax* (taks) laws for the colonies. Taxes are money that must be paid by people for the support of the government. Most of these taxes were on goods brought into the colonies. The colonists felt these taxes were unfair. They did not have representatives in Great Britain's government, and so they had no way to vote against these taxes.

British Actions and Colonial Reactions

The British government passed the Sugar Act in 1764. This *act* (akt), or law, placed a tax on

sugar and some other goods that came from Great Britain. The colonists were troubled.

A year later the British government passed the Stamp Act. The Stamp Act required colonists to buy government stamps. These stamps had to be put on all newspapers and business papers. The Stamp Act led to much protest from the colonists. Groups called the Sons of Liberty and the Daughters of Liberty were formed. Members of these groups spoke up about the rights of the colonists. Not one penny was ever collected by the British from the Stamp

Act! Finally in 1766, the government repealed, or ended, the Stamp Act.

In 1767 the British government passed the Townshend Acts. Goods from Great Britain, such as glass and paper, were taxed. Again the colonists protested! They fought back with a *boycott* (boi′kot). The boycott meant the colonists refused to buy, sell, or use any goods from Great Britain. This hurt the business of British merchants. British troops were sent to Boston to help the tax collectors.

Bad feelings developed between the British troops and the citizens of Boston. A fight broke out in March of 1770. Shots were fired into the crowd. Five townspeople, including a former slave, Crispus Attucks, were killed by the British soldiers. They may have been the first people to die for American independence. Speechmakers called the event the Boston Massacre. The people of Boston demanded that the troops leave their city.

The British government repealed the Townshend Acts. Then, in 1773, the government passed the Tea Act. This act forced the colonists to buy tea from only the British East India Company. Again the colonists reacted. On December 16, 1773 in Boston, a group of colonists

At the Boston Tea Party, colonists disguised as Indians cried, "Boston Harbor a teapot tonight!" Angered by the loss of their cargo, the British closed the harbor.

dressed as Mohawk Indians. They climbed aboard the British tea ships and dumped 342 chests of tea into Boston Harbor. This was the famous "Boston Tea Party". From Boston to Charleston colonists joined in the tea boycott.

The British government was outraged by the Boston Tea Party. It closed the port of Boston as punishment and sent a British general to rule Massachusetts. Other colonies sprang to the aid of Boston. Food and supplies were smuggled in to the people of Boston. The colonies began to unite against British rule. The word *independence* (in′di pen′dəns) began to be heard. Independence means the freedom from control of another country.

Two Meetings in Philadelphia

The colony of Massachusetts called all the colonies together to consider taking action. Representatives from all the colonies except Georgia attended the First Continental Congress at the State House in Philadelphia on September 5, 1774. The Congress wrote a letter to King George. The representatives asked the king to open the port of Boston. They also asked him to allow them to decide about their own taxes. They said that the colonies would not trade with Great Britain until the king agreed to grant all of these requests.

In England, George III refused to do what the colonists were asking. He did not answer the letter.

The colonists called for another meeting at the State House in Philadelphia on May 10, 1775. They hoped that the Second Continental Congress would be able to settle the matter.

The War for Independence

During this time things in Boston were growing worse. British soldiers were stationed in the city. British warships lay in the harbor. Samuel Adams, John Hancock, and other colonial leaders encouraged the people of Boston not to give up hope.

Fighting at Lexington and Concord

In April 1775, General Gage, the British commander, heard that the colonists had stored guns and powder at Lexington and Concord in Massachusetts. He heard also that Adams and Hancock were hiding in Lexington. Gage decided to destroy the supplies. He declared that he would send Adams and Hancock to Great Britain to be hanged as rebels. He called them "rebels" because they would not obey the British laws. We call the colonists who were working for freedom "patriots."

Patriots in Boston found out Gage's plans. Paul Revere and William Dawes were sent to warn the people. They rode all night, waking the colonists and telling them to arm themselves. Samuel Adams and John Hancock escaped the approaching British army.

The British arrived in Lexington early the next morning. A little band of minutemen waited for them on the village green. Minutemen were colonists who could be ready to fight even with only a minute's notice.

The minutemen were badly outnumbered. They began to withdraw. Then a shot rang out! No one knows who fired that first shot. But on this April day in 1775, war between Great Britain and its colonies began. More shots followed.

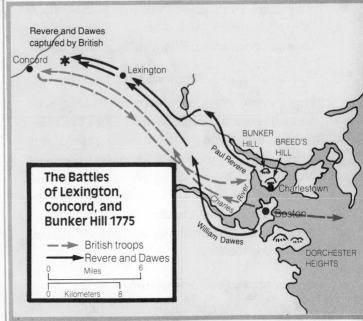

The Battles of Lexington, Concord, and Bunker Hill 1775

Revere and Dawes captured by British

Concord

Lexington

BUNKER HILL

BREED'S HILL

Paul Revere

Charlestown

Charles River

Boston

William Dawes

DORCHESTER HEIGHTS

- →→→ British troops
- →→→ Revere and Dawes

0 — Miles — 6

0 — Kilometers — 8

A statue of Paul Revere stands in Boston, Massachusetts, near the start of his famous ride to warn patriots of the British army's approach. William Dawes took another route to spread the warning.

Several minutemen were killed or wounded before the British marched on toward Concord.

More minutemen met the British army at a bridge in Concord. A short but bitter battle followed. This time the British had to retreat. They pulled back to Boston without capturing the colonial leaders or the supplies.

The Battle of Bunker Hill

On the morning of June 16, 1775, General Gage woke to an unpleasant surprise. Overnight patriot troops had taken possession of a hill near Boston.

Three thousand British soldiers started up the hill. The patriots were told not to use their ammunition until necessary. Their ammunition was gunpowder, shot, and cannon balls.

Twice the British marched almost to the top of the hill. Twice they were driven back by a rain of shots. The third time they charged up the hill only a few shots were fired at them. The patriots had used up their ammunition! They had to retreat.

This battle is known as the battle of Bunker Hill. But it was really fought on Breed's Hill, a smaller hill to the east. The colonists lost the hill, but the battle proved that they had a chance to win against the British army. They needed training, arms, ammunition, and a good leader.

Washington as Commander of the Army

News of two important events reached the Second Continental Congress meeting in Philadelphia. Ethan Allen's troops had captured the British fort, Ticonderoga, on Lake Champlain in New York. They took a cannon, guns, and ammunition. The other news was that the patriots had fought well at Bunker Hill. The leaders from Boston decided that a commander was needed for the army.

George Washington had been an able leader in the French and Indian War. Congress made him commander in chief of the army.

The Declaration of Independence

A committee of five was chosen to write a paper declaring American independence. All gave the problem much thought, but a young Virginian, Thomas Jefferson, wrote most of the declaration. It stated the colonists' complaints against the king and their reasons for wanting indepen-

Representatives of the thirteen colonies accepted the Declaration of Independence. The original document is displayed in the National Archives Building in Washington.

dence. This document was the Declaration of Independence.

On July 4, 1776, the Declaration of Independence was adopted by the Congress. A few days later, colonists heard the declaration that had been accepted. They celebrated the birth of a new nation, the United States of America.

No longer was the war only for rights of the colonists. Now it became the War for Independence. This war is sometimes called the Revolutionary War since the colonists revolted against the king.

Thomas Jefferson

Thomas Jefferson was the author of the Declaration of Independence. He was also an architect, inventor, and educator.

Jefferson designed the University of Virginia, the Virginia state capitol building, and his home, Monticello. He was a farmer who used modern methods of farming. He experimented with new crops.

Jefferson was also an inventor. He designed the swivel chair and the dumb-waiter. A dumb-waiter is used to carry dishes of food from a basement kitchen to an upstairs dining room.

Jefferson had one of the best collections of books of his time. His library became the Library of Congress in Washington, D.C. The public education system of Virginia was established by Jefferson. Later, Jefferson became the third President of the United States.

Jefferson considered the writing of the Declaration of Independence and of a law that established religious freedom in Virginia to be among his finest accomplishments.

Thomas Jefferson followed several European styles in designing his home, Monticello. Inside the house visitors can see many of the mechanical devices Jefferson invented.

Early Days of the War

George Washington's army lacked everything an army needs. The cannon, guns, and ammunition Ethan Allen captured at Ticonderoga were a great help. These supplies were moved to Boston. The hills overlooking Boston were fortified with the cannon. The British leaders ordered their troops to leave the city. Ships took them to Halifax, Nova Scotia.

Washington and his army marched on south. On Long Island, New York, they met the British again. The Americans were defeated. But Washington retreated, or pulled his army back. He saved most of his soldiers.

Then began a chase across New York and New Jersey. The British army was large and well-trained. For 2 months the Americans retreated. Washington and the Americans crossed the Delaware River into Pennsylvania.

The British, led by Lord Cornwallis, returned to New York. Some soldiers stayed in Trenton,

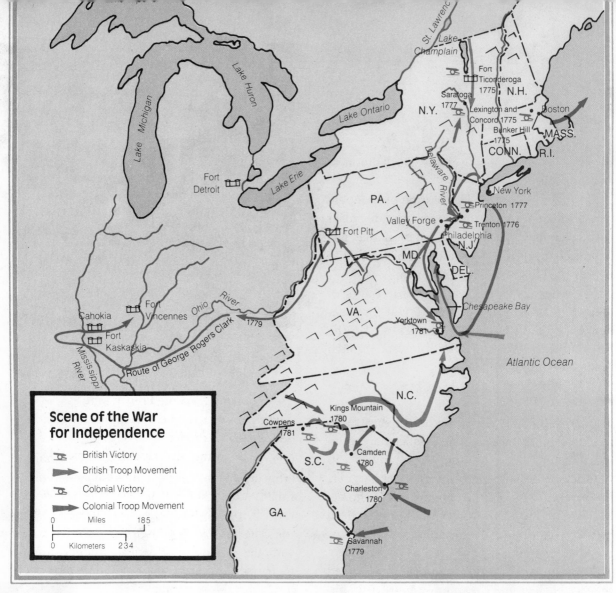

**Scene of the War
for Independence**

British Victory

British Troop Movement

Colonial Victory

Colonial Troop Movement

0   Miles   185

0   Kilometers   234

Fort
Detroit

Fort
Vincennes

Cahokia

Fort
Kaskaskia

Route of George Rogers Clark

1779

Ohio River

Mississippi River

Lake Michigan

Lake Huron

Lake Erie

Lake Ontario

St. Lawrence

Lake Champlain

Fort Ticonderoga 1775

Saratoga 1777

N.Y.

N.H.

Lexington and Concord 1775

Boston

Bunker Hill 1775

MASS.

CONN.

R.I.

New York

Princeton 1777

PA.

Valley Forge

Trenton 1776

Philadelphia

N.J.

Fort Pitt

MD.

DEL.

VA.

Chesapeake Bay

Yorktown 1781

Atlantic Ocean

N.C.

Kings Mountain 1780

Cowpens 1781

S.C.

Camden 1780

Charleston 1780

GA.

Savannah 1779

Delaware River

In the War of *Independence* major battles
were fought in most of the colonies.
Some important battles were also fought
in the West. Name some famous battle
locations. Why were most battles fought
on the coast?

New Jersey, to watch for the Americans. Most
of them were Hessians (hesh′ənz), or German
soldiers hired to fight the Americans.

During the night boat loads of American
soldiers led by Washington moved across the
Delaware. Early the next morning they surprised the Hessians and captured Trenton. A
few days later they won another victory at
nearby Princeton, this time against the British.

The war did not go well for the Americans the
next year. The British army took Philadelphia and
then settled down to spend winter there. Washington's army was camped at Valley Forge, a few
miles away.

The winter of 1777–1778 was bitterly cold. At Valley Forge Washington's troops lacked warm clothing. There was not enough food. Many were ill. About 3,000 died that terrible winter. Congress sent no money, food, or clothing to Valley Forge. How could Washington explain this to the troops? While the British officers and soldiers were living comfortably in Philadelphia, the American soldiers froze in huts and tents.

Washington held the army together. Baron von Steuben (bar'ən von stoō'bən), a trained soldier from Germany, helped drill the American troops. By spring he had turned the working people who made up the American troops, into a well-trained army.

Women During the Revolutionary War

Washington needed soldiers. Many farmers left their land to fight. Women and children tended the farms. Abigail Adams ran the family farm while her husband, John, served in Congress. Some women served on the battlefield. Margaret Corbin's husband was killed at Fort Washington. Although wounded, Margaret took her husband's place firing a cannon. Nanye'hi, a Cherokee woman, served as scout and spy. Thousands of women helped in making shot and gunpowder and supplying horses and food.

Blacks During the Revolutionary War

More than 5,000 blacks enlisted in the American army. Blacks fought at Lexington and Concord, Bunker Hill, Trenton, Saratoga, and in other major battles. Both the British and the colonials recruited blacks for their armies. Other blacks served at sea in America's tiny navy.

The Battle of Saratoga

One bit of good news gave General Washington courage to bear the hard days at Valley Forge. He heard that Americans had won an important battle at Saratoga, New York. In October 1777, they had defeated a British army led by General Burgoyne (bər goin'). Until this time the Americans had been losing battle after battle. The victory at Saratoga was important because it gave the Americans confidence.

Help from France

Congress sent Benjamin Franklin to France to ask for help. When the French king heard of the victory at Saratoga, he decided to send an army and ships to America.

The Marquis de Lafayette (mar'kwis də laf'ē et'), a young French noble, had already been helping. He was thrilled by the colonists' fight for freedom. He hired soldiers, bought a ship, and arrived in America in April 1777.

The Winning of the Northwest

The war spread to colonies west of the Appalachians in the Northwest Territory. This huge area stretched from the Ohio River north to the Great Lakes and west to the Mississippi. Find the Northwest Territory on the map of the War for Independence on page 80.

Pioneers had settled south of the Ohio River in what is now Kentucky. At that time the land belonged to Virginia. The British armed American Indians. Some Indians fought against the settlers who were a threat to their lands.

But the Iroquois League, a group of tribes, could not decide which side to support. Those in the League who sided with the British had their villages destroyed by the Americans under Washington's orders. Most of the Mohawks and Cayugas (kā yōō′gəz) and some of the Tuscaroras (tus′kə rôr′əz) moved to Canada. The Oneidas (ō nīd′əz) moved to what is now Wisconsin. Some of the Senecas (sen′ə kəz) moved to Pennsylvania and present-day Oklahoma. The Onondagas (on′ən dô′gəz) and most Senecas and Tuscaroras stayed in New York.

Captain George Rogers Clark had a plan for stopping the British and Indian threat. He sent scouts to find out about the British forts. They reported that there were not many soldiers to guard the forts. Then he gathered American troops at Fort Pitt in the spring of 1778. They traveled down the Ohio River almost to the Mississippi. Then they marched overland to Kaskaskia (ka skas′kē ə), Cahokia (kə hō′kē ə), and Vincennes (vin senz′). Trace their route on the map of the war on page 80. Clark succeeded in taking the most important forts in the Northwest Territory. But could they be held with so few troops?

The British commander in Detroit marched south with a large force. He took Vincennes back from the Americans. He decided to wait until spring to attack the other forts.

Clark's only chance was to surprise the British again. His march across the swampy, flooded plains that February was one of the hardest in history. For 16 days the troops waded, often up to their shoulders, in icy streams. But they surprised the enemy and took Vincennes again. They drove the British north. Thus Clark and the small army won land for the Americans.

Fighting in the Southern Colonies

Neither side had won great victories in the northern or middle colonies. The British knew that many wealthy colonists still sided with Great Britain. Such colonists were called Tories or Loyalists. General Cornwallis, the British commander, felt sure these Tories would help the British. He decided to carry the war south where he hoped to find Tory support.

The British had little trouble taking Savannah, Georgia. The few patriots left in Charleston, South Carolina, also had to surrender. One after another, important places on the coast of Georgia and South Carolina fell. As Cornwallis marched inland, Tories joined the British army.

There were no large armies in the South to stop Cornwallis. But small bands of patriots made life hard for the British. They began slowly to wear the British down.

Cornwallis's army moved northward and westward until it reached the highlands of South Carolina. On Kings Mountain patriots surprised the British and almost destroyed their army.

General Greene's Plan

Washington sent General Nathanael Greene to help the southern patriots. Greene had too few soldiers to defeat Cornwallis in battle. Greene decided to make Cornwallis chase him.

Again and again Greene led the American army close to the British camp. Cornwallis would prepare for battle, only to find the Americans gone. When the British commander realized that he had been tricked, he was miles from the coast where his ships lay. He hurried north to attack Virginia.

General Greene's plan had worked. In 3 months he had taken part of Georgia and most of South Carolina from the British army.

The Trapping of Cornwallis

Lafayette was in charge of the American forces in Virginia. Like Greene, Lafayette planned to wear down Cornwallis's army. After chasing Lafayette all through Virginia, Cornwallis settled down at Yorktown. He waited for help from New York. The map of the War for Independence on page 80 shows that Yorktown is on a peninsula in Chesapeake Bay.

Lafayette's troops surrounded Yorktown. The French, not the British, fleet sailed into

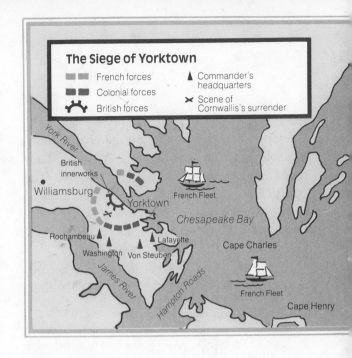

The Siege of Yorktown

▨ French forces	▲ Commander's headquarters
▰ Colonial forces	✕ Scene of Cornwallis's surrender
⌒ British forces	

Chesapeake Bay. Washington marched American soldiers from New York to Virginia. They took their position north of Yorktown. The British troops were trapped on the peninsula!

The Americans and the French began firing on Yorktown on October 9, 1781. Day by day

After the war the United States stretched from the Atlantic Ocean to the Mississippi River. Look back to page 74. What changes had taken place since 1763?

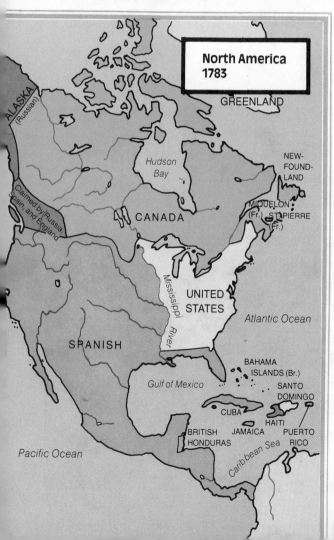

North America 1783

the British defenses crumbled under the cannon fire. Their ammunition began to run low. They saw that the Americans were moving nearer. Cornwallis realized he was beaten.

On October 19, 1781, General Cornwallis surrendered to General Washington. With France's help, the thirteen colonies had defeated powerful Great Britain!

A Free and Independent Nation

After the surrender at Yorktown, American and British representatives met in Paris, France, to settle the terms of peace. In 1783 Great Britain gave up its claim to the thirteen colonies. The United States was recognized as an independent nation.

The map of North America on this page shows how large a country the Americans had won.

Do You Know?

1. Why was the French and Indian War fought? What were the terms of the 1763 treaty?
2. What actions of the British government led to the Declaration of Independence?
3. What victory made the Americans feel that they had a chance to win?
4. How were Cornwallis and the British trapped in Yorktown?

To Help You Learn

Using New Words

surrender   treaty

tax   boycott

act   independence

constitution

The phrases below explain the words listed above. Number a paper from 1 through 7. After each number write the word that matches the definition.

1. An agreement between groups of people or nations
2. Freedom from the control of another country
3. Money that must be paid by people to support the government
4. A law
5. To give up control of
6. To refuse to buy, sell, or use any goods, as a protest
7. A group of written laws governing a nation or a state

Finding the Facts

1. How did manufacturing cities grow up along the fall line?
2. What was England's first permanent settlement in America? When was it founded?
3. What three events occurred in 1619?
4. What person or group founded each of England's thirteen colonies in North America?
5. Which colonies were founded for religious freedom?
6. Why did Great Britain begin to enforce tax laws after the French and Indian War?
7. How did colonists in each colony keep informed of what was happening in other colonies?
8. How and where did the War for Independence begin? Who was chosen to command the American army? Why was he chosen?
9. What was the Declaration of Independence? Who wrote most of it? When was it adopted?
10. Where did Washington's army spend their worst winter? What good news brought them hope?
11. How was the war won in the South? Where did Lord Cornwallis surrender to General Washington?

Learning from Maps

1. Look at the map of early settlements on page 57. Why was New Amsterdam a good place for a trading post?
2. Use the map on page 80 as you answer these questions about the War for Independence: When was the battle of Saratoga? How far west did Clark go? How far south did the fighting go?
3. Use the map of North America on page 84. What was the western boundary of the United States in 1783?

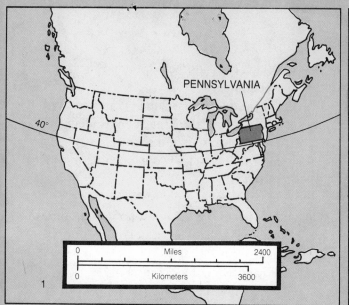

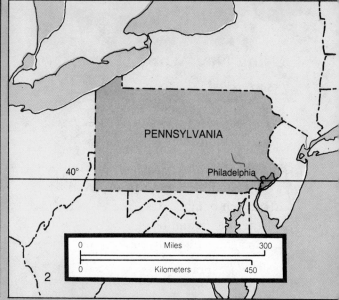

4. Most maps have a scale of miles (kilometers). This helps you tell how far one place is from another, and if one map is drawn on a larger scale than another.

Maps drawn on a larger scale give more information about a smaller area than maps drawn on a smaller scale. Find Pennsylvania on the two maps above. Which map is drawn on a larger scale?

Take a piece of paper with a straight edge. Lay it across the widest part of Pennsylvania on map 2. Mark it at both ends of the state. Now hold the straight edge along the distance scale on map 2. How wide is Pennsylvania? Now do the same thing for map 1. Is Pennsylvania the same width on this map also?

Using Study Skills

1. **Time line:** The following events are not listed in the right order. Find the date for each. Then write them in the correct order on a time line.
   - Battle of Saratoga
   - William Penn and Quakers arrive in Pennsylvania
   - Great Britain gives up thirteen colonies
   - Dutch arrive in New Netherland
   - First Continental Congress meets in Philadelphia
   - French and Indian War begins
2. **Outline:** An outline helps you see the plan of a book, a unit, or a part of a unit. It also helps you review materials. Copy the outline and complete it.

French and Indian War 1756–1763
  I. Reasons for starting
     A. Great Britain and France wanted to control North America
     B.
  II. Important battles
     A. French and Indians defeated Braddock
     B. British captured forts on Lake Ontario
     C.
     D.
  III. Treaty of 1763
     A.
     B. France gave Louisiana to Spain

Thinking It Through

1. Americans owe a debt to people like Anne Hutchinson and William Penn. What freedoms do we have today which they helped gain?

     The Mayflower Compact, the Connecticut Constitution, and the town meeting helped to give us another freedom. Explain.

2. The House of Burgesses in Virginia was important in American history. Explain why.

3. Explain how the colonists, with a poorly equipped army, were able to win against a highly trained British army.

4. Why is what has happened in the colonial days so important to us today?

Projects

1. *Yankee Doodle* was a song that was first sung during the War for Independence. Learn to sing other songs that were sung during that war.

2. The Research Committee might learn more about one of the leaders and battles of the War for Independence.

     The Explorers' Committee could show on maps where the armies were when the battle was fought.

3. Imagine you are an early settler. Write a letter to relatives who did not come to America telling them about your experiences. Tell how you spend your days.

4. The Reading Committee might ask the librarian for books about life in the colonies and books about the War for Independence.

5. Make an outline map of the United States by tracing the map on pages 92 and 93. Write in the names of the thirteen colonies, the important rivers, lakes, and settlements. Label the Atlantic Ocean. The map of early settlements on page 57 will help you. Keep this map for use as you study other sections of your text.

3 A Growing America

Unit Preview

The United States gained its independence from Great Britain. However, the job of setting up a new form of government for the nation was difficult. The states did not want to give up their rights. So at first American leaders established a central government with limited powers. But this government did not work well. Then American leaders met in Philadelphia. They created a strong central government. Power was divided among three branches, or parts. George Washington was elected as the first President. He chose the site for our national capital, Washington, D.C.

The young nation grew. New lands were added. Eventually, the United States stretched from the Atlantic to the Pacific Ocean. The growing country had to face serious problems, however. America fought a second war with Great Britain for freedom of the seas in 1812. Trouble developed within the United States as well.

Disagreements arose between North and South over slavery and the right of a state to leave the Union. In 1861, war broke out between northern and southern states. The southern states set up their own government. The Union was divided in a civil war.

Fighting continued until 1865. Abraham Lincoln was able to save the Union and end the practice of slavery. The United States survived and grew into a strong nation.

Things to Discover

If you look carefully at the picture, map, and time line, you can answer these questions.

1. The map shows how the United States extended its borders. What country borders the United States on the north? On the south?
2. The picture shows the Capitol in Washington, D.C., where the United States Congress meets. The Constitution established the Congress. When was the Constitution adopted?
3. Against what country did Congress declare war in 1812?
4. How long did the Civil War last?

Words to Learn

You will meet these words in this unit. As you read, you will learn what they mean and how to pronounce them. The Word List will help you.

abolitionist	free state
amendment	House of Representatives
blockade	inaugurate
cabinet	legislature
capital	ratify
Capitol	republic
carpetbagger	secede
compromise	Senate
Confederacy	slave state
convention	Supreme Court
elect	tariff

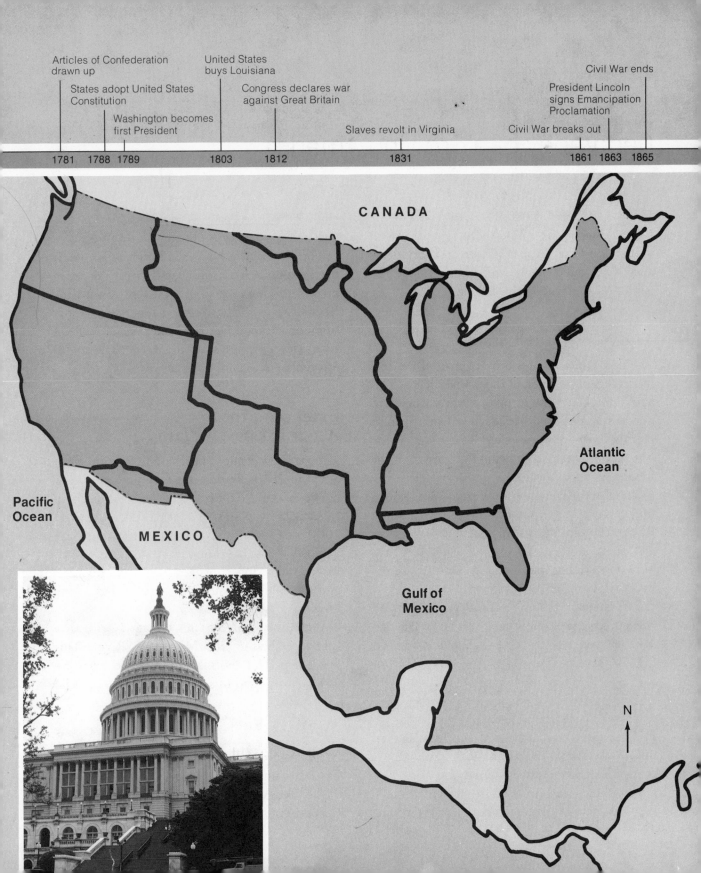

Articles of Confederation
drawn up

States adopt United States
Constitution

Washington becomes
first President

United States
buys Louisiana

Congress declares war
against Great Britain

Slaves revolt in Virginia

Civil War ends

President Lincoln
signs Emancipation
Proclamation

Civil War breaks out

1781　1788　1789　　　　　1803　　1812　　　　　　1831　　　　　　　　1861　1863　1865

CANADA

Atlantic
Ocean

Pacific
Ocean

MEXICO

Gulf of
Mexico

N

1
Geography of a Growing America

The map on page 91 shows the growth of the United States. In 1783 there were thirteen states along the Atlantic Coast. Seventy years later the United States stretched from the Atlantic Ocean to the Pacific Ocean.

The New United States

The new United States took control of the former British lands west of the Appalachians. This land stretched west from the Appalachians to the Mississippi River. It reached from Spanish Florida in the South to the Great Lakes in the North. See the map showing the growth of the United States on page 91.

The Ohio River is an important waterway in this region. It is a branch of the Mississippi River. The Ohio flows through land that is flat and gently rolling. The soil is dark and rich. Summers are hot but rainfall is plentiful. In the winter it is cold and snowy.

The land south of the Ohio River is hilly and rugged. But near the Gulf coast, it is flat and low. The soil is sandy and the climate is warm in the Gulf Coastal Plain.

The Louisiana Purchase

In 1803 the United States bought from France the land known as Louisiana. With this one purchase, the United States doubled in size. This huge piece of land stretched from the mouth of the Mississippi River north to Canada. It included the area between the Mississippi in the East and the Rocky Mountains in the West.

The land of the Louisiana Purchase is mostly flat or rolling. The soil changes from black, to brown, to gray as you go westward toward the Rockies. The northern region generally is hot in summer. Sometimes in winter severe snowstorms sweep south from the Arctic. The southern region is usually warm all year.

Extending the Atlantic Coastal Plain

The United States purchased Florida from Spain in 1819. Florida is a long, low peninsula between the Atlantic Ocean and the Gulf of Mexico. Few places in Florida are more than 100 feet (30 m) above sea level. Because the peninsula has no mountains, northern winds sometimes bring cool weather in winter. But Florida's climate is subtropical and it has a long growing season.

When the United States bought Florida, the land stretched to the Mississippi River. This western part of Florida was given to what are now Alabama and Mississippi so they, too, could have a Gulf coastline.

Reaching the Pacific

Great Britain and the United States both claimed the land known as the Oregon Country. Eventually both countries agreed on the border between

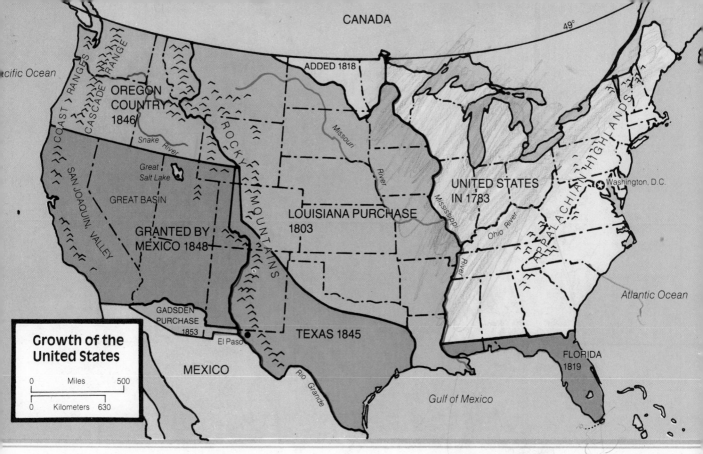

Growth of the
United States

Miles
0   500

Kilometers
0   630

CANADA

49°

Pacific Ocean

ADDED 1818

OREGON
COUNTRY
1846

Snake River

Great
Salt Lake

GREAT BASIN

SAN JOAQUIN VALLEY

COAST RANGES   CASCADE RANGE

GRANTED BY
MEXICO 1848

GADSDEN
PURCHASE
1853

El Paso

MEXICO

Rio Grande

ROCKY MOUNTAINS

Missouri River

LOUISIANA PURCHASE
1803

TEXAS 1845

Gulf of Mexico

Mississippi River

Ohio River

UNITED STATES
IN 1783

Washington, D.C.

APPALACHIAN HIGHLANDS

Atlantic Ocean

FLORIDA
1819

Beginning with the thirteen colonies, the United States added land until the country reached from the Atlantic Ocean to the Pacific Ocean. How long did it take the United States to get the land you see on this map?

the United States and Canada. This border is the 49th parallel of latitude. The Oregon Country was south of this border and became part of the United States in 1846. The nation now stretched from the Atlantic Ocean to the Pacific Ocean.

Most of the Oregon Country is made up of rugged mountains, high plateaus, and fertile mountain valleys. The Coast Ranges are mountains near the Pacific coast. The western slopes of the coast ranges are rainy. Great forests of Douglas fir grow there.

The eastern slopes are drier with fewer forest lands. East of these mountains is another range called the Cascades (kas kādz′). Between these two mountain ranges lies a fertile valley. A high, rugged plateau lies east of the mountains. The Snake River has cut canyons into this plateau.

Stretching to Mexico

Texas had been the northern part of Mexico. But in 1836 the Texans revolted. Texas became an independent republic. When Texas became part of the United States in 1845, war broke out between the United States and Mexico. The war ended in 1848. Mexico was defeated. As part of the peace treaty, Mexico gave up the lands that are now California, Nevada, Utah, most of Arizona and New Mexico, and portions of Colorado and Wyoming. The United States agreed

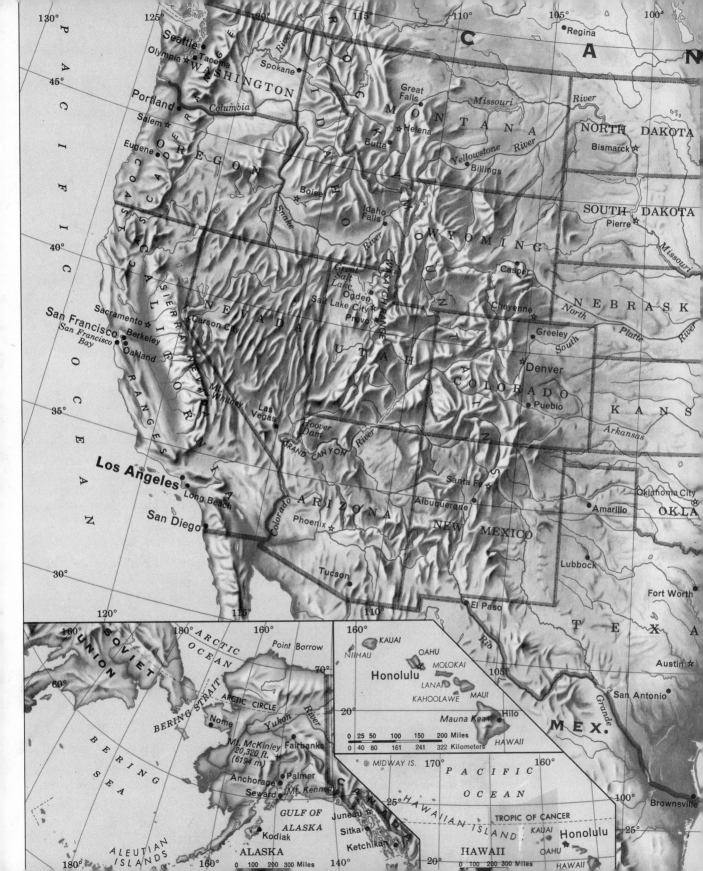

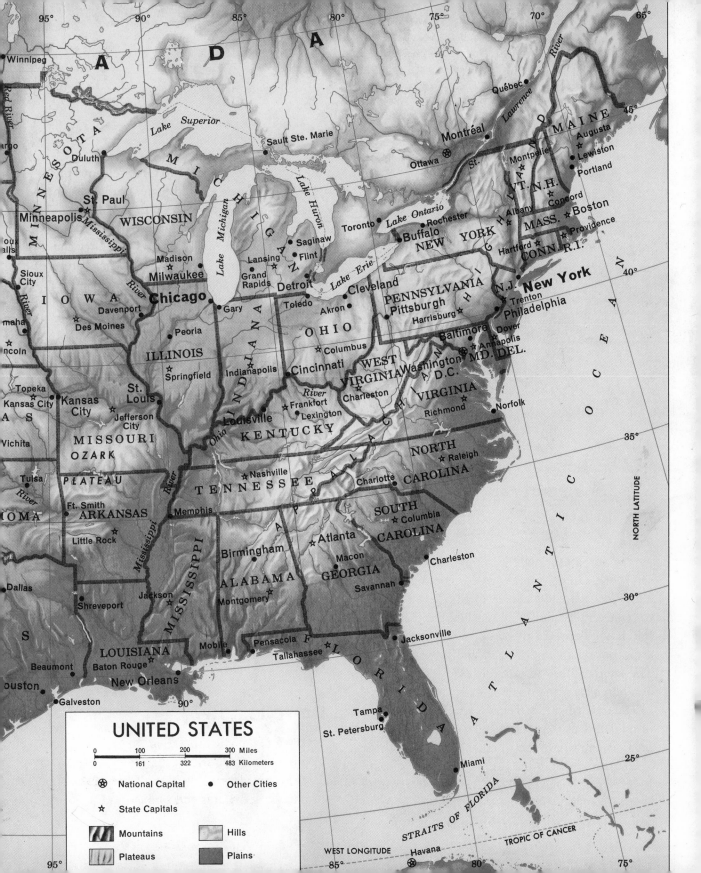

Redwood trees are among the oldest and tallest trees in the world. Some are 300 feet (90 m) tall. Many of them began to grow 13 or 14 centuries ago.

to pay for these lands. Several years later, in 1853, the United States agreed to purchase an additional piece of land from Mexico in order to build a railroad. This was called the Gadsden Purchase. This land today makes up the southernmost portions of Arizona and New Mexico. The southern border established by the Gadsden purchase is the one that exists today.

The eastern part of Texas is warm with plenty of rainfall. But the central and western parts are on a plateau where the weather is dry.

The Rio Grande (rē′ō grand) means "Great River" in Spanish. The Rio Grande flows south from Colorado. It begins to flow southeast around El Paso (el pas′ō), Texas. From El Paso to the Gulf of Mexico the Rio Grande forms the border between the United States and Mexico.

The land granted by Mexico in 1848 extends from the Rocky Mountains to the Pacific Ocean. The southern part of this land is dry and warm all year. There are deserts in some areas where only cactus and plants that need little water can grow.

North of the dry area high plateaus and rugged mountains fill the landscape. Also in this region is the Great Basin. The Great Basin is a region where rivers flow inland rather than toward the sea. Great Salt Lake is at the lowest part of the Great Basin.

The part of the land granted by Mexico that borders the Pacific is now called California. Northern California has a mild and moist climate. Great forests grow on the western slopes of its mountain ranges. Redwood and giant sequoia (si kwoi′ə) trees grow here. The eastern slopes of these mountain ranges are drier with fewer forests.

Southern California is warm with dry summers and rainy winters. Between the mountain ranges of southern California lies one of the most fertile valleys on earth. It is called the Central Valley.

Do You Know?

1. What is the climate like in the land of the Louisiana Purchase?
2. What river forms the border between the United States and Mexico?

2
A New Plan of Government

When the colonists were ruled by Great Britain, they had assemblies to make some of their laws. When Americans declared their independence from Great Britain, each state kept its assembly. But there was no plan for uniting the states under one government.

The Articles of Confederation

In 1781 a group of patriots drew up the Articles of Confederation (kən fed′ə rā′shən) which provided for a plan of government. It allowed for a Congress to be made up of representatives from all the states. This Congress was to become the central government.

Under the Articles of Confederation, Congress had limited powers. Americans had rebelled against Great Britain because they believed the king and the lawmakers of Great Britain had too much power. Therefore, they did not want their new central government to be too powerful.

The Articles stated that Congress could declare war and make peace treaties, but it could not force people to join the army. It could borrow money from other countries, but it could not collect taxes to pay its debts. Congress could ask the states for money, but it could not force them to pay it. It could not control trade between the states or between the United States and a foreign country. Nor could it prevent the states that had no gold or silver from issuing paper money. Paper money without

gold or silver in the bank to back it was worthless. Congress could pass laws, but it had no way of making people obey them.

The states had as much, or more, power than Congress. Each state elected a group of representatives called a *legislature* (lej′is lā′chər). A legislature is a group of persons who have the power to make laws for a state or a country. But the power of the states led to problems. The state legislatures began to use their power against one another. New York made people from other states pay taxes on goods that they sold in New York. New Jersey would not accept paper money made in Pennsylvania. Maryland and Virginia quarreled over the use of the Potomac River. States had disputes about roads, bridges, boundaries, and debts. Congress could not stop the quarrels.

Under the Articles of Confederation the new states acted like thirteen separate countries. During the War for Independence they had worked fairly well together. Now it seemed they could not agree on anything.

George Washington and other leaders were worried. They knew that the central government was too weak. They began to plan for a central government with more powers.

Meetings were called to discuss the problems of the new nation. Many states refused to send delegates to them. Finally, twelve states were persuaded to send delegates to a meeting in Philadelphia. The delegates hoped to find a way of improving the Articles of Confederation.

Thirty-nine of the 42 delegates still at the Constitutional *Convention* stood before George Washington to sign the Constitution.

The Constitutional Convention

The *convention* (kən ven′shən), or meeting held for a common purpose, opened on May 25, 1787, when 55 delegates had arrived in Philadelphia. They came from every state except Rhode Island. At the convention were some of the most respected people in the United States. Most of them had fought to make our nation free. Now they meant to put it on a firm foundation. George Washington was chosen to be in charge of the convention. During the convention the delegates decided to plan a new form of government.

From May until September they worked behind closed doors. It was hard to agree on a plan of government. Each suggestion was discussed carefully. There were heated arguments. Benjamin Franklin, the oldest delegate, often helped to make peace at the convention.

The weeks became months. Some delegates had to return to their homes or to their work. The others continued to debate until a new plan of government was put into writing.

On September 16, 1787, Independence Hall in Philadelphia was the scene of an important event. On a table in front of George Washington lay the new plan of government. It was the Constitution of the United States. The weary delegates were ready to sign it. They had created the foundation of a strong central government. They felt that with it the United States could become a great nation.

One after another the delegates stepped to the table and signed the Constitution. The new form of government was ready for the thirteen states to adopt.

Adopting the Constitution

At least nine of the thirteen states had to *ratify* (rat′ə fī) or approve, the Constitution before it could become the law of the land. The delegates took copies of the Constitution to their state legislatures.

Getting the Constitution ratified was not easy. Some of the lawmakers objected because many powers had been taken from the states and given to the national government. The national government, or government of the whole nation, is also called the federal government. Other delegates complained that certain rights for which they had fought were not clearly promised in the Constitution. Some of those who favored the Constitution wrote a series of articles defending it. These articles are now known as the *Federalist Papers*.

It was James Madison who spoke out for ten measures to protect certain freedoms. They were added to the Constitution. Laws added to the Constitution are *amendments* (ə mend′ments).

An amendment becomes a law when three-fourths of the states ratify it.

The first ten amendments are called the Bill of Rights because they protect a person's rights or freedoms. Among the freedoms protected by the Bill of Rights are freedom of religion and freedom of speech. The right of the people to meet together peacefully is also protected. Other rights, such as the right to a fair trial, protect persons tried in court.

Delaware was the first state to ratify the Constitution. By June 1788 nine states had approved it. The United States Constitution became the law of the land. By 1790 all thirteen states had adopted the Constitution. The Bill of Rights was approved in 1791. The young country had a new form of government.

Our National Government

According to our Constitution the national government is divided into three parts, or branches. The three branches are called the legislative (lej'is lā'tiv), executive (eg zek'yə tiv), and judicial (jōō dish'əl).

Three Branches of Government

The legislative branch makes the laws. The law-making body is called Congress. Congress is made up of two houses. One is the *Senate* (sen' it) and the other is the *House of Representatives* (rep'ri zen'tə tivz). Members of these two houses of Congress meet in a building called the *Capitol* (kap'it əl) in Washington, D.C. Each state sends two members to the Senate. Members of the Senate are called senators. Senators are elected to six-year terms. The vice-president of the United States heads the Senate, but has no vote unless the senators are equally divided on an issue.

Members of the House of Representatives are called representatives. They are chosen according to the number of people in a state. A state with a large population has more representatives than a less populated state.

Representatives are elected to two-year terms. The House of Representatives is headed by the Speaker of the House. This person is chosen by the representatives.

The executive branch of the national government is headed by the President of the United States. The President must see that the laws are carried out. The President may ask Congress to pass new laws.

The President chooses a group of persons to help with the duties of the executive branch. This group is called the *cabinet* (kab'ə nit). Members of the President's cabinet are called secretaries (sek'rə ter'ēz). Over the years the cabinet has become a part of the presidency even though it is not mentioned in the Constitution.

The President is chosen every 4 years. Only a person born in the United States can be President. If for some reason the President is unable to complete a term of 4 years, the vice-president finishes the term. The President is also the commander in chief of the armed forces of the United States.

The judicial branch is often called the "watchdog" of national government. The *Supreme* (sə prēm') *Court,* our country's highest court,

The *Congress* passes the laws.

The *President* enforces the laws.

The *Supreme Court* makes judgments about the laws.

decides whether a law is in keeping with the Constitution, or constitutional. If a law is not constitutional it does not remain a law. The Supreme Court of the United States is made up of nine justices, or judges. The chief justice heads the Supreme Court. Each justice is appointed by the President for a life term.

Each branch of the national government has its own powers. Each branch can check the power of the other two branches. This system of checking keeps any one branch from becoming too powerful.

Powers of the Government

The Constitution gives the national government certain powers. The states are left with the remaining powers, unless they are denied by the Constitution. The following powers are among those given the national government: to control trade with foreign nations and among the states, to coin money, to set up post offices, to declare war, to enter into treaties, and to raise and support an army and a navy.

The delegates to the Constitutional Convention in Philadelphia tried to draw up a lasting form of government. They succeeded. The Constitution which they planned in the summer of 1787, with some changes or amendments, is still our form of government. The government that it set up is a *republic* (ri pub'lik). A republic is a nation in which the people govern through

The power of governing the United States is divided among three branches. The Congress, the President, and the Supreme Court are equal and independent.

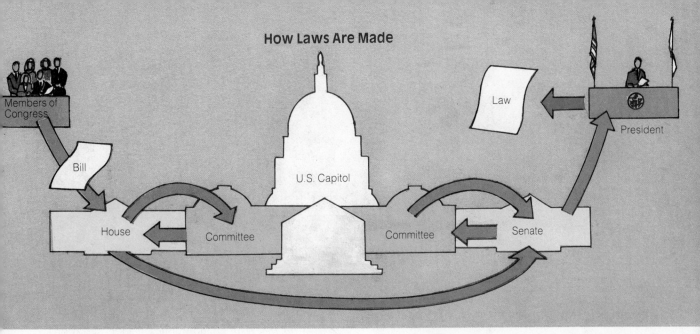

How Laws Are Made

This diagram shows how a bill becomes a law. If the bill was introduced in the *Senate*, where would it go next?

the representatives they have chosen. A republic has a president or other elected head of government.

How Laws Are Made

Laws are made by the two houses of Congress. A law is first called a bill, or a proposed law. A bill is introduced into either house of Congress. It is sent to a committee. The committee studies the bill carefully and makes some changes. Then the committee presents the bill to the whole house.

If the majority of the members of one house of Congress pass the bill, it is sent to the other house of Congress. If the other house makes any changes, the bill is sent to a joint committee, made up of members from both houses. A *compromise* (kom′prə mīz′) is worked out. A compromise is the settlement of a disagreement by having both sides give up some part of their claims or demands.

Then both houses vote on the compromise bill. If it is approved by both houses, the bill is

sent to the President. The President studies the bill carefully. If the President signs it, the bill immediately becomes a law.

If the President vetoes, or refuses to sign it, the bill is sent back to Congress. Both houses of Congress vote again. If two-thirds of both houses vote for the bill, it becomes a law.

Putting the Constitution to Work

George Washington had led our fight for independence. When a better form of government was needed, he helped plan it. When the new republic was set up, the people *elected* (i lekt′əd), or voted for, George Washington as their first President.

New York City was chosen to be the *capital* (kap′it əl), or city where the laws for a nation or state are made. President Washington would live in New York City. Congress and the Supreme Court would also meet there. Later, the capital was moved to Washington, D.C.

Government and military leaders stood on the balcony of Federal Hall with George Washington when he was *inaugurated*.

Inaugurating the First President

After the end of the War for Independence, George Washington returned to his home at Mount Vernon, Virginia. He loved his home and hoped to spend the rest of his life there with his family. But in the spring of 1789 he was on his way to New York City. He was to be *inaugurated* (in ô′gyə rāt′əd) as the first President of the United States. To inaugurate someone is to officially install him or her in office.

Washington made the journey on horseback and by coach. All along the way people came out to cheer him. He crossed the Hudson River to New York City in a brightly decorated boat. Guns from the ships in the harbor fired a salute as he landed.

On April 30, 1789, great crowds gathered to see George Washington inaugurated. How they cheered when he appeared on the balcony of Federal Hall! New York City had given this building to the nation. With Washington were Vice-President John Adams, and Judge Robert R. Livingston. Judge Livingston stepped for-

ward, and silence fell over the crowd. Then he read the President's oath of office. This oath of office is a solemn promise to carry out the laws of the Constitution. When Washington repeated the final words of the oath, the people began to cheer. The first President of our country had been inaugurated!

Washington, D.C.

President Washington and other leaders wanted a capital city where government would be the main business. Southerners wanted to have the capital in their part of the country. Northerners wanted it in the North.

Two members of Washington's cabinet helped decide where the capital would be. Alexander Hamilton of New York was Secretary of the Treasury. Thomas Jefferson of Virginia was Secretary of State. Often these men did not agree. However the two secretaries decided to work together on this important issue. They agreed to reach a solution as quickly as possible.

Hamilton persuaded northern congressmen to vote for a southern capital. This is what Jefferson wanted. In return, Jefferson got southern congressmen to agree that our national government should pay the debts of the states from the Revolutionary War. This pleased Hamilton.

Congress voted to build the capital on the Potomac River. President Washington chose the spot where the city, named for him, now stands. Land on both sides of the Potomac was set aside. This area is the District of Columbia.

The city of Washington was carefully planned. The Capitol, the building in which Congress meets, is the center of the city. It stands on a hill. The President's home and other government buildings are near the Capitol.

George Washington

You probably know that George Washington was born on February 22. That day is celebrated as a holiday in most of the states in our country.

Washington's parents were living on a farm in Virginia when he was born. While he was growing up, George went to school. He also learned how to ride and shoot. He admired his oldest brother, Lawrence, who had been an officer in the British navy. George hoped to go to England and join the navy too.

Before George was 12 years old, however, his father died. The plans to go to England had to be forgotten. George had to manage the family farm.

While George was in his teens, the land west of the Piedmont and the Appalachians was being explored. People were needed to survey, or measure, the land. Washington decided to learn how to survey.

Lawrence Washington had a plantation on the Potomac River in Virginia called Mount Vernon. George often spent time there and become acquainted with his brother's friend Lord Fairfax. Lord Fairfax owned a large tract of land west of the Blue Ridge Mountains in present-day Kentucky. George was only 16 years old when Lord Fairfax hired him to help survey these western lands.

On surveying trips George learned how to live in the forest. He saved his money to buy land. Each day he wrote in a diary.

George was 20 years old when his brother Lawrence died and left him the plantation at Mount Vernon. George married Martha Custis, a young widow with two children. For the next 20 years, except when he was fighting in the French and Indian War, George lived at Mount Vernon. His crops, cattle, and fine horses were famous throughout Virginia.

This stately white mansion was the center of life at George and Martha Washington's estate, Mount Vernon.

Artist Gilbert Stuart painted these famous portraits of George and Martha Washington in 1796, just one year before President Washington retired from office.

After the French and Indian War Colonel Washington became an important person in Virginia. The people elected him to the House of Burgesses. They wanted him to help make laws for the colony.

When delegates were sent to the First Continental Congress in Philadelphia, Virginia sent Colonel Washington. He was sent to the Second Continental Congress also. Like most colonists at that time, he thought the colonies ought to try to get along with England. After the battle of Bunker Hill, however, Washington accepted the command of the army and led the colonies in the struggle for independence.

The war lasted 6 years. These years were the hardest in Washington's life. He met many defeats, and he and his troops endured a terrible winter at Valley Forge. But General Washington never gave up. In the end the army was victorious. Through it all the army respected and loved their great leader.

After the war Washington returned to Mount Vernon. The plantation was soon running well. He invented a new plow, grew better fruit trees, and improved a breed of cattle. People from all parts of the world visited Mount Vernon. Then the country called Washington to serve again.

As President, Washington served the country well for 8 years, or 2 terms. He refused to accept a third term and retired to his home. Less than 2 years later George Washington died. People deeply mourned the death of the man who was "first in war, first in peace, and first in the hearts of his countrymen."

Do You Know?

1. Why was the government of the United States weak under the Articles of Confederation?
2. Who wrote the Constitution? When and where was it written?
3. How was the Constitution adopted?
4. What is the Bill of Rights?
5. What was the first capital city of our country?

Before You Go On

Using New Words

elect   amendment
convention   cabinet
Senate   compromise
legislature   ratify
republic   inaugurate
Supreme Court   House of
Capitol   Representatives
capital

The phrases below explain the words or terms listed above. Number a paper from 1 through 14. After each number write the word or term that matches the definition.

1. A meeting held for a common purpose
2. The part of Congress which has the most members
3. The highest court in our country
4. A group of people, chosen by the President, to help with the duties of the executive branch
5. A group of persons chosen to make laws
6. The part of Congress made up of two members from each state
7. To vote for a person for an office
8. To approve
9. A nation in which the people govern through their chosen representatives
10. To put into office
11. A law which is added to the Constitution
12. The city where the laws for a nation or state are made
13. The building where members of the United States Congress meet
14. Settlement of a disagreement by having each side agree to give up some part of its claims

Finding the Facts

1. How does the land south of the Ohio River differ from the land near the Gulf coast?
2. What is the climate of Florida?
3. What line of latitude forms part of the border between the United States and Canada?
4. What is the climate of Texas like?
5. What is the climate of California like?
6. What new plan of central government began in 1781?
7. Why did delegates in Philadelphia try to improve the Articles of Confederation?
8. Who was in charge of the convention held in Philadelphia in 1787?
9. Which was the first state to ratify the Constitution?
10. Which branch of the national government makes the laws? Which branch sees that the laws are carried out? Which branch decides whether a law is in keeping with the Constitution?
11. Where was George Washington inaugurated?

3

Winning Freedom of the Seas

The United States had broken its ties with Great Britain. Now its manufacturers and merchants needed new markets. Americans also wanted the products of distant lands. American ships began to visit the seaports of Europe and Africa. But people missed the products of the Far East that British ships used to bring.

Growth of Trade

Merchants of the United States decided to open trade with Asia. Less than 10 years after the United States became a nation, a ship from the port of New York City reached China. Not to be outdone, Boston merchants fitted up two ships for trade with the Far East. Captain Robert Gray commanded one of the ships.

Captain Gray's Voyage to China

Captain Gray sailed southward along the coasts of North and South America and around Cape Horn. He stopped for furs on the west coast of North America. He then sailed across the Pacific Ocean to Hawaii and China. His was the first ship to carry the flag of the United States across the Pacific Ocean. He exchanged furs for tea, spices, and silk.

Gray returned by Magellan's and Drake's route around Africa. See the map showing the routes taken in search of the Far East on page 34. Gray was the first American to sail around the world. His voyage helped promote trade between China and the United States.

The War of 1812

Americans soon began to trade with Great Britain again. Merchants also built up valuable trade with France. Both these European countries needed our raw materials. Americans needed their manufactured goods.

Then Great Britain and France went to war. Each planned to cut off the other's trade. The British began to seize American ships headed for France. The French captured American vessels bound for England. Because of this European war, the United States was losing ships and goods.

The British began stopping American vessels in the middle of the ocean and searching them. They seized any British sailors they found. Sometimes they took American sailors and forced them to work on British ships.

"This is an insult!" said a group of Americans, known as the War Hawks. "We must fight Great Britain!" But the United States was not prepared for war. Its army was small and poorly trained. Its navy had only 15 ships. The British fleet had about 1,000 vessels. But the War Hawks persuaded Congress to declare war against Great Britain in 1812.

The Saving of the Northwest

Early in the war the British invaded from Canada and captured Detroit. It looked as though they might take the whole Northwest. A British fleet lay on the north shore of Lake Erie, in Canada. Oliver Hazard Perry, a young naval officer,

In the War of 1812 the *Constitution* gained fame as a fighting ship. This painting shows "Old Ironsides" winning a battle against the British ship *Guerrière*.

was ordered to stop the British from coming across the lake. The Congress sent shipbuilders to help Perry. With new ships and sailors, Perry defeated the British in a difficult naval battle. "We have met the enemy and they are ours," was the message Perry sent to Congress.

General William Henry Harrison's army then drove the British out of Detroit back into Canada. The American Northwest had been saved.

Victories by the American Navy

The Americans were doing better at sea than on land. Even before the victory on Lake Erie they had won several sea battles in the Atlantic Ocean.

The few ships of the United States navy did not dare meet the strong British navy. So American ships went out by ones or twos. If they met many enemy ships, they sailed away as fast as they could. If they met only one, they attacked.

The most famous of these fighting ships was the *Constitution*. The *Constitution* won so many battles it became a terror to the British navy. The United States proudly nicknamed it "Old Ironsides." The *Constitution* was said to be so sturdy that cannonballs would bounce off its sides. When the war ended, "Old Ironsides" was taken to the navy yard in Boston. Time and again there was talk of wrecking the old ship. Each time some people remembered its deeds in the War of 1812, and it was spared. Today the *Constitution* is docked on the Charles River, near Boston. Visitors can go aboard the grand old ship.

The Burning of Washington, D.C.

In the last year of the war the British tried several times to enter the United States. One British fleet tried to bring soldiers from Canada across Lake Champlain. They were defeated

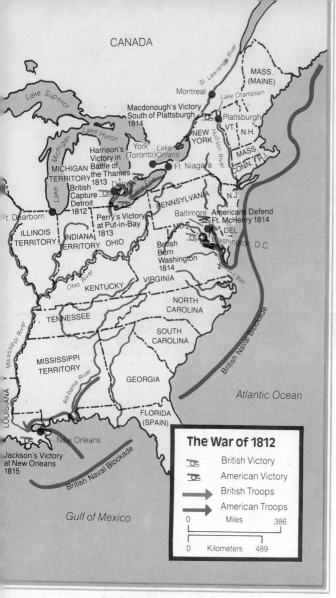

The War of 1812

⚔	British Victory
⚔	American Victory
➡	British Troops
➡	American Troops

0 Miles 386

0 Kilometers 489

In the War of 1812, battles were fought on both land and water. Name some famous battle locations. What battles were won by the Americans?

both on land and on Lake Champlain. This ended British attacks from the north.

In the East, British ships landed an army on the shore of Chesapeake Bay and marched to Washington, D.C., our nation's capital.

As the British army approached, President James Madison and First Lady Dolley Madison fled Washington, D.C. They took as many valuables with them as possible. The British burned the President's house, called the White House; the Capitol; and other government buildings.

The Battle at Fort McHenry

Then the British started toward Baltimore to capture the city. Troops in Fort McHenry, near Baltimore, were determined to turn back the British ships.

When night came British ships tried to get past the fort in the darkness. The watchful Americans saw them. Fort McHenry's cannon roared. British guns returned the fire. The battle raged all night.

An American watched the battle from a British ship where he was being held. The first dim light of morning showed the American flag still flying over the fort. The British attack had failed. This watcher, Francis Scott Key, jotted down a poem which had been forming in his mind as he watched the fight. The poem, "The Star-Spangled Banner," was later set to music. It became our national anthem.

Jackson and the Battle of New Orleans

Another British fleet, carrying a large army, tried to capture New Orleans, near the mouth of the Mississippi River. General Andrew Jackson was sent to stop the British.

Jackson was a good soldier. He had fought in the War for Independence as a volunteer at the age of 13. He and his brother were held prisoners by the British for some months. When the War of 1812 broke out, he was eager to fight.

This view of the battle of Fort McHenry shows the American flag and "the bombs bursting in air." The British ships in the harbor failed in their attack.

Jackson gathered an army of pioneers from Tennessee and Kentucky and marched south. They reached New Orleans before the British. There they were joined by sailors and pirates from the Gulf coast. There were French people from Louisiana and two groups of black soldiers. They were ready for the British army. When the British came, they were defeated by the Americans.

The Results of the War

Jackson's victory at New Orleans was not necessary to win the war. The battle of New Orleans was fought after the war had ended. In those days communications were very slow. News had not reached New Orleans before the battle. Representatives of the United States and Great Britain had signed a peace treaty in Bel-

gium in December, 1814. The War of 1812 was the last war between Great Britain and the United States.

During the War of 1812 the United States built a navy. The United States won the right to sail the oceans without interference. The United States had also proved to the world that it was truly an independent nation.

Do You Know?

1. Why did the United States go to war with the British in 1812?
2. How did "The Star-Spangled Banner" come to be written?
3. What did the Americans gain by the War of 1812?

4
The Civil War

The people who wrote the Constitution held different opinions about government. They knew that there would be many disagreements in a republic. But they hoped that people with different ideas would discuss their differences.

Quarrels that Divided the Nation

Some people thought the national government had too much power. They believed that the states had lost too many of their rights. These and other problems led to heated discussions in Congress. At first these quarrels were settled by compromise. Finally the quarrels became so bitter that no compromise could be reached. In 1861 the Civil War broke out. A civil war is a war between citizens of the same country.

The Quarrel over Tariff

The first quarrel was about *tariff* (tar′if). A tariff is a tax paid on goods brought into a country from foreign countries. The manufacturers of the North wanted a high tariff put on products brought in from other countries. These goods would then sell at a higher price than those made in America. This would make it easier for northern manufacturers to sell their products because they would be cheaper than foreign goods. The South did little manufacturing. People of the South bought many goods from Europe. They wanted no tariff on foreign goods so that the price of these goods would be low.

In 1828 Congress passed a tariff act. This pleased the people of the North, but it angered Southerners. Southern states threatened to *secede* (si sēd′), or withdraw from the Union, as the United States was called then. Fortunately, Congress was able to reach a compromise. No states seceded from the Union.

The Quarrel over Slavery

The second quarrel was harder to settle. By 1776 many Americans, both in the North and in the South, felt slavery was wrong. It might have disappeared gradually if the cotton gin (cot′ ən jin) had not been invented.

This machine could clean as much cotton in a day as 50 workers could by hand. Much more cotton could be produced. Since there was a growing market for cotton, southern planters began to plant more and more cotton. This meant that more slaves were needed to work in the cotton fields.

There were many Northerners who did not want slavery to spread. The Ohio River formed the boundary between "slave" and "free" states. *Slave states* were those where slaves were used. In *free states* no slaves could be owned. There were fifteen slave states where 4 million slaves belonged to about 350,000 slave owners. In these same states there were 6 million people who held no slaves. There were also thousands of free blacks.

Some Americans felt that owning slaves for any reason was wrong. They wanted to abolish,

Frederick Douglass worked to abolish slavery with speeches and articles in his newspaper. Harriet Tubman led more than 300 slaves to freedom.

or do away with, slavery altogether. These people were called *abolitionists* (ab´ə lish´ə nists). Abolitionists wanted all slave owners to set their slaves free at once.

Three Black Leaders

Three black leaders tried to do something to free their people. In 1831, a black slave preacher, Nat Turner, led a revolt in Virginia. His rebel army fought well, but lost. In the end Nat Turner was captured and hanged.

Frederick Douglass, a free black, hoped to abolish slavery by telling people of its evils. He edited an abolitionist newspaper called the *North Star*. In the newspaper he suggested that an "underground railroad" be set up. An underground railroad is a means of helping slaves escape to freedom. Hiding places, or "stations," were provided along routes for runaway slaves. The slaves were fed and taken from one point to another until they reached Canada. Slaves escaped to Canada because there was a law in the United States stating that runaway slaves had to be returned to their owners if captured.

Some people risked their lives to help slaves escape. One of these was Harriet Tubman. After escaping as a slave herself, she returned many times to lead other slaves to freedom. Harriet Tubman became known as the "Moses" of her people because she led so many slaves to freedom. She freed more than 300 slaves.

Agreement by Compromise

For a while there was an equal number of slave states and free states. But the United States continued to grow, adding new lands. The addition of lands caused the question of slavery to flare up again. Were the settlers to be allowed to keep slaves in these new lands? Were new states to enter the Union as free or as slave states?

In 1803 our country bought the land known as Louisiana from France. Later, Texas and other lands owned by Mexico were added. The question of slavery in the new lands was settled by a compromise. A few years later Congress passed a law allowing the people in each new state to decide whether they wanted slavery or not.

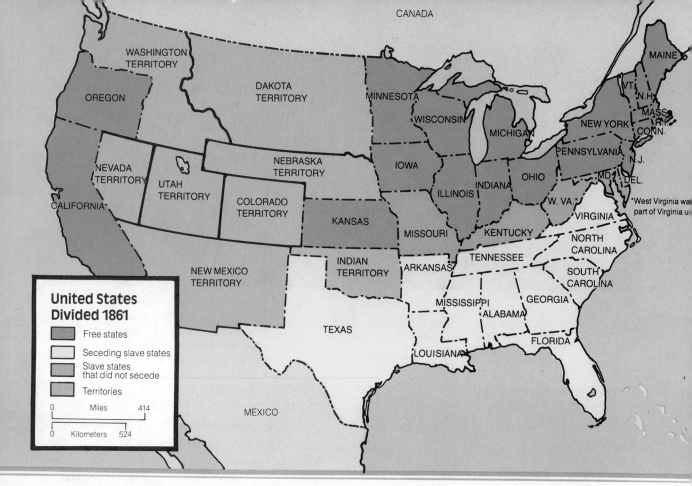

The states were divided over the issue of slavery. Which *slave states* seceded from the Union? How many states were *free states?*

Election of a Republican President

In 1856 a new political party was organized. The Republican party, as it was called, became popular in the North and Northwest. The original aim of the new party was to keep the country united and the new lands free from slavery.

The slaveholders in the South were worried about this new party. They were afraid that a Republican president might also try to do away with slavery in slave states. Many Southerners also feared the possibility of rebellion by the slaves themselves. In 1859 John Brown led a small group in an attack on Harpers Ferry in Virginia. Brown wanted to get the weapons stored there. He planned to give them to slaves so that they could fight for their freedom. The attack failed, but Southerners saw Brown's raid as a sign of what the future might bring.

Abraham Lincoln

On February 12, 1809, Abraham Lincoln was born in a log cabin in Kentucky. Abe lived there until he was seven. Then the Lincoln family moved to Indiana. Two years later Nancy Lincoln, Abe's mother, died.

Abraham Lincoln argues against slavery at one of the 1858 debates with Stephen Douglas. How did the debates help Lincoln to become a national leader?

After a while, Abe's father married Sarah Bush Johnston. She helped Abe learn to read and write. Later, whenever his father could spare him from work, Abe went to school.

Even though he went to school only 2 or 3 months a year, Abe was always reading. He would borrow books from neighbors to read at night.

When Abe was 21, the Lincoln family moved to Illinois. Abe worked as a clerk in a store for several years. Then he bought a store of his own. But Lincoln's store was not a success. He was in charge of the post office for a while. Later he became a surveyor.

After trying many kinds of work, Lincoln made an important decision. He decided to run for the Illinois legislature. He had tried once before, but was defeated. This time he succeeded. Lincoln's experience in the state legislature convinced him that good laws were important. He began to study law and opened an office in Springfield, Illinois.

Lincoln stayed in the Illinois legislature for 8 years. Then he was elected to the House of Representatives in Washington, D.C., and served one term. Back in Springfield, Lincoln returned to his law office. He became one of Illinois' leading lawyers.

Lincoln was very concerned about the country's problems. He knew the question of slavery was dividing the nation. He felt that slavery should not be allowed in new lands. Lincoln ran for the United States Senate as a Republican. He had to run against Stephen Douglas. In 1858, Lincoln challenged Douglas to a series of debates.

The speeches given by the two men were reported throughout the country. Although Lincoln lost the election, he became very well known. Lincoln's belief that the Union must be preserved impressed many people. He also became known for his statements against slavery. In 1860 the Republicans asked Abraham Lincoln to run for President. He was elected.

On February 3, 1861, the wives and children of Union soldiers at Fort Sumter were sent to New York for safety. Two months later Confederate forces attacked the fort.

Secession of the South

Many Southerners believed that a state had the right to leave the Union. "The South is not being fairly treated," many Southerners said. "We will secede!"

South Carolina was the first to secede. Six other states quickly followed. These seven states formed a new government called the *Confederacy* (kon fed′ər ə sē), or the Confederate States of America. Four more southern states joined the Confederacy within a few months' time. The map of the divided United States on page 110 shows our country at the time Lincoln became President. In 1863 western Virginia broke away from Virginia and stayed in the Union. It became the state of West Virginia.

President Lincoln was inaugurated on March 4, 1861. Jefferson Davis became President of the Confederate States of America.

The War Begins

Fort Sumter, in Charleston Harbor, South Carolina was held by Union troops. On April 12, 1861, the Confederate army fired on the fort. The Union troops could not hold the fort and surrendered. Firing on Fort Sumter started the Civil War.

Confederate soldiers, in gray uniforms, were fighting for the right of a state to secede. Union soldiers, dressed in blue, wanted to save the Union. Both sides were sure the war could not last long. But the war went on for 4 bitter years.

Many people felt that the Union had a great advantage in the Civil War. The Union had a larger population and more factories than the Confederacy. But the Confederacy had advantages too. It had well-trained military leaders. These leaders were fighting on familiar ground. The Confederacy had fine riders for the cavalry. The Union army was made up of many factory workers. They would be fighting far from home on unfamiliar ground.

Early Stages of the War

President Lincoln knew that the Confederacy needed supplies from Europe. So he ordered a *blockade* (blo kād') of southern ports. A blockade is the closing of an area to prevent people or supplies from going into or out of it. Charleston in South Carolina, Savannah in Georgia, and New Orleans in Louisiana were the chief ports in the South. Union warships fired on any ships that tried to enter or leave.

An early plan of Union leaders was to capture Richmond, Virginia, the Confederate capital. They felt that this would end the war. Again and again the Union army advanced toward Richmond. Again and again it was defeated by the Confederate army commanded by General Robert E. Lee of Virginia.

Famous Civil War photographer Mathew Brady recorded many war scenes. Here are Union infantry troops and free blacks in front of their tent between battles.

A Comparison of the Union and the Confederacy

FACT BOX 1

	The Union	The Confederacy
States	24 (including 4 border states that were slave states, and West Virginia, which became a state in 1863)	11
Population	22,000,000	9,000,000 (including 3,500,000 slaves)

Look at the two fact boxes. Why did many people feel that the Union had a great advantage in the Civil War?

The Confederacy had a smaller population and fewer factories than the Union. But the Confederacy had advantages too. It had well-trained military leaders. These leaders were fighting on familiar ground. It had people used to outdoor living. It had fine riders for the cavalry. The Union army was made up of many factory workers. They would be fighting far from home on unfamiliar ground. They were not used to living off the countryside. They depended on long supply lines. The war would not be a short one. It would last for four bitter years.

FACT BOX 2

1. For every acre (ha) of farmland in the Confederacy the Union had 2 acres (0.8 ha).

2. For every mile (km) of railroad track in the Confederacy the Union had about 3 miles (4.8 km).

3. For every factory the Confederacy had, the Union had seven factories.

4. For every ton of iron the Confederacy produced the Union produced 24 tons (21.6 metric tons).

Robert E. Lee

Robert Edward Lee's earliest memories were of a plantation with a large house and sloping lawns. This was in Stratford, Virginia, where he was born on January 19, 1807.

The Lee family moved to Alexandria, Virginia, when Robert was still young. Here he met, and later married, Mary Custis, the great-granddaughter of Martha Washington.

No one was surprised when young Robert chose to join the army. At 18 he entered the military academy at West Point on the Hudson River in New York. Many of our nation's army officers were trained at West Point. During the war with Mexico Lee served our country well. Later he became head of West Point.

Lee believed that keeping slaves was wrong. He did not believe that states should secede from the Union. However, he was a Virginian. The time would come when Lee would have to take sides in the quarrel.

At the time when Confederate soldiers fired on Fort Sumter, Lee was a colonel in the army of the United States. Lincoln asked Colonel Lee to take a command in the Union army. Lee loved the United States. But he loved Virginia too, and Virginia had seceded from the Union. What was he to do? Should he take a command in the Union forces and fight against Virginians? Or should he help defend Virginia against the Union? He decided that it was his duty to serve Virginia.

In a letter to President Lincoln, Lee expressed his sorrow at having to refuse the honor of commanding the Union forces. He resigned from the United States Army.

Robert E. Lee is pictured in his uniform as an officer of the Army of the United States. When the Civil War began, however, he took command of the Confederate Army.

Jefferson Davis made Lee the commander of the Army of Northern Virginia. Later Lee became commander in chief of all Confederate forces.

All through the Civil War, Lee tried to bring victory to the Confederacy. He was a splendid leader. For 2 years he never lost a battle. Then at Gettysburg, Pennsylvania, Lee's forces suffered a major defeat. Trying to attack the larger Union forces, Lee lost one-third of his troops. It was one of the worst battles in the war for both sides. President Lincoln honored the brave soldiers who died there in 1863 when he gave his Gettysburg address.

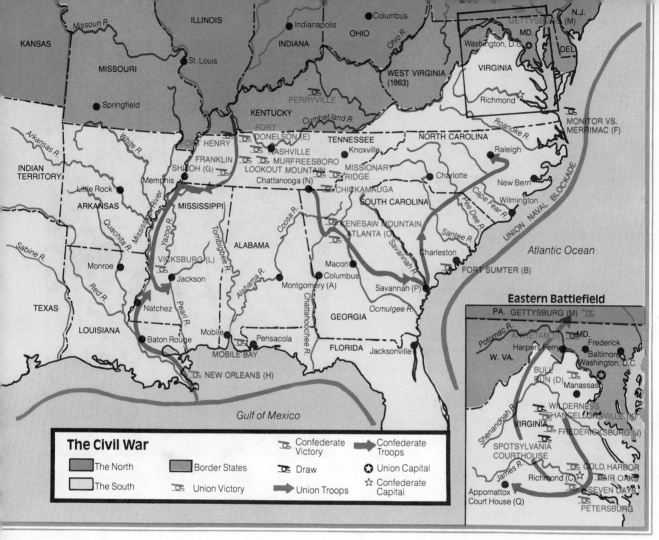

The Civil War

- ▨ The North
- ▨ Border States
- ▢ The South
- ⚓ Confederate Victory
- ⚓ Draw
- ⚓ Union Victory
- ➤ Confederate Troops
- ➤ Union Troops
- ✪ Union Capital
- ☆ Confederate Capital

Eastern Battlefield

Most Civil War battles took place in the Southern slave states. Which states saw the most fighting? Which Northern state was the site of a crucial battle? Where did that battle take place?

For 4 years Lee was able to keep the Union army out of Virginia too. Lee realized the Confederacy was lost, and he surrendered.

After the war Lee set to work to help unite the country. He became president of Washington College (now called Washington and Lee University) in Virginia. He urged the students to forget the war and think of themselves as Americans, not as citizens of a particular state or region. Robert E. Lee died in 1870.

The War in the West

In 1863 Union ships were blockading southern ports. The Union hoped to divide the Confederacy by taking the towns on the lower Mississippi River. Admiral David Farragut (far′ə gət) took New Orleans on April 25, 1862. On July 4, 1863, General Ulysses S. Grant took Vicksburg and smaller towns on the Mississippi. By the end of 1863 the Mississippi Valley was in Northern hands. The South was cut in two.

The Civil War   1861–1865

1861
February
Mississippi, Florida, Alabama, Georgia, Louisiana, and Texas joined South Carolina to form the Confederate States of America (CSA). MONTGOMERY (A) was the first capital.

April
The Confederates forced Union troops (USA) to surrender FORT SUMTER (B). Virginia joined the Confederacy. Lincoln ordered southern ports blockaded.

May
Arkansas, Tennessee, and North Carolina seceded. RICHMOND (C) became the capital of the Confederacy.

July
Union troops were defeated near BULL RUN (D).

1862
February
General Ulysses S. Grant's troops captured FORT DONELSON (E).

March
Battle between the *Monitor* (USA) and the *Merrimac* (CSA) ended in a draw (F).

April
Grant defeated Confederate forces at SHILOH with great losses (G). Admiral David Farragut (USA) captured NEW ORLEANS (H).

June
After the Seven Days' Battle near RICHMOND (C). General George McClellan (USA) was forced to retreat.

August
Union forces were defeated in second battle of BULL RUN (D).

September
General Robert E. Lee's (CSA) invasion turned back in battle near ANTIETAM CREEK (I). Lee withdrew to Virginia. (Lee was the commanding officer of the main Confederate army.)

December
Union forces unsuccessfully attacked Lee at FREDERICKSBURG (J).

1863
March
Grant was placed in charge of all the Union armies.

May
Lee and General "Stonewall" Jackson (CSA) defeated Union forces at CHANCELLORSVILLE (K).

May 22–July 4
After a six-weeks' siege by Grant, VICKSBURG (L) surrendered. Union forces won control of the Mississippi River and the Confederacy was split in two.

July
Lee's invasion of Pennsylvania ended in defeat at GETTYSBURG (M). Union forces put down riots against the draft in NEW YORK CITY.

November
Grant defeated Confederate troops near CHATTANOOGA (N). Tennessee came under Union control.

1864
May–June
Grant's forces advanced toward RICHMOND (C).

May–December
General William T. Sherman's troops invaded Georgia, moved from ATLANTA (O) to SAVANNAH (P) destroying much in their path.

1865
April
Richmond was taken by Union forces. The main army of the Confederacy, under Lee, surrendered at APPOMATTOX COURT HOUSE (Q).

The Emancipation Proclamation

On January 1, 1863, Lincoln signed the Emancipation Proclamation (i man′sə pā′shən prok′lə mā shən). The aim of this declaration was to emancipate, or free, the slaves in the Confederacy. The slaves in the border states—Missouri, Maryland, Kentucky, Delaware—were not freed.

The Emancipation Proclamation had little immediate effect. But as the war moved south, slaves were freed. Roughly 200,000 former slaves became Union soldiers or sailors. About 38,000 blacks lost their lives in battle.

End of the Civil War

Since General Grant had been successful in the West, Lincoln made Grant commander of all the Union forces. Grant began making plans to bring the war to a close. His plan was to lead an army into Virginia and take Richmond. At the same time, General William Sherman would cut the eastern Confederacy in half and weaken it further.

Look at the map of the Civil War and the outline of its important events on these pages. You can see that Grant's plan succeeded. In September 1864, General Sherman captured

Almost four years to the day after the war began, General Lee surrendered to General Grant. The ceremony took place at the home of Wilmer McLean in Appomattox, Virginia.

Atlanta, Georgia. Sherman's army then burned and destroyed farms and homes from Atlanta to the coast. Sherman then marched north to join Grant in Virginia.

General Grant attacked Richmond with a huge army. General Lee's army was smaller. They were exhausted and poorly equipped. Lee realized that it was useless to continue the bloodshed.

On April 9, 1865, General Lee surrendered to General Grant at Appomattox (ap′ə mat′ əks), in Virginia. The Civil War was over.

After the War

Northerners and Southerners both suffered greatly during the war. But the Union had been saved. The question of whether a state could

118

secede from the Union had been settled. Our nation could not be divided. Slavery was abolished forever!

Death of Abraham Lincoln

Peace came, and President Lincoln made plans to unite the country. He believed the South had suffered enough. He wanted it to be taken back into the Union. But Lincoln did not live to carry out his plan. Five days after the war ended he was sitting in a theater in Washington, D.C., enjoying a play. Suddenly a shot rang out. The President had been shot by John Wilkes Booth, an actor. Abraham Lincoln died the next morning. The nation lost a great leader; the South lost a good friend.

Problems of the South

The war was over, but the South was in ruins. Returning soldiers found their homes burned, their fields trampled and destroyed. They had no money to hire workers. Southerners had to find ways to rebuild. This time of rebuilding is known as Reconstruction.

The government passed a law forbidding anyone who had fought in the Confederate army to vote or to hold office. The South was divided into sections that were ruled by Union army officers. Troops were sent by the government to enforce the law. They stayed in the South for many years.

Blacks had freedom but they still had problems. No one had made any plans to help the freed slaves. Some stayed on with their former owners. Others went from place to place looking for work.

Amendments to Help the Freed Blacks

Between 1865 and 1870 Congress passed three amendments to the Constitution. The Thirteenth Amendment stated that all slaves were free. The Fourteenth Amendment made all blacks citizens. The Fifteenth Amendment gave black men the right to vote. The Constitution allowed black men to vote and hold office.

Many Northerners moved south after the Civil War. They carried their possessions in bags made of carpet. They were called *carpetbaggers* (kar′pit bag′ərz). Some of the carpetbaggers were honest businesspeople. But others saw a chance to make money from the problems of the South. They pretended to be the freed slaves' friends. They helped blacks get elected to office, hoping to control them.

A number of blacks were elected to Congress during this period. The black lawmakers passed many good laws. For example, they introduced free education for all children. Other laws were passed that provided help for the poor. Projects to help those who had no jobs were begun.

There were also Southerners who worked with blacks and northern Republicans to pass these laws. They were called "Scalawags" (skal′ ə wags) by Southerners who believed they were too helpful to the blacks.

Reconstruction Ends

Now that blacks were free, most people were satisfied. The armies were removed from the South. Congress passed a law allowing those who had been Confederate soldiers to vote in national elections and to send representatives to Congress. Reconstruction ended in 1877.

Soon after the Civil War, blacks won seats in Congress. These men represented voters in Mississippi, Alabama, Florida, Georgia, and South Carolina.

Some white people in the South then took steps to get blacks out of office. They threatened and forced blacks from their positions. They kept most blacks from voting, so that white legislators were elected. It was a long time before blacks in southern states were elected to office again. It was also a long time before southern states voted for a Republican. Because the southern states voted the same way on many important issues, they came to be called the "Solid South."

Do You Know?

1. What were the most important causes of the Civil War?
2. Tell who each of the following was: Jefferson Davis, Robert E. Lee, David Farragut, Ulysses S. Grant, William Sherman, John Brown.
3. How did the war end? When did it end?

To Help You Learn

Using New Words

secede
Confederacy
carpetbagger
tariff
free state
blockade
amendment

compromise
republic
capital
slave state
abolitionist
Capitol

The phrases below explain the words or terms listed above. Number a paper from 1 through 13. After each number write the word or term that matches the definition.

1. A state that did not permit slaves to be owned
2. Settlement of a disagreement by having each side agree to give up some part of its claims
3. A state that allowed slaves to be used
4. A law that changes the Constitution
5. A person who wanted all slaves freed
6. A tax on goods brought into a country
7. To withdraw from an organization
8. The nation formed by the states that seceded from the Union
9. The city where the laws for a nation or state are made
10. A Northerner who moved to the South after the Civil War
11. A nation in which the people govern through their chosen representatives
12. The building in which the United States Congress meets
13. The closing of an area to prevent people or supplies from going into or out of it

Finding the Facts

1. What purchase doubled the size of the United States?
2. What occurred at the convention held in Philadelphia in 1787?
3. What does each part, or branch, of the national government do?
4. What are the first ten amendments called? What do they protect?
5. Why did Congress declare war against Great Britain in 1812?
6. What were the results of the War of 1812?
7. Why was the South opposed to a tariff on foreign goods? Why was the North in favor of a tariff on foreign goods?
8. What was the escape route used by slaves called? Who was Harriet Tubman?
9. Why was the Republican party founded? Who became the first Republican President of the United States?
10. Who became President of the Confederate States?
11. Where did the Civil War begin?
12. What was the Emancipation Proclamation?
13. What three amendments to the Constitution helped blacks?

Learning from Maps

1. Turn to the map on page 91 showing the growth of the United States. When did the United States obtain Florida? From what country did the United States get land in 1848? Did our country add the Oregon Country before or after it added Texas? Which purchase came first, Louisiana or Gadsden? How many years passed between these two purchases?

2. Look at the map of the Civil War on page 116. In what part of the country did most of the fighting of the Civil War take place? Where was the northernmost battle fought? What city was the Confederate capital? What city was the Union capital?

About how far apart are these two cities?

Use the map and the list of Civil War events on pages 116–117 to answer these questions. Which side won both battles at Bull Run? Where was the first Union victory? Where was the battle of Shiloh? Which side won at Shiloh? Where was the battle of Chancellorsville? Which side won at Chancellorsville?

Using Study Skills

1. **Diagram:** Study the diagram below. Then answer the questions.
   The winds blowing in from the Pacific Ocean are warm and carry moisture. As they rise and pass over the top of the

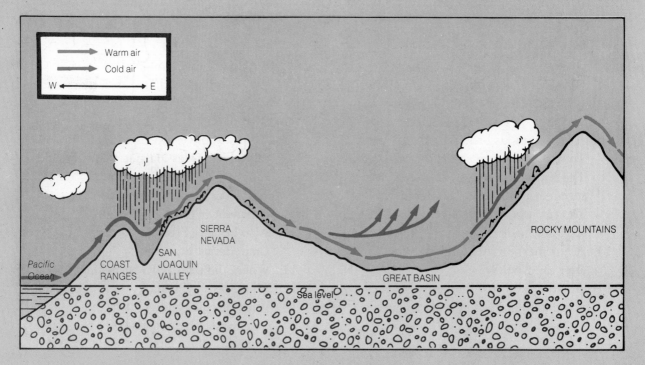

mountains, they grow cool and clouds form. The clouds then drop their moisture in the form of rain or snow. As the winds continue to blow, they force their way under the warm air of the valley. The warm air rises, clouds form, and rain falls again. But now the clouds have less moisture and the rainfall is less. Why is the land farthest from the ocean a desert area?

Why are the west sides of the Coast Range, the Sierra Nevada, and the Rockies covered with more trees than the east sides? Why is the Great Basin such a dry area? Why are there few clouds there?

From what direction do the winds tend to blow in the United States?
2. **Time Line:** Copy the time line for this unit. Put in the dates for these events: Abraham Lincoln elected President; Constitutional Convention held; Mexico grants land to United States; Bill of Rights approved

Thinking It Through

1. Why did the founders divide the power of the central government into three parts instead of placing it all in one part?
2. The battle of New Orleans was fought more than 2 weeks after the War of 1812 was over. How did this happen? Why would it not happen today?

3. When the Civil War ended, President Lincoln urged that the southern states not be punished. What might have happened if Lincoln had not been killed?

Projects

1. Have the Research Committee find out more about the steps a bill must go through before it becomes a law. The committee might make a chart showing the steps and the role of the three branches of government in the law-making process.
2. Many people played important roles during the Civil War. Among them were Dorothea Dix, Phillip Sheridan, George Meade, Clara Barton, Charlotte Forten, "Stonewall" Jackson, George McClellan, and Sojourner Truth. Read about one of these people or a person mentioned in the text. What did the person you chose do during the Civil War?
3. The United States has had many different flags during its history. Work in groups. Have each group find out about one of the following flags: American flag at the time of the Constitution, American flag of 1818, the Great Star flag, Union flag during the Civil War, and four Confederate flags during the Civil War.

Make pictures of the flags and label each for a classroom display.

4 Moving Ahead

Unit Preview

After the Civil War, Americans were ready to go on with the building of the nation. As American industry grew, so did American cities. People moved to the cities from small towns and farms. Immigrants came from other countries. Cities grew quickly.

The automobile and other inventions changed the lives of Americans. Americans were free to move about more. They no longer had to live near their work.

As trade with other countries increased, the United States became concerned about what was happening in other parts of the world. The United States began to play a leading role in world events. During the 1900s, the United States became involved in two world wars and two Asian wars. But the nation also worked toward world peace.

Americans made great progress in protecting the rights of its citizens. Women got the right to vote and moved toward full equality in every part of American life. Blacks, Spanish-speaking Americans, and other groups made progress in obtaining their civil rights.

One area of increasing concern in the world and in our country is energy. Providing heat, light, and power requires the use of much energy. New energy sources are being developed. People also realize that the resources we have must be used wisely. They know that conservation must be practiced by all.

Things to Discover

If you look carefully at the picture, map, and time line, you can answer these questions.

1. The areas highlighted on the map represent major population centers in the United States. As cities grew, it was not always clear where one city ended and another began. Where are the largest of these population centers located?
2. What two countries signed a peace treaty in 1978?
3. When did World War II begin? When did this war end?
4. How many years after World War I ended did World War II begin?
5. When was the Civil Rights Act passed?

Words to Learn

You will meet these words in this unit. As you read, you will learn what they mean and how to pronounce them. The Word List will help you.

assembly line	industry
canal	megalopolis
census	migrant worker
civil rights	nuclear energy
communism	pollute
democracy	segregate
depression	suburb
dictator	technology
free enterprise	uranium
Hispano	

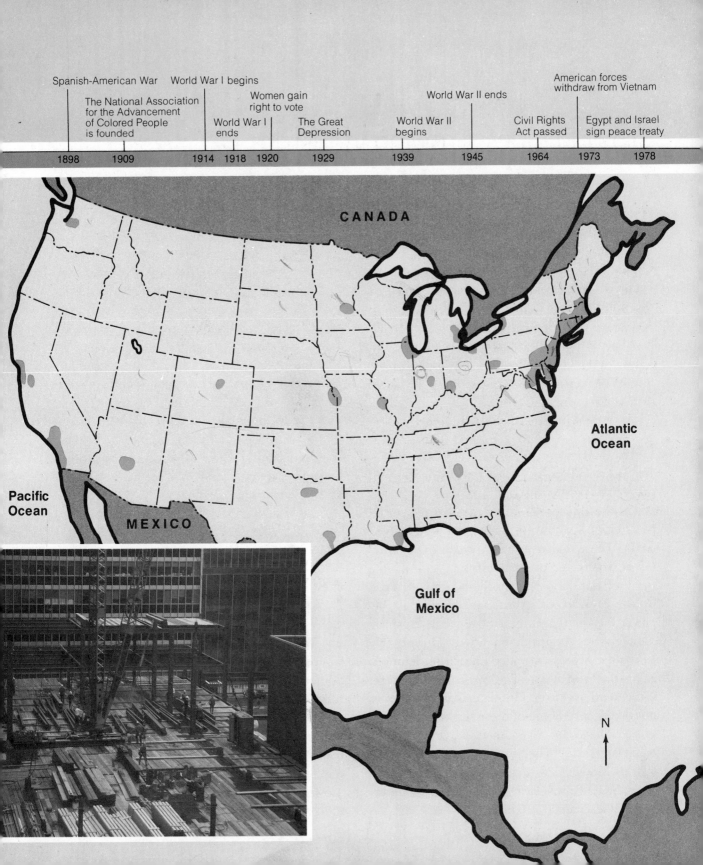

Spanish-American War   World War I begins

The National Association
for the Advancement
of Colored People
is founded

Women gain
right to vote

World War I
ends

The Great
Depression

World War II ends

World War II
begins

Civil Rights
Act passed

American forces
withdraw from Vietnam

Egypt and Israel
sign peace treaty

1898   1909   1914 1918 1920   1929   1939   1945   1964   1973   1978

CANADA

Pacific
Ocean

MEXICO

Atlantic
Ocean

Gulf of
Mexico

N

1

Growing Cities, Growing Industries

People worked hard to rebuild and unify America after the Civil War. It was time to move ahead. In 1790 the first *census* (sen′səs) of the United States was taken. A census is an official count of people. Every 10 years a census is taken in the United States. In 1790 there were 4 million Americans. Most of them were living in small settlements or on farms. Today the United States has more than 220 million people. Most of these people live and work in or near cities.

Early Cities

The Aztec, Maya, and Inca Indians had developed cities before the coming of the Europeans. When the Europeans came, they too began to build cities. Cities were built along the Atlantic coast. These cities grew through trade with Great Britain and other countries.

Cities were also built in the South and West by the Spanish. St. Augustine, Florida, is the oldest city in the United States. The Spanish founded St. Augustine in 1565. During the 1770s the Spanish founded church settlements along the west coast. The Spanish used these settlements to protect their claims in what is now California. Some of these settlements, such as San Diego and San Francisco, grew to become large cities. The Spanish founded Santa Fe in what is now New Mexico. Unlike other early cities, Santa Fe was far from the ocean. Santa Fe is the oldest capital city in the United States.

More Cities Grow

Rivers, such as the Ohio, were used by westward bound settlers. Settlements were located on river banks to serve the needs of river travelers and those who chose to settle in the region. When the steamboat was invented, river traffic increased. People moved and settled on farms and ranches. Food and other products of the West were shipped east. Goods manufactured in eastern factories were shipped west. River towns were important in this trading. Many grew into major cities, such as Cincinnati, Ohio; Louisville, Kentucky; Memphis, Tennessee; and Kansas City, Missouri. Locate other cities that grew up on rivers on the map of the United States on pages 92–93.

People and goods moved east and west by *canal* (kə nal′). A canal is a waterway that is built to connect two bodies of water. Towns were established along canals just as they were along rivers.

A few roads were built. Inns were started along these roads to serve the needs of travelers. Towns were begun where roads crossed, or where ferries carried travelers across rivers. Sometimes cities grew up at places where one form of travel met another.

After the Civil War, railroad building increased. Many cities were started to serve the needs of railroad workers and travelers. As the rails stretched west, so did urban, or city, growth. Western farmers and ranchers sent food and cattle to eastern markets. Cities grew

Thousands of immigrants arrived in New York City in 1906. They were part of the second wave of immigrants who came from southern and eastern Europe at the turn of the century.

where cattle trails met railroads. Some river cities became important railroad cities. Chicago, Illinois; St. Paul, Minnesota; and Omaha, Nebraska, grew rapidly after the railroads were built. No longer were large cities to be found only on the coasts.

Some cities grew because of their natural surroundings. Mining towns started near places rich in minerals. Factory towns were built near waterfalls. Lumber towns began near forests.

Industrial Growth and Immigration

The growth of cities after the Civil War was tied to the growth of *industry* (in′dəs tre) in America. Industry refers to manufacturing and other businesses. Machines were gaining widespread use in manufacturing. Machines could produce goods quickly and cheaply. But America was not made by machines. America is the work of

people. People were needed to run the machines and work in the factories. People and factories came together in cities.

Factories grew rapidly in the cities located near sources of raw materials and means of transportation. The cities acted like magnets. They attracted people seeking jobs. Farmers from rural areas and thousands of immigrants headed for America's cities.

Americans All

Between 1790 and 1860 about 5 million immigrants entered the United States. Most of these people were from northern Europe. By the end of the century, almost half of the immigrants were from southern and eastern Europe. The people who immigrated were seeking work and a new life. They were seeking opportunity.

The immigrants settled in the cities. Life was not easy for the immigrants when they got to America. Most immigrants were poor. Many

Many immigrants moved to the Midwest to find jobs in the factories of cities, like Chicago in Illinois. Today, Chicago is home for people from Poland, Ireland, Germany, and the Soviet Union.

did not speak English. Many were not used to living in crowded apartments. New immigrants looked for people from their homeland. They wanted to be near people who spoke their language and shared their traditions. Soon neighborhoods of people from the same country grew up in the cities. These areas were usually poor. The people could not afford to live anywhere else.

European immigrants crossed the Atlantic Ocean. Most settled in the East. They were from Great Britain, Ireland, Italy, the Netherlands, France, Sweden, Russia, Switzerland, Poland, Germany, and Austria-Hungary. Immigrants from China and Japan crossed the Pacific Ocean and settled in the western part of the country. Immigrants from Mexico crossed the southern border of the United States. Mexican-Americans and Chinese-Americans helped build the railroads in the West and Southwest.

Immigrants are part of this country's history. They have changed America. Their skills and talents have helped the country grow. Each immigrant group brought traditions and customs to share with those who were already here. Between 1861 and 1930 almost 33 million immigrants arrived in the United States. Many of them passed by the Statue of Liberty in New York. The sight of the Statue of Liberty meant freedom and a new life for them.

Today immigrants still come to America. They no longer come in the millions. There is now more freedom and opportunity in other countries. But the United States still welcomes people who have little freedom at home, people who cannot worship as they please, and those who are victims of war. Cubans, Vietnamese, and people from other Latin American countries, are among the most recent immigrants to this country.

Labor Unions

The jobs brought about by the rapid industrial growth in the late 1800s and early 1900s were hard. Factories were noisy and often unsafe. Many factory workers worked as long as 12 to 13 hours a day. Working 6 days a week was common. Men, women, and children all worked in the factories. Some children even worked in the mines.

Laws were eventually made to protect children. Conditions in the factories remained poor, however. A worker might be fired if he or she asked for better working conditions or for more money. So workers agreed to band together to form labor unions. Workers could then act as a group. They could protect themselves from long hours, loss of jobs, and poor working conditions. Local labor unions joined together to form national labor unions. As industry expanded, the power of the labor unions also became stronger.

Jane Addams

Settlement houses were set up to help solve the problems of the immigrants. One of these community centers was Hull House in Chicago. Jane Addams, a social worker, opened this house for immigrants in 1889. She fed hungry people, took care of sick people, and gave English lessons to immigrants. Hull House also had a playground, a kindergarten, a library, and a meeting room. Jane Addams and other people, called reformers, helped establish child labor laws. These laws protected children against harsh working conditions in factories.

Americans Prosper

In the early 1900s living and working conditions were poor. But within a generation life got better for most Americans. Americans were healthier and were living longer. They were better clothed, better fed, and better educated. They worked fewer hours to produce the goods they needed. More people, not just the rich, had leisure time. People had time to enjoy sports, art, and music.

Cities Today

Throughout most of the twentieth century, cities continued to grow. As they became larger, they became more crowded. In some places today it is difficult to know where one city ends and another begins. Cities are connected by thousands of miles of highways. A large urban area made up of a number of nearby cities is called a *megalopolis* (meg'ə lop'ə lis). One megalopolis stretches from Boston to Washington, D.C.

Greater income and the automobile have enabled people to move away from the center of large cities. Many people go to cities for work, shopping, and entertainment. But they live in smaller communities, called *suburbs* (sub'urbz). A suburb is a community close to, or on the outer edge of, a city. The suburbs are not as crowded as the cities. They are often newer and cleaner. There are fewer cars and less noise.

Many businesses and services of the cities followed people to the suburbs. As people and businesses began to move away from the large cities, life in the cities changed too. Some city

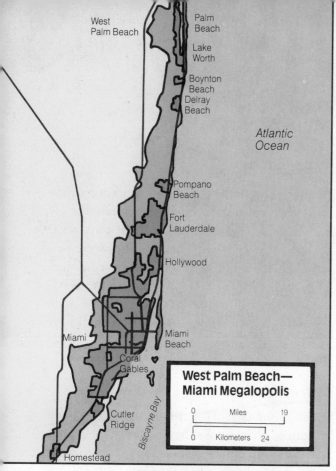

Some cities on this map form a *megalopolis* along the eastern coast of Florida.

Industrial and Technical Progress

Business and industry developed rapidly after 1865. It was truly a time of progress. Inventions and discoveries speeded up industrial growth. The lives of Americans were changed too. Improvements in transportation, communication, and power production continue to shape the way we live and work.

Progress Through Inventions

Many different inventions helped American industry grow. Generators were invented to produce electricity. With electric power, factories could turn out products quickly and cheaply. When Thomas Edison made the first electric light bulb in 1879, electricity became important in homes as well as in factories throughout the world.

Just before 1900 Americans began traveling in automobiles. Within 20 years cars were a familiar sight.

Henry Ford had developed a way to make automobiles quickly and inexpensively. Workers and machines were lined up. The cars and parts then passed by on a belt. Each worker was responsible for adding a particular part to the car as it passed by. This system of production is called the *assembly line* (ə sem′blē līn′). Since cars could be made more quickly, they became less expensive.

The lives of American changed. Almost every family could afford a car. People no longer had to live near their jobs. Thousands of people went to work on the assembly lines. Thousands

businesses lost their customers. Factories moved away from cities to suburban areas with lower rents. In many neighborhoods unskilled workers were left without jobs. Buildings were left in need of repair. Yet many people could not afford to live anywhere else. Because they became costly to repair, many buildings were left vacant. Entire neighborhoods became run-down.

The movement away from cities may begin to slow down. Many people are again finding it preferable to live in the cities. Gasoline prices have risen sharply. Traveling to and from a job in the city has become more expensive. Living in a city also puts people closer to theaters, museums, and other cultural places.

Thomas Edison here holds an electric light bulb, one of 1,100 devices he invented during his 60-year career. His lab in Menlo Park, New Jersey, has a model of this bulb.

more opened gas stations, diners, and other businesses to serve a population that could move about at will.

With the airplane flights of Wilbur and Orville Wright in 1903, a whole new way of travel began. Improved transportation was important for industry too. Raw materials and finished products could be moved faster and farther.

Communications also improved. In 1876 Alexander Graham Bell invented the telephone.

With telephones, radio, and television, instant communication was possible.

A new source of power was discovered in 1938. In that year scientists succeeded in splitting an atom of an element called *uranium* (yoo rā′nē əm). Uranium is a radioactive element found in a certain mineral. An atom is a very small part of all matter. It is so small that it cannot be seen. When an atom is split, it produces a great deal of energy in the form of heat.

Complex machines and indicators with lights and dials help control-room workers operate *nuclear* power plants.

Energy produced by splitting atoms is called *nuclear energy* (nōō′klē ər en′ər jē). Nuclear energy was first used in making bombs for war. But people soon began to find other ways to use this new power source. Today a number of nuclear power plants generate electricity.

Technology

Using knowledge and skills to build useful machines is known as *technology* (tek nol′ə jē). One of the results of technology is the computer. A computer is a machine that works out problems rapidly, using information and instructions that it has received and stored. The very first computer was built in 1835. It worked slowly because electric power was not yet available. After World War II, the technology for modern computers began developing at a fast rate. Computers became smaller, and they could handle more information in a shorter time. Today computers are used to do many kinds of work. Business records can be stored in computers. Mail can be sorted by computers at the post office. Computers are used to help doctors perform tests. Advanced computers even direct satellites in space.

Do You Know?

1. What city is the oldest city in the United States? What city is the oldest capital city in the United States? Who founded these cities?
2. How did cities attract people?
3. Why did so many immigrants come to the United States between 1860 and 1930?
4. How did Henry Ford make cars quickly and inexpensively?

132

2
The United States Looks Beyond Its Borders

In the years that followed the Civil War, Americans began to put the nation back together again. Americans also began to look at what was going on around them in other countries.

The Spanish-American War

Cuba, an island southeast of Florida, was controlled by Spain. The Cubans had been unhappy with Spanish rule. A revolution began. Arms were sent to the Cubans by Americans. Some of the rebels were American citizens. An American battleship, the *Maine,* was sent to Cuba.

In February of 1898, the *Maine* exploded in Cuba's Havana (hə van′ə) Harbor. The explosion killed 260 American sailors. To this day, no one knows what really caused the explosion. But many Americans thought it was an act of war.

The United States declared war on Spain. Victories came swiftly to the Americans. The war lasted only 115 days. During that time Commodore George Dewey captured the Philippine Islands from Spain. Theodore Roosevelt became famous by leading a charge up San Juan (san′ hwän′) Hill in Cuba.

The peace treaty gave Cuba freedom from Spain. Spain turned over control of the Philippine Islands, Puerto Rico (pwer′tō rē′kō), Guam (gwäm), and some small islands in the Pacific to the United States. As a result the United States now controlled lands far beyond its borders. It was recognized by other nations as a world power.

Trade with Other Countries

By the early 1900s trading with other countries had become important to the United States. To trade with Japan and China, ships from Atlantic ports had to travel around South America. Like the early European explorers, the United States sought a short route to the Far East. The narrow strip of land connecting North and South America was chosen as the best place to build a canal.

It was a huge undertaking to cut across 27 miles (43 km) of land. But in 1914, Americans completed the building of the Panama Canal. It connected the Atlantic and Pacific oceans. Now ships could save thousands of miles in their journeys from one ocean to the other.

The First World War

In 1914 war broke out in Europe. A group of nations, called the Central Powers, fought another group of nations, called the Allies (al′īz). The Central Powers were led by Germany and Austria-Hungary. The Allies were led by Great Britain, France, and Russia.

At first, the people of the United States did not want to enter into the war. But in 1915, the British ship *Lusitania* (lo͞o′sə tā′nē ə) was sunk by a German submarine. Many Americans went down with the ship. The mood of America changed. Americans were coming closer to war. In 1917, President Wilson asked the United

The *Lusitania* docks in New York in 1907. Eight years later, it was torpedoed by a German submarine. The United States entered World War I soon after.

States to join in "a war to end all wars". This war is called the First World War or World War I.

Most of the fighting took place in Belgium (bel′jəm), France, Italy, and what is now Poland. Both sides suffered great losses. The starving and poorly-equipped Russian army left the battlefield and returned home. A revolution took place in Russia in 1917. The new government began peace talks with Germany.

The arrival of fresh American troops turned the tide of the war. The German army was beaten back by the American army. On November 11, 1918, the German leaders agreed to stop fighting. Each year the end of the First World War is celebrated as Veterans Day.

The Great Depression

After the war, Americans prospered. Factories produced great amounts of goods. There were jobs. Because people had jobs, they could afford to buy more goods. America's factories soon produced more goods than people could buy. Factories then cut back production and people lost their jobs. People and businesses could not afford to pay back the money they had borrowed.

In 1929 the world entered a period of economic *depression* (dē presh′ən). A depression is a time when there is little business and much unemployment. Banks were forced to close. Factories and businesses were shut down. Many people lost their jobs and the money they had in the bank. Some people even lost their homes. It was a time of great fear.

Franklin Delano Roosevelt was elected President in 1932. He told the Americans, "the only thing we have to fear is fear itself." President Roosevelt had a plan called the New Deal.

The New Deal had many parts. It created jobs. With money earned from jobs, people could buy more. Factories began to produce more goods. They hired more workers. It took several years for the country to recover from the depression. But finally it was back on its feet again. The New Deal worked.

The Second World War

Germany invaded Poland in 1939. Two days later, France and Great Britain declared war on Germany. Later, the Soviet (sō′vē et′) Union, fought Germany too. The Soviet Union was the new name for Russia. Italy and Japan supported Germany. These three nations were called the Axis (ak′sis). Two of these nations were ruled by a *dictator* (dik′tā′tər), or ruler who has absolute power. Adolf Hitler ruled Germany, Benito Mussolini (bə nē′tō moos′ə lē′nē) ruled Italy. Prime Minister Tojo (tō′jō) ruled Japan.

German armies overran and occupied most European countries. Japan invaded China. Hitler began to treat Jews and Slavic peoples harshly. They were used as slave labor in factories. Most were sent to concentration camps where millions were put to death or starved. This mass destruction of human beings became known as the Holocaust (hol′ə kôst′).

During World War II more than two million women worked in war industries. These women are operating milling machines that finished parts for fighter planes.

As in World War I, at first the United States did not want to get involved. But on December 7, 1941, Japanese bombers attacked Pearl Harbor, an American naval base in the Hawaiian Islands. Many American ships were sunk. The next day the United States declared war on Japan. A few days later the United States declared war on the other Axis countries.

The Allied armies of the United States, Great Britain, the Soviet Union, France, and China closed in on the Axis armies. Battles were fought in Europe, in North Africa, and in the Pacific.

The Allies began to fight their way toward Germany from the west and the east. Facing defeat, Hitler killed himself in May 1945. Germany surrendered. The war in Europe was over. Germany was divided into sections and occupied by the Allies.

Representatives from nations throughout the world meet in the General Assembly of the United Nations. This special session was called to discuss limiting weapons.

President Franklin D. Roosevelt of the United States died shortly before the war in Europe ended. Harry S. Truman, who was the Vice-President, became President.

As the war in Europe was coming to an end, the war against Japan continued. America had developed a new powerful weapon, the atomic bomb. One bomb could destroy a city. President Truman feared that thousands of Americans would die as the battles went on. He wanted to stop the war. In August 1945 President Truman ordered that an atomic bomb be dropped on Hiroshima (hēr′ō shē′mə). The Japanese city was destroyed. A few days later a second atomic bomb was dropped on Nagasaki (nä′gə sä′kē). More than 100,000 people were killed by the force of the bombs. The Japanese surrendered and World War II was over.

Building a Better World

The end of World War II left much of Europe and Japan in ruins. The United States wanted to help the people of these countries. Programs began which sent aid to the war-weary nations. The European countries and Japan became productive again. Today, Western Europe and Japan are our allies and partners in trade.

Ties between the United States, Canada, and 13 nations of Western Europe were made stronger by the creation of NATO. NATO stands for the North Atlantic Treaty Organization. The NATO agreement says that each member country will aid another member if that member is attacked.

World War II showed that countries should work for peace and settle their differences without war. Countries all over the world joined in

1945 to form the United Nations. The United Nations tries to settle disagreements by discussion, not fighting. The task is difficult. Sometimes the United Nations has been able to keep peace. At other times, the United Nations has not been successful. Yet most nations feel the United Nations gives them a chance to talk over their differences. The United Nations offers one way to work for peace among the nations of the world.

Relations with the Soviet Union

At the end of World War II, tensions between the governments of the United States and the Soviet Union began to grow. The United States was founded on a belief in *democracy* (di mok′rə sē), or government by the people. A democratic government was established to represent the people and to protect their rights and freedom. The economic system in the United States is called the *free enterprise* (frē′en′tər-prīz′), or private enterprise, system. Under the free enterprise system, citizens can own property and businesses. They can decide where to work and what kind of work they want to do.

The system of government in the Soviet Union is called *communism* (kom′yə niz′əm). Under communism the government owns all factories, machines, and resources. Communism is also an economic system. In this system, the government runs all factories and stores. Citizens cannot own businesses. The government decides how industries will be run and where people will work.

The government of the Soviet Union would like other countries to become communist. The American government would like to see more democracies in the world. Conflicts between the systems of democracy and communism grew stronger during the 1950s. The period was called the "cold war." This was a time when there was no open warfare, but when the countries did not trust one another. The tense feelings between the United States and the Soviet Union began to ease in the 1970s.

But in 1980, the Soviet Union sent troops into the country of Afghanistan (af gan′ə stan′). The United States and other nations protested the invasion. They refused to take part in the 1980 Summer Olympics that were held in the Soviet Union. The United States also stopped trading some products with the Soviet Union.

The Korean War

Since World War II there have been wars that resulted from the struggle between communism and democracy. One of these wars took place in the early 1950s in Korea.

Korea is a peninsula on the eastern coast of Asia. China borders this nation on the north. At the end of World War II, Soviet troops occupied North Korea. American troops occupied South Korea. After the American and Soviet troops left the region, North Korea invaded South Korea. The United Nations sent troops to defend South Korea. Americans and South Koreans made up most of these troops. Chinese communists entered the war and attacked the United Nations forces.

In 1953 the United Nations and the communists agreed to a truce. Korea was divided into two separate nations. North Korea had a communist government. South Korea set up a democratic government.

The War in Vietnam

The struggle between communism and democracy also led to a war in Vietnam, another country in Southeast Asia. Vietnam had once been a colony of France. In 1954 the French were forced to leave Vietnam. The country was divided into two parts. North Vietnam was controlled by communists, and South Vietnam was controlled by noncommunists.

North Vietnam began a struggle for the control of all Vietnam. A civil war was the result. Communist countries, including the Soviet Union, supported North Vietnam. The United States sent troops to help South Vietnam.

As the number of American troops increased, so did protests over our involvement in the war. Many people felt that Americans should not take sides in another country's civil war. But not all Americans felt this way. Others felt the spread of communism must be stopped. The American people became divided over participation in the Vietnam war. American forces withdrew from Vietnam in 1973.

Relations with China

Since 1949 the People's Republic of China has had a communist government. When the Chinese communists took over, Americans were not permitted to enter China. But in the early 1970s relations between China and the United States improved. In 1972 President Nixon visited China. Since then more Americans have visited China, and trade between the two countries has increased.

The Middle East

Much of the world's concern centers around a region called the Middle East. Rich oil deposits lie in this region. Trouble exists between Israel (iz′rē əl) and the surrounding Arab nations in this area.

The United States has supported Israel since it was created in 1948. But the United States hopes to bring peace to the entire Middle East. In 1979, with the help of the United States, Israel and Egypt (ē′jipt), an Arab nation, signed a peace treaty. While many problems remain in the Middle East, the agreement was a big step toward bringing peace to the area.

Actions for Peace

President John F. Kennedy challenged the American people. He said, "Ask not what your country can do for you—ask what you can do for your country." He was the youngest person ever elected President of the United States. Unfortunately, his term as President was short. John Kennedy was assassinated (ə sas′ə nāt′ed) in November of 1963. Many people all over the world were saddened by his death. He had developed programs to promote peace in the world.

People of all ages can join the Peace Corps. In 1962 President John Kennedy greeted a group of elderly volunteers at the White House. Everyone in the group was between the ages of 60 and 76.

In 1961 the Peace Corps was founded by President Kennedy. The Peace Corps sends people to developing nations to help them improve their agriculture, education, and industry. President Kennedy also began the Alliance for Progress. The Alliance for Progress sends aid to South and Central American countries. The United States gives or loans money to countries in many parts of the world. Food and emergency supplies are sent to countries where there are crop failures or earthquakes. American people often help during such disasters.

Do You Know?

1. Why was the Panama Canal built?
2. What countries led the Central Powers in World War I?
3. What is Pearl Harbor? What happened there in 1941?
4. What actions ended the war with Japan in World War II?
5. When was the United Nations formed? Why?

Before You Go On

Using New Words

suburb

nuclear energy

democracy

communism

canal

megalopolis

technology

depression

assembly line

census

industry

free enterprise

dictator

uranium

The phrases below explain the words or terms listed above. Number a paper from 1 through 14. After each number write the word that matches the definition.

1. A ruler who has absolute power
2. A waterway that is built to connect two bodies of water
3. A community close to, or on the outer edge of, a city
4. Government by the people
5. An official count of the people in a country
6. A large urban area made up of a number of nearby cities
7. A system of government under which all property and goods are controlled by the government
8. A time when there is little business and much unemployment
9. A radioactive element
10. The use of knowledge and skills to build useful machines
11. A word that refers to manufacturing and other businesses
12. Energy produced by splitting atoms
13. A method of manufacturing in which each worker is responsible for adding a particular part to the product as it moves by on a belt
14. An economic system which allows citizens to own property and businesses

Finding the Facts

1. Which American Indians built cities in America before the Europeans came?
2. What form of travel helped cities such as Chicago and Omaha to grow rapidly?
3. What are some of the problems immigrants faced when they settled in America?
4. What invention enabled people to live farther away from where they worked?
5. Why did the United States become involved in the Spanish-American war?
6. When did World War I begin? When did the United States enter the war?
7. How did the Great Depression affect Americans?
8. Why did the United States become involved in World War II?
9. What war took place in Asia in the early 1950s?
10. From what war were American troops withdrawn in 1973?
11. What do Peace Corps volunteers do?
12. What organization was set up in 1945 to help settle disagreements among nations?

3
Recognizing Human Rights

Individual rights and freedoms have been important to people in America for hundreds of years. However, not everyone in the United States has enjoyed full *civil* (siv′əl) *rights.* Civil rights are the individual rights of a citizen such as freedom of speech, the right to vote, and equal protection under the law. An important part of American history has been the struggle to extend civil rights to all Americans.

Civil Rights for Blacks

The Emancipation Proclamation and the Thirteenth Amendment freed the slaves. Citizenship was granted to those who had been slaves through the Fourteenth Amendment. The Fifteenth Amendment stated that no citizen could be denied the vote because of race, color, or having been a slave. In spite of these amendments, blacks had difficult problems. Many cities of the United States had laws to *segregate* (seg′rə gāt′), or separate, blacks and whites. In some states, public places such as beaches and restaurants were separated into black and white areas. Schools admitted only whites or blacks to their classes. Some businesses would not hire blacks. All of this segregation denied civil rights to blacks.

Under the leadership of many black Americans, black people began to gain their civil rights. In 1954, the Supreme Court ruled that schools must not be segregated. A series of civil rights acts was passed by Congress. The most

important was the Civil Rights Act of 1964. This act outlawed segregation in public places such as schools, parks, beaches, restaurants, and libraries. The act gave equal opportunities to everyone, regardless of race.

In 1964 also, the Twenty-fourth Amendment was passed. After the Civil War, some states required people to pay a tax before they could vote. This law was a hardship for poor people, including those who had been slaves. For many years people who had been slaves had little voice in their government. The Twenty-fourth Amendment made this voting tax unlawful in national elections. In 1965 the Voting Rights Act did away with literacy tests, or tests of the ability to read and write, in elections. These two laws helped protect voting rights of blacks.

Martin Luther King, Jr.

In 1955 Rosa Parks, a black, refused to give up her bus seat to a white in Montgomery, Alabama. She was arrested because of this. Other blacks, led by Dr. Martin Luther King, Jr., of Atlanta, Georgia, refused to ride the city buses. The following year a federal court ruled that segregated buses were no longer allowed.

In the early 1960s Dr. Martin Luther King, Jr., made speeches and led marches to demand civil rights for blacks. Both blacks and whites joined in these marches. Dr. King believed that fighting for civil rights should be done without violence. He was awarded the Nobel Prize for Peace in 1964.

Dr. Martin Luther King, Jr., waves to some of the 250,000 people who marched on Washington, D.C., in 1963. The marchers, including 60,000 whites, staged this peaceful demonstration to demand *civil rights* for blacks.

Dr. King took part in many peaceful gatherings. In 1963 he led a march on Washington, D.C. More than 200,000 blacks and whites heard Dr. King speak. He said he had a dream in which black and white children would grow up in an America of peace, equality, and justice.

In 1968 Martin Luther King, Jr., was killed. King's work was carried on by his followers. Coretta King, wife of Martin Luther King, Jr., continues to bring the message of peace and justice to Americans. We celebrate January 15, Dr. King's birthday, as Martin Luther King, Jr. Day.

The NAACP

Many groups work for the ideals set forth by Dr. King and other black leaders. One major black organization is the National Association for the Advancement of Colored People, or NAACP for short. This association was founded in 1909. The NAACP promotes the rights of black people throughout the nation.

During the 1900s progress has been made by the United States in granting blacks their civil rights. Blacks have served in the President's cabinet, on the Supreme Court, and in Congress. They have held high positions in the armed forces. Blacks are recognized for their contributions to art, science, education, and sports.

While there has been progress, there is much more to be done to achieve racial equality. More than 1,500,000 black families live in poverty. Black youths make up the greatest number of people in America who are out of work. The job of solving these problems is a task not only for blacks. It is a task for all Americans.

Women marched for voting rights in New York City, 1912. Eight years later, an amendment guaranteed women's right to vote. Today's supporters of women's rights are both women and men.

Women's Rights

Women, too, have struggled to gain equal rights. The Constitution did not provide women with the right to vote. Beginning in the 1840s, women joined together to win this right. A Women's Rights Convention was held in 1848 in Seneca Falls, New York. The convention, or meeting, was organized by Lucretia (lū krē′shə) Mott and Elizabeth Cady Stanton.

Before women could vote, an amendment to the Constitution had to be ratified. Groups began organizing to work for this amendment. Meetings were held. A women's newspaper was published. Finally, in August of 1920, the Nineteenth Amendment was passed. Women had gained the right to vote.

The struggle for equal rights for women continues. Many women and men in the 1970s and 1980s worked to ratify a new amendment to the Constitution. This amendment, called the Equal Rights Amendment, or ERA for short, states that equality shall not be denied on account of sex. When three-fourths of the states ratify it, the ERA will become a law.

Organizations have been formed to present the views of women. In 1966, Betty Friedan founded the National Organization for Women, or NOW for short. NOW works to advance women's rights and equality in America, especially in job opportunities and equal pay. Such goals are important, because more than half of American women work outside the home.

Since the Nineteenth Amendment passed, more women have been active in government. They have been elected to Congress. Women have served as governors of states and mayors of such cities as Chicago and San Francisco. Women have been appointed to the President's cabinet. Some have held high positions in the army and the navy. More people have begun to recognize the achievements of women in art, science, education, and sports.

Spanish-Speaking Americans

Next to blacks, the largest minority group in the United States are *Hispanos* (his pan′ōz), or Spanish-speaking people. Most Spanish-speaking Americans are of Mexican, Puerto Rican, or Cuban descent. Although these three groups share a common language, they have different backgrounds.

Mexican-Americans

The largest group of Hispanos in the United States are the Mexican-Americans. Many people came from Mexico into what is now the southwestern United States in the 1600s and 1700s. Even more came in the 1900s. Today most Mexican-Americans live in California and Texas. More than a half-million Mexican-Americans live in Los Angeles, California. In recent years the first Mexican-Americans have been elected to serve in Congress.

Many Mexican-Americans found jobs as *migrant* (mī′ grant) *workers,* or seasonal farm workers. Migrant workers travel from one orchard or field to another to gather crops. Because the migrant workers only stay in one place for a short time, their children are not able to stay in school for very long. The migrant workers and their families had other problems too.

César Chávez

One migrant worker who recognized the problems of his co-workers was César Chávez (sā′ zär chä′ vās). Chávez knew that farm workers were not being paid enough. In many places crops would be sprayed with chemicals to kill insects. It was dangerous for workers to go into such fields.

To help farm workers get a fair wage and safe working conditions, Chávez organized a labor union. Like Dr. Martin Luther King, Jr., he believed in nonviolence. Chávez wanted to make changes in a peaceful way. To get the farm owners in California to recognize the union, Chávez organized a boycott. He asked Americans to boycott, or not buy, the grapes of those

César Chávez, United Farm Workers'
President, talks to workers and supporters
at Modesto, California. How were
Chávez's and Dr. King's ideas for change
alike?

farm owners who did not sign an agreement
with the union. The plan worked, but it took 3
years. César Chávez continues to work for
the United Farm Workers' Union in other states.

Puerto Ricans

You have read that Puerto Rico became a terri-
tory of the United States after the Spanish-
American war in 1898. Today, the people of
Puerto Rico elect a governor and representa-
tives to make their laws. All Puerto Ricans are
American citizens. In the 1950s many Puerto
Ricans began to move to the United States.

Most Puerto Ricans moved to cities in the
Northeast, like New York, and the Midwest,
like Chicago. It is often difficult to get good jobs

in the cities. Many Puerto Ricans do not speak English. They are not used to the life in cities because many have lived and worked on farms. Children who speak Spanish at home have to learn English to understand their teachers at school.

Today, many schools have special programs for their Spanish-speaking students. Puerto Ricans have learned new skills and found better jobs. Some have started their own businesses.

Cubans

In 1959 there was a revolution in Cuba led by Fidel Castro (fēdel' cäs'trō). Castro became the leader of a communist government. About 700,000 Cubans came to the United States after Castro came to power. Most of these people settled in Florida. Many also went to New York and New Jersey. But the immigration was not allowed to continue. The United States stopped trade with Cuba. The two countries broke all ties.

In 1980, however, Castro allowed Cubans to leave the country once again. Thousands of Cubans came to the United States. They were reunited with their families.

Other Groups Work to Gain Rights

Other groups have worked to extend their rights. In 1968 the Indian Civil Rights Act was passed. This act extended the Bill of Rights to American Indians living on land set aside by the government.

Elderly people often were treated unfairly because of their age. People confined to wheel-chairs found it difficult to get in and out of public buildings, buses, trains, and planes. All of these groups, and others, are continuing to bring their needs to the attention of the American people.

Since the 1960s things have begun to change. For example, public buildings, such as libraries and schools, had ramps built for the handicapped and the elderly. A plan was set up to help people over 65 years of age pay for medical care. A law was passed allowing people to work until they are 70 years of age instead of having to retire at the age of 65.

The Constitution we have today is the same Constitution written in Philadelphia in 1787. But it has been amended many times. Some of these amendments have extended rights to more and more Americans. People around the world who struggle for their own human and civil rights look to America for encouragement.

Do You Know?

1. How were public places in some states segregated?
2. Who was the black civil rights leader who believed in nonviolence?
3. What does the Nineteenth Amendment do? When was it passed?
4. What does NOW stand for? Who was its founder?
5. What are the three largest groups of Hispanos in the United States?

146

4
Energy and Ecology

As America became industrialized, it began to use its resources more rapidly. At first no one thought America would ever run out of resources such as timber and water. Trees were cut down to build homes and factories. But new trees were not planted. Many factories dumped their chemical wastes into rivers. Wastes *pollute* (pə loot') the water. To pollute means to make unclean. Factories and automobiles poured smoke into the air. The air became polluted. Sometimes coal was mined by stripping away the valuable topsoil which covered it. Most Americans are just beginning to realize that resources must be used wisely.

The Need for Energy

When George Washington became President there were only a few kinds of energy used to do work. The muscle power of humans and animals was important for getting much work done. There was also the energy of wind and falling water. Wood was used for heat.

The industrialization of America was made possible because new kinds of energy were developed. Steam and electricity could be made by burning coal, oil, and natural gas. At first these new forms were cheap.

Since industry needed large amounts of cheap energy, many resources were used up. Trees were cut down to fuel steamboats. Coal was mined as fuel for railroad engines and was used to make steel for rails. Oil became a cheap

source of energy and was used widely. Today, America does not produce enough oil to fill its needs. Much oil has to be imported from other countries.

Americans are learning that care must be taken in using sources of energy. They also realize that new forms of power must be found.

A manufacturing plant disposes of wastes by dumping them in a stream. Name other sources of *pollution* which endanger the environment.

The Massachusetts Electric Company installed these solar collector panels at a family home in Worcester to learn how well they could adapt an older house to solar heat. A new bank in Minnesota has solar energy panels in its design.

New Energy Sources

To meet the increased energy needs of our country, Americans are searching for new energy sources.

Some of these "new" sources are really not new at all. Wind power has been used for many years in some parts of our country. Pumping water was one job windmills could do. Today, wind power is used to run electric generators.

One of the most promising energy sources is clean, safe, and in endless supply. That source is the sun. The sun sends out huge amounts of energy in the form of rays. The energy from the sun's rays is called solar energy. It can be used to heat homes and cook food. Solar-powered batteries can be used in radios. To use solar energy, it must first be collected and stored. This involves expensive equipment. But scientists are studying how to do this with lower cost.

The earth itself provides energy in the form of underground steam and hot water. This is called geothermal (jē′ō thur′məl) energy. Pipes transport the steam and hot water to the surface where it can be used to heat homes.

Other sources of energy come from using natural resources in new ways. In the coal gasification (gas′ə fə kā′shən) process, hot coal is blasted with air and steam. This produces gas that can be burned as fuel.

Grains such as corn can be used to make alcohol (al′kə hôl). The alcohol is mixed with gasoline. The mixture is called gasohol (gas′ə hôl). It is a clean-burning fuel that can be used instead of pure gasoline.

You read about nuclear energy in an earlier section. An important use of nuclear energy is producing electricity. At nuclear power plants, atoms are split inside nuclear reactors. The heat produced inside the reactors is used to make steam. Then the steam is used to run turbines. Turbines are machines that generate, or produce, electricity.

Nuclear power plants need to be kept safe. The materials used in the reactors are radioactive. Radiation is harmful to people and the environment. It is very important that the reactors be kept shielded to prevent the escape of any radiation.

After the materials are used in the reactor, they must be disposed of carefully. The used materials still give off radiation. Some waste materials have been buried deep in the earth. Some have been buried at sea. If leaks occur, harmful radiation can escape.

Conservation

Americans use more energy per person than any other people on the earth. Most of the energy we use comes from oil or natural gas. Scientists think that we may run low on oil around the year 2000.

Scientists say there are two ways to meet our future energy needs. One way is to explore and develop other sources of energy, such as solar energy. The other way is to practice conservation with our present resources. Conservation means a preserving of what we have and not wasting it. Conservation is easy when it becomes a habit. All Americans may not be able to do research on solar energy, but all can practice conservation.

Do You Know?

1. Where does geothermal energy come from?
2. What are some uses of solar energy?
3. What is gasohol?
4. What is the coal gasification process?
5. Why must the wastes from nuclear power plants be disposed of carefully?

To Help You Learn

Using New Words

nuclear energy	democracy
civil rights	dictator
communism	free enterprise
pollute	Hispano
segregate	migrant worker

The phrases below explain the words or terms listed above. Number a paper from 1 through 10. After each number write the word or term that matches the definition.

1. Government by the people
2. The rights of a citizen such as freedom of speech and the right to vote
3. Separate
4. Make unclean
5. A ruler who has absolute power
6. Energy produced by splitting atoms
7. A Spanish-speaking person
8. A system of government under which all property and goods are controlled by the government
9. An economic system which allows citizens to own property and businesses
10. A seasonal farm worker

Finding the Facts

1. How often is a census of the United States taken?
2. Where did settlements and cities tend to develop in the United States?
3. What are suburbs?
4. How did immigrants help America?
5. Where in the United States have many Spanish-speaking people settled?
6. Who is César Chávez? How has he helped migrant workers?
7. Who invented the telephone? The electric light bulb?
8. What is a computer? Name some ways computers are being used today.
9. What does Veterans Day celebrate?
10. What were two opinions held by Americans about the Vietnam war?
11. What action did the United States take when the Soviet Union invaded Afghanistan?
12. What does NAACP stand for? What does this organization do?
13. Why was the Civil Rights Act of 1964 important?
14. What does ERA stand for? What does it state?
15. What did the Indian Civil Rights Act of 1968 do?
16. When George Washington became President, what kinds of energy did people use to do work?
17. How does nuclear energy produce electricity? What are some problems of nuclear power plants?
18. What is solar energy? Why is it a promising energy source?
19. How is wind power used today?
20. What is conservation? Why is it so important to conserve resources?

Learning from Maps

1. Turn to the map of the United States on pages 92–93. What large cities are located on the following rivers: Ohio, Mississippi, and Missouri?
2. "Boswash" is a name given to the megalopolis stretching from Boston to Washington, D.C. Use the map of the United States on pages 92–93 to identify the major cities within "Boswash." Make a list of them.
3. Use the population distribution map on page 448 and the map of the United States on pages 92–93. Identify a megalopolis around Lake Michigan and one in southern California.
4. Use a world map or a globe to answer these questions. What four large islands make up Japan? On which island is each of the following cities: Hiroshima and Nagasaki? On what continent are North Korea, South Korea, and Vietnam? What countries border Israel?

Using Study Skills

1. **Graph:** Look at the graph below. What does the graph show? From where did most immigrants come between 1871 and 1880? Between 1961 and 1968? Was the percentage of immigrants from Asia more or less between 1961 and 1968 than it was between 1871 and 1880?

Immigrants to the United States

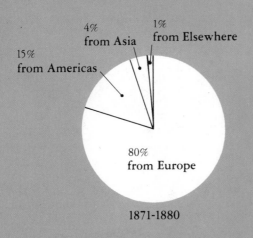

4% from Asia
1% from Elsewhere
15% from Americas
80% from Europe

1871-1880

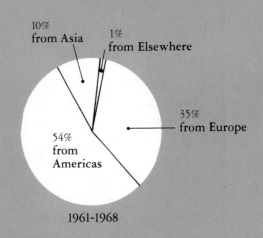

10% from Asia
1% from Elsewhere
35% from Europe
54% from Americas

1961-1968

2. **Time Line:** The following events are not listed in the right order. Copy the statements in the right order. Skim this unit to find the dates.

   Panama Canal completed
   President Nixon visits China
   First United States census taken
   Franklin D. Roosevelt elected President.
   Peace Corps founded

3. **Outline:** Copy the outline of the two world wars below. Reread the text and complete the outline.
   I. World War I
   A. Central Powers
   1. Germany
   2.
   B. Allies
   1.
   2.
   3.
   4.
   II. World War II
   A. Axis
   1.
   2.
   3.
   B. Allies
   1.
   2.
   3.
   4.

4. **Chart:** Look at the chart of Presidents of the United States on page 458. Who was President when World War I ended? When Pearl Harbor was bombed? When Germany surrendered at the end of World War II? When the Civil Rights Act of 1964 was passed?

Thinking It Through

1. Each numbered event was the cause of a lettered event. Match the events.
   (1) Japanese bombers attacked Pearl Harbor.
   (2) Black leaders protested the practice of segregation.
   (3) The battleship *Maine* exploded in Cuba.
   (4) Atomic bombs were dropped on Japan.
   (5) Natural resources may be used up.
   (a) World War II ended.
   (b) Americans practice conservation.
   (c) The United States entered World War II.
   (d) The Spanish-American War began.
   (e) Congress passed several Civil Rights Acts.

2. During the 1970s many immigrants arrived from Vietnam. In 1980 many immigrants arrived from Cuba. These immigrants were placed in camps until American sponsors were found for them. If you sponsored an immigrant, how might you help that person get settled in our country?

3. Make a list of what you feel are the ten most important inventions. Then arrange your list in order of importance to you. The first item on your list should be the invention you feel is most important. Why did you choose it?

4. In 1907 an American automobile cost $2,123. Henry Ford offered a model for $850 in 1908, $540 in 1914, and $290 in 1924. Why do you think Ford was able to sell his cars at lower prices?

Projects

1. The Research Committee might find out what each person below invented. Use books from your school library. Thomas Edison, Isaac Singer, Wernher Von Braun, Garrett Morgan, George Eastman, Lewis Latimer, Anna Baldwin, Vladimir Zworykin, Christopher Sholes, Jan Matzeliger

2. Work in two groups. One group can find out more about World War I. The other can find out more about World War II. Each group might find out about leaders, important battles, and organizations created to deal with war-time problems. Each group might also make a map showing how countries were divided during the war.

3. Many people have helped groups to gain civil rights. The Reading Committee might like to find a book or story about the following people: William E. B. Du Bois, Gloria Steinem, Max Cleland, Jesse Jackson, Vine Deloria, and Maggie Kuehn.

4. Report to the class. Make a list of the ways you can practice conservation at home. Make another list of ways that you can help your school save energy. Make a conservation poster of one item on the list.

5 The Northeastern States

Unit Preview

The Northeast has two regions. In the New England section, there are Maine, New Hampshire, Vermont, Massachusetts, Connecticut, and Rhode Island. In the Middle Atlantic states, there are New York, Pennsylvania, New Jersey, and Delaware.

The settlers in the northeastern states were skilled at making things, and there were rivers to provide power for mills, and later, factories. The rivers also helped to develop trade among settlements, and later, among cities. American manufacturing began in the Northeast, and it has remained an important manufacturing region.

Improved methods of transportation developed in the Northeast. The Erie Canal was built to connect New York City and the Great Lakes region. Steam power was used to run boats and trains. Railroads linked cities of the Atlantic Coastal Plain with midwestern cities like Chicago.

New York City, the largest city in the United States, is in this region. Other large cities are located in the Northeast. These cities grew as industries developed. Immigrants came from many countries to live and work in the cities.

Fishing, lumbering, quarrying, and farming are occupations of the northeastern states today. But their manufacturing and mining make the northeastern states a great industrial and commerical region of the United States.

Things to Discover

If you look carefully at the picture, map, and time line, you can answer these questions.
1. How many states are in the Northeast?
2. What ocean borders the states of the Northeast?
3. The picture shows Pittsburgh, a large northeastern city in Pennsylvania. What natural feature might explain why the city grew up there?
4. When did the Erie Canal open? How many years later did the St. Lawrence Seaway open?
5. When was the first oil well drilled in the United States?
6. What country borders some of the northeastern states?

Words to Learn

You will meet these words in this unit. As you read, you will learn what they mean and how to pronounce them. The Word List will help you.

anthracite	quarry
bituminous	shaft mining
coke	slag
electronics	smelt
export	spinning jenny
import	strip mining
lignite	suffrage
locomotive	textile
merchant marine	tourist

154

Samuel Slater's
spinning mill built

Erie Canal opens

First American steam
locomotive built

First oil well drilled
in United States

National Woman Suffrage
Association founded

Philadelphia begins
urban renewal

St. Lawrence Seaway opens

Winter Olympics held
in Lake Placid

1793   1825 1830   1859   1869   1945 1959   1980

CANADA

Atlantic
Ocean

Pacific
Ocean

MEXICO

Gulf of
Mexico

N

1
Geography of the Northeastern States

The Northeast has two regions. The first to be settled was New England. This name is a reminder that its earliest settlers came from England. The New England states are Maine, New Hampshire, Vermont, Massachusetts, Connecticut, and Rhode Island.

The other region, the Middle Atlantic, gets its name from its location. Look at the eastern coastline of the United States on the map on page 93. You can see that the Middle Atlantic states are about midway between the north and south ends of the Atlantic coast. These states are New York, New Jersey, Pennsylvania, and Delaware.

Both regions have irregular coastlines, a broad coastal plain, mountains, valleys, and flat lowlands. The Northeast has a rich source of water power in its hundreds of lakes, streams, and rivers.

Land Surface

The surface of the Northeast is not level. The soil is thin and covered with rocks. A great glacier, or sheet of ice, caused this. Thousands of years ago this glacier covered the northern part of North America. For years it was very cold there, and the land lay under the great sheet of ice. Slowly, very slowly, the glacier moved southward. As it moved, it wore down the tops of mountains, carrying rocks and soil with it.

The weather grew warmer. The ice and snow began to melt. Water filled the hollow places

scooped out by the glacier. It formed rivers and lakes. Millions of large rocks were left where they were dropped by the melting ice.

The Piedmont

The map of the Northeast on page 157 shows the land surfaces or natural regions. A map which shows the natural regions is called a physical map. A physical map uses different colors to represent the different natural regions. The key, or guide, is in the lower righthand corner. What color represents plains, or lowlands? The lowland along the Atlantic coast is called the Atlantic Coastal Plain. Where are there more lowlands? West of the Atlantic Coastal Plain are hills and mountains called the Appalachian Highland. What color is used to show the highland? What color means high mountains? Where are high mountains found on the map of the Northeast?

West of the Atlantic Coastal Plain is the Piedmont region. A piedmont, as you remember, is an upland region between a plain and mountains. The Piedmont in North America lies between the Atlantic Coastal Plain and the Appalachian Highland. It extends from the Hudson River south to central Alabama.

The Appalachian Highland

West and north of the Piedmont the land rises to form the Appalachian Highland. It is made up of many mountain ranges with gentle slopes and rounded peaks. Forests cover most of the

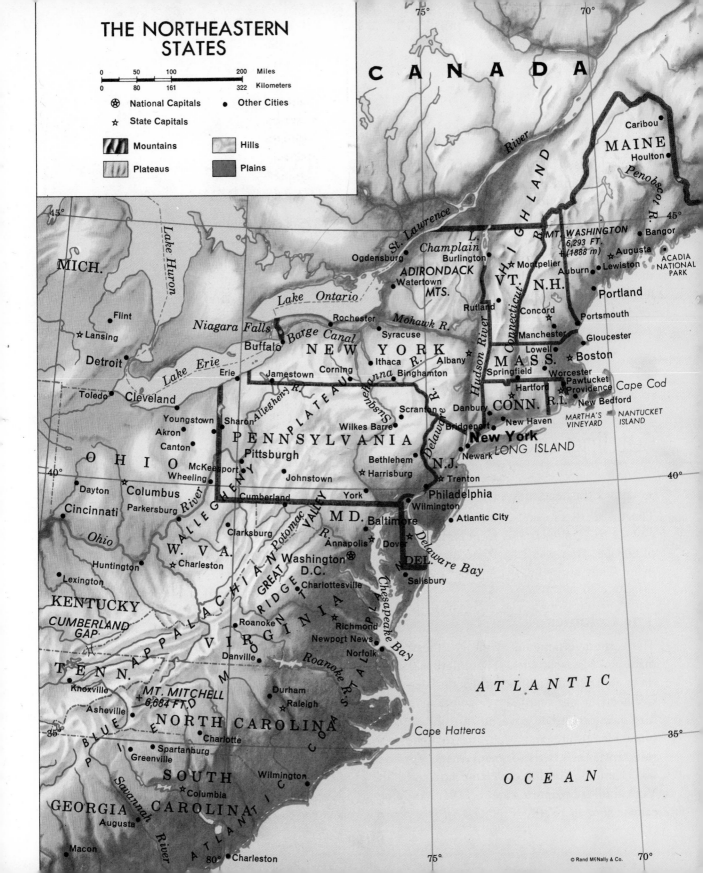

THE NORTHEASTERN STATES

				Miles
0	50	100	200	Miles
0	80	161	322	Kilometers

⊛ National Capitals   • Other Cities

☆ State Capitals

Mountains   Hills

Plateaus   Plains

CANADA

MICH.

Lake Huron

MAINE

Caribou

Houlton

Penobscot R.

HIGHLAND

MT. WASHINGTON
6,293 FT.
(1888 m)

Bangor

Ogdensburg   St. Lawrence River   L. Champlain   Burlington   ☆ Montpelier   Augusta   Lewiston   ACADIA NATIONAL PARK

ADIRONDACK
MTS.

Watertown

VT.   N.H.   Auburn

Portland

Rochester   Mohawk R.   Rutland   Concord ☆   Portsmouth

Niagara Falls   Barge Canal   Syracuse   Hudson River   Manchester   Gloucester

Buffalo   NEW YORK   Ithaca   Albany   Lowell   MASS.   ☆ Boston

Flint

☆ Lansing

Detroit

Lake Erie   Erie   Jamestown   Corning   Binghamton   Springfield   Worcester   Pawtucket   Cape Cod

Toledo   Cleveland   PLATEAU   Susquehanna   Scranton   Danbury   Hartford   CONN.   R.I.   Providence   New Bedford

Delaware R.   Bridgeport   MARTHA'S   NANTUCKET
VINEYARD   ISLAND

Youngstown   Sharon   Allegheny R.   Wilkes Barre   New Haven

Akron   PENNSYLVANIA   New York   LONG ISLAND

OHIO   Canton   Pittsburgh   Bethlehem   Newark

McKeesport   Johnstown   Harrisburg ☆   N.J.

Dayton   Columbus ☆   Wheeling   Cumberland   York   Trenton

Cincinnati   Parkersburg   ALLEGHENY River   Philadelphia

Ohio   Clarksburg   Potomac   M.D.   Baltimore   Wilmington

W. VA.   R.   Annapolis ☆   Dover   Atlantic City

Huntington   ☆ Charleston   Washington   D.C. ⊛   DEL.

Lexington   GREAT   RIDGE   Charlottesville   Chesapeake Bay   Salisbury

KENTUCKY   APPALACHIAN   VALLEY   Delaware Bay

CUMBERLAND
GAP   Roanoke   Richmond ☆   Newport News

TENN.   VIRGINIA   Danville   Norfolk

Knoxville   MT. MITCHELL   Roanoke R.s.   ATLANTIC

Asheville   6,684 FT.   Durham   Cape Hatteras

BLUE   NORTH CAROLINA   Raleigh

Charlotte

Spartanburg   Wilmington   OCEAN

Greenville

SOUTH   Columbia ☆

GEORGIA   CAROLINA

Augusta   Savannah River

Macon   Charleston

© Rand McNally & Co.

75°   70°

45°

40°

35°

80°   75°   70°

Appalachians. The highest New England peak, Mount Washington, is in New Hampshire. It is more than 6,000 feet (1,800 m) above sea level. Mount Washington is snow-covered during the winter.

Good farmland is found in the wide valleys of the Appalachian Highland. The largest, most fertile area is the Great Valley. This valley extends south from eastern Pennsylvania.

2
Settling the Northeastern States

The first settlers came to the northeastern region of the United States from many countries of Europe. They wanted a chance to earn a good living. They wanted to live in freedom.

The Colonies

The earliest settlements in the Northeast were made in Massachusetts. The Pilgrims landed there in 1620. Neighboring Rhode Island and Connecticut were settled a few years later. Before they established governments of their own, New Hampshire and Maine were under the rule of Massachusetts for many years. Vermont was claimed by both New Hampshire and New York until it became a state in 1791. Maine became a state in 1820.

New York was originally a Dutch colony. Later it was divided into three colonies—New York, New Jersey, and Delaware. People from Sweden were the first to settle in Delaware. Pennsylvania was settled by William Penn, an English Quaker.

After the Revolutionary War, the colonies developed a new plan of government. They became the states we are studying now.

Transportation

The rivers and lakes of the Northeast helped the region become a manufacturing center. Manufacturing means making goods by machines. Water power ran the early factories. The lakes and rivers provided excellent transportation.

By the early 1800s, the lands around the Great Lakes were being settled. The new settlers there needed the goods that were manufactured in New York. They wanted to trade their farm products for the things they needed.

But in those days it took a long time to move products from one place to another. And it was very expensive. What was needed was a cheap means of transportation.

Water has always been the cheapest means of transportation. The region had plenty of waterways. How could the settlers living around the Great Lakes make the best use of them? How could they get their farm products and raw materials to New York City in the cheapest and easiest way?

New York City is located at the mouth of the Hudson River. People who settled to the north took their products down the Mohawk and Hudson rivers to New York City. Steamboats were a popular means of river travel after Robert Fulton proved that steam power could run boats. Fulton tested his steamboat, the *Clermont,* on the Hudson River.

The Erie Canal

"A canal between the Hudson River and Lake Erie would give us a waterway connecting the Great Lakes with the Atlantic Ocean." So spoke Governor Clinton of New York in 1817.

In 1825 the first boat moved along the Erie Canal and down the Hudson. The Erie Canal provided an easy, cheap means of transportation between the Great Lakes region and New York City. Find the Erie Canal on the map of early transportation routes on page 239.

A *locomotive* steams swiftly along the New Portage Railroad near Cresson, Pennsylvania. Train connections between faraway areas made the world seem smaller.

The Early Railroad

Sending goods by water is slow. Soon people wanted faster means of transportation. Hard roads had been built to connect the cities of the Atlantic coast with the lands west of the Appalachians. Carriages and wagons carried passengers and freight along these roads. But vehicles drawn by horses are also slow.

Then English inventors built a railroad steam engine which could move on its own power. It was called a *locomotive* (lō′kə mō′tiv). In 1829 a locomotive was brought from England to the United States. Peter Cooper, an American, improved it. The following year he built *Tom Thumb,* a small steam locomotive which could pull a train of coaches.

Soon railroads were built connecting the cities of upper New York State with New York City. Boston, Philadelphia, and other eastern cities also built railroads. By 1861 most cities of the Atlantic Coastal Plain were connected with Chicago and other cities west of the Appalachians. In 1869 the Atlantic and Pacific coasts were joined together with iron rails. Today railroads connect all parts of the country.

Other Waterways

Trains are fast, but water transportation is cheaper. Manufacturers of heavy machinery wanted the cheaper water transportation. So New York State built an improved waterway called the New York State Barge Canal. The canal extends 800 miles (1,280 km) from Lake Champlain and the Hudson River to Lakes Erie and Ontario. This system of canals, rivers, and lakes includes the Erie Canal. Heavy goods are sent on flatbottomed boats called barges.

Until recent years large ocean-going ships could sail up the St. Lawrence River only as far as Montreal. West of Montreal canals had been built to carry smaller ships around the rapids in the river. A large modern ship could not use the canals.

A ship traveling from Erie, Pennsylvania, to Montreal, Quebec, on the St. Lawrence Seaway passes under eight bridges. How many locks does it go through? Where is the water level highest? Where is it lowest?

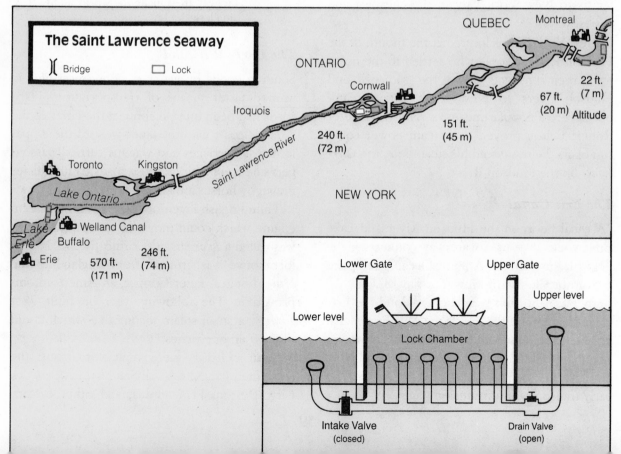

Life was often difficult for immigrants who came to the United States at the turn of the century. Many lived in apartments and earned money at low-paying jobs. This family is making artificial flowers.

Canada and the United States decided to work together and widen these canals and deepen the river channel. The St. Lawrence Seaway was opened in 1959. Now ocean ships can reach Buffalo and cities farther west on the Great Lakes.

Growth of Industry

Industry refers to manufacturing as well as other businesses. It also means the making of, or working with, certain kinds of products. Examples are the automobile industry, the coal industry, and the *tourist* (toor'ist) industry. A tourist is a person who travels for pleasure. Still another meaning of industry is any kind of work which provides us with what we want or need. Mining, building, farming, and transportation

are all industries. Later in this unit, you will read about the chief industries of the Northeast.

The Northeast became a region of rapidly growing industries for two reasons. The first reason was that improvements in transportation lowered the cost of sending goods. The lower cost made it possible for industries to produce more goods. The second reason for the growth of industry was that a large number of workers lived in the northeastern states. Industries need many people to work in factories and provide services. More workers meant an increase in the production of goods.

During the 1830s more and more iron was needed for farming tools and railroad tracks. By the middle 1800s the iron industry, especially in Pennsylvania, had grown very large. The United States began trading its iron products with other countries of the world. By the late 1800s our country had become one of the largest industrial countries in the world.

Growth of Cities

As industries in the northeastern states grew, more people were needed to work in factories. So the population of the cities grew. Improved farm machines meant that fewer farmers were needed to supply the same amount of food. So many farmers moved to cities to become factory workers.

A large number of immigrants arrived in our country from Europe in the nineteenth and twentieth centuries. These people came in ships that often landed in New York City first. Many stayed there while others settled in Boston, Philadelphia, and Pittsburgh. The immigrants often crowded into run-down parts of cities. They could not afford better housing.

During the 1900s a large number of blacks also moved to the northeastern states and other northern states. At that time these states had more industries than southern states had. The blacks wanted to find jobs in industries of the Northeast. So they too settled in cities.

Women's Rights

As you remember, during the first half of the 1800s people began to work together for equal rights for women. They demanded that women be given the same opportunity for an education as men. They resolved to organize and work for women's *suffrage* (suf'rij), or right to vote.

A large meeting was held in Worcester, Massachusetts, in 1850. It was organized by Lucy Stone and Paulina Wright Davis. Men as well as women attended. They came from nine states. It was the first national meeting held to discuss equal rights for women.

Susan B. Anthony, Leader for Women's Rights

Susan B. Anthony was born in Adams, Massachusetts, in 1820. She became a teacher. She was interested in working for change in our country. Susan felt strongly that women must be given rights equal to those of men.

Susan began to make speeches across the country. She published a weekly paper on women's rights. In 1869 Susan and Elizabeth Cady Stanton founded the National Woman Suffrage Association. The Association was against the Fifteenth Amendment of the Constitution. This amendment gave black men the right to vote. But it did not give black or white women this right. The National Woman Suffrage Association believed that all women should have the right to vote, just as men had.

162

Susan B. Anthony wrote and spoke convincingly for women's *suffrage*. Though she did not live to see the results of her work, her efforts were successful.

In 1872 Susan voted in New York. It was her way of testing the Fifteenth Amendment. She was arrested, tried, and fined for breaking the law. But Susan refused to pay the fine because she felt that the law was wrong. She was not put into jail.

All her life Susan B. Anthony worked for the right of women to vote. She died in 1906. Fourteen years later, the Nineteenth Amendment was added to the Constitution. This law gave women the right to vote. In 1979 the United States government issued the Susan B. Anthony coin in her honor.

Do You Know?

1. What advantage does water transportation have over trains? What advantage do trains have over water transportation?
2. What three groups of people moved to cities in the Northeast to work in factories?
3. What right was given to women by the Nineteenth Amendment?

Before You Go On

Using New Words

locomotive   suffrage
tourist

The phrases below explain the words listed above. Number a paper from 1 through 3. After each number write the word that matches the definition.

1. The right to vote
2. A person who travels for pleasure
3. An engine which can move on its own power

Finding the Facts

1. How did the glacier that moved over North America long ago change the surface of the northeastern states?
2. What is a piedmont?
3. Where is the highest mountain peak in New England?
4. In which present-day northeastern state were the earliest settlements made?
5. Who started the colony of New York?
6. When did the Erie Canal open? What did it provide?
7. What American built a small steam locomotive which could pull a train of coaches?
8. Why did New York State build the New York State Barge Canal?
9. What two countries worked together on the St. Lawrence Seaway?
10. Name two reasons why industries grew in the northeastern states.
11. What caused cities in the northeastern states to grow?
12. Where was the first national meeting on equal rights for women held? Who organized the meeting?
13. What did Susan B. Anthony work for most of her life?

3
Living and Working in New England

Maine, New Hampshire, Vermont, Massachusetts, Rhode Island, and Connecticut make up the New England states. The population map of the United States on page 448 shows that many people live in Massachusetts, Connecticut, and Rhode Island.

Manufacturing

Manufacturing is the leading industry of New England. Thousands of people make a living by working in mills and factories. The chief products are made from cloth, metal, leather, and lumber. New England is also a leader in the manufacturing of electronic equipment.

Textiles

Weaving cloth is called *textile* (teks′tīl) manufacturing, or the textile industry. This was an early industry in New England. At first spinning was done by hand. Only one thread was spun at a time. By 1793 Samuel Slater had a *spinning jenny* (jen′ē) set up in a mill on a river near Pawtucket (pô tuk′it), Rhode Island. A spinning jenny could spin many threads at a time. Machine-made thread could be sold more cheaply.

Then power looms, or weaving machines, were invented. The first power loom in our country was built in Waltham (wôl′tham), Massachusetts, in 1814. Thread could then be spun and cloth woven by power machines in textile mills or factories.

The first spinning and weaving machines were run by water power. Mills were built at waterfalls and rapids. Then steam replaced water power. Coal from Pennsylvania began to be used in furnaces to make steam. Now most textile machines are run by electricity.

Textile mills need raw materials such as linen, silk, cotton, and wool. The early settlers of New England raised sheep for wool. Today New England mills need more wool than their farms can supply. They get wool from our Rocky Mountain states and other lands.

For years, New England had more textile factories than any other part of the United States.

At *textile* mills giant mechanical looms weave cloth from thread at very high speeds. Mill workers keep the machines supplied with spools of thread.

But during the 1800s manufacturers began building textile factories in the South to be closer to the cotton region. The factories provided jobs, and the number of workers increased. By the 1940s the South had more textile mills than New England. But the textile industry is still important in the New England states today.

Metal Products

Many New England settlers were skilled metal workers. They made small articles such as jewelry and watches. Today articles of iron, copper, brass, gold, and silver are made in Connecticut cities. More production of metal articles has helped to make up for lost business in textiles. It has also created jobs for more workers.

Typewriters, brushes, and machinery for mills and factories are made in New England. Some cities also make articles of sterling silver. Sterling is the name for fine, almost pure, silver.

Leather Products

Colonial shoemakers cut, shaped, and sewed every pair of shoes they sold. The hides and skins they used came from the animals raised nearby. The leather they used was made in small factories called tanneries. There the hides were treated, or tanned, with the juices of wood and the bark of certain trees to soften them. Later they were dyed.

Today large factories take the place of shoemakers and village factories. Hides and skins reach New England by truck and railroad from our West. Ships bring more from South America. Goods brought in, or imported, from other

These leather pieces have been tanned and dyed. They may be cut and sewn to make jackets, coats, shoes, or boots.

countries are called *imports* (im′pôrts).

Leather articles are still manufactured in parts of New England. Massachusetts ranks second and Maine sixth in the nation in leather manufacturing. Shoes are the leading leather product. Some of the region's leather products are sent to other countries. Goods sent out of a country are called *exports* (eks′pôrts).

Forest Products

New England has large forests in certain areas. Spruce, pine, hemlock, birch, ash, and maple are some of the trees in these forests. Spruce logs make good paper. Lumber, made from other kinds of trees, is used to make ships, toys, and other articles. New England's forests furnish lumber for everything from ships to toothpicks to paper products.

In colonial times Bangor, Maine, was a great lumber market. Maine is still famous for its lumber, ranking sixth in the nation. Today Maine has many very large paper mills.

Much of New England's paper is used in books, magazines, and newspapers. Towels, napkins, and wrapping paper are also made.

Do you like maple syrup and maple sugar? These products are made from the sap, or juice, of the sugar maple tree. The Indians taught the settlers how to bore small holes into the trunks of the trees and to put spouts into the holes. Then they hung buckets under the spouts to catch the sweet, flowing sap. The sap is boiled to make maple syrup. With longer boiling it becomes maple sugar. Vermont is still famous for fine maple sugar and syrup.

Electronics

New England has many factories that produce electronic products. *Electronics* (i lek tron′iks) is a branch of the science of electricity. It has made possible such inventions as television, radio, sound motion pictures, tape recorders, and small calculators. It has also made possible radar, X ray machines, and computers. When you make a long-distance telephone call, electronic

An *electronics* worker assembles the wires for a device that will guide airplanes by remote control. Working with electronic circuits is detailed and complicated.

devices amplify, or strengthen, your voice. When a door opens as you walk toward it, photoelectric cells are at work. All such modern wonders are based on electronics.

Stone Quarrying

Granite, marble, and slate are used for buildings. These valuable kinds of building stone are found in New England. Many people make a living by cutting these stones. The open pit where stone is cut is called a *quarry* (kwôr′ē).

Stone used for building is found in huge solid layers. Great pieces must be loosened by blasting with dynamite. Special saws run by machinery can then cut them into blocks. The blocks are too large and heavy to be hauled far. So quarries must be near rivers or railroads.

Vermont is among our country's leaders in quarrying granite, marble, and slate. The largest granite quarries in the United States are near Barre, Vermont. Granite is a good, hard material for building monuments and public buildings. Marble comes in a variety of colors. Slate is used for floors, shingles, and roofs. Other important minerals dug from quarries in New England are clay, sand, and gravel.

Farming

New Englanders can raise only a small part of the food they need. Most of the farms are small because the land is hilly and the soil is rocky.

In the early days farmers tried to raise grains, vegetables, fruit, livestock, and poultry. They tried to supply people with all kinds of foods. That is, they engaged in mixed farming. More and more people went to work in factories. Farmers had to feed many more people. So each began raising just a few crops to sell in city markets. Such farmers did what is called specialized farming.

Farmers began to do specialized farming for two reasons. The first reason was that they realized some crops grew better than others. Farmers could raise more of these than of other crops. The other reason was that city people would buy more of certain foods than of others.

Farms near large cities, called truck farms, raise vegetables and fruits for city markets. These farms are small. Produce is grown out of doors in summer and in greenhouses in winter.

In winter tomatoes, lettuce, celery, and strawberries are grown in these greenhouses.

Dairy farming is an important business. It provides milk, cream, butter, and cheese. Vermont is the leading dairy state in New England. The hillsides of New England have pastures for dairy cattle. Hay and corn are grown on the less hilly parts. Much of the corn is cut while it is still green and stored in tall buildings, called silos. Corn from the silos and hay are used to feed the cattle all winter.

Poultry farms specialize in raising chickens, eggs, ducks, and turkeys. The hundreds of poultry farms in Connecticut, Vermont, Rhode Island, and Massachusetts send their products to cities in New England and New York.

Fruit orchards dot the hilly New England landscape. Fruit trees will grow on hilly land where farm machinery cannot be used. Apple trees are not easily killed by frost. Apples are the most important fruit crop in New England where frost comes early.

Potatoes grow well in sandy soil and cool, moist summers. The soil and climate of Aroostook (ə rōos′ took) County, in northern Maine, are just right for them. On their large potato farms Maine farmers use machinery to plant and harvest crops.

Tobacco, too, needs good soil and special care. In New England, only the Connecticut River Valley is suited to its growth. A leaf tobacco good for cigar wrappers is grown there.

Cranberries will grow only in wet lands. Maine, Cape Cod, and the nearby islands of Nantucket and Martha's Vineyard are famous for cranberries.

Products of the
Northeastern States

Fishing

Even before the settlers arrived, people came to New England to fish. The shallow waters off the coast of New England are fine places to fish. Billions of small fish come to these waters to feed on sea plants. Larger fish, like cod, halibut, and haddock, come to eat the smaller fish. The large fish are caught and sold in many city markets. While most fish is sold fresh, some fish is frozen and shipped to other places.

Some of the fishing areas are far from the coast. Fishing there is called deep-sea fishing. Fishing fleets leave coastal cities to do deep-sea fishing early in spring. There are boats with both sails and motors in the fleet. Each ship carries several small rowboats, called dories. Every morning fishers leave the ship in dories. At sunset they return to the ship. The day's work is done when the fish is packed in ice or stored in ice-cold, or refrigerated, rooms. When these

Fishers from New England may spend weeks at a time on deep-sea fishing boats like this one. Why do you think sea gulls follow the boats?

rooms are filled, the fishing fleet returns to its port.

Many countries have laws to protect their fishing waters. The United States has laws stating that no other country can fish within 200 nautical miles (370 km) of our shore without permission.

Inshore fishing means fishing within 2 or 3 miles (3 or 5 km) of the coast. Inshore fishers go out in their small motorboats. They bring in the catch each night.

In the quiet waters of New England's bays and inlets several kinds of shellfish, or animals that live in shells, are found. Clams, oysters, crabs, and lobsters are shellfish. Massachusetts furnishes many clams. Maine is famous for its lobsters.

Lobsters are caught in traps, called lobster pots. The pots are made so that lobsters can swim into them, but they cannot get out. Fishers usually bait the pots with fish. Because so many are being caught along our eastern coast, lobsters are now raised to replace those caught. The eggs are gathered and kept in quiet, inland ponds until they hatch. The baby lobsters are then put into bays and into the mouths of rivers. They grow there until they are large enough to catch.

Two other products of inshore fishing are scallops and clams. Scallops swim by moving their shells. They grow in beds off the southern shore of New England. Scallops are scooped up with dredges or gathered with rakes. Clams live in the sands along the seashore. Today clams, too, are growing scarce. According to a Massachusetts law, clams can now be dug only at certain times.

Recreation

Would you like to spend a vacation in New England? Many people do. The beaches along the coast are fine places to go. New England has beautiful mountains, forests, lakes, and rivers. Hunters and skiers visit these spots in the winter. People like to go there in summer to camp and fish.

The states and our national government have set aside large parks, forests, and seashores for the people's recreation. New England has many such recreation areas. White Mountain National Forest, in New Hampshire, and Green Mountain National Forest, in Vermont, are two of these. Acadia (ə kā′dē ə) National Park, situated along the coast of Maine, has many summer visitors. Cape Cod, Massachusetts, was named a National Seashore in 1961.

People interested in the history of our coun-

A wooden lobster pot usually is baited with fish. One end of the pot has a net shaped into a funnel. The lobster can go through the funnel to reach the fish but cannot find the opening again to escape.

try visit New England, where many events in our early history took place. Some landmarks still remain. Furniture, tools, and costumes of early days may be seen in museums.

Major Cities

New England is an industrial area, and manufacturing is a major activity of its cities. The seaports of this region are centers for shipbuilding, fishing, and transporting goods. Lumber mills, quarries, and textiles are still important industries, as they were in colonial times.

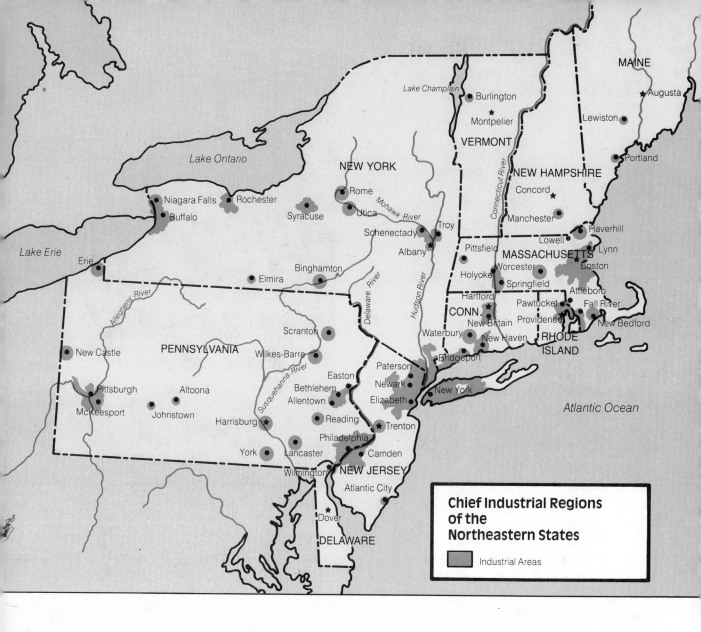

Chief Industrial Regions of the Northeastern States

Industrial Areas

Boston is the largest city in New England and the capital of Massachusetts. As the largest industrial center in New England, Boston has many factories. Making machinery, medical instruments, and processed foods are important industries. Printing, publishing, banking, and insurance firms are also there. Boston is second among the world's busiest wool markets. It is a major fish market. The Port of Boston is the busiest in New England.

Providence (prov′ə dəns) is the capital and largest city of Rhode Island. It is a major manufacturing center and seaport in New England. Providence is one of the world's most important centers for the making of costume, or inexpensive, jewelry. Machinery, metals, silverware,

172

Factories, office buildings, and homes all line the waterfront of Boston. Many people enjoy sailing boats on the Charles River.

and textiles are also made in Providence.

Hartford is the capital of Connecticut, So many insurance firms are located in Hartford that it is often called "Insurance City." Factories of Hartford make aircraft equipment, machinery, metal products, and chemicals. Bridgeport is the largest city in Connecticut. Machine tools, brass products, and electrical equipment are made there. It has a port on the Pequonnock (pi kwon′ək) River.

The capital of Maine is Augusta. It has shoe factories as well as cotton, paper, and lumber mills. Printing and poultry-processing are carried on there. Processing means preparation. In Augusta, poultry is prepared for sale.

Portland is Maine's largest city. Its factories make printed material, clothing, metal products, electronic parts, and processed foods. Portland's harbor is the closest in the United States to Europe. It is the second busiest oil-shipping center on the Atlantic. It is a fishing fleet base, and a center for shipping seafood and potatoes.

Concord, the capital of New Hampshire, has granite quarries and printing plants. Its factories make electronics, leather, and wood products. The largest city in New Hampshire is Manchester (man′ches′tər). It is the state's chief manufacturing center. Boots, shoes, and cotton and woolen goods are made there.

Vermont's capital is Montpelier (mont pēl′yər). It has insurance firms, granite industries, and printing plants. Plastics and machinery are made there. The largest city in Vermont is Burlington. Its factories make cereal and aircraft equipment.

Do You Know?

1. What is mixed farming?
2. What products come from New England's forests?
3. What is meant by the textile industry?
4. How are hides tanned or made into leather?
5. Name three products of the electronics industry.

173

4

Living and Working in the Middle Atlantic States

New York, New Jersey, Pennsylvania, and Delaware make up the Middle Atlantic states. The Middle Atlantic area has good harbors and important trade centers.

Do you know how many people live in the United States? About one-sixth of them live in the Middle Atlantic states. The many large cities tell us that the Middle Atlantic states are one of our most important manufacturing regions. Find this section on the population map of the United States, page 125, and the map of industrial regions of the Northeast on page 172. Comparing these maps shows that a large population and industry go together.

Mining

What a treasure chest of natural resources the Appalachian Highland is! See the map of early settlements in the Northeast on page 57. Iron ore, coal, limestone, slate, and some natural gas are found there. Early settlers discovered iron ore. They used charcoal as fuel to *smelt* (smelt) the iron ore. Smelting means separating the iron metal from its ore by heating.

Later, coal was found close to the iron ore. Coal then took the place of charcoal in smelting iron. The United States leads the world in coal production.

The Story of Coal

In the early days of Pennsylvania, so the story goes, two people were hunting near where

Wilkes-Barre and Scranton now are. Night came, and they built a small fire between two black stones.

"This will scare wild animals away and keep us warm," they said. "The stones will keep the fire from spreading."

In the night the hunters began to feel very warm. "How strange!" they said. "Our fire should be out by this time."

Instead of a small fire they saw a large blaze! Puzzled, they went closer. "The black stones are burning," the hunters said. "They must be coal." The hunters were right. They had discovered a large field of *anthracite* (an′thrə sīt′), or hard coal.

Two other important kinds of coal are *bituminous* (bī too′mə nəs), or soft, coal, and *lignite* (lig′nīt), or brown coal. The map on page 175 shows where these two kinds of coal are found in our country. Do we have more bituminous coal or more lignite coal? In what states is lignite found?

Methods of Mining

Two methods are generally used to mine coal. One method is *strip* (strip) *mining.* This method is used when the coal beds lie close to the earth's surface. Giant power shovels or other earth-moving equipment remove the layer of earth covering the coal. The coal is broken up, usually by explosives, and loaded into trucks.

Some coal lies in the ground in layers separated by rock. A deep shaft has to be cut through the rock to reach the coal. Elevators built in the shafts lower miners and machinery to tunnels, which lead to the coal. These tunnels are lighted with electricity. Small electric trains run on tracks in these tunnels. They carry workers, tools, and coal to and from the elevators. This kind of mining is called *shaft* (shaft) *mining.*

Most of the work in mines today is done by machinery. Miners use large machines run by electricity to cut the coal into squares. Holes are made with electric drills, and dynamite is put into them. The dynamite blasts the coal out in lumps. Usually machines load the lumps into cars, and the electric train hauls them to the shaft. In the early years of mining, this hard work was all done by people and mules. Some mines are still old-fashioned and dangerous.

Strip mining has been used to mine coal here. This way of mining is a good way to get coal, but it causes problems. Notice how bare and empty the earth looks. With no plants growing in it the soil easily can be blown or washed away. The places where coal is found in the United States are shown on the map below. In which states of the Northeast is *bituminous* coal found?

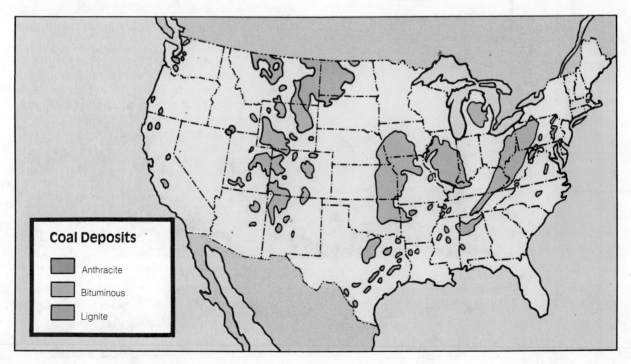

Coal Deposits

- Anthracite
- Bituminous
- Lignite

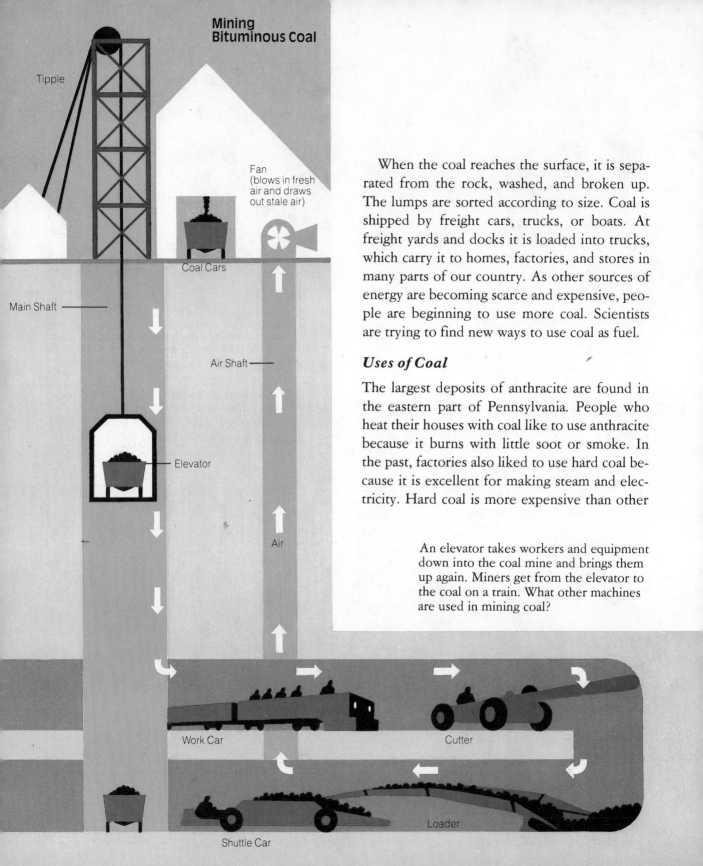

Mining Bituminous Coal

Tipple

Fan (blows in fresh air and draws out stale air)

Coal Cars

Main Shaft

Air Shaft

Elevator

Air

Work Car

Cutter

Shuttle Car

Loader

When the coal reaches the surface, it is separated from the rock, washed, and broken up. The lumps are sorted according to size. Coal is shipped by freight cars, trucks, or boats. At freight yards and docks it is loaded into trucks, which carry it to homes, factories, and stores in many parts of our country. As other sources of energy are becoming scarce and expensive, people are beginning to use more coal. Scientists are trying to find new ways to use coal as fuel.

Uses of Coal

The largest deposits of anthracite are found in the eastern part of Pennsylvania. People who heat their houses with coal like to use anthracite because it burns with little soot or smoke. In the past, factories also liked to use hard coal because it is excellent for making steam and electricity. Hard coal is more expensive than other

An elevator takes workers and equipment down into the coal mine and brings them up again. Miners get from the elevator to the coal on a train. What other machines are used in mining coal?

kinds of coal because it is scarce. How does this help to explain why anthracite is rarely used in industry today?

Until recently bituminous coal from the Allegheny Plateau was used to run most of the manufacturing machinery of the Northeast. It makes more soot and smoke than hard coal. But it is cheaper. Bituminous coal is the main fuel in power plants. It is used as fuel in some homes and furnishes power to thousands of factories. Tar, pitch, and dyes are made from bituminous coal. It can be changed into products such as cement, perfume, and paint.

Oil and Gas Production

Oil is very important today. The first oil well in the United States was drilled in Titusville (tīt′əs vil), Pennsylvania, in 1859. The discovery of oil caused great excitement. Soon other wells were drilled. Gas was also found with the oil. For many years the Allegheny Plateau furnished more oil and gas than any other part of our country. Today this region supplies only a small part of the oil and gas that we use.

Where does most of our oil come from today? The map of oil fields on page 292 will show you. Name some uses of oil.

Shipbuilding

Shipbuilding was important along the Atlantic coast from the time the first settlers arrived. Ships then were sailing vessels and were made of wood. Lumber was plentiful in the American forests.

The swiftest, most beautiful of sailing vessels was the clipper ship. The first clipper ships were built in the 1840s. Because clipper ships had very large sails, they could travel at a fast "clip," or speed. The long, slender ships cut through the water with ease. The nation's *merchant marine* (mur′chənt mə rēn′) first became important in the time of the clipper ships. The merchant marine is the fleet which carries on the trade of a nation. It delivers goods to ports around the world. The United States Merchant Marine Academy is at Kings Point, New York.

But the fastest clipper ships could not keep up with steamships, which were driven by engines. Next, steel replaced wood for ships. Shipbuilding remained important in cities like Philadelphia, which was near coal and iron-ore fields. Camden, New Jersey, and Chester, Pennsylvania, are also important shipbuilding centers.

Textiles

People in the crowded industrial areas east of the Appalachians needed textiles. Eastern Pennsylvania had fuel and water power. But there were few raw materials at hand. The many railroads and rivers made transportation easy. "It would pay us to bring in the raw materials if we built textile mills here," said manufacturers.

Today textile mills are found in New York, Pennsylvania, and New Jersey. These three states are among the top ten textile-producing states in our country. In addition, factories in these states make much clothing, which is sold in stores throughout the world.

Manufacturing

The Middle Atlantic states are among the leading industrial states in our country. Industries grew there because the region had many natural resources, a good location, and a large number of workers.

About one-third of the population in the Middle Atlantic states works in manufacturing. Pennsylvania manufactures iron and steel, machinery, transportation equipment, and metal products. New York and New Jersey manufacture food products and clothing. Many food products are manufactured in Delaware as well. The Middle Atlantic states manufacture chemicals, electrical equipment, paper, and paper products. Much printing and publishing are done there.

Iron and Steel Milling

The making of iron and steel and of iron-and-steel products became the leading industry of the highlands of Pennsylvania. This area has hundreds of rivers for transporting goods. It once had abundant deposits of coal and iron ore. Today, however, Pennsylvania's mines can no longer supply its factories with enough raw material. Iron ore is brought from the region around Lake Superior and from western South America.

Iron is the basic ingredient used in the steel industry. Which northeastern states have large amounts of iron? How does this relate to the large number of steel mills in the area? Where are our copper deposits?

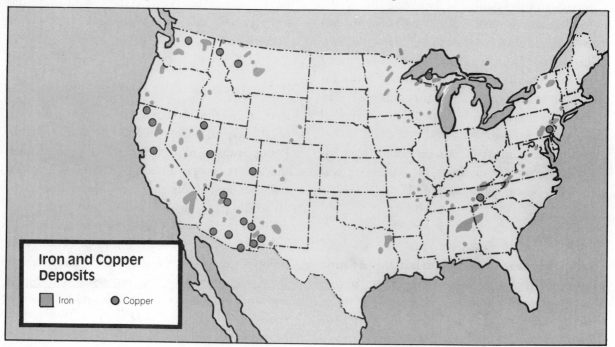

Iron and Copper Deposits

Iron   Copper

The Story of Iron and Steel

Smelting iron ore and making steel are two different industries. Smelting, as you know, means heating the ore to separate the iron metal from its ore. At one time charcoal and coal were used as fuel to melt the ore. Today *coke* (kōk) and limestone are used in smelting iron ore. Coke is made by slowly heating soft coal in airtight ovens to take out the gas, tar, and oil. What is left is coke. Coke, when used as fuel, produces much greater heat than coal does.

The ore is smelted in tall, round buildings called blast furnaces. They are made of steel and lined with brick. Iron ore, coke, and limestone are poured into a blast furnace. As these minerals slowly pass down the furnace, blasts of hot air are blown into it. The coke burns with great heat and the ore and limestone melt. The melted rock joins with the limestone, forming *slag* (slag). The slag, when melted, is lighter than the melted iron, so it floats on top.

The melted iron is drawn from the bottom of the furnace and poured into molds. The iron cools in the molds and hardens into bars. The iron can be made into usable articles. It is also made into steel. Steel is tougher and harder than iron.

To make steel, the bars of iron are melted again, or the hot liquid is used before it hardens. Small amounts of carbon are added. Metals such as nickel or chromium may be added. This is all melted in a large furnace. The hot liquid steel is run off into molds to harden into ingots (in′gəts), or bars.

Do you know why the steel industry is so important in the United States? The manufac-

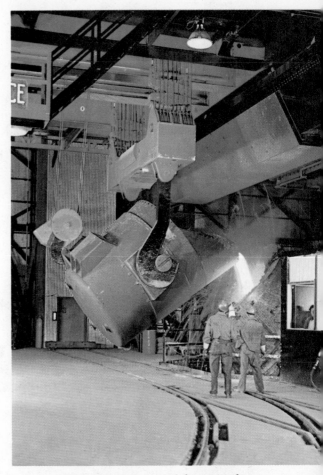

Melted steel is poured from the furnace. It is liquid and white-hot. Workers must wear protective clothing. Later, the molten metal will be formed into sheets or bars.

ture of automobiles, airplanes, ships, and locomotives depends on the steel industry. Skyscrapers are built with steel for the framework. Trains run on steel rails. Today the steel industry in the United States is modernizing. It is doing this to meet competition from the steel industry in Europe and Japan.

Philadelphia
An Old City with a New Face

The year was 1682. A group of people led by William Penn met together to plan a city called Philadelphia. The plan called for straight streets and many parks. More than 260 years later another group of people met together to replan the same city. Philadelphia had changed a great deal in 260 years. Narrow streets had become jammed with traffic. Many people no longer came into the city to shop. Large areas had become run-down.

Philadelphia was one of the first large cities to do something about its urban problems. Streets were widened, and travel into the city was made easier. Neighborhoods were rebuilt according to a special plan. The plan called for more than tearing down old buildings and putting up new ones. Many old buildings were left standing and were restored. New buildings were designed so they did not look out of place in old neighborhoods.

Philadelphia has much to be proud of. It is the largest city in Pennsylvania. Our Declaration of Independence was signed there. Our Constitution was written there. For a while the city was our nation's capital.

Philadelphia's location near water helped it become a busy seaport. Woolen mills and shipyards were built. Later it became a leading manufacturer of railroad engines. Today the city's factories turn out iron and steel products, textiles, and chemicals. It is near the largest oil-refining region on the Atlantic coast. █

Oyster fishers pour their catch into storage bins for the trip to market.

Farming

Crops grow well on the Atlantic Coastal Plain, in the Hudson Valley, on the Piedmont, and on the Lake Plain south of Lakes Ontario and Erie. These regions have good soil and a mild climate. Their farms help to supply city people with the fresh food they need.

Two important kinds of farming in the Middle Atlantic states are dairy farming and poultry farming. New York and Pennsylvania rank among the top ten states as producers of dairy cattle. Pennsylvania ranks among the top ten states in the production of eggs. Peaches, pears, and apples are grown in New Jersey and Delaware. Farmers in western New York grow fruits and grapes.

The sandy soil and mild climate of the Atlantic Coastal Plain are well suited to truck farming, or the raising of produce for market. The melons, strawberries, tomatoes, and other vegetables of New Jersey, Delaware, and Long Island are famous in the Northeast.

Truck farms on Long Island specialize in potatoes, cabbage, and other vegetables. Cranberries grow on New Jersey marshes. Eastern Pennsylvania produces tobacco. Why do each of these areas specialize in certain crops?

Fishing

You know that both deep-sea and inshore fishing are carried on all along the coast. But in the shallow, quiet waters off Long Island and Delaware a special kind goes on—fishing for oysters. When oysters are first hatched, they swim about looking for something to which they can cling. Baby oysters fasten themselves to rocks and shells. Often thousands of them are found growing close together at the bottom of a bay or a sound. Such places are called oyster beds.

There is a large market for oysters. So many people make a business of raising them. They collect thousands of eggs in large tanks. When the baby oysters hatch, they are put into shallow waters. Here they grow to full size. This takes 3 to 4 years. Then they are ready for market. Other shellfish come from this region. Long Island waters produce fine scallops. New Jersey has many clams, lobsters, and crabs.

Some oyster fishers go out in small boats and gather the oysters with long-handled rakes. Others have boats which are fitted with strong iron dredges run by machinery. Dredges scoop up great bagfuls at a time. Oysters are packed in ice and shipped to inland cities and towns.

Major Cities

The cities of the Middle Atlantic region are important manufacturing centers. Products are made from steel, paper, chemicals, and textiles. Banks, insurance firms, and printing plants provide services for our country and the world. With its airports and harbors, this area is part of a great transportation network.

Buildings tower above New York City, a center of art, industry, fashion, music, and literature. It is also a busy international port.

New York City is the largest city in the United States and one of the five largest cities in the world. The people of this great city come from many different ethnic backgrounds.

Publishing books and magazines is an important industry. There are more printing plants in New York City than in any other city in our nation. As a world financial center, many corporations and banks have their headquarters in New York. New York City is also known as a center of fashion. The clothing and textile industries employ many people. Other industries include food products, furniture, chemicals, paints, and paper products.

Many tourists visit this city to enjoy its museums, theaters, and art galleries. The Port of New York is one of the world's largest and busiest. New York City also has two major airports.

Albany is the capital of the state of New York. It is one of the state's leading transportation centers. Its busy port on the Hudson River makes it an important industrial and shipping center. Many people in Albany have government jobs. Others work in factories that make brass products, medicines, and paper products.

More cameras and film are made in Rochester (roch′es′tər) than in any other city in the world. Other factories in Rochester make instruments, dental equipment, electronic equipment, food products, clothing, and textiles.

Pittsburgh, Pennsylvania, is a river port. It stands where the Monongahela (mə non′gə hē′lə) and Allegheny rivers join to form the Ohio River.

Pittsburgh is Pennsylvania's second largest city. Nearby coal mines and iron ore deposits helped Pittsburgh become one of the world's greatest steelmaking centers. It is one of the world's largest makers of aluminum, machinery, and safety equipment. Plate glass, used for windows, is another important product of the Pittsburgh area. Glass is made from certain sands. The sand and clay in this area are exactly right for making glass. Dishes, bricks, and tile are manufactured from clay found near Pittsburgh. A number of Pittsburgh's products are transported on its rivers.

The capital of Pennsylvania is Harrisburg. A large number of people there work for the government. Many others work in clothing and shoe factories. Steel is also an important industry, as it is in Pittsburgh.

New Jersey's capital is Trenton. It has many factories. Making electrical goods, metal products, machinery, and rubber products are leading industries. Trenton is also a printing and publishing center. About one-third of the people there work for the government.

Newark is New Jersey's largest city. It is the third largest insurance center in the United States and a major banking center. Newark has many factories. The chief industries make electrical equipment, metal products, and processed foods. Newark is a leading New Jersey port and air cargo center.

Wilmington is Delaware's largest city. It is one of our country's largest chemical and petrochemical centers. A petrochemical is made from petroleum or natural gas. Wilmington's factories make automobiles, steel, plastics, dyes, textiles, and rubber and leather products. Dover, the capital of Delaware, is in a rich farming region. Its chief industries are canning, airplane repairing, and rubber products.

Recreation

Many people visit the Middle Atlantic states each year. Like New England, the Middle Atlantic states have beautiful mountains, forests, lakes, and rivers. People visit these spots in the winter to hunt and ski. Many people attended the Winter Olympic Games held at Lake Placid in New York State in 1980.

People go to the Middle Atlantic states in the summer to camp, fish, and enjoy boating. The beaches along the Atlantic coast have many vacationers. Both the states and the federal government have set aside lands for parks, forests, and recreation. One such area is the Allegheny National Forest in Pennsylvania.

Tourists enjoy the Middle Atlantic states because of an interest in our country's history. This region played an important part in colonial times, during our war for independence from Great Britain.

Do You Know?

1. What is the difference between iron and steel? What are some uses of steel in our everyday life?
2. What are the chief products of Pennsylvania?
3. What are two kinds of farming in the Middle Atlantic states?

To Help You Learn

Using New Words

slag
bituminous
anthracite
coke
imports
merchant marine
exports
quarry
locomotive

shaft mining
smelt
lignite
spinning jenny
electronics
strip mining
textile
suffrage

The phrases below explain the words or terms listed above. Number a paper from 1 through 17. After each number write the word or term which matches the definition.

1. Brown coal
2. The right to vote
3. Woven cloth
4. Goods and products brought in from another country
5. A way of mining coal when it is close to the earth's surface
6. An early machine which could spin many threads at a time
7. An open pit from which stone is cut
8. Goods and products which are shipped out of a country
9. A special branch of electricity used in industry
10. Ships which carry on the trade of a nation
11. Heating ore to separate the metals from the ore
12. What is left after the iron is smelted ✓
13. Soft coal ✓
14. Coal from which gas has been removed
15. Hard coal
16. A way of mining coal through a deep hole
17. An engine which can move on its own power

Finding the Facts

1. What highland is located in the northeastern states?
2. In what state is the Erie Canal?
3. What has always been the cheapest means of transportation?
4. What did Peter Cooper build?
5. Who founded the National Woman Suffrage Association in 1869?
6. What is the leading industry of New England?
7. Which New England state is famous for lumber? Which is famous for maple sugar?
8. Where are the largest granite quarries in the United States?
9. What is the capital of each New England state? What is the largest city of each?
10. Where are the largest deposits of anthracite? What are two methods of mining coal?
11. What are some uses of bituminous coal?
12. What helped industries grow in the Middle Atlantic states?
13. What are two important kinds of farming in the Middle Atlantic states?

185

14. What is the largest city in our country?
15. What is the capital of each Middle Atlantic state? What is the largest city of each?

Learning from Maps

1. Study the map of the northeastern states on page 157. Which natural regions extend through the whole Northeast? Which do not? What country lies north of the northeastern states? What ocean is at the east? Which of the Great Lakes border this region?
2. On the map of the United States on pages 92-93 locate the northeastern states. Between what parallels of latitude do the northeastern states lie?
3. Look at the map of forest regions of our country on page 357. What kinds of forests are in the northeastern states? Which kind of forest grows along the coast between Massachusetts and Delaware?
4. Look at the map of iron and copper deposits on page 178. Which northeastern states have deposits of iron? Which have copper deposits?

Using Study Skills

1. **Graph:** What does the graph on page 187 show?

   About how many tons of coal were produced in 1974? Was this more or less than the amount produced in 1972?

   In what year was the least amount of coal produced?

   Did the amount of coal produced between 1973 and 1976 increase or decrease? About how much less coal was produced in 1972 than in 1976?
2. **Diagram:** Look at the diagram showing coal mining on page 176. What kind of coal does the diagram show being mined? What machines do the miners use in the mine? How does fresh air get into the mine and stale air get out?
3. **Chart:** Make a chart like the one for Maine below, for the other northeastern states. Find the population figures, the capital, and the year of admission to the Union for each state on page 59. Find the largest city and the chief occupations of each state by using your text, an almanac, and encyclopedias.

State	Population	Capital	Admitted to Union	Largest City	Chief Occupations
Maine	1,124,700	Augusta 21,000	1820	Portland 63,000	lumbering, leather goods, farming, fishing

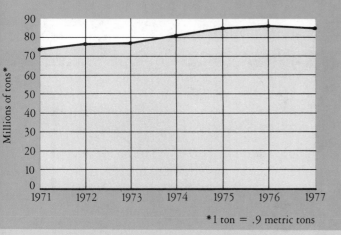

Production of Bituminous Coal in Pennsylvania, 1971-1977

Millions of tons*

90
80
70
60
50
40
30
20
10
0

1971 1972 1973 1974 1975 1976 1977

*1 ton = .9 metric tons

Thinking It Through

1. You remember that coal and iron ore were found together in eastern Pennsylvania. There were also many swift streams in this area. Can you explain how these things helped manufacturing to grow rapidly in this region?

2. Industries grew in the northeastern states for many reasons. If you could start a new business, what kind of business would you like to start? Where would you like to start your business? What things would you consider before choosing a location?

3. People who are interested in the history of our country visit buildings and landmarks in the northeastern states where events in our early history took place. Why is it important to save historical buildings and landmarks? Explain your answer.

4. Philadelphia was one of the first large cities to do something about its urban problems. If you could work on a committee to replan your city, what would you want done? Why?

Projects

1. Have the Reading Committee ask the librarian for help in finding books about life in the northeastern states. There are many interesting books about early settlers, American Indians, cities, and industries.

2. The Explorers' Committee might find out more about the clipper ships and the fast runs they made to China. They should try to find pictures of particular ships, such as the *Flying Cloud* or the *Sea Witch*.

3. The Research Committee might find more information about coal. What steps are being taken to make coal mining safer and to make coal burn more cleanly? What is being done to develop America's coal reserves? You might write the Department of Energy in Washington, D.C.

4. Many people from the northeastern states have made important contributions to our country. Work in small groups. Have each group find out about one of the following people: Edmund Muskie, Beverly Sills, Calvin Coolidge, Bella Abzug, Washington Irving, Reggie Jackson, Shirley Chisholm, Molly Pitcher, Mary Cassatt, and Howard Pyle. What contribution did each person make? Share what you find with the class.

5. If you cannot get a large outline map of the United States, make one by tracing the map on pages 92 and 93. Write in the names of the northeastern states, the important rivers, lakes, and cities. Label the Atlantic Ocean. Show the capital of each state with a star.

6 The Southeastern States

Unit Preview

The southeastern region of the United States is a vital agricultural and growing industrial area. The southeastern states in this region are Virginia, West Virginia, Maryland, North Carolina, South Carolina, Georgia, Kentucky, Tennessee, Alabama, Mississippi, and Florida.

The first lasting English settlement in America was made in this region. English people kept coming to the Southeast long after the first settlement. Spanish people were the first settlers in Florida. As the coastal lands became more populated, pioneers moved inland. The Indians of the region were forced to give up their land. The government had many Indian groups moved to places farther west.

Before the Civil War the southeastern states were called the "land of cotton." Today many products besides cotton are shipped from the Southeast. Forests grow fast in the warm climate of the Southeast, and lumbering is an important industry. After iron and coal were found near Birmingham, Alabama, it became a steel center. Many other industries have developed in the Southeast. The government project called TVA has helped to develop some industries as well as farming.

With all its industry, the Southeast remains a major farming region. But farming has changed too. Cotton and tobacco fields now share the land with orchards and with fields of soybeans, peanuts, corn, sweet potatoes, and other crops.

Things to Discover

If you look carefully at the picture, map, and time line, you can answer these questions.
1. What ocean borders some southeastern states? What body of water is south of these states?
2. What white fluffy crop shown in the picture grows well in the southeastern states?
3. When did the United States buy Florida?
4. What happened to the Cherokees in 1838?
5. How many years after the first airplane flight did the first people land on the moon?

Words to Learn

You will meet these words in this unit. As you read, you will learn what they mean and how to pronounce them. The Word List will help you.

basin	growing season
bauxite	legume
boll	naval stores
cannery	phosphate
citrus fruit	rayon
cotton belt	reservoir
crop rotation	sharecropper
cultivator	soil erosion
dam	soybean
dehydration	subtropical land
flood plain	tenant farmer
frontier	tung oil
gap	

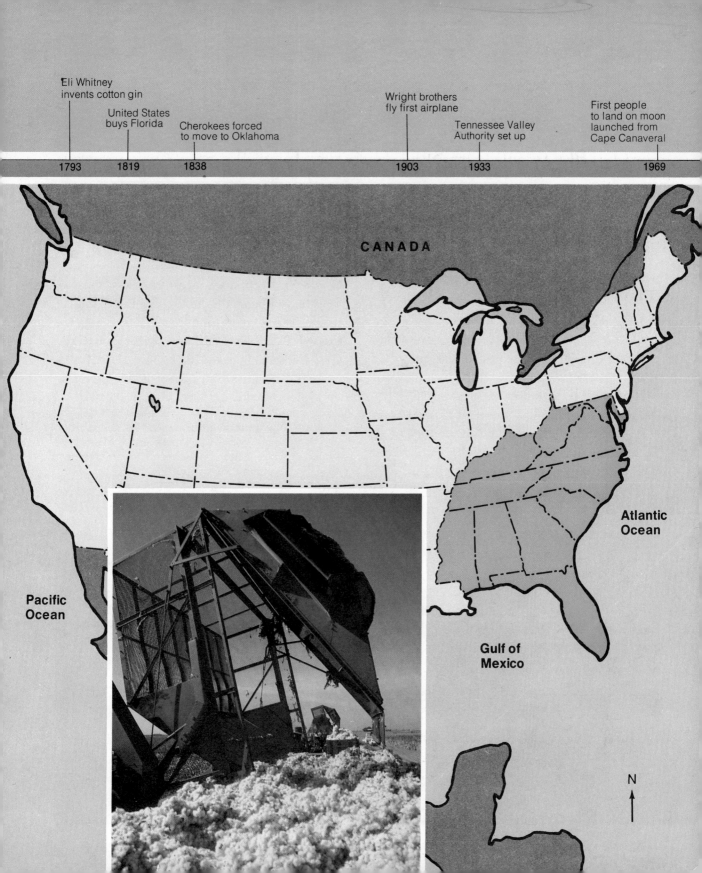

Eli Whitney
invents cotton gin

United States
buys Florida

Cherokees forced
to move to Oklahoma

Wright brothers
fly first airplane

Tennessee Valley
Authority set up

First people
to land on moon
launched from
Cape Canaveral

1793   1819   1838   1903   1933   1969

CANADA

Pacific
Ocean

Atlantic
Ocean

Gulf of
Mexico

N

1

Geography of the Southeastern States

The southeastern states have an irregular coastline, and hills and mountains inland.

The Lowlands

A large part of the southeastern states is a lowland. It is made up of the Atlantic Coastal Plain, the Gulf Coastal Plain, and the Mississippi *Flood* (flud) *Plain*. A flood plain is land covered by water when rivers overflow their banks. The Atlantic Coastal Plain and the Gulf Coastal Plain join in Florida. These two plains are really one large plain. It stretches along the eastern and southern coasts of the southeastern states.

The only way to tell where the Atlantic Coastal Plain ends and the Gulf Coastal Plain begins is by seeing which way the rivers flow. On the map of the southeastern states opposite find the Potomac, the James, and the Savannah rivers. These rivers flow through the Atlantic Coastal Plain. The Alabama River drains the Gulf Coastal Plain and flows into the Gulf of Mexico. The Mississippi River is the largest of the rivers that flow into the Gulf of Mexico.

Flat-bottomed boats called barges carry heavy loads of products on the Mississippi River. These goods are delivered to cities along the Mississippi *Flood Plain*.

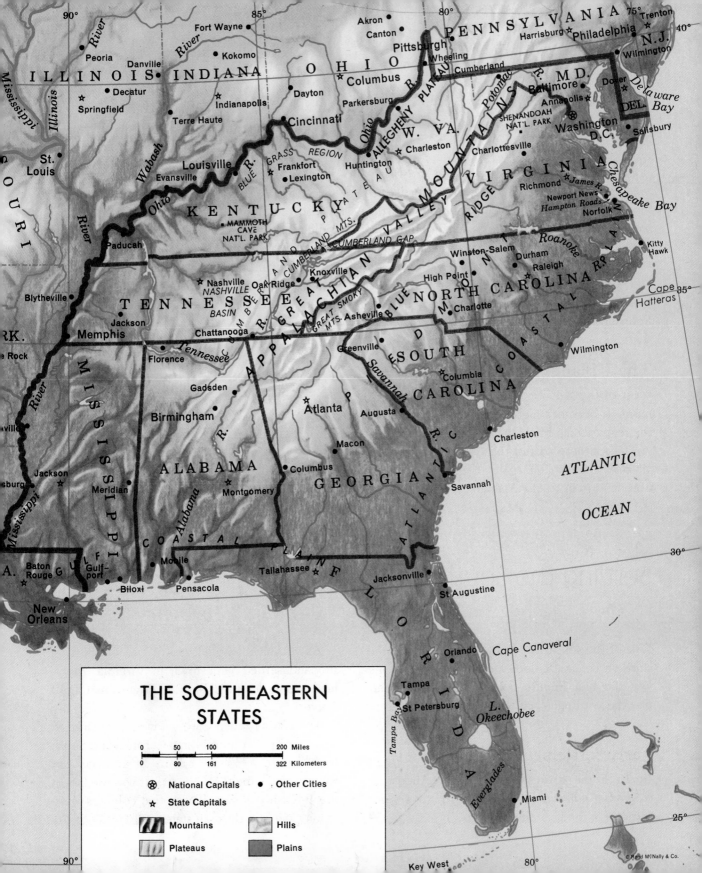

THE SOUTHEASTERN STATES

0	50	100	200	Miles
0	80	161	322	Kilometers

⊗ National Capitals   • Other Cities

☆ State Capitals

Mountains   Hills

Plateaus   Plains

© Rand McNally & Co.

Find the Blue Grass Region and the Nashville Basin on the map. These low, fertile regions are separated from each other by the western stretches of the Appalachian Highland. Because they are surrounded by higher lands, they are called *basins* (bā′sinz).

The Great Valley lies in the heart of the Appalachian Highland. It extends from eastern Pennsylvania to central Alabama.

The Uplands and Highlands

West of the Atlantic Coastal Plain is the Piedmont. It becomes higher as it stretches toward the Appalachian Highland.

The southern part of the Appalachians forms an almost unbroken chain of mountains from Maryland to northern Alabama. The mountains west of the Blue Ridge Mountains and the Great Valley are the Cumberland Mountains. These mountains have a *gap* (gap), or narrow valley through which it is easy to travel. The gap is known as Cumberland Gap.

The northern part of the Appalachian Highland is sometimes called the Allegheny Plateau. The southern part is the Cumberland Plateau.

Do You Know?

1. What states make up the Southeast?
2. What three plains make up the lowland of the southeastern states?
3. What is the northern part of the Appalachian Highland called? The southern part?

2
Settling the Southeastern States

Five of the southeastern states were among the thirteen original colonies of our country. One was the first English colony settled. Another was the last English colony settled.

Early Settlements

In 1565 the Spanish founded St. Augustine (ô′gəs tēn′), Florida, the oldest permanent white settlement in the United States.

As you have learned, in 1607 colonists from England settled Jamestown in Virginia. Maryland was settled in 1634 by an Englishman, Lord Calvert.

The colony called Carolina was quite large. It was later divided into North Carolina and South Carolina. In 1733 the colony of Georgia was founded by James Oglethorpe. It was the last of the English colonies. These five colonies were among the first thirteen states.

Growth of the Southeastern States

Settlers continued to come to the southeastern colonies from England, Scotland, Ireland, and Germany. The rapid growth of the coastal areas led settlers to move inland to the Piedmont.

To the west was the Appalachian Highland. Land companies bought large tracts of land beyond the mountains from the British government. The companies offered pioneers large sections of land for low prices.

Main Routes to the West

The long, high ridges of the Appalachian Highland were hard to cross. But the pioneers found and used four natural routes to the West, as shown on the map of these routes on this page.

In New York, the Hudson and Mohawk rivers provided a route through the mountains. This route led to the Lake Plain and the Great Lakes waterway.

In Pennsylvania and Maryland, pioneers followed the crude traces of roads—cut by Britain's armies—to the forks of the Ohio.

In Virginia and North Carolina, the pioneers followed rivers to their sources in the Appalachians. Once through the mountains, pioneers found themselves in the Great Valley. They traveled along this valley and river bottoms to the Cumberland Gap. It offered easy passage to the hilly uplands of Kentucky and Tennessee.

In South Carolina and Georgia, pioneers followed the coastal plain westward around the Appalachian Highland. However, this route led them through territory claimed by Spain.

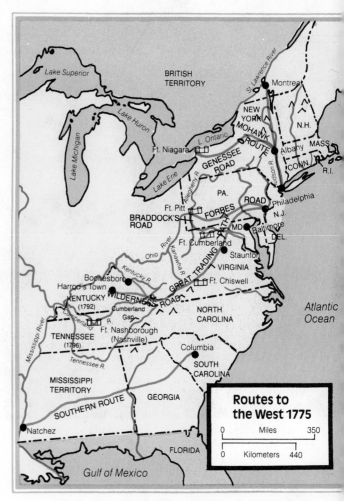

Follow the main early routes to the West. Locate the rivers on the map. Which routes followed rivers part of the way? What route crossed the mountains?

Settling the Frontier

As the Coastal Plain, the Piedmont, and the Great Valley became more densely populated, many pioneers decided to move west. They constantly moved onward to the everchanging

193

Pine-covered mountains rise steeply above the deep valleys and ridges of Virginia. Settlers found rich farmland in the valleys of the Appalachian Highland.

frontier (frun tēr′). The settled region of a country lying along the border of an unsettled region is called a frontier.

Daniel Boone and James Robertson led the first groups of settlers through Cumberland Gap. They settled the land west of the Appalachian Highland. At first, these new settlements were claimed by Virginia and North Carolina. Soon after our country became independent,

Kentucky and Tennessee became states of the United States. Kentucky became a state in 1792, Tennessee in 1796.

Settling Alabama and Mississippi

Cotton grew well in Georgia and the Carolinas. The factories of old England and of New England needed raw cotton. So southerners planted cotton on most of their land. Because they did not know how to use fertilizer, their land wore out. A search for new cotton lands led the planters into what are now Alabama and Mississippi.

Planters rushed to the cotton-growing region between Georgia and the Mississippi River. At first, Congress ruled this region. When enough people had settled here, two new states were formed. In 1817 Mississippi became a state. In 1819 Alabama became a state.

Indians of the Southeastern States

The Creek Indians lived in what are now Alabama and Georgia. When settlers began to move onto Creek lands, the Indians became angry. They attacked Fort Mims in Alabama. United States soldiers, led by Andrew Jackson, fought back. They defeated the Creeks who were then forced to move to present-day Oklahoma.

The Seminole (sem′ə nōl′) Indians lived in what is now Florida. When they heard about the Creeks, the Seminoles decided to take action to keep their lands. This decision started the First Seminole War. Jackson led some soldiers across the border of Florida and took several Spanish forts. He forced Spain to give up its claim to the territory. In 1819 Spain decided to sell Florida to the United States for 5 million dollars. But Jackson did not conquer the Indians.

Several years later, the Second Seminole War broke out. After 2 years of fighting, Osceola (äs′ē ō′lə), the Seminole's chief, was captured. The Seminoles continued to fight until they were nearly ruined. Many of the survivors moved to Oklahoma. Others stayed in Florida.

The Cherokee (cher′ə kē) Indians lived in the Carolinas and Georgia. Following the War for Independence, settlers began to move onto Cherokee lands. More settlers arrived after gold was discovered there. Georgia asked the United States government to force the Cherokees off their lands. The Cherokees asked for help from the United States Supreme Court. But the Court ruled against the Indians. The Court stated that the Indians lived on the land, but did not own it.

Later, Congress made a treaty forcing the Cherokees to be moved to what is now the state of Oklahoma. The 1838 march of the Cherokees became known as the "Trail of Tears." Almost 4,000 people died because of starvation and disease. Look at the map of Indian removal on page 230. Trace the route the Cherokees followed to the West.

The Story of Cotton

In colonial times the rice and indigo plants were the chief money crops in South Carolina and Georgia. Then cotton-spinning mills were built in the North. The mill owners there and in England wanted more cotton. They bought all the cotton southerners sent to market and wanted more. Before long cotton was the chief money crop in the South. Plantation owners wanted more slaves to work in the fields.

But the cotton had to be free from seeds before it was sold. Removing the seeds from the cotton by hand was slow work.

Eli Whitney, a young New England schoolteacher, was visiting a Georgia plantation in 1793. Whitney realized that if a machine could be invented that would remove the seeds from the cotton, much more cotton could be cleaned in a shorter time. Whitney invented such a machine, called a cotton gin. It cleaned as much cotton in a day as 50 people could by hand.

What a change that invention caused! Planters as far north as Virginia began to raise cotton. Still the factories wanted more. Planters then moved to cotton lands west of the Appalachian Highland. The cotton-growing region became known as the *cotton belt* (belt). Find the cotton belt on the map on page 202.

Again demands for more slaves increased. Slave traders brought more blacks to the South to provide cheap labor. Many farmers felt that they could not make money from growing cotton without the cheap labor provided by slaves. So slavery continued. Disagreements about it became one of the causes of the Civil War.

Sharecroppers and Tenant Farmers

Before the start of the Civil War, planters had no trouble getting workers. As their plantations grew, they bought more slaves. After the war there were no slaves. There were few workers to be hired on farms. Besides, the planters had little money to pay the workers. How could they run their plantations?

The system that developed was called sharecropping. A planter's land was divided. The planter kept part and divided the rest into small farms which were rented. The planter gave each renter a cabin, a mule, a plow and other farming tools, and food. In return, the workers tended the planter's land. After the harvest, workers shared all the crops with the owner of the land. Such workers came to be known as *sharecroppers* (sher′krop′ərz).

A planter often also had *tenant* (ten′ənt) farmers on the land. Tenant farmers, too, were given small plots to work. But they owned their tools and work animals. They paid their rent with either crops or money.

George Washington Carver, Plant Expert

George Washington Carver was born near Diamond Grove, Missouri, about 1861. He was the son of slaves. He worked while in college to earn money for his education. After college Carver became a teacher of agriculture at Tuskegee (tus kē′gē) Institute in Alabama.

The land in Alabama was worn out. It had been used only for growing cotton. Carver restored minerals to the soil by planting other kinds of crops.

Carver found that peanuts, sweet potatoes, and pecans grew well in the Alabama soil. He then taught farmers what he had learned. Carver found how to make more than 400 products from peanuts and sweet potatoes, and more than 75 products from pecans. His improvements completely changed agriculture in the Southeast.

Carver continued to work at Tuskegee, studying ways of better farming. After his death in 1943, Congress set aside January 5 as a day to honor George Washington Carver.

George Washington Carver had a laboratory at Tuskegee Institute. Here he worked many hours each day to carefully test all of the products he made from pecans, sweet potatoes, and peanuts.

Growth of Transportation

As the southeastern states grew, transportation improved. Better roads and more railroads were built. They helped carry raw materials to the North. They carried food grown in the West to the South where food was needed.

Then a new kind of transportation developed. In December 1903, Wilbur and Orville Wright came from Dayton, Ohio, to make the first successful airplane flight at Kitty Hawk, North Carolina. They chose Kitty Hawk because it was one of the windiest places in the country. It had sandy hills which were free of bushes and trees. The work of the Wright brothers led to the air travel we enjoy today.

During the 1950s and 1960s our country became interested in space exploration. Scientists worked with engineers to design long-range

Orville Wright had to lie flat on the frame to control the airplane he and his brother built. The Wright brothers' plane is now in a museum in Washington, D.C.

missiles. Launchings were made from a missile-testing center at Cape Canaveral on Florida's Atlantic coast. The climate there allows launchings to be made all year long. Nearby islands provide bases for stations to track launched spacecraft. In 1969 the first people to land on the moon were launched from Cape Canaveral at the John F. Kennedy Space Center.

Do You Know?

1. Why did settlers use the Cumberland Gap?
2. Why did more and more landowners plant cotton?
3. What is Cape Canaveral?

Before You Go On

Using New Words

tenant farmer   frontier
flood plain   cotton belt
sharecropper   basin
gap

The phrases below explain the words or terms listed above. Number a paper from 1 through 7. After each number write the word or term that matches the definition.

1. Any low region surrounded by higher lands
2. The region of a country lying along the border of an unsettled region
3. Lowland that is often covered by water when rivers overflow their banks
4. A person who pays rent for farmland with either crops or money
5. A narrow valley in mountains
6. Area in the South where cotton grows well
7. A person who works on another's farm and shares crops with the landowner

Finding the Facts

1. What kind of coastline do the southeastern states have?
2. In which state do the Atlantic Coastal Plain and the Gulf Coastal Plain meet?
3. How can you tell where the Atlantic Coastal Plain ends and the Gulf Coastal Plain begins?
4. Where is the Great Valley?
5. Where is the Cumberland Gap?
6. Which five southeastern states were among the thirteen original states of our country?
7. Who led the first groups of settlers through Cumberland Gap?
8. How was Florida added to the United States?
9. What Indian tribe was forced to move to Oklahoma in a march known as the "Trail of Tears"?
10. What did Eli Whitney invent?
11. What crops did George Washington Carver introduce to the southeastern states?
12. How did railroads help the southeastern states?
13. Who made the first successful airplane flight in 1903? From where was it made?
14. From where were the first people to land on the moon launched?
15. Where did the Creek, Cherokee, and Seminole Indian groups live? Where did many of them have to go?

3

Living and Working in the Southeastern States

The population maps on pages 125 and 448 show that almost one-fourth of America's people live in the Southeast. Beginning in the 1950s, more and more people have found jobs in the new industries of the Southeast. Some people work on farms, in forests, or in orchards.

The Tennessee Valley Authority

The Tennessee Valley is the land drained by the Tennessee River and its tributaries. It once had good soil, forests, minerals, and navigable rivers. But poor farming methods robbed the soil of plant food. Many trees were cut or burned down. Heavy rains caused floods which carried off the topsoil. Fertile fields became barren. They were cut by gullies, or ditches. This washing away of soil is known as *soil erosion* (i rō′zhen). Our government sent scientists to see what could be done to save the valley.

In 1933 the government set up an organization known as the Tennessee Valley Authority, usually shortened to TVA. The TVA had offices in Knoxville, Tennessee. TVA planned ways to prevent floods, stop soil erosion, plant trees, and make better use of the natural resources.

The work of the TVA was started by building more *dams* (damz). A dam is a wall or bank built across a river to stop its flow. Wilson Dam, at Muscle Shoals in Alabama, had been built in 1925, before this experiment began. The dams hold back the waters so the rivers do not overflow their banks and cause floods. *Reservoirs* (rez′ər vwärz′), or lakes, are formed behind the dams. Water from the reservoirs is allowed to flow into the streams when the rivers are low. This makes them navigable at all times. Power plants were built at the foot of some dams. These plants generate (jen′ ə rāt′), or make, electricity. The electricity generated in the plants supplies power and light to factories, towns, and farms in a 200-mile (320 km) area.

Trees were planted on the bare slopes. These new forests help check soil erosion and prevent floods. Experts showed farmers how to plow land in order to keep soil from being carried away in heavy rains. They showed farmers how to fertilize the land and rotate crops. TVA has done much to improve farming methods in the Tennessee Valley.

TVA has also brought electric power to the valley and helped it change into an industrial region. Factories and factory towns have grown up throughout the farming sections. The TVA project has saved millions of dollars by preventing floods. It has helped develop water power in many states of the South.

Farming in the Southeast

Most of the land in the Southeast is coastal plain. Only a small area is too rugged for farming. The climate and rainfall there are favorable

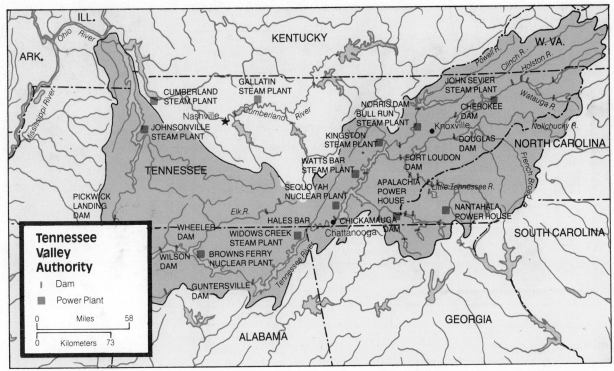

The Tennessee Valley Authority (TVA) built *dams* to control floods and power plants to generate electricity along the Tennessee River. What states benefit from TVA?

for farming. The rainfall map on page 17 shows the amount of rainfall the southeastern states get. The surface and climate make it possible to grow many different crops in these states.

The Cotton Belt

Cotton must have certain conditions to grow. Cotton needs a very special climate. It must have a *growing season* (sē′zən) of at least 200 days. The growing season is the part of the year when crops can be grown outdoors. It is the time between the last killing frost in the spring and the first killing frost in the fall. Most farm crops do well with a shorter growing season than cotton must have.

Cotton must also have between 20 and 60 inches (51 and 152 cm) of rainfall. If the plants get too much rain, they rot. With too little, they wither and die. The rain must come in spring and early summer. Rain in late summer or early fall rots the cotton fiber. It makes harvesting the cotton a difficult task.

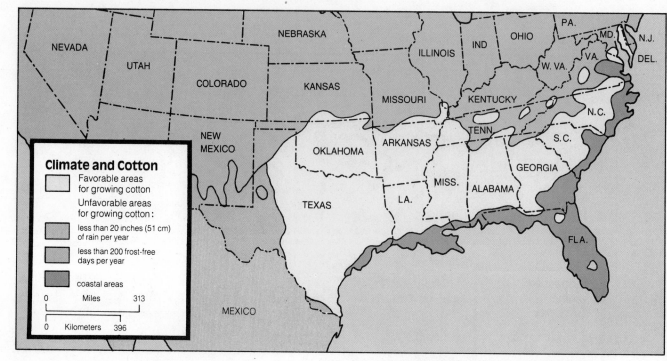

NEVADA
UTAH
COLORADO
NEW MEXICO
TEXAS
MEXICO

NEBRASKA
KANSAS
OKLAHOMA

ILLINOIS
IND
MISSOURI
ARKANSAS
LA.
MISS.
ALABAMA

OHIO
PA.
KENTUCKY
W. VA.
VA.
MD.
N.J.
DEL.
TENN.
N.C.
S.C.
GEORGIA
FLA.

Climate and Cotton

◻ Favorable areas for growing cotton

Unfavorable areas for growing cotton:

▨ less than 20 inches (51 cm) of rain per year

▨ less than 200 frost-free days per year

▨ coastal areas

0   Miles   313

0   Kilometers   396

The area where cotton is the leading crop is called the *cotton belt.* What kind of climate does cotton need? How many states are in the *cotton belt?*

Today small farmers usually own the land they work. Instead of raising the same crops on the same land year after year, they practice *crop rotation* (rō tā′shən). That is, if they have raised cotton for 2 or 3 years, they plant a different crop. Some crops, like cotton, rob the soil by using up its richness. Other crops, like soybeans and peanuts, put plant food back into the soil. By rotating crops, a farmer builds up the soil. However, cotton is still grown on many farms in the Southeast.

From Planting to Market

Part of the Southeast is near the tropics. See the physical map of North and South America, page

13. We speak of land near the tropics as *subtropical* (sub trop′i kəl) *land.* In the subtropical part of the cotton belt, planting can begin in February. Farther north it is April before danger from frost has passed.

After the soil is plowed and broken up, seeds are sown by drills. Later, machines called *cultivators* (kul′tə vā′tərz) are used to loosen the soil and uproot the weeds. Cultivators are pulled between the rows of cotton by tractors.

Eight or ten weeks after the seeds are planted, the cotton belt is a sea of blossoms. At first the blossoms are white, then pink, and then red. In a few days the blossoms fall off. Small seed pods, called cotton *bolls* (bōlz), form in their places. Late in August the cotton bolls start to burst open, showing white, fluffy fibers.

Cotton picking begins when the first bolls open. Long ago people picked the cotton. Today almost all the cotton is picked by machines.

Near most large cotton fields is a large building where the seeds are taken out of the cotton. The machine that separates the fiber from the seeds is a cotton gin. Another machine presses it into bales, wraps the bales in heavy cloth, and ties them with steel bands.

A bale of cotton weighs about 500 pounds (225 kg). Before they are shipped, the bales are put into another machine which presses the cotton together tightly. This makes the bales much smaller and easier to handle. They are then stored in warehouses ready to be shipped.

Uses of the Cotton Plant

Years ago people learned to make cloth from cotton fibers. Now useful products are also made from cotton seeds. Cottonseed oil is used in cooking, in making soap, and as salad oil. Cottonseed cake makes excellent cattle feed. It can be ground up to make a cheap fertilizer.

Short cotton fibers sometimes stick to the seeds. These fibers are too short to make good cotton cloth. They are often used in making *rayon* (rā′on). Rayon is a type of cloth that looks and feels much like silk. The stalks of the cotton plant are used in making paper.

Tobacco

The first money crop raised in our country was tobacco. The method of growing and preparing the crop has not changed very much. Raising tobacco is hard work. The tiny seeds must be started in seedbeds. Each plant is then set out in the field by hand or by machine. The growing plants are carefully tended. When ripe, the leaves are picked and taken to barns or sheds for curing, or drying. This prepares the leaves for market.

Tobacco is usually cured in one of two ways. Sometimes the leaves are hung in sheds. These sheds either have walls made of slats or no walls at all. Tobacco dried this way is "air-cured." In the Carolinas tobacco is often dried by stoves or furnaces. Tobacco treated this way is "heat-cured." The dried tobacco is taken to market towns. It is sold at a public sale to buyers from tobacco factories.

North Carolina and Virginia make up one of the chief tobacco regions in the country. North Carolina's farms produce more tobacco than those of any other state. Another tobacco region is in Kentucky and northern Tennessee.

Mixed Farming

In recent years southern farmers have turned to new kinds of farming. They still grow cotton and tobacco. They also raise many kinds of grains, fruits, and vegetables for market. They keep farm animals and poultry and raise feed for them. The crops and animals they raise on mixed farms help to build up worn-out soil.

Certain plants, like peas and beans, which grow in pods, are called *legumes* (leg′yoomz). Legumes are grown on many farms in the South.

An important legume is the *soybean* (soi′bēn′). The first soybeans were brought here from China. Many uses have been found for

Processing Cotton

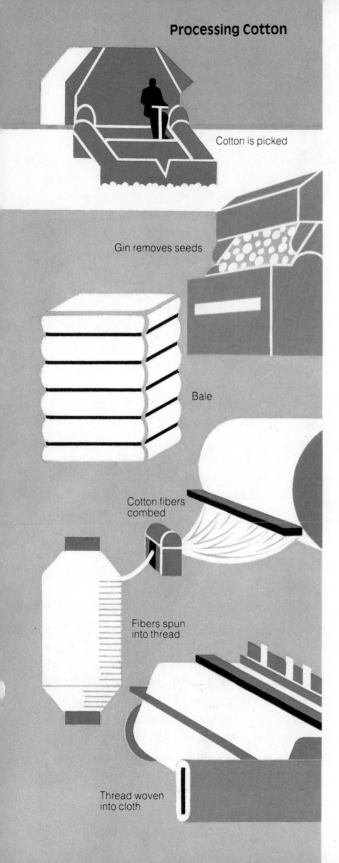

Cotton is picked

Gin removes seeds

Bale

Cotton fibers combed

Fibers spun into thread

Thread woven into cloth

Production of Cotton in the United States 1970-1977

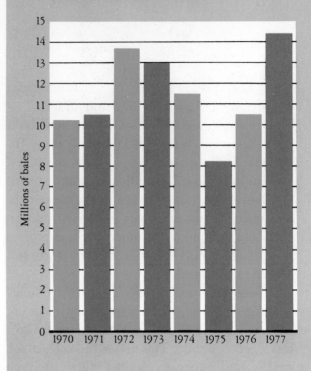

Millions of bales

1970 1971 1972 1973 1974 1975 1976 1977

The graph above shows how cotton production has changed from year to year. What are some causes of these changes? The steps in processing cotton are shown in the diagram at the left. Which of these steps would take place inside a textile mill?

soybeans. They are ground into flour and used in cakes and bread. Soybean oil is used to make a variety of paints, varnishes, and plastics.

Peanuts are also legumes. They have pods which grow and ripen underground. The low, sandy coastal plain of southeastern Virginia and of North Carolina is fine for growing peanuts. They also grow well in Alabama and Georgia. As you remember, George Washington Carver introduced the growing of peanuts to farmers in the region.

Many pecans are raised in the Southeast. Tall pecan trees grow wild along the Gulf Coast.

This is a farm in Tennessee. In plowing the fields, the farmer has followed the natural curve, or contour, of the land's surface. This will help prevent *soil erosion*.

They are cultivated in only a few southern states. Pecan nuts have thin shells. This makes it easy to get the meat out. Bags of pecan nuts are shipped to all parts of our country.

The tung tree is a native of China. The trees are also grown in the United States for needed *tung* (tung) *oil*. Tung oil is pressed from the seeds found in tung nuts. This oil is used in making paint, varnish, and plastics. Large groves of tung trees grow in Mississippi and Florida. They supply most of the tung oil used by manufacturers in the United States.

Fruits and Other Special Crops

Almost every kind of fruit you can think of grows in the Southeast. South Carolina raises and ships more peaches than any other state except California. Fine peaches also grow in Georgia and Alabama and in the Great Valley in Maryland and Virginia. The Great Valley in Virginia is famous for apples as well as peaches. There are also many apple orchards in West Virginia.

Not many parts of our country are warm enough to raise oranges, grapefruit, lemons, and

205

limes. These *citrus* (sit′rəs) *fruits* need a tropical or subtropical climate. More than one-half of all the citrus groves in the United States are in Florida. They produce more than two-thirds of our citrus fruits.

The owner of a citrus grove is always worried until the fruit is ripe. One frost can ruin an entire crop. Lemons and limes are most easily killed.

Huge packing sheds are built near the citrus groves all through the citrus-growing regions. Some of the fruit is washed, sorted, packed in boxes, and shipped to big cities. Tampa and Orlando are cities in Florida where citrus fruits are packed and shipped. Juices are prepared for market too. Plants for processing canned frozen juice are often located near citrus groves.

Other special crops of the southeastern states are sweet potatoes, sugarcane, and rice. Growing sweet potatoes began to pay after the work of George Washington Carver. He made bread, starch, glue, candy, plastics, and other things from sweet potatoes. Then farmers in Mississippi, Alabama, and other states in the region could make money by growing sweet potatoes. Drying sweet potatoes is also an important industry.

Sugarcane needs a hot, wet climate and fertile soil. Find the Everglades on the map of the Southeast on page 191. These great swamplands in southern Florida are being drained. Sugarcane grows well in these wet lands and is an important crop in Florida.

Some rice is grown along the Gulf Coast. The swampy, warm conditions on this coastal plain are good for rice-growing.

Livestock Raising and Dairy Farming

Southerners have always raised livestock. Today numerous farms in the Southeast have pigs. Many farmers also raise poultry, cattle, horses, sheep, and bees.

Raising horses was a paying business before the automobile was invented. The Bluegrass Region of Kentucky is still famous for fine racing and riding horses. Fine horses are also raised in Virginia.

Dairy farming is an important industry in most of the Southeast, especially in the northern part. There are many dairy farms east of the Appalachians. The coastal plain of Maryland has large dairy farms. The Piedmont of Maryland and Virginia and the Great Valley are other important dairy regions. The hilly sections of West Virginia supply dairy products to nearby cities.

Raising beef cattle is becoming important in Kentucky, Georgia, and Florida. The largest beef-cattle ranches east of the Mississippi River are in Florida. Cowhands care for great herds of cattle on the grasslands north of Lake Okeechobee (ō′kə chō′bē). Hog raising is important in South Carolina and Georgia.

Many mules are raised in the Southeast. Mules are smaller, tougher, more sure-footed, and cheaper than horses. They are used on some farms and in mines.

Large flocks of sheep graze in Virginia, West Virginia, Tennessee, and Kentucky. Sheep are raised for meat and wool.

Poultry is raised in the Southeast. Many of the chickens raised for eating come from the Southeast.

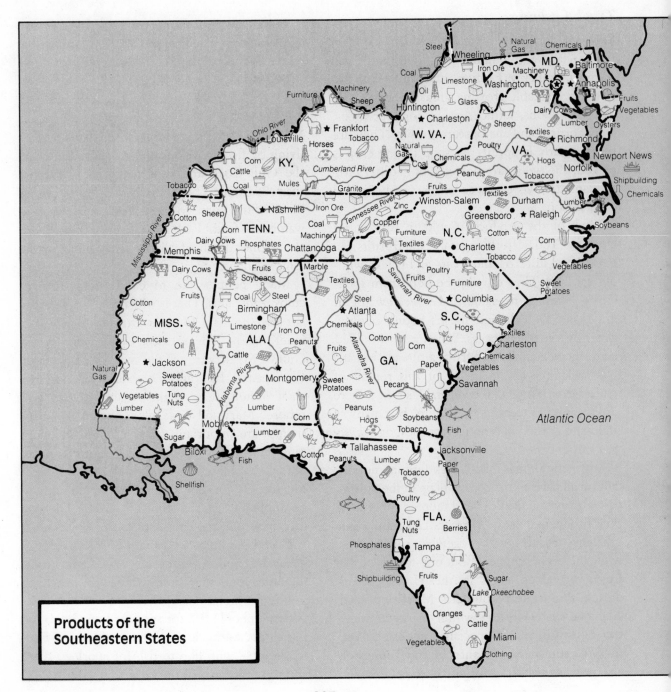

**Products of the
Southeastern States**

Steel
Natural Gas
Chemicals
Wheeling
Coal
Iron Ore
Machinery
MD.
Baltimore
Oil
Limestone
Washington, D.C.
Annapolis
Huntington
Glass
Charleston
Sheep
Dairy Cows
Lumber
Oysters
Fruits
Vegetables
Furniture
Machinery
Sheep
W. VA.
Textiles
Richmond
Frankfort
Ohio River
Louisville
Tobacco
Horses
Natural Gas
Chemicals
VA.
Hogs
Norfolk
Newport News
Corn
Cattle
KY.
Cumberland River
Coal
Peanuts
Tobacco
Shipbuilding
Tobacco
Coal
Mules
Granite
Fruits
Textiles
Chemicals
Nashville
Iron Ore
Tennessee River
Zinc
Winston-Salem
Durham
Lumber
Cotton
Sheep
TENN.
Coal
Copper
Greensboro
Raleigh
Soybeans
Mississippi River
Corn
Machinery
Furniture
N.C.
Cotton
Corn
Dairy Cows
Phosphates
Chattanooga
Textiles
Charlotte
Memphis
Fruits
Marble
Poultry
Tobacco
Vegetables
Dairy Cows
Soybeans
Textiles
Fruits
Furniture
Sweet Potatoes
Cotton
Fruits
Coal
Steel
Steel
Columbia
MISS.
Birmingham
Atlanta
S.C.
Chemicals
Oil
Limestone
Chemicals
Hogs
Jackson
ALA
Iron Ore
Cotton
Corn
Charleston
Cattle
Peanuts
Fruits
GA.
Paper
Chemicals
Sweet Potatoes
Alabama River
Montgomery
Sweet Potatoes
Pecans
Vegetables
Natural Gas
Savannah
Vegetables
Tung Nuts
Oil
Lumber
Corn
Peanuts
Lumber
Atlantic Ocean
Sugar
Mobile
Lumber
Cotton
Soybeans
Fish
Biloxi
Fish
Peanuts
Lumber
Jacksonville
Shellfish
Tallahassee
Tobacco
Paper
Poultry
Tung Nuts
FLA.
Berries
Phosphates
Tampa
Shipbuilding
Fruits
Sugar
Lake Okeechobee
Oranges
Cattle
Vegetables
Miami
Clothing

Truck Farming

Spring comes early to the Atlantic Coastal Plain of Maryland and Virginia. The light, sandy soil warms up quickly. Farmers have made it an important vegetable-growing area. Cabbages, tomatoes, onions, lettuce, sweet corn, potatoes, strawberries, and melons are grown. They are planted early in spring. As soon as one crop is picked, the fields are plowed and another crop is planted. Two or three crops can be raised each season.

Most of the produce is sold in large cities close by. Today fresh vegetables and fruits can be shipped in refrigerator cars and trucks without spoiling. They can also be kept from spoiling by canning, freezing, or *dehydration* (dē'hī drā'shən). Dehydration means taking out the water by a special process. When water is added later, the vegetables and fruits are ready to eat.

Maryland is in the heart of this region of truck farms. Some of the vegetables raised there are shipped to markets elsewhere. But many of them are canned in canning factories, or *canneries* (kan'ər ēz).

Refrigeration has made truck farming important on all parts of the coastal plain in the Southeast. Refrigerated trucks and railroad cars transport products quickly. Farmers can supply the northern markets with vegetables during the winter. Florida supplies about one-fourth of the fresh vegetables eaten in the United States during the winter. Southern Mississippi and Alabama share Florida's winter markets. Many truck farms in Florida specialize in raising potatoes and strawberries. Kentucky and Tennessee also grow strawberries for northern markets.

Some southern farmers still raise one or two money crops. The change to mixed farming has made farming in the Southeast more profitable.

Fishing

Many people in the southeastern states make a living by fishing. Along the Atlantic Coast and the Gulf Coast the continental shelf is more than 75 miles (120 km) wide. Hundreds of kinds of fish come to these warm, fairly shallow waters to feed. Each year fishers there catch about one-fourth of all the fish caught in the United States.

Many people like to eat oysters, shrimp, crabs, and clams. That is why there is a big market for shellfish. Oysters grow best in warm, quiet waters. The greatest oyster beds in the Gulf of Mexico are off the coast of Mississippi. Chesapeake Bay and Delaware Bay are the chief oyster areas on the Atlantic Coast. Baltimore, Maryland and Biloxi (bə läk'sē), Mississippi are important oyster-packing and shipping cities. Shrimp, too, like warm waters. Shrimp boats are a common sight in the Gulf of Mexico. Oysters and shrimp are packed in ice to be shipped fresh, and some are frozen. They are usually sent to the cities east of the Rockies.

Clams and crabs are caught off the shores of Delaware and Chesapeake bays. Sea trout, flounder, mullet, and red snapper are caught in southern waters.

Some people fish for sport or fun. Game fish live in the waters around the peninsula of Florida. People who like to fish for sport go there and to other parts of the Gulf.

Large machines help workers load logs on trucks. The trucks deliver the logs to nearby mills or to railroad cars to be carried to other parts of the United States.

Lumbering

What a huge forest most of the Southeast was when the first colonists arrived! Coastal lands were covered with softwood trees, chiefly yellow, or southern, pine. Oak, hickory, maple, and other hardwoods grew on the cooler uplands. Gum, sycamore, and cottonwood grew along the rivers and in the bottom lands of the Mississippi. Cypress was found in the swamps. What is now our Southeast was once the largest stretch of forest lands in our country. It is still a fine forest region.

Trees grow easily in the Southeast because of the warm climate and abundant rain. Forests grow faster in that section than in other parts of our country. Today one-fourth of our lumber comes from the forests of the Southeast. To replace those that are cut down, new trees are planted.

Cutting Lumber

Most lumbering in the Southeast is done on the coastal lowlands. Look at the product map on page 207 to see what states have important lumber industries.

Roads and railroad tracks are run into the forests to the lumber camps. Logs are loaded on flat cars or on trucks and carried to the mills. Because of the mild climate, lumbering goes on in these forests of the Southeast in both winter and summer.

The logs are sawed and made into boards in mills close to the lumber camps. For many years the boards were sent to factories in the North or exported. Today the Southeast has its own factories for the making of furniture and other wood products. But the forests still supply much of the lumber used in other parts of the United States.

Inside a lumber mill, special machines cut logs into boards and neatly stack them for shipment. Most of the lumber will be used later by the construction industry.

Uses of Lumber

The gum of the pine tree is made into turpentine, tar, and resin. In colonial days these products were known as *naval* (nā′vəl) *stores*. Naval stores were used in shipbuilding at that time. Today the gum of the pine tree is used in making linoleum, paper, and soap. Tar is used for paving and roofing. Turpentine is used to mix paints. The pine forests of northern Florida, southern Georgia, and Alabama supply most of the naval stores now needed.

Tall, straight pines make good telephone poles and boards for building purposes. Yellow pines can be turned into wood pulp. Wood pulp is made by grinding wood and mixing it with water. Wood pulp is used to make paper, especially newsprint, the paper used in newspapers. Wood pulp is also used to make rayon.

Oak, maple, and other hardwood trees from the Appalachians make excellent lumber for houses and furniture. Gumwood is shaved into thin layers and made into berry boxes, fruit baskets, and barrels.

The forests of this region supply the furniture-making factories, pulp and paper mills, and rayon plants of the Southeast with lumber. They also send lumber to factories in other parts of the world.

Mining

The Southeast has many natural resources. For 200 years the land was used chiefly for farming. Mining is now an important industry in the Southeast.

Coal, Oil, and Gas

The coal-deposits map on page 175 shows that a bituminous coal field lies under almost the whole Appalachian Highland. This is the largest coal field in the world. It extends into Kentucky, West Virginia, Virginia, Tennessee, and Alabama. Kentucky and West Virginia mine the largest amounts of coal each year.

Many mining towns have grown up in these states. Much of the coal mined is used to make electricity for power in factories of the southeastern states. Some coal is shipped north or exported. Often, coal is sent by water because it is cheaper to ship heavy goods by water than by railroad. Norfolk and Newport News, Virginia's largest seaports, export more coal than any other cities in the United States.

The oil and natural-gas fields of the Appalachian Highland also extend into West Virginia and Kentucky. These fields help furnish power and fuel for the glass and chemical factories of West Virginia. Oil fields are also located in the Gulf coastal area. Some oil is pumped from offshore deposits in the Gulf. Look at the map of oil deposits on page 292.

Other Minerals

You have learned that iron ore, coal, and limestone are used in making steel. Large amounts of all three are found close together in northern Alabama. The Great Valley near Birmingham is one of the richest iron-ore areas in our country. You know that coal is mined in this region and that limestone is found throughout the Great Valley. Much limestone lies near Birmingham. With these resources Birmingham has become a great iron-and-steel city.

The Southeast has other minerals in addition to coal, oil, gas, and iron. One of these is *phosphate* (fos′fāt). Phosphates are minerals needed for growth by plants and animals. Worn-out soil often lacks phosphates. Southern farmers use a great deal of fertilizer, some of which is made from phosphate rock.

Large amounts of phosphate rock are found in Tennessee and Florida. The world's largest deposits of this rock lie near Tampa Bay, in Florida. Here the rock is so near the surface that it can be scooped up with power shovels. Not all the phosphate rock is made into fertilizer. Some is made into a substance that puts "fizz" in soft drinks. One kind of baking powder also contains phosphate.

Building stones, mainly marble and granite, are quarried in Georgia, Tennessee, Virginia, and Alabama. In northern Georgia is a bed of building stone 60 miles (96 km) long and several miles wide. Pure white and pink marble is quarried there. This marble is in great demand for statues and public buildings. Granite is used for large buildings, bridges, monuments, and curbstones because it is so hard.

Graphite, zinc, and lead are mined in the Southeast, too. Graphite is a soft, black, greasy mineral. It is chiefly used in making "lead" pencils. Tennessee has many deposits of zinc.

Manufacturing

Until the middle 1900s most of the people in the Southeast made their living by farming. The map on page 215 shows that all the southeastern states now have industrial regions.

The Southeast has rich raw materials, a good climate, good transportation, and a great number of workers and markets. Industries need all

Machine parts are made from metal in this manufacturing plant in Tennessee. Workers use precise cutting machines to shape each part to exact measurements.

these. That is why many northern factories moved to the Southeast during the 1900s.

A few factories were moved before the 1900s. Among them were textile mills from New England. Small towns grew up around the early mills and factories. At first each town manufactured just one kind of article, depending on the kind of raw materials nearby. Some southern towns still specialize in one or two products. However, large factories in the Southeast now makes many kinds of goods.

One leading industry today is the manufacture of chemicals. Another leading industry is food processing. Other industries manufacture textiles, furniture, clothing, iron and steel, and paper products.

Vacationing

Many people visit the Southeast each year. They enjoy the beaches along the Atlantic and Gulf coasts. They vacation among the beautiful mountains, forests, lakes, and rivers.

Four national parks have been set aside in the southeastern states. The parks are visited by hundreds of people. Everglades National Park is in southern Florida. It is the largest subtropical wilderness and swamp in the United States. The Great Smoky Mountains National Park stretches along the border between North Carolina and Tennessee. It is a wooded highland. Mammoth Cave National Park, in Kentucky, is a huge cave with miles of passageways and an underground river. It has beautiful natural formations and lakes. Shenandoah National Park, in Virginia, is part of the Blue Ridge Mountains.

The Lincoln Memorial, Washington Monument, and Capitol are points along a line through the central area of Washington, D.C. Museums and other government buildings are close by.

People interested in our country's history visit the Southeast. Many important events of the past took place in these states.

Washington, D.C.

Washington, D.C. is the capital of the United States and the center of our national government. Members of Congress, members of the Supreme Court, and the President work in Washington, D.C. This city has many museums and interesting buildings. Washington, D.C. is an attraction for visitors from all over the world. Many businesses and organizations are located in this important city.

The great dome at the top of the Capitol can be seen from almost every part of Washington. Congress meets in the Capitol to make laws for the whole United States.

Near the Capitol is the Library of Congress, one of the finest libraries in the world. On the other side of the Capitol is the National Archives (är′kīvz) building, where our nation's records are kept. The Declaration of Independence and our Constitution are kept there. They are in a case covered with a special kind of glass to protect them.

For many years, the Supreme Court met in a special room in the Capitol. Now the Court meets in a white marble building with eight graceful columns.

On Pennsylvania Avenue, about one mile (1.6 km) from the Capitol, stands the White House. Our President lives and works in the White House while in office. The President's house is a fine building with deep porches surrounded by rolling lawns and shady trees.

Most of the people in Washington work in the government. They help in the task of running the country. Government is the main business of the capital.

Washington is also a city of monuments. The most famous of these are the Washington Monument and the Lincoln Memorial. The Jefferson Memorial, the newest of the three, is also a well-known Washington landmark.

The Washington Monument is a tall shaft made of marble and granite. It rises more than 500 feet (150 m) above the ground. From the windows near the top there is a fine view of the city.

A wide lawn slopes from the Washington Monument to a clear, deep pool. Its waters reflect the Washington Monument and the Lincoln Memorial, which stands at its other end. Wide marble steps lead to a hall in the Lincoln Memorial. Here is a large statue of President Abraham Lincoln. A ray of light seems always to fall on the quiet marble figure seated on the marble chair. People seldom talk as they look at this statue. Lincoln's eyes are kind and his smile friendly. He seems to say, "Come closer. I like people. Come and talk with me."

The head of Jefferson's huge statue almost touches the ceiling in the Jefferson Memorial.

Everything else seems small next to this statue. It reminds visitors of Thomas Jefferson's belief in democracy, the idea that all people are created free and equal. Visitors leave thinking of the kind of democracy Jefferson wanted when he wrote the Declaration of Independence.

Washington, D.C., has many other points of interest. The Museum of African Art is located in Washington. The Smithsonian (smith sō' nē ən') Institution is one of a number of other museums. Ford's Theater is the place where President Lincoln was shot. Plays, music, and dance are enjoyed at the Kennedy Center for the Performing Arts.

Chief Cities

Three of the twenty largest cities in the United States are in the Southeast. These cities are Baltimore, Maryland; Washington, D.C.; and Memphis, Tennessee.

Coast Cities

In early colonial times towns were built along the Atlantic Coast. Many of the towns started then are important cities today.

Baltimore, Maryland, on Chesapeake Bay, became an early trade center. Today it is the largest city in the Southeast. Baltimore ranks next to Birmingham in making iron and steel. Baltimore's factories make everything from heavy machinery and airplanes to railroad cars, chemicals, and food products. Fruit, vegetables, and seafood are canned there. The factories make the cans for these foods. Almost every kind of industry is found in Baltimore.

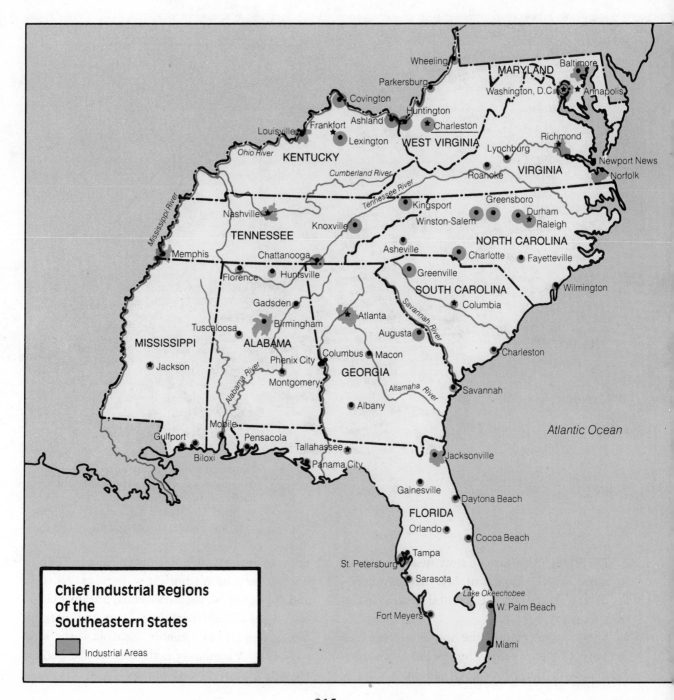

Chief Industrial Regions of the Southeastern States

Industrial Areas

Wheeling
MARYLAND
Baltimore
Parkersburg
Washington, D.C.
Annapolis
Covington
Huntington
Ashland
Charleston
Louisville
Frankfort
WEST VIRGINIA
Richmond
Lexington
Lynchburg
Newport News
Ohio River
KENTUCKY
VIRGINIA
Norfolk
Cumberland River
Roanoke
Tennessee River
Kingsport
Greensboro
Nashville
Durham
Knoxville
Winston-Salem
Raleigh
Mississippi River
TENNESSEE
NORTH CAROLINA
Memphis
Asheville
Charlotte
Fayetteville
Chattanooga
Florence
Huntsville
Greenville
SOUTH CAROLINA
Wilmington
Gadsden
Atlanta
Tuscaloosa
Birmingham
Augusta
Savannah River
Charleston
MISSISSIPPI
ALABAMA
Columbus
Macon
Jackson
Phenix City
GEORGIA
Alabama River
Montgomery
Altamaha River
Savannah
Albany
Atlantic Ocean
Mobile
Gulfport
Pensacola
Tallahassee
Biloxi
Panama City
Jacksonville
Gainesville
Daytona Beach
FLORIDA
Orlando
Cocoa Beach
Tampa
St. Petersburg
Sarasota
Lake Okeechobee
W. Palm Beach
Fort Meyers
Miami

Miami Beach has many hotels along the Atlantic coast. People from northern states enjoy visiting here during winter months. The weather is warm enough for swimming and outdoor sports.

There are many dairy farms near Annapolis (ə nap′ə lis), the capital of Maryland. Annapolis is the home of the United States Naval Academy.

The physical map of the southeastern states on page 191 shows that Chesapeake Bay is connected with the Atlantic Ocean by a narrow neck of water called Hampton Roads. This is one of the nation's busiest waterways. Norfolk and Newport News, in Virginia, are on Hampton Roads. Together they form the nation's largest shipbuilding center. Norfolk is the largest city in Virginia. It is the site of the biggest naval base in the United States.

To the south are Charleston, South Carolina, and Savannah (sə van′ə), Georgia. They are shipping and manufacturing cities. Both produce cotton textiles, wood pulp, other wood products, and fertilizer.

Jacksonville and Tampa, in Florida, are manufacturing and trade centers. Jacksonville, on the Atlantic Coast, makes cigars, articles of wood, and naval stores such as tar, pitch, and turpentine. It is Florida's largest city. Tampa's manufacturing plants package processed food. Phosphate ore is mined and exported from the port of Tampa.

Miami (mī am′ē), on the eastern coast of Florida, is a famous tourist city, which is also important for its ready-to-wear clothing factories. Many people fled to Miami from Cuba in the late 1950s and 1960s. Many Cubans settled in Florida.

Mobile (mō′bēl), Alabama, on Mobile Bay has one of the finest harbors on the Gulf Coast. From Central America comes *bauxite*, (bôk′sīt), the ore from which aluminum is made. Aluminum, fertilizer, cotton, and lumber products are exported. Mobile is the port for Birmingham.

Appalachian Cities

Birmingham, Alabama, is the chief manufacturing center of the southern Appalachian area. Birmingham and its neighboring cities form a large industrial region. This is a region of mining and quarrying, coking and smelting, making steel, and manufacturing iron-and-steel goods. Birmingham, Alabama's largest city, produces chemicals, transportation equipment, and processed food.

Chattanooga (chat′ə noo′gə) and Knoxville (noks′vil′), in eastern Tennessee, manufacture heavy machinery, as well as smaller articles. These cities also produce cotton goods.

Wheeling, West Virginia, and Charleston, the capital of West Virginia, are railroad centers and river ports. They are on the Appalachian Highland, where coal and oil are found. They manufacture products from oil and iron and steel. Charleston is noted for making chemicals.

Piedmont Cities

Many industrial cities in the Piedmont are old market towns. They turned to manufacturing because they were close to raw materials and had water power.

Richmond, Virginia's capital, is one of the oldest manufacturing cities of the Southeast. Richmond's factories make tobacco products, cotton goods, rayon, and paper.

Winston-Salem and Durham (dur′əm), in North Carolina, lead the world in tobacco products. Greensboro (grēnz′bur′ō), North Carolina, also started by making tobacco products. Today it is a cotton textile center, too.

Charlotte (shär′lət), the largest city in North Carolina, is the center of a group of busy towns. They specialize in cotton textiles, rayon, and knitted goods. Columbia, the capital and largest city of South Carolina, produces textiles and fertilizers.

High Point, North Carolina, was one of the first southern cities to manufacture furniture on a large scale. Today it remains a leading furniture-making center. It also makes textiles, hosiery, mirrors, paints, and shipping containers.

217

Atlanta
A Modern Boom Town

Few southern cities suffered more in the Civil War than Atlanta, the capital and largest city of Georgia. In the battle of Atlanta, the city was burned to the ground and all but destroyed. But Atlanta rose from its ashes. Today it is a booming business capital of the southeastern states.

More than 1,500 factories are located in Atlanta. They make everything from iron-and-steel goods to chemicals and textiles. Canneries in Atlanta can peaches and other southern farm products. In addition to industry, many large nationwide businesses have established their headquarters there.

Atlanta is an inland city far from the coast. No navigable river is nearby. Yet it is a transportation center. In 1837, Atlanta was chosen as the location of the southern end of a railroad. Atlanta developed as a transportation and trade center. Many farm and factory products go through Atlanta. It has one of our country's busiest airports.

Atlanta's mild climate and booming industries attract many people to the city. With the help of the national government, the city set up neighborhood centers to help people find jobs. ■

River Cities

Louisville (loo′ē vil′), Kentucky, and Memphis (mem′fis), Tennessee, are river ports. They were both market centers in early times. Now they are manufacturing and trade centers. Each is the largest city in its state. Louisville, on the Ohio River, early became a market for the products of neighboring regions. Tobacco products, furniture, paints, and varnishes, electrical goods, bricks, and tile are made there. Louisville also makes baseball bats.

Memphis, Tennessee, is a large Mississippi River port. It began as a shipping port for cotton from the nearby farms and lumber from the surrounding bottom lands. Now it has many factories too. The factories make cotton goods and cottonseed products. Memphis is the world's largest market for cotton and hardwood.

Huntington, West Virginia, is a port city on the Ohio River. It is the largest city in the state.

Montgomery (mont gum′ər ē), the capital of Alabama, is also a river port. Jackson, the capital and largest city of Mississippi, lies on the Pearl River. Both cities are manufacturing and trade centers. Many oil companies have offices in Jackson because of the nearby oil fields. Montgomery also makes lumber products.

Other Cities

Nashville, the capital of Tennessee, lies in the center of the Nashville Basin. Dairy farmers in this region sell their products in Nashville.

Horses are bought, sold, and traded in Lexington, Kentucky, and in Frankfort, the state capital. Raleigh, the capital of North Carolina, is a tobacco center. The capital of Florida is Tallahassee (tal′ə has′ē). Many of the people there have government jobs. Tallahassee is also a trading center for dairy foods, fruits and nuts, and lumber.

In some places in the Southeast, entirely new cities have been built. They are called "satellite (sat′əl īt), communities" because they are on the edge of large metropolitan areas like Washington, D.C. However, they do not depend on the metropolitan areas. These communities have their own industries and are self-sufficient. One famous satellite community is Reston, Virginia. It is a carefully-planned small city with parks, lakes, and other recreation areas. Another similar community is Columbia, Maryland.

Do You Know?

1. Why did the government set up the Tennessee Valley Authority?
2. Why do farmers in the Southeast states practice crop rotation?
3. Why do trees grow easily in the southeastern states?
4. What minerals are found in the southeastern states?
5. What cities in Virginia form a large shipbuilding center?

To Help You Learn

Using New Words

bauxite   phosphate
boll   cultivator
dam   crop rotation
gap   growing season
rayon   citrus fruit
legume   subtropical land
cannery   dehydration
soybean   naval stores
reservoir   soil erosion
frontier   cotton belt
tung oil

The phrases below explain the words or terms listed above. Number a paper from 1 through 21. After each number write the word or term which matches the definition.

1. A place like a lake, formed behind a dam, where water is stored
2. A narrow valley in mountains
3. A mineral needed for growth by plants and animals
4. The region of a country lying along the border of an unsettled region
5. The ore from which aluminum is made
6. Turpentine, tar, and resin made from the gum of the pine tree
7. A wall or bank built across a river to stop the flow of water
8. The washing away of soil by heavy rains or floods
9. Area in the South where cotton grows well
10. The time of year when crops can be grown outdoors
11. Land that lies near the tropics
12. A way of building up the soil by planting different crops on the same land every 2 or 3 years
13. A kind of legume first brought to this country from China
14. A vegetable, such as peas or beans, that grows in pods
15. A machine used to loosen the soil and uproot weeds
16. Small seed pod of the cotton plant
17. Oil made from the nuts of a tree
18. The removal, or taking out, of water by a special process
19. Oranges, lemons, and grapefruit
20. A cloth that looks and feels like silk
21. A factory where food is prepared and canned

Finding the Facts

1. What plains make up the lowland of the southeastern states?
2. What highland forms an almost unbroken chain from Maryland to Alabama?
3. Describe the land in the Bluegrass Region and the Nashville Basin.
4. What four routes did pioneers use to cross the Appalachians?
5. What crop caused planters to rush to present-day Mississippi and Alabama?

6. Why did the Creek Indians attack Fort Mims in Alabama? What was the result?
7. How are tenant farmers and sharecroppers alike? How are they different?
8. Why was the cotton gin so important?
9. Who improved agriculture in the southeastern states?
10. What did Orville and Wilbur Wright do in 1903? Why did they choose Kitty Hawk?
11. How has the Tennessee Valley Authority helped conservation?
12. What are some uses of the cotton plant?
13. What was the first money crop raised in our country?
14. What legumes, nuts, and fruits are grown in the Southeast?
15. Why are the southeastern coastal states a good fishing area? What shellfish are shipped to other parts of the country from the Southeast?
16. What different products are obtained from trees in the southeastern states?
17. What is phosphate used for?
18. Why did many northern factories move to the southeastern states?
19. What are some famous monuments in Washington, D.C.?
20. What is the capital of each southeastern state? What is the largest city of each?

Learning from Maps

1. On the map of the United States on pages 92–93 locate the southeastern states. Between what parallels of latitude do the southeastern states lie?

2. Turn to the map of the southeastern states on page 191. What body of water borders the southeastern states on the east? What body of water borders them on the south? Where are mountains found? What is the highest peak? Which southeastern state is entirely plains?

3. Look at the map of the TVA on page 201. What river flows through this area? What dams are in Alabama?

4. Now look at the cotton-belt map on page 202. Which southeastern states grow the most cotton? Turn to the rainfall map on page 17 to find how much rain the cotton belt gets.

Using Study Skills

1. **Time Line:** Arrange the following events in the correct order. Your text will help you find when each event took place.
   Kentucky becomes a state
   Alabama becomes a state
   Atlanta chosen as railroad location
   Tennessee becomes a state

2. **Chart:** Make a chart of the southeastern states like the one you made for Unit 5, page 186.

3. **Graph:** Look at the graph on page 204. In which year was the least amount of cotton produced? In which year was the greatest amount of cotton produced?
   Did the amount of cotton produced between 1971 and 1972 increase or decrease? Did the amount produced between 1973 and 1974 increase or decrease?

How much cotton was produced in 1973? About how much more was produced in 1974 than in 1971?

4. **Diagram:** Look at the diagram showing cotton processing on page 204. Arrange the steps below in the correct order.
   Gin removes seeds
   Cotton is picked
   Fibers are spun into thread
   Threads are woven into cloth
   Cotton fibers are combed

Thinking It Through

1. After the invention of the cotton gin slavery developed rapidly. If the gin had not been invented, do you think slavery might have gradually disappeared? Why or why not?
2. During the 1900s many northern factories moved to the southeastern states. How did this change the southeastern states? What might this region be like if factories had not moved there?
3. Birmingham, Alabama, is often called the "Pittsburgh of the South." How do you explain this?
4. Many Americans are moving to the "Sunbelt." The southeastern states make up part of the "Sunbelt." Why do you think people choose to move to this area?

Projects

1. You might like to make a classroom movie which tells the story of cotton. To do this, you need a roll of narrow shelfpaper. On the paper draw pictures one under the other, beginning with the planting of cotton seed and ending with pictures of finished goods made from cotton. Write short captions. Fasten each end to a short stick and show your movie.
2. Many historical buildings are still standing in the Southeast. Find as many pictures of these as you can in magazines and newspapers. Make a scrapbook or put them on a bulletin board and put labels under them.
3. The Research Committee might find out more about the Indian groups mentioned in this unit. How did the Indians live before they were forced to leave their lands? How did their lives change when they moved?
4. Pretend you work for the government of a southeastern state. Make a pamphlet explaining why a certain factory should set up a plant in your state. Include pictures in the pamphlet. Decide which state you work for and what factory you desire.
5. The Reading Committee might ask the librarian for books about the southeastern states. Try to get books about the pioneers, the Indians, the TVA, and the people you read about in this unit.

Unit Preview

In 1783 the United States reached from the Atlantic Coast to the Mississippi River. Most people lived near the Atlantic Coast. But pioneers already were looking westward.

Part of today's North Central region was, in 1783, the Northwest Territory. Five North Central states were carved from this region: Illinois, Indiana, Ohio, Michigan, and Wisconsin. After the Louisiana Territory was bought, seven other North Central states were formed from this territory: Minnesota, Iowa, Missouri, North Dakota, South Dakota, Nebraska, and Kansas.

The government set up a plan so sections of the territories could become states. Many people moved into the territories to get the free land offered by the government.

Settlers found in the region of the North Central states some of the world's best corn and wheat lands. It has remained so, but it has also become a great industrial region. The discovery of iron ore opened up this area to industrialization.

Good transportation systems have helped industries and farms in the North Central states. The Mississippi River provides a waterway for shipping products to the sea. Barges can move the products south to New Orleans. The St. Lawrence Seaway, connected with the Great Lakes, also offers access to the sea. Ocean-going ships can move between the Great Lakes and the Atlantic Ocean.

Things to Discover

If you look carefully at the picture, map, and time line, you can answer these questions.

1. How many states are in the North Central region?
2. When did Congress set up a plan of government for the Northwest Territory?
3. What important type of work done in the North Central states is shown in the picture?
4. What natural features form part of the border for some North Central states?
5. How was travel made easier after 1811?
6. What important raw material for industry was discovered in the region? When?
7. Marietta, Ohio, was the first settlement in the Northwest Territory. When was it founded?
8. When was the Louisiana Territory purchased?

Words to Learn

You will meet these words in this unit. As you read, you will learn what they mean and how to pronounce them. The Word List will help you.

bran	reaper
combine	seed drill
disk harrow	sod
expedition	sterilize
linseed oil	surplus product
open-pit mining	taconite
pasteurize	territory
prairie	threshing machine
processing	toll

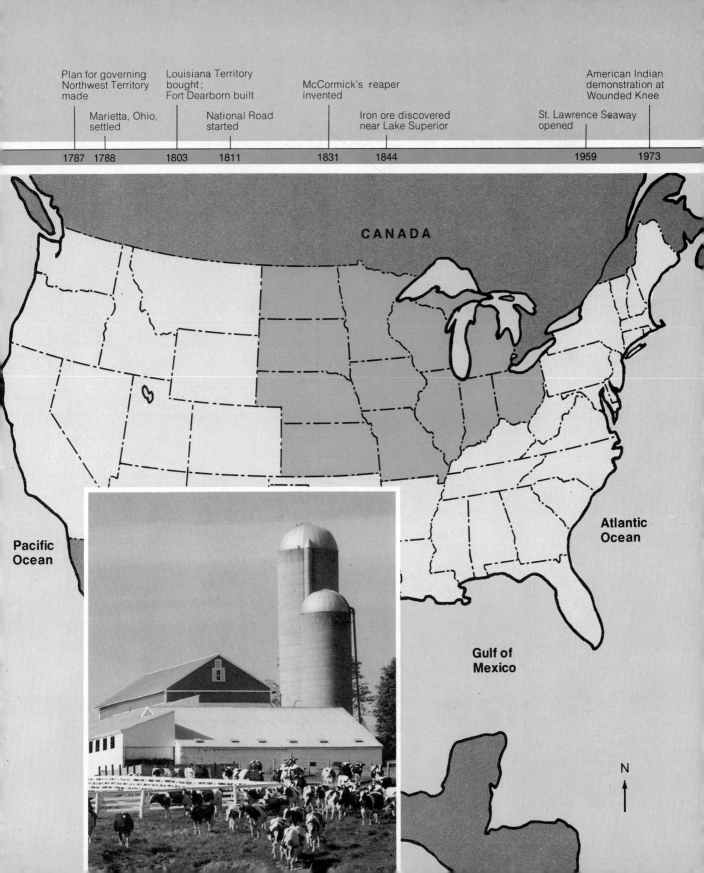

Plan for governing
Northwest Territory
made

Marietta, Ohio,
settled

Louisiana Territory
bought;
Fort Dearborn built

National Road
started

McCormick's reaper
invented

Iron ore discovered
near Lake Superior

St. Lawrence Seaway
opened

American Indian
demonstration at
Wounded Knee

1787 1788   1803   1811   1831   1844   1959   1973

CANADA

Pacific
Ocean

Atlantic
Ocean

Gulf of
Mexico

N

1

Geography of the North Central States

The North Central states are Ohio, Michigan, Indiana, Illinois, Wisconsin, Minnesota, Iowa, Missouri, Kansas, Nebraska, and North and South Dakota. Almost everywhere you go in the North Central states you see farms of one kind or another. These twelve states produce food for millions of people. Some of these states also have great industries which use the raw materials of the region.

Lakes and Rivers

The North Central states are fortunate to have great water highways. In these states are Lakes Superior, Michigan, Huron, and Erie, four of the five Great Lakes. These busy lakes make up one of the most important inland waterways in this country.

The Great Lakes are connected with each other by small rivers and lakes. They are also connected with the St. Lawrence River, which flows into the Atlantic. This forms a waterway from the middle of North America to the Atlantic Ocean.

Much of our nation's greatest river system, the Mississippi, flows through the North Central states. It drains the wide central plain between the Appalachians and the Rockies.

Giant concrete dams have been built on the Missouri River, the largest tributary of the Mississippi. Behind the dams are artificial lakes. These dams and lakes help control floods, furnish electric power, and provide water for irrigation. The Missouri River is navigable as far as

Chicago, Illinois, is on the west side of Lake Michigan. It is the largest city in the North Central states.

Sioux City, Iowa. It flows into the Mississippi just north of St. Louis.

At Cairo, Illinois, the Ohio River joins the Mississippi. Starting at Pittsburgh, the Ohio River is navigable its entire length. The Ohio and Missouri rivers help make the Mississippi a mighty river.

Soil and Surface

Thousands of years ago the great glacier that covered northern North America covered much of the North Central states. As it moved southward, it left thin soil, bare rocks, and hills in some places. For the most part it left deep, rich soil and stretches of level and gently rolling land. Because of the deep, rich soil farmers there can grow good crops. The level and gently rolling land makes it easy for farmers to use machinery. It also keeps the soil from being washed away easily by rain.

Most of the North Central states is lowland. These states are part of a plain that stretches for more than 1,000 miles (1,600 km) from the Appalachians to the Rockies. See the map of these states on page 227 and the map of the United States on pages 92 – 93 .

A rough, hilly region extends southward from Canada into Michigan, Wisconsin, and Minnesota. This is a region of lakes, forests, and rocks. Eastern Ohio is part of the Allegheny Plateau. Southern Missouri is part of the hilly Ozark Plateau. In southwestern South Dakota, the Black Hills break the stretch of rolling plains. These hills are higher than the Appalachians but lower than the Rockies.

Climate

The North Central states have a favorable climate for farming. The summers are usually hot and the winters cold. But the northern part of this region has longer, colder winters and shorter, cooler summers than the southern part. The growing season is about 4 months long in the northern part. In the southern part it is 6 months long. This is long enough for wheat, corn, and oats to grow and ripen.

The rainfall of these states is also favorable for growing many kinds of crops. Most of this region receives between 20 and 40 inches (51 and 102 cm) of rainfall each year. A few places receive more than 40 inches (102 cm). Western North Dakota, South Dakota, Nebraska, and Kansas receive less than 20 inches (51 cm) a year. Farmers there plant crops that need small amounts of rain to grow, or they irrigate their crops.

The differences in the growing season, rainfall, and temperature make parts of the North Central states better suited to one crop than to another. Because of these differences it is possible to raise a variety of crops and livestock.

Do You Know?

1. What are the twelve North Central states?
2. What is the surface of the North Central states like?
3. What great waterways are in these states?

2
Settling the North Central States

George Rogers Clark and those with him, you remember, captured the Northwest Territory from the British during the Revolutionary War. This territory stretched from the Ohio River north to the Great Lakes and as far west as the Mississippi River. Find this area on the map of the Northwest Territory on this page.

The Northwest Territory

The Northwest Territory was first claimed by France. Then the British defeated the French and gained control of it. After the Revolutionary War it became part of the new nation, the United States of America.

Several eastern states claimed part of the Northwest Territory. It had been granted to them, they said, in their colonial charters. But Maryland, which had no western lands, did not favor these claims.

"We are now under one government," Maryland declared. "All western lands should belong to the national government, not to the states."

New York led the way by giving up its claims to the western lands. One by one, the other states gave up their claims, too. The land then became a *territory* (ter′ə tor′ē) of the United States. A territory is a settled area, not yet a state, which is governed by Congress.

Plan of Government

In 1787 Congress made a plan of government for its new land. By this plan the Northwest Territory, as the whole land was called, was to be divided into smaller areas which could become states. The plan had three steps.

At first the whole territory would be controlled by Congress. A governor, secretary, and three judges would make the laws and see that they were carried out.

When there were 5,000 voters in an area, the settlers could elect their own assembly. They could make their own laws and raise money by taxes. They would also elect a representative who would advise Congress about their affairs. An area so organized became a territory.

Five states were formed from the Northwest Territory. What are they? What rivers border this territory? How do you think it got its name?

When such a territory had 60,000 free inhabitants, it could become a state. The people would write their own constitution. When Congress approved it, the territory would join the Union as a new state. It could then send a representative to Congress to help make the laws. Best of all, the new state would have the same rights that the old states had. The plan also promised the settlers certain rights in helping to govern themselves.

This plan of government was very successful.

Indians lost their land when settlers moved west. From what part of the Northwest Territory did the Indians first move? The Trail of Tears is the path the Cherokees took to Oklahoma.

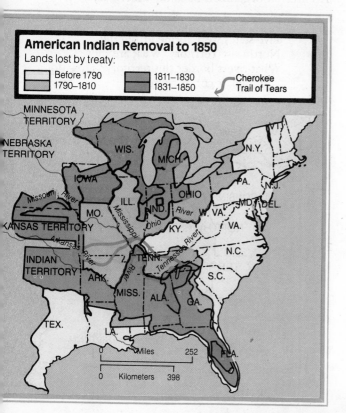

American Indian Removal to 1850

Lands lost by treaty:
- Before 1790
- 1790–1810
- 1811–1830
- 1831–1850
- Cherokee Trail of Tears

It was used as a pattern in all new territories of the United States.

Settling the Northwest Territory

Besides making a plan for governing the Northwest Territory, Congress had to decide how the land was to be settled. Should it be sold or given away to settlers? The struggling young nation needed money. So it sold large tracts of land to people who formed land companies. These companies would make money by selling the land to settlers.

First settlements in Ohio

One of the first land companies was formed by a group of citizens in Boston. They bought 1,500,000 acres (600,000 ha) of land along the Ohio River. General Rufus Putnam, who fought in the Revolution, was their leader.

General Putnam and those with him made their settlement at the mouth of the Muskingum River in 1788. They named it Marietta. It was the first settlement in the Northwest Territory under the new plan.

Another settlement made on the Ohio River was Cincinnati. Later Moses Cleveland made a settlement on Lake Erie. Find these towns on the map of the Northwest Territory, page 229.

War with the American Indians

As people moved into the Northwest Territory, they settled on lands that belonged to the American Indians. The Indians fought to keep their lands. The British, who hoped to get back the Northwest Territory, also urged the American Indians to fight the settlers. President Washington sent General Anthony Wayne to protect the settlers. At the battle of Fallen Timbers, General Wayne defeated a group of American Indians made up of the Shawnees (shô nēz′), Ottawas (ot′ə wəz), Chippewas (chip′ə wäz), and Potawatomis (pot′ə wot′ə mēz). The American Indians were forced to move from most of the Ohio region.

Settlers kept moving westward taking more American Indian lands. Tecumseh (ti kum′sə), a Shawnee chief, worked to help American Indians keep their lands. But soldiers led by William Henry Harrison defeated a group of Shawnees at the battle of Tippecanoe. The Indians were forced to move from what is now Indiana.

The last fighting in the Northwest Territory that involved the Indians was the Black Hawk War. The Sauk (sôk) and Fox Indians were defeated. They were forced to leave what is now Illinois and move to a reservation in Iowa.

Routes to the Western Lands

Settlers now poured into the region north of the Ohio River. There were four main routes used by the pioneers to get beyond the Appalachian Mountains. Beyond the mountains, the Ohio River became the great highway to the Northwest. Tens of thousands of settlers used this river to reach the western lands.

Look at the map of routes to the west on page 193. Pioneers followed the Great Valley, through the Cumberland Gap, to the Kentucky River. They followed this river northwest to the Ohio River. From the Great Valley, pioneers also followed the Kanawha River to the Ohio.

Two rough roads across Pennsylvania and Maryland led pioneers to Fort Pitt, now Pittsburgh, on the Ohio River.

Pioneers from New England and New York traveled west along the Hudson and Mohawk rivers to Lake Erie. Some continued westward along its southern shore. Others traveled on the lake. This route provided the easiest way through the mountains. After the Revolutionary War, this lowland route became important. Pioneers traveled on foot, on horseback, by covered wagon, and by boat.

Transportation by Boat

One kind of boat used by the pioneers was a flatboat. It was a flat-bottomed boat with square ends. Another kind of boat that carried pioneers was a keelboat. It was longer and narrower than a flatboat. It had a narrow platform on each side. People walked along the platform and pushed the boat through the water with long poles. Some keelboats had masts and sails that could be used too.

Moving in Covered Wagons

Those who traveled by covered wagon had to plan carefully. Heavy furniture had to be left behind. But the wagon was big enough to carry household goods and farming tools. It could carry seed corn and enough food for the long journey west.

Covered wagons were shaped like boats. They were higher at both ends than in the middle. The wheels were large. Over the tops of the wagons were curved bows which supported white canvas covers. Strong oxen pulled the

Covered wagons were a good way for families to move their belongings. These settlers are crossing the plains to the West. What animals did they take with them? Why?

wagons slowly. The rough roads made the wagons sway from side to side.

Life in a New Settlement

The pioneers had to find a place to live. Some wanted to settle in villages and towns. Others looked for farms.

Farmers often settled near a river or stream. Fine crops could be grown on the rich, level land of the river valley. The river could be used for travel.

Some farmers chose a spot where large trees grew. They thought the soil was fertile because trees grew there. Besides, trees furnished wood for building houses and fences. They also supplied fuel for the fireplace.

Other settlers were happy when they found a grassy meadow or an open place in the forest.

Here crops could be planted with little trouble. The land did not have to be cleared of trees and bushes.

As soon as possible, they planted a small patch of corn. Corn was the pioneers' best crop. It could be eaten by people as well as by animals. Corn husks were made into mattresses for the beds. The cobs were often used for fuel.

A House-Raising

Food and shelter were the things settlers needed most. Their first shelter was often a log hut with only three walls. The other side of the hut was open. The roof sloped to the ground. Such log huts sheltered many pioneers until they could build a better home.

Good neighbors were very important in helping build a more permanent home. People were glad to help new neighbors get settled.

232

There was much work to be done. Trees had to be cut down and underbrush, or thick bushes, cleared away to make room for the new home. Logs had to be carefully chosen, trimmed of branches, and cut to the right lengths.

The neighbors began to arrive early in the morning. They chopped down trees and rolled the logs to the clearing. Then they cut the logs to the right length and notched them so that they would fit together. Four logs were laid to form a foundation. Walls were made by putting one log on top of another to a height of 7 or 8 feet (2.1 or 2.4 m). The roof was made by placing poles to form a gable. The poles were then covered with shingles.

Willing hands made the work go fast. By sunset the one-room cabin was finished. The family was glad to have their new home.

Husking and Quilting Bees

Neighbors helped one another with other jobs that were too big for one family to do alone. Sometimes neighbors gathered for a husking bee. Husking meant taking the husks or outside leaves from the ears of corn. Two teams would race to husk a pile of corn. After the husking bee everyone would enjoy supper. Later everyone would enjoy a lively square dance.

A quilting bee provided another occasion for neighbors to get together. Quilts are bedcovers. The top covers of quilts are usually of patchwork, or small bright scraps of cloth sewed together. The bottom cover is often a piece of plain cloth. Layers of cotton or wool are placed between covers. Then the covers are quilted, or stitched together in lines or patterns.

Pioneers could build a log house in one day. Everyone helped. Men and women had many things to do until the job was done. What activities do you see?

Marketing Goods

By the early 1800s thousands of people had settled in the Northwest Territory. Fields of grain and pasture lands had taken the place of forests. Villages and towns had sprung up.

More corn, tobacco, hogs, sheep, and wheat than the settlers could use, or *surplus products* (sur′plus′ prod′əkts), began to be raised on the farms. People in towns and cities of the East wanted to buy these surplus products. But it cost too much to send them across the Appalachians to the eastern cities.

The pioneers in the Northwest Territory found a way to solve their problem. Many of their farms were along the Ohio River, or along the streams flowing into it. Transportation on it was easy and cheap.

"Our corn, tobacco, and pork can be loaded at our own landing," they said proudly. "Our boats can float downstream on the Ohio to the Mississippi and on down to the port of New Orleans.

"Ships come to New Orleans from Europe, the West Indies, and cities along our Atlantic Coast. We can get a good price for our products by sending them to New Orleans."

As time passed, settlers in the Ohio Country sold more and more of their products in New Orleans. They bought manufactured goods and other things they needed. So trade grew up between the Ohio settlers and the merchants of New Orleans, the great Mississippi River port.

The Louisiana Purchase

No sooner had the farmers found a place to sell their surplus products than they faced another problem. New Orleans and the land west of the Mississippi belonged to Spain.

While Washington was President, Congress made a treaty with Spain. With this agreement settlers could send their products down the Mississippi. They could land their goods at New Orleans without paying a tax.

Then the news came that Spain had given New Orleans and all the Louisiana Territory to France.

France was a great, powerful nation. It could stop the trade at New Orleans if its leader wished.

President Jefferson greatly feared that this might happen. He was also afraid that the farmers might even try to capture New Orleans themselves. That would mean war with France!

President Jefferson sent James Monroe to France to join our representative there. He hoped they could persuade France's leader to sell New Orleans and the land around it. To everyone's surprise, France offered to sell not only New Orleans but all the Louisiana Territory. This vast plains region stretched from the Mississippi River to the Rocky Mountains.

The United States agreed to buy the Louisiana Territory. It would pay 15 million dollars for the region.

When the United States bought Louisiana Territory in 1803, it doubled the size of the young nation. Much of the region of our North Central states was part of this territory. The great Mississippi River system and the rich land it drained became part of our nation.

Exploring the Louisiana Territory

Little was known about this huge region west of the Mississippi. President Jefferson asked Meriwether Lewis to lead an *expedition* (eks′pə dish′ən), or exploring party, into the region. See the map of this expedition, page 235.

Young Meriwether Lewis was President Jefferson's private secretary. He asked William Clark to go with him on this important expedition. William was the younger brother of George Rogers Clark.

The President asked Lewis and Clark to trace the Missouri River to its source, or beginning. He also wanted them to cross the mountains and find a way to the Pacific Ocean. As they traveled, they were to take careful notes about the soil, climate, animals, plants, and minerals.

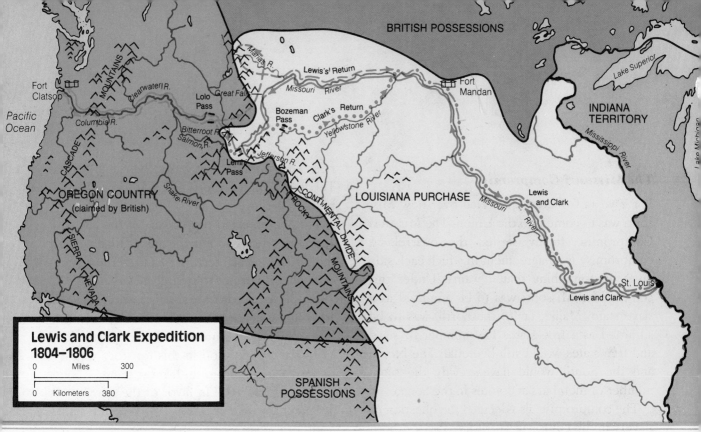

**Lewis and Clark Expedition
1804–1806**

0   Miles   300

0   Kilometers   380

Meriwether Lewis and William Clark explored the Louisiana Territory for two years. Why do you think the explorers took separate routes back?

The President also hoped they would gain the good will of the Indians living in the region.

The reports and maps that Lewis and Clark brought back gave much information. People began to realize what a huge, rich country lay beyond the Mississippi. They called it the new West. The journey of Lewis and Clark also gave our country a claim to the land between the Rocky Mountains and the Pacific Ocean. This was known as the Oregon Country.

New States: Ohio, Indiana, Illinois

By 1803 so many people lived in Ohio that Congress allowed it to enter the Union as a state. Ohio was the first state to be made from the Northwest Territory. Because the plan of government for the Northwest Territory did not permit slavery, Ohio came in as a free state. Within the next 15 years Indiana and Illinois also came in as free states.

Problems in the New West

Pioneers kept moving west. When they found much of the land in the Northwest Territory taken up, they settled in Louisiana Territory.

In 1818 Missouri asked to join the Union. It had been settled by people from the South who had slaves. So Missouri wanted to come in as a slave state. As yet no law had been made about slavery in the Louisiana Territory. Also our country had the same number of slave states as free states. This balance would be upset if Missouri became a slave state.

The Missouri Compromise

For 2 years Congress quarreled over how Missouri was to come into the Union. The Missouri Compromise finally settled the quarrel. A compromise is an agreement in which each side gives up something that it wants. Under this compromise Missouri was to be admitted as a slave state. Maine, far to the north, was to be admitted as a free state. The number of slave and free states would still be equal. The North and the South would have exactly the same number of members and votes in the Senate.

The compromise also decided the question of slavery in the Louisiana Territory. The southern boundary of Missouri was to be the dividing line between slave and free states. All new states formed north of this line except Missouri were to be free states. New states formed south of this line would be permitted to have slaves.

Kansas and Nebraska

For a while the slavery question in the Louisiana Territory appeared to be settled. Two states had been formed in this region. Each had entered the Union as the compromise stated.

Arkansas was admitted in 1836 as a slave state. It was south of Missouri. Iowa came in as a free state in 1846. It was north of Missouri. People thought the Missouri Compromise would continue to work. They were disappointed.

In 1854 a new law was presented to Congress. This law stated that the land bordering Missouri on the west and lying just north of its southern boundary would become two territo-

ries. The southern part was to be called Kansas Territory. The northern part was to be the Nebraska Territory.

No one objected to this part of the law. But another part caused much trouble. It stated that the settlers in each territory had the right to decide whether or not to permit slavery.

People began taking sides at once. "Kansas and Nebraska are north of the line agreed upon in the Missouri Compromise," said Northeners. "The slavery question in this territory was settled by that compromise. It must stand."

Southerners were in favor of the new law. It gave a chance for another slave state and more Southern senators.

Slavery became more of a problem than ever. Even the members of Congress quarreled about it. But they finally passed the law.

People soon learned what the new law meant. Neither Northerners nor Southerners were concerned about Nebraska. Everyone thought it would be a free state. In Kansas the story was different. Find Kansas on the map of the North Central states on page 227.

Since the settlers themselves could decide whether the state was to be slave or free, the race was on. Northern settlers rushed in hoping to make it a free state. Southern planters hurried there to win it for slavery. For almost 7 years there were bitter quarrels and arguments between the two groups. At last Kansas came into the Union as a free state.

Quarrels of this kind led to bitter feeling between the North and the South. As you know, the difference of opinion over slavery led to the Civil War.

Cyrus McCormick invented a *reaper* that helped farmers cut grain faster than they could cut it by hand. Cyrus is shown behind his reaper when it was tried out in 1831. People were surprised and delighted to see that the reaper really worked.

Farming on the Prairies

When the pioneers went beyond the Mississippi, they found a new kind of land. They saw miles of gently rolling plains covered with tall, thick grass. These grassy plains were called *prairies* (prer′ēz). On and on the prairies stretched. Trees were few, except along the rivers.

Some settlers chose land for their farm along the streams where there were trees. Others settled on the open prairies. It was hard work breaking the thick *sod* (sod). Sod is the part of the soil containing grass and its roots. The pi-oneers raised fine crops from the rich prairie soil. The prairie grass made good hay for pasture. Logs were scarce. Many pioneers built their homes of sod.

Cyrus McCormick, Inventor

When people learned that fine crops could be grown on the prairies, more settlers came. But harvesting had to be done by hand. It was slow, hard work. A *reaper* (rē′pər) was needed for cutting grain. Such a harvesting machine was built by Cyrus McCormick.

Cyrus was born in Virginia in 1809. There he watched his father try many times to make a reaper. Cyrus, too, began to work on the machine. He finally succeeded in 1831.

Then Cyrus McCormick moved to Chicago, Illinois, so that he could be near the prairie farms where wheat was grown. Cyrus built a factory in Chicago that made reapers.

Many farmers began to use the McCormick reaper because it saved time and money. Later, a new and strong steel plow was invented. With it the tough prairie sod could be plowed more easily. Then people by the thousands came to these grassy plains.

Free Land to Settlers

The United States doubled in size when it bought Louisiana Territory. When people wanted any of the new land, they had to buy it from the government. After a while they began to say, "The United States owns a great deal of land. Much of it has no settlers. The government should give some of it to us."

. In 1862, during the Civil War, Congress passed the Homestead Act. This was a law that permitted a person to select 160 acres (64 ha) of government land. At the end of 5 years the land belonged to the person if that person planted crops on it and lived on it.

When the Civil War ended, thousands of soldiers returned to their homes. Some wanted to begin a new life on land of their own. The Homestead Act helped them. Many families went west and lived on this government land. Some blacks also went west after the Civil War. Most settled in Kansas and started farms.

Losing More Land

Once again as people moved westward they took American Indian lands. Fighting between the American Indians and the soldiers took place. Each side won some battles. The Sioux (soo) defeated General George Custer at the battle of Little Bighorn in Montana. But later, Sitting Bull and other Sioux were trapped by the soldiers at Wounded Knee Creek in South Dakota.

Many American Indians live in the North Central states today. Most live in South Dakota. During the 1970s some American Indian groups demanded the return of some of the lands taken from them in the past. In 1973 at Wounded Knee, South Dakota, the American Indian Movement drew attention to the Indians' problems and demands. This group held the town against federal agents for 71 days. Finally the government promised to study their complaints.

Travel by Road

Today it is easy for us to travel. The pioneers were not so fortunate, however. They had to find ways to get from one part of the country to another.

The first roads followed paths made by the American Indians or wild animals. Some pioneers blazed trails through the forests. Later, these trails were widened and improved. New roads were also built. On some, logs were laid side by side. Others were made of boards or thick planks. Still others were built of stone and gravel.

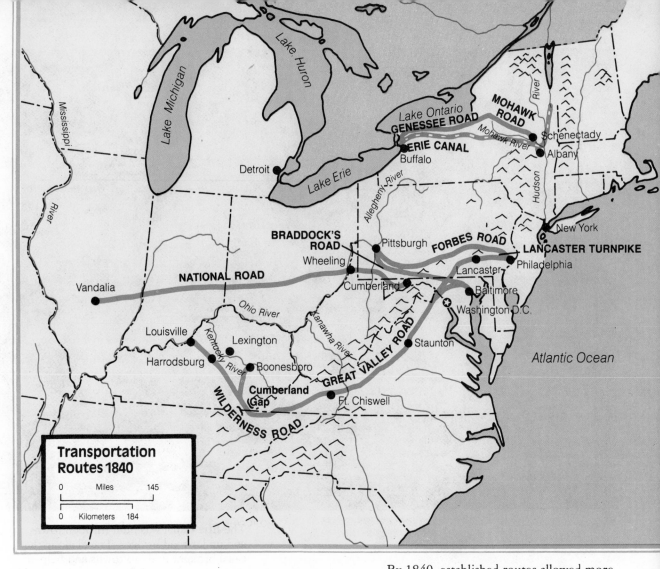

Transportation Routes 1840

0 Miles 145

0 Kilometers 184

By 1840, established routes allowed more people to move to the West. Settlers beyond the Appalachians used these routes to send their products east.

The National Road

One of the best and most important highways of its time was built by our government. This fine road was about 30 feet (9 m) wide. It was built of broken stone with stone bridges across the streams. Because the government built it, it was called the National Road.

The National Road began at Cumberland, Maryland, and went to Wheeling, on the Ohio River. It was extended westward across Ohio,

Indiana, and Illinois to Vandalia. Later, another road was added to extend the National Road to St. Louis on the Mississippi River. This was the first time our government had built a road. Find this road on the transportation map on this page. It is part of U.S. 40 today.

Travel was heavy on the National Road. Big covered wagons pulled by powerful teams of horses moved freight on it. Over it rolled farm wagons, market wagons, and buggies. Cattle,

The Erie Canal was built through towns and under road bridges. Travel along the canal brought trade to towns and helped them grow. How did boats move through the canal?

sheep, and hogs were driven to market over the road, and thousands of pioneers used it to travel westward. Later, railroads extended westward. As the railroads were built, the National Road became less important.

Toll roads

Many of the improved roads were built by business people to make money. They charged a *toll* (tōl), or money, for using the road. There are toll roads today run by governments.

Travel by Water and Rail

For years people wondered, "Can boats be moved without sails or oars?" When the steam engine was invented, people began to try to run boats with steam power.

The Clermont

In 1807 Robert Fulton proved that steam power can run boats. His boat, the *Clermont*, started in New York and puffed its way up the Hudson. The *Clermont* reached Albany in 32 hours. Here at last was a boat that did not depend on the wind. It was moved by steam power. It could even travel against the wind. This made upstream travel faster and easier. Within a few years steamboats traveled on all the important waterways.

The Erie Canal

Travel by water is cheaper than travel by land. Where there were no waterways, people often dug canals to connect bodies of water. Many canals were built during the first half of the 1800s.

The most famous was the Erie Canal, which connected the Hudson River with Lake Erie. See the transportation map, page 239. It was an all-water route between the Great Lakes and the Atlantic Ocean. Eastern merchants and manufacturers used it to send goods and supplies to the North Central states. Meat, lumber, and grain from these states went through the canal to eastern cities. Thousands of pioneers traveled part of the way to the West on the canal.

Early Railroads

By the 1830s railroads were coming into use. The first railroads were built in the East. They usually joined one town with another.

Passengers rode in cars built like stagecoaches. These early trains were uncomfortable and not very safe. The windows had no glass. The cars swayed, and it was hard for passengers to keep their seats. Sparks and cinders sometimes burned holes in clothes.

As time passed, safer, longer railroads were built. Towns and cities grew up along the railroad tracks.

The St. Lawrence Seaway

The Great Lakes and the St. Lawrence River are shared by Canada and the United States. Ships of the two countries use the lakes, their canals, and connecting rivers.

For years the people of Canada and the United States hoped to make the St. Lawrence River a seaway. To do this both the river and the waterways between the Great Lakes had to be deepened and widened. Then ocean-going vessels could sail from the Atlantic Ocean directly to cities on the Great Lakes.

In 1959 their dream came true. The two governments worked to make the St. Lawrence and the waterways between the lakes usable for larger ocean-going ships. Narrow places were widened and shallow places deepened. Canals and dams were built. It was like adding a new seacoast to many cities of the United States.

Do You Know?

1. Where was the Northwest Territory? What states were made from it?
2. What plan of government did Congress set up for this territory?
3. Why did pioneers need a Mississippi port?
4. What was the Louisiana Purchase?
5. What was the Missouri Compromise? How did the law of 1854 change it?

Before You Go On

Using New Words

sod   territory
toll   expedition
prairie   surplus product
reaper

The phrases below explain the words or terms
listed above. Number a page from 1 through 7.
After each number write the word or term that
matches the definition.

1. A settled area, not yet a state, that is
   governed by Congress
2. An exploring party
3. That which is left when needs are satisfied
4. A small sum of money paid for use of a
   road
5. A grassy plain
6. The part of the soil containing grass and its
   roots
7. A machine for cutting grain

Finding the Facts

1. Why are the North Central states an
   important farming region?
2. When would a territory become a state?
3. What Shawnee chief worked to help
   American Indians keep their lands?
4. What purchase did the United States make
   in 1803 that doubled the size of our
   country?
5. What agreement decided the question of
   slavery in the Louisiana Territory?
6. Why did Cyrus McCormick build a reaper
   factory in Chicago, Illinois?
7. How did the Homestead Act help to settle
   the West?
8. What road began in Cumberland,
   Maryland, and extended to St. Louis?
9. Who built the first successful steamboat?
10. Why was the Erie Canal important?
11. What is the St. Lawrence Seaway?

3
Living and Working in the North Central States

Farming is a very important business. It helps to feed people throughout the world. Rich farmlands make the North Central states a valuable part of our country. A large number of people make their living on farms in these states.

Important Crops

The greatest corn-growing region of our country is in the North Central states. It is called the corn belt. It stretches from Ohio to the central part of Nebraska. Find it on the map of the corn belt on page 244. Here you will find more fields of corn than of any other crop.

Throughout the corn belt the growing season is at least 5 months long. Most kinds of field corn need this much time to grow and ripen before the heavy frosts come. A heavy frost usually kills plants or stops their growth. The hot summer days and nights of the corn belt are good for corn. There are frequent showers, especially in May and June. The rich soil, the level and gently rolling land, the long growing season, and plenty of rain are just right for corn. These things combine to make the corn belt the best corn-growing region in the world.

Harvesting corn is an easy job with the help of a mechanical picker. This machine picks the corn, removes the husks, and drops the corn in a wagon.

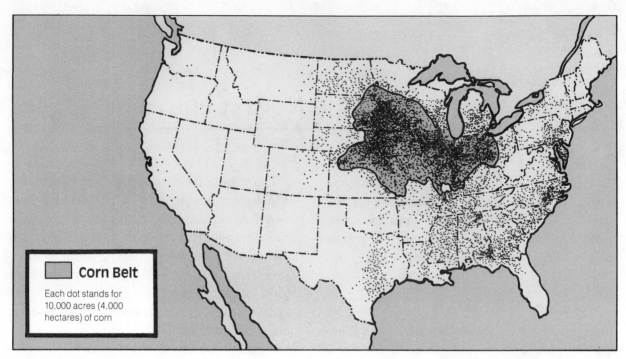

The area shaded in orange is commonly known as the corn belt. Other states grow corn too, but conditions for growing corn are best in the North Central states. Does corn grow where you live?

Besides corn, you will see fields of soybeans, oats, wheat, and hay. The farmer sells most of these crops. Soybeans are made into oil, soybean flour, and other products. A large percentage of oleomargarine comes from soybean oil. The cake left after the oil is pressed out of the beans is used to feed livestock. Iowa usually leads in growing corn in our country. Illinois is first in soybeans. Many other states in the region also raise soybeans.

Many corn-belt farmers raise cattle, hogs, and poultry to supply their own families. Indiana leads the North Central states in egg production. There are many dairy farms in the corn belt. Fresh milk and butter are sold in cities nearby. Cheese making is also a big industry.

More hogs are raised and fattened in the corn belt than in any other part of our country.

Many farmers also raise beef cattle. They send them to meat-packing centers. Some centers are Omaha, Kansas City, East St. Louis, St. Paul, St. Joseph, Des Moines, Sioux City, Cincinnati, and Ottumwa.

Uses of Corn

Most of the corn and some of the other kinds of grain are fed to animals. Instead of selling the grain, the farmers fatten their animals with it and then send them to market. Meat brings a higher price than does grain. The corn belt is the greatest meat-producing area of our country. Can you see why it is sometimes called the "meat belt"?

Corn is also made into corn bread, hominy, or mush. Breakfast cereal, syrup, and corn starch are other corn products. Paper and wallboard are made from the stalks and leaves. Even the cobs are ground and used.

Farm Work

In spring a farmer uses a tractor to plant crops. Attached to the tractor is a *disk harrow* (har′ō). The harrow has sharp steel disks shaped like saucers with cutting edges. These sharp disks make the soil fine and smooth. Using a disk harrow is faster than plowing.

Sometimes fertilizer is spread across the fields. It adds richness to the soil and brings a bigger yield of corn. Then the corn planter attached to the tractor makes furrows in the ground and drops the seeds at the same time. The cultivator loosens the soil so that rain can soak in. It also digs up the weeds.

During the summer the farmer cuts the alfalfa. This plant makes good hay. After it dries in the sunshine for several days, it will be baled and hauled to the hay barn. The farmer also harvests the oats. A *combine* (kom′bīn) cuts the ripe oats and separates the grain from the straw and chaff at the same time. The farmer uses a combine to cut all the grain on the farm.

In fall the farmer drives the tractor down the rows of corn. Behind the tractor the corn picker gathers the big yellow ears of corn. The corn picker husks the corn and puts it into the wagon.

Our Nation's Breadbasket

Every day millions of Americans eat bread made of wheat grown in the fields of the North Central states. The greatest wheat-growing region in our country is in these states. It is sometimes called our nation's "breadbasket" because so much wheat is grown there.

Wheat was not grown in America until the seed was brought from Europe. In colonial days it was grown in the northeastern part of our country. As the pioneers moved west, wheat growing spread with them. When farmers moved into Ohio, Indiana, and Illinois they found that wheat grew well in these states.

Later, when settlers reached North Dakota, South Dakota, Nebraska, and Kansas, they found good wheat land there. The soil was rich, the land was cheap, and the climate was fine for wheat. Because there was less rain than farther east, this region was better for wheat than for corn. Wheat soon became the most important crop in that region.

Wheat Farming Develops

In early days farmers in the North Central states did not have machinery to help them. Much of their work was done by hand. The farmers worked as much land as they could plant and harvest. Wheat must be harvested as soon as it is ripe; so most wheat farms were small.

During the 1800s the reaper and other new and better farm machines were put on the market. In the 1840s planting machines, called *seed drills* (drilz), were invented. These seed drills planted the seed faster and more evenly. They planted many rows at a time.

By this time, also, the iron plow had replaced the wooden plow. Still later, plows were made of steel. The steel plows easily broke up the tough sod of the prairies.

Harvesting was speeded up by the invention of the *threshing* (thresh'ing) *machine*. The threshing machine separated the kernels of wheat from the stalks. Before this time threshing had been done by beating the stalks or by driving animals over them. With a threshing machine a few people could do the work of many. Work that had once taken several days could be done in a few hours.

These new and improved machines brought about changes in farming. Work on the farm began to be done by machines pulled by horses. Later the farmers used tractors. Farms grew larger. Farmers did not have to work as hard as when they did all work by hand.

Wheat farms today are very large. Many are 300–400 acres (120–160 ha) in size. Some farms are 500–1,000 acres (200–400 ha). Many are even larger.

Today's Wheat Lands

The map of the wheat belt on this page shows that wheat is grown in many parts of the North Central states. This is called the wheat belt. Notice that the dots are closest together in Kansas and North Dakota. These are the two leading

The wheat belt stretches across the United States. What state lies completely in a shaded area? Where is most winter wheat grown? Can you name the state that grows the most spring wheat?

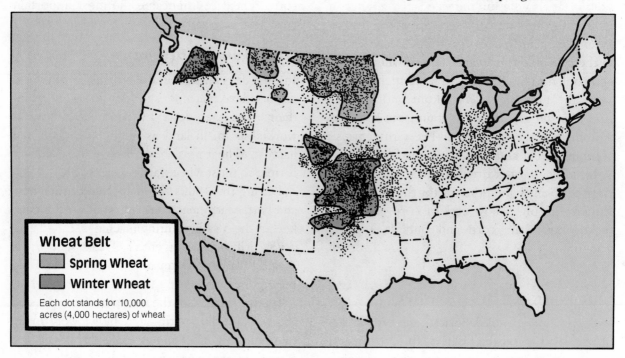

Wheat Belt

■ Spring Wheat

■ Winter Wheat

Each dot stands for 10,000 acres (4,000 hectares) of wheat

Farmers using *combines* can harvest many acres of wheat in a day. These machines can even cut wheat on hilly land.

wheat-growing states. Bismarck, the capital of North Dakota, is a shipping center for nearby wheat farms and cattle ranches. Topeka is the capital of Kansas. It is one of the wheat belt's shipping centers. Topeka has flour mills, meat-packing plants, and railroad shops which are among the world's largest.

The wheat-growing region around Kansas is called the winter-wheat region. It extends into Nebraska, Colorado, Oklahoma, and Texas. Winter wheat is sown in autumn and harvested in summer.

Two important manufacturing centers in the winter-wheat area are Omaha and Lincoln. Omaha is one of the largest wheat-storage areas in the United States. Lincoln, the capital of Nebraska, has large flour mills.

North Dakota is the center of the spring-wheat region. This region extends into Minnesota, South Dakota, Montana, and also into Canada. Winters there are too long and too cold for wheat to be sown in the autumn. Instead it is sown in spring and harvested in late summer.

Pierre, the capital of South Dakota, is a trade center for nearby farms. A railroad center and the second largest city in South Dakota is Rapid City. The largest city in South Dakota is Sioux Falls. This city is a trade center. It also has large meat-packing plants.

A Wheat Farm

Autumn is a busy time of year in the winter-wheat region. The farmer drives the tractor across the broad, level fields. Attached to it is a harrow. When the ground has been cut into very fine pieces, the farmer will sow the wheat.

The farmer attaches the tractor to the seed drill to sow the wheat. In the long box across the top of the drill are both seed wheat and fertilizer. As the tractor pulls the drill, the seeds and fertilizer slide down the many little tubes to the ground. A small disk at the bottom of each tube makes a furrow into which the seeds and fertilizer fall. Chains dragging behind the drill pull the loose topsoil over the seeds.

The wheat seeds sprout in a short time. The broad fields soon grow green and look as though they are covered with grass. Wheat plants are several inches tall by the time cold weather comes.

Toward the end of June the wheat is ready for harvest. The farmer harvests the wheat with a combine. The combine cuts the wheat and threshes it at the same time. It cuts the heads from the wheat stalks and shakes out the kernels of wheat. The chaff and the straw are left on the field. Later the straw will be tied into bundles or bales by another machine. The threshed wheat is stored in a bin in the combine. When the bin is full, the golden grain is dumped into a truck.

The wheat is hauled to town to be stored in the grain elevator. This tall building is called an elevator because the wheat is carried up, or elevated, to the top and dumped in. Buckets on a moving belt carry the wheat up.

The grain elevator is a good place for storing wheat to keep it dry, fireproof, and away from mice and rats. Later, the wheat will be shipped to grain markets or to flour-milling cities.

Farmers in the wheat region carry on mixed farming. This means they do not depend on one crop for their living. They use some of the land for pasture and some for crops to feed and fatten the livestock. The crops are usually wheat, corn, oats, and alfalfa and other hay crops. If the farm is farther west, where there is less rain, the farmer would raise sorghum in place of corn. Sorghum is a canelike grass raised for grain and feed. It does not need as much moisture as corn.

There are many risks in farming. Farmers cannot always depend on the weather. Winter snows act like a blanket. They protect the wheat plants. But too little snow may allow the roots of the wheat to freeze. Dry weather in spring keeps the wheat from growing well. If there are hot, dry winds while the kernels are forming, the kernels shrink. Heavy rains at harvest time may knock the seeds from the heads and beat the stalks to the ground. Grasshoppers and other insects may destroy the wheat. A plant disease called wheat rust may attack it. If any of these things happens, the wheat crop is poor, and the farmer loses money.

Raising Spring Wheat

In Montana, North Dakota, South Dakota, and Minnesota spring wheat is raised. Wheat grows well in the deep, rich soil of this almost level land. The rainfall is light, but there is enough for wheat. The rain comes in the spring and early summer when the wheat needs it more than at other times.

The work in the spring-wheat region is much like that in the winter-wheat region. In autumn farmers plow and prepare their fields for planting. When spring comes, they plant the wheat as fast as possible.

Spring-wheat farmers often raise oats, barley, and hay, as well as wheat. Some raise flax. The flax in this area is raised for its seed. From the crushed flaxseed *linseed* (lin'sēd') *oil* is made.

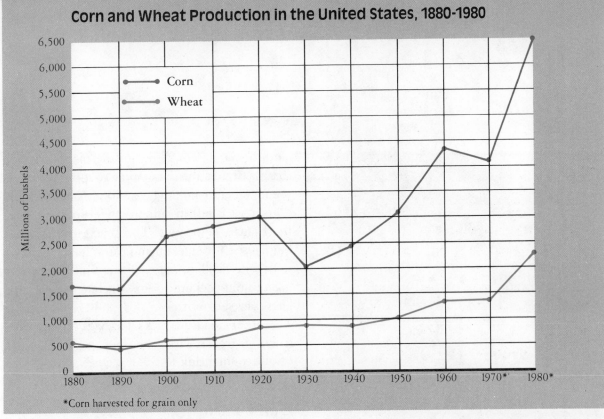

Corn and Wheat Production in the United States, 1880-1980

Millions of bushels

Corn
Wheat

*Corn harvested for grain only

This graph compares the production of corn and wheat over a long period of time. Which crop has always given more bushels? During which two periods did corn production fall?

Linseed oil is used to make paint and varnish. Many farmers, especially in the eastern part of the spring-wheat region, keep dairy cows.

Flour Milling

In the early days, farmers took their grain to millers for grinding into flour. The mill was usually built beside a stream or river. The moving water turned the big wheel on the outside of the mill. This wheel was connected with the millstones inside. As the big wheel went round and round, the heavy millstones ground the wheat into flour.

Today, most flour mills are run by electricity. Wheat from hundreds of small elevators is shipped to modern mills in big cities. It is stored there in giant elevators. A wide, moving belt carries the grain from the elevators to the top of the nearby mill. Then pipes take it from floor to floor. On the way down it passes through many machines.

From the time the wheat enters the mill until it leaves as flour, machines do all the work. Machines clean and wash the wheat and remove any dirt, sticks, or stones mixed with it. Other machines grind the wheat into flour.

In a modern mill the wheat passes between many sets of steel rollers. Each time it passes through a set of rollers it is ground a little finer. After each grinding, it is sifted. The fine silk

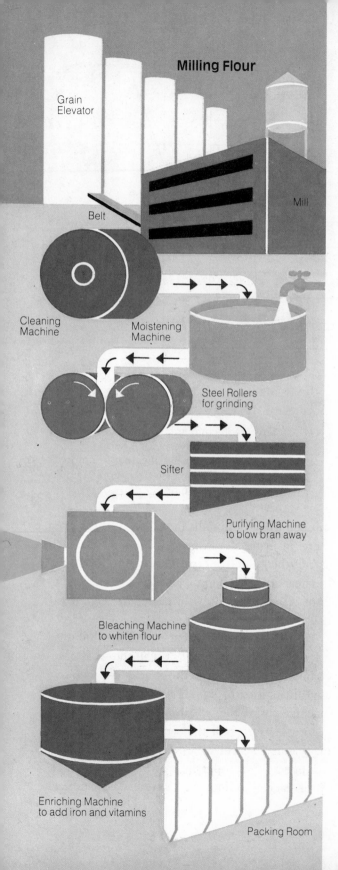

Milling Flour

Grain Elevator

Belt

Mill

Cleaning Machine

Moistening Machine

Steel Rollers for grinding

Sifter

Purifying Machine to blow bran away

Bleaching Machine to whiten flour

Enriching Machine to add iron and vitamins

Packing Room

cloth of the sifters takes out the pieces of *bran* (bran). Bran is the dark outer coat of the wheat seed. When whole-wheat flour is made, this outer coat is left in. When white flour is made, the bran is taken out. The bran is not wasted but is used for chicken and cattle feed.

When the flour is very fine and smooth, it goes to the packing room. Machines put it into bags, sacks, or boxes.

Workers load the sacks and bags of flour into trucks or freight cars. The flour goes to all parts of our country and to other lands.

Dairy Farming

You can see by the map of dairy farms on page 251 that the North Central states have many dairy farms. Wisconsin produces more milk than any other state. It is also first in cheese making. Madison, the capital of Wisconsin, is in the heart of Wisconsin's dairy region.

Minnesota has many dairy farms. It leads the nation in butter making. Minneapolis is the largest city in Minnesota, and St. Paul is the capital.

Iowa is also a leading butter producer. The capital and largest city of Iowa is Des Moines (də moin'). Des Moines is a trade and manufacturing center. It makes farm machinery and cereal products and has meat-packing plants. Many farm magazines and business papers and journals are published there.

Wheat grains go through many stages to become flour. Grinding rollers break up the kernels. What does the bleaching machine do?

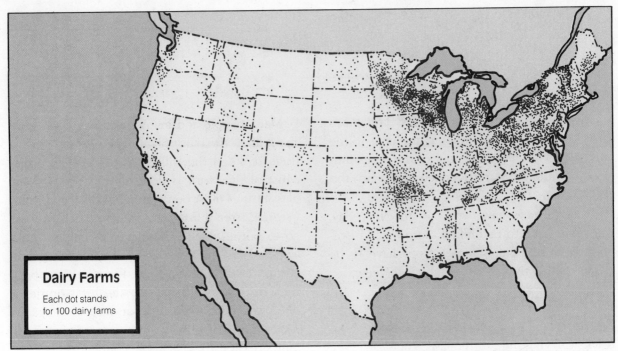

Dairy Farms

Each dot stands for 100 dairy farms

Dairy farms are found in all the states. Where are the densest areas of dairy farming? Find these areas on the crop regions map, page 19. What crop is often grown in dairy farming areas?

The dairy-region land is not as level as the land in the corn belt. Some parts are hilly and rough. Others are swampy or have many lakes. Winters are longer and colder than in the corn belt. Much hay is grown there. Dairy cows instead of beef cattle graze in the grassy pastures. There are creameries and cheese factories instead of grain elevators and stockyards in the towns. But the dairy region is as important as the corn belt.

A Dairy Farm

Sometimes there is a stream flowing through a dairy farm. Cows need plenty of water to drink. There are hayfields, cornfields, and fields of oats or other grains. Cows need grain as well as grass and hay to give rich milk.

Hay is cut green and allowed to dry in the sun before it is stored for winter feed. Oats and other grains are also raised for winter feed. The straw left after these grains are threshed is used as bedding for the cows.

The tall, round building that looks like a tower is the silo. Winter feed for the cattle is stored in the silo. Corn, clover, and alfalfa are cut while they are still green. A machine chops up the cornstalks, clover, and alfalfa into little pieces. It blows the pieces through a pipe into the silo.

The milkhouse is near the barn. This building is kept spotlessly clean. Today most dairy farmers use milking machines to milk their own cows. Anna Baldwin, a United States farmer, made the first suction milking machine. Later a Scottish inventor made a milking machine like those used today.

251

On large farms glass or stainless steel pipes carry the milk from the milking machines to the milkhouse. The milk runs out of the pipes into cans or into large, refrigerated tanks in the milkhouse.

Dairy farmers have work to do every day. The cows have to be milked morning and evening. In spring and summer crops have to be raised to feed the cows throughout the year.

The Dairy Plant

Perhaps you have seen large refrigerator tank trucks carrying milk to the city. They can carry milk long distances. They keep it cold until it reaches the dairy plant. Milk is also carried by railroad cars. Huge glass-lined tanks inside these cars keep the milk cold and clean.

Many people and many machines work with the milk at the dairy plant. There everything is done to keep the milk clean, pure, and safe. Most of the work is done by machinery. The glass bottles must be thoroughly clean and then *sterilized* (ster'ə līzd') to kill germs before they go to bottle-filling machines. The milk is *pasteurized* (pas'chə rīzd') or heated, to kill certain germs. Then it is cooled and put into the bottling machines. Each clean, sterilized bottle is filled with milk and capped at once.

Some milk is put into paper containers. This milk is pasteurized also. The containers are sterilized before they are filled. Then they are

Swiss cheese is made from fresh, sweet milk. Cheesemakers separate the solid parts of the milk from the liquid part to form the cheese.

dipped in hot paraffin, a kind of wax. Paraffin makes them strong and keeps them from leaking. When the containers are filled, they are put into wooden boxes, ready to be sent to grocery stores or to your home.

Some dairy farmers live too far away to send fresh milk to the city. Some of them separate the rich, yellow cream from the milk and sell it to creameries. There it is made into butter. Farmers sometimes sell their fresh milk to cheese factories.

Dairying in the Past and Today

When our country was first settled, most farmers carried on general farming. They raised grains and other crops. They kept a few cows to furnish milk, butter, and cheese for themselves. Sometimes they had more than they could use. At the village store they traded what they did not need for groceries and other supplies. Other farmers kept a few extra cows. They sold their surplus milk and butter to regular customers in towns and cities.

After a while farmers became interested in dairying as a business. They brought good breeds of dairy cattle from Europe. These cows gave more and richer milk. The invention of the cream separator made it easier for them to separate cream from milk. A test for butterfat helped farmers decide which cows were giving the richest milk. They received a better price for the milk which had more butterfat in it. Refrigerator cars made it possible to send dairy products longer distances. Milking machines made it easier for farmers to have large herds. Milk and cream are used in many ways. The milk may be used fresh. It may be made into ice cream, cottage cheese, butter, and cheese, or into evaporated, condensed, or powdered milk. Many products have been made from milk by treating it in special ways. These products include paint, cloth, glue, and plastics.

Vineyards and Orchards

Many people think of the Great Lakes only as a fine water highway. Fruit growers along the shores of Lake Michigan and Lake Erie value them for another reason. The lakes help to make these shores a fine fruit region.

Winds in the northern part of the United States come mostly from the west. Before these westerly winds reach the fruit lands, they have been blowing over water. In spring the water of the lakes is cold. The winds are cooled by blowing over this cold water. This slows down the blossoming of the fruit trees until there is little danger of frost. If frost kills the blossoms, the trees will bear no fruit.

During the summer the water in the lake is heated by the sun. In the fall the water stays warm long after the land has cooled. Winds blowing over this warm water take the warm air with them. This protects the orchards and vineyards until the fruit ripens. Find the fruit-growing region on the products map on page 254.

Lumbering

When settlers first came to the Northwest Territory, forests covered most of the land east of the Mississippi River. The pioneers cut down

**Products of the
North Central States**

the trees. They built their homes, barns, and fences of them. From trees they made flatboats, keelboats, and canoes. They used some for fuel. Many trees were cut down to make room for fields of grain or just to clear the land.

The settlers did not realize they were ruining our forests. So far as they knew, there were trees enough to last forever. They could not know that a time would come when people would need to conserve, or save, the forests of the United States.

Lumbering was an important industry in the region around the Great Lakes by the time the Civil War ended. In the winter lumberers cut down trees and sawed them into logs. They hauled them in wagons to the frozen rivers and streams. Sometimes oxen or horses dragged them over icy roads. In spring the ice in the riv-

ers melted. Then the lumberers moved the logs down the rushing rivers to the sawmills.

The mills were usually built where rapids or falls in the river furnished power. Factories using wood to make carriages, furniture, and wagons often grew up near the mills.

Lumber from these forests helped build many cities and towns along the Great Lakes. It helped build new settlements on the treeless plains of Missouri and Kansas, too.

Like the pioneers, lumberers seemed to think these forests would last forever. Often they cut down all the trees in a region but used only the best timber. The rest was left on the ground to rot.

Once these forests produced much lumber. Today only a little lumbering is done in the Great Lakes region. Other forests there have been set aside as national forests so they are protected. Through careful cutting and the planting of young trees, the Great Lakes region may again be an important source of lumber.

Mining in the North Central States

The North Central states contain mineral riches the pioneers never dreamed were there. These mineral resources are important for this region, and for the whole country.

The United States, as you have read, is one of the world's leading manufacturing nations. But manufacturing would not be possible without plentiful supplies of such minerals as coal, iron, lead, petroleum, and zinc.

Lead, Zinc, and Other Minerals

Missouri leads our country in the production of lead. This soft, heavy, bluish-gray metal is used to make storage batteries, paint, and pipes. It is also used around electric wires and in nuclear energy plants to protect people from the deadly rays. There are many lead mines in the Ozark Plateau. Find this plateau on the map of the North Central states on page 227.

The Ozark Plateau also produces zinc. Zinc is used in electric batteries and in paint. It makes a good coating for iron, because it does not rust easily.

Lead and zinc are two important mineral resources. What North Central states have deposits of these metals? Much lead and zinc is found farther west, but it is used by industries of the North Central states.

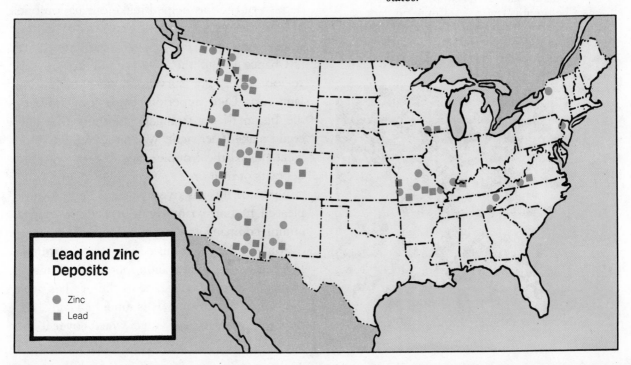

Lead and Zinc Deposits

● Zinc

■ Lead

The oil fields here supply some of the gasoline, fuel oil and natural gas needed in the North Central states. Look at the map of oil fields and pipelines on page 292. In which states might you expect people to make a living in the oil industry today?

The coal map on page 175 shows that bituminous coal is found in these states. The fields in Indiana, Illinois, and eastern Ohio are among our nation's leading coal fields. They supply fuel to run factories and to heat homes and offices. Some coal is sent to lake ports for shipment. Deposits of brown-black coal, a soft coal known as lignite, are found in the Dakotas.

South Dakota leads our nation in gold production. At Lead, in the rich Black Hills region, is the largest gold mine in the United States.

This is what natural copper looks like before it is *processed*. Copper is dark gold in color and is made into many different things. Jewelry is sometimes made with copper. What coin is entirely made of copper?

Limestone, sand, and clay are also found in this region. Limestone, as you know, is used to make cement and iron. Sand is used in making glass. Clay is made into bricks and pottery.

Long before Europeans came to this country, American Indians mined copper in northern Michigan. When the French came, they were more interested in looking for furs. They did nothing with the copper.

Years afterward the Michigan copper mines became the most important in our country. Today Michigan does not produce as much copper as it once did.

Iron Ore, a Great Mineral Resource

Our nation's greatest iron-mining region is near the western end of Lake Superior. See the iron and copper map on page 178. This great deposit of ore has helped make our nation one of the greatest producers of iron ore in the world.

Chance led to the discovery of iron in this region. One day surveyors were measuring land near Lake Superior. Their compass needle began to act strangely. Nothing they did could make it act right. When they tried to find what caused the trouble, they discovered large deposits of iron ore.

News of this discovery spread. People were pleased to find so much iron. They formed a mining company and began to mine the ore.

Some of the ore is buried deep in the ground. It is reached by shafts and tunnels, which make it expensive to mine. Some of the ore lies near the top of the ground. It is mined cheaply, for the layers of earth and gravel which cover it are

Open-pit mining is used to mine iron ore in parts of Minnesota. The ore is taken by trucks or railroad cars to docks on Lake Superior. Ships carry the ore to iron and steel centers.

easily stripped off. Large power shovels scoop up the ore. As they dig deeper and deeper into the ground, they make a huge pit or hole. This method of mining is called *open-pit mining* (mī′ning). The largest open-pit mine in the world is in Minnesota, about 70 miles (112 km) northwest of Duluth.

Most of the ore from this region is shipped from the lake ports of Duluth and Superior. Find them on the map of the Great Lakes waterway system on page 258. Long trains of freight cars loaded with reddish-brown ore move from the mines to these ports. They move out on the great loading docks high above the water and then dump the ore into bins beneath the tracks. For 8 months of the year the Great Lakes are free of ice. During this time freighters carry the ore to such iron-and-steel centers as Gary, Indiana, and Detroit and Cleveland, Ohio. From Cleveland and other places on the Great Lakes some of the iron ore is sent to Pittsburgh. What route does it follow?

Miners know that the rich ores around Lake Superior cannot last forever. After long, hard work they learned how to take the iron out of certain kinds of rock. One of these iron-bearing rocks is called *taconite* (tak′e nīt).

Taconite has small amounts of iron scattered through it. To use the iron in a blast furnace, it must be removed from taconite rocks in a special way. After the rock is mined, it is ground and crushed into a powder as fine as flour. The iron is removed and formed into small balls of nearly solid iron. When the balls are baked, they are ready to go into blast furnaces. There is a good supply of taconite in Michigan, Wisconsin, and Minnesota. The Lake Superior region can supply iron for many years to come.

Many workers are needed to mine these ores and process them. Mining companies have built houses, shipping centers, churches, schools, power plants, and other buildings near their plants. In this way whole new towns have grown up.

A Trip Through the Great Lakes

The Great Lakes are one of the world's busiest and most important inland waterways. They provide cheap transportation for shipping. Let us follow a freighter with a cargo of iron ore as it goes down the Great Lakes from Duluth to Cleveland.

On lake freighters the space between the pilot house and engine room is called the hold. Cargo is carried in the hold. We can look down through the hatches, or openings in the deck, into the hold.

The ore-loading dock rises above us as our ship anchors by it. Steel chutes, or tubes, from bins in the dock are let down through the openings into the hold. Soon reddish-brown ore comes rumbling and thundering down the chutes. Within a few hours the last of the ore thunders into the hold. Then all of the hatches are covered. The freighter is ready to leave.

Rapids, Locks, and Canals

The map on this page shows the Great Lakes and the rivers and other narrow waterways that connect them. Rapids and waterfalls in the connecting waterways made it hard to travel on the lakes in early times. The Welland Canal was dug around Niagara Falls so that boats could go be-

The map shows some of the routes used to take products from the Great Lakes to the sea. The diagram below shows the different altitudes of the Great Lakes. How do ships move to another level?

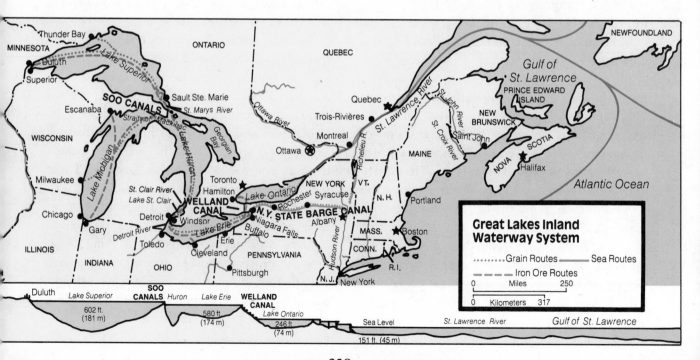

258

This freighter on Lake Superior near Silver Bay, Minnesota, is filled with iron ore. It will travel the Great Lakes Inland Waterway System to its final destination.

tween Lake Erie and Lake Ontario. The Soo Canals were built around the rapids in St. Marys River, which joins Lake Superior and Lake Huron. One canal is on the United States side of the river. The other is on the Canadian side.

Lake Huron is 22 feet (7 m) lower than Lake Superior. Ships passing through the canals are lifted or lowered that distance. This is done by giant locks. Locks are large boxes set up in the canal. They are made of concrete with a gate at each end. The locks are part of the canal.

Through the Soo Canals

The freighter enters Lock No. 3. The water in it is at the level of Lake Superior. Slowly our ship glides into the lock. We notice that the gate in front of us is closed. Then the heavy gate behind us swings shut. We are cut off from the rest of the canal. Slowly the water is let out of the lock. The freighter sinks lower and lower.

We see more and more of the walls of the lock. At last the water in the lock is level with the water in St. Marys River. The big gate in front of us swings open. With a short blast of our whistle we steam out of the lock. We continue on our way down the quiet, tree-lined St. Marys.

From St. Marys River we steam across Lake Huron. Then we pass through the St. Clair River and Lake St. Clair.

Delivering the Iron Ore

The freighter passes through the Detroit River and into Lake Erie. We soon enter Cleveland's outer harbor. There we pull alongside a row of huge machines. These are cranes with giant scoops attached to them. Each scoop takes about 20 tons (18 metric tons) at a bite. The hatch covers come off. The freighter will be unloaded in a few hours.

Vacation Lands

The Great Lakes and the lands around them are good places for rest and play. The sandy beaches and the beautiful scenery along the lakes attract thousands of summer visitors. They stay at motels, hotels, and tourist camps along the shores.

Some people like to take a cruise on the big passenger ships. Others find pleasure in sailing boats or using speedboats on these lakes. Still others find good fishing in the region. Sand dunes in Indiana and Michigan also attract visitors to the Great Lakes region.

Each year many people visit the national parks of the North Central region. Isle Royale National Park is a Michigan island in northern Lake Superior. Its woods have many animals and plants. Voyageurs National Park in northern Minnesota is known for its fishing. Wind Cave National Park is located in the Black Hills of South Dakota. The park has American Indian sites in addition to an interesting cave.

Cities, Manufacturing, and Trade

The North Central states are one of the important manufacturing regions of the country. From their forests, mines, and farms come raw materials to be made into usable products in their factories.

Many factories in the North Central states get power from oil or natural gas. The map on page 292 shows the main oil pipelines. The region's factories use electricity, too. In many places, coal is burned to make this electricity. Electricity is also made in nuclear energy plants.

Beautiful Birch Lake near Ely, Minnesota, is fine for canoeing and fishing. Besides the Great Lakes, the North Central states have many smaller lakes people can enjoy.

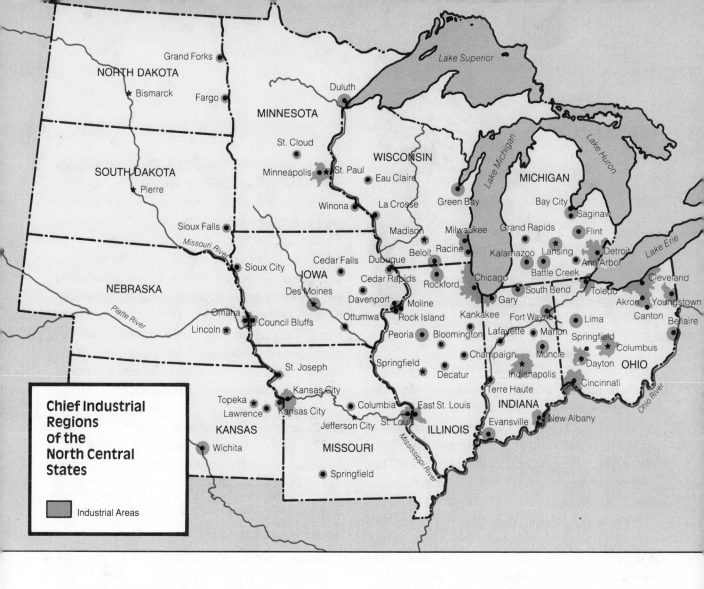

Chief Industrial
Regions
of the
North Central
States

Industrial Areas

Tens of thousands of people in this region earn their living by *processing* (pros'es sing) food. Processing means preparing food for marketing. Meat packing is a leading industry in many cities and towns. Flour mills are scattered throughout the wheat lands. Illinois, Michigan, and Minnesota have canneries, where vegetables are canned or quick-frozen.

Factories making farm machinery have also grown up in these states. Transportation costs are less when this heavy machinery is made near farms where it is used.

Manufacturing and Trade Centers

Many cities of the North Central states have gained importance through manufacturing. But they also serve as trade centers for the people of the area. Farmers take their products to nearby cities and sell them. In the cities they buy the things they need. People from smaller communities also shop in cities near them.

Many other mills and factories in this area depend upon iron and steel for the products they make. Indianapolis, the capital of Indiana, needs iron and steel for its automobile parts, trucks,

Like most major cities in the North Central states, Milwaukee, Wisconsin, has large railroad yards.

airplane motors, and heavy machinery. Indianapolis also makes chemical products and has meat-packing and vegetable-canning plants.

Wichita, Kansas, is an important farm machinery and airplane manufacturing center. This city, which lies in the oil fields, also makes oil-well equipment.

Milwaukee, Wisconsin's largest city, manufactures much heavy machinery. Because it is on Lake Michigan, it has cheap water transportation for its shipping. Some of Milwaukee's leading products are automobile frames, large gas engines, power shovels, and tractors. The people of Milwaukee also manufacture food products, leather goods, paper products, and other goods.

Some industries in the North Central region get their raw materials from other parts of our country or even from foreign lands. The rubber industry of Akron, Ohio, gets its natural or crude rubber from across the ocean. Akron is often called the rubber capital of the world because so many rubber products are made there. The leading product is automobile tires.

Columbus, the capital of Ohio, is another trade and manufacturing city in this area. It makes much mining machinery. It has machine shops, meat-packing plants, and other factories. Cincinnati, on the Ohio River, is well-known for its soap, machine tools, and other products.

Omaha, on the Missouri River, is another river port. It is the largest trading and manufacturing city in Nebraska. To it come products from the surrounding farms. Omaha has become one of the largest livestock markets in the nation. It is also an important grain market. Most of its manufacturing is connected with the processing of food. There are also many insurance companies located in Omaha.

The North Central states have many very large cities. All are important in manufacturing. Let us look at the largest of these cities.

Chicago, Great City on Lake Michigan

Chicago, near the southern end of Lake Michigan, is one of the three largest cities in our country. Both France and England once claimed the land where Chicago now stands. In 1783 this land became part of the United States. Twenty years later Fort Dearborn was built at the mouth of the Chicago River. When steamboats and railroads came, Chicago grew rapidly.

Many settlers from the East journeyed to Chicago by boat and made their homes on the nearby prairies. In a few years they were sending their surplus grain and cattle to Chicago. Some of these products were used in Chicago, but many were shipped to busy cities in the East. In exchange, these cities shipped manufac-

262

The trading and industrial city of Detroit, Michigan, is built out to the very edge of the Detroit River. Recently the people of Detroit rebuilt this waterfront area.

tured goods to Chicago. This growing city soon became the trading center for the rich farming region around it. Today it is the most important marketing center in the North Central states.

Chicago is the greatest railroad center and air center in our nation. It is also easily reached by trucks, river barges, and lake freighters.

In the Chicago area many foodstuffs are prepared for market. Corn is made into all kinds of corn products. Chicago is the center for this industry. It is also a busy grain market. Chicago leads all our cities in the manufacture of farm machinery. It is also an important iron-and-steel center. Chicago's position on the Great Lakes provides cheap transportation for bringing raw materials to its factories. The finished products can also be shipped out cheaply to all parts of the world.

Detroit, the Motor City

When the French were in the Northwest, they built a fort and trading post on the narrow river between Lake Erie and Lake St. Clair. Today the city of Detroit stands where the old fort stood. It is one of the country's largest cities.

Detroit's good location on the Great Lakes makes it a fine industrial and trading center. Detroit ranks first in the manufacture of automobiles. So many automobiles are made in Detroit that it is called the Motor City. Other important products of Detroit's factories are machinery, brass and bronze products, tools, chemicals, medicines, and paints.

Automobiles and their parts are also manufactured in the Michigan cities of Flint, Pontiac, and Lansing. Lansing is the capital and trade center for surrounding farms.

St. Louis
Gateway to the West

St. Louis, Missouri became the "Gateway to the West" after the Louisiana Purchase. Wagon trails led out from St. Louis. Steamboats once docked at St. Louis. Major overland trails to the western lands also began in St. Louis. Western products were sent to St. Louis to be distributed over the country by river and land. St. Louis was an important Missouri and Mississippi River port.

Today St. Louis is still the Mississippi River's most important inland port. Diesel-powered towboats push barges up and down the river between St. Louis and New Orleans. The barges are loaded with products. Do you remember why shippers like to send heavy materials by water?

The Missouri River, too, continues to help St. Louis. Look at the map on page 261 showing the industrial regions of the North Central states. What cities shown here are on the Missouri River? Why is St. Louis a good outlet for their river trade?

As in the past, the city is still a major railroad center. Airlines and good highways make reaching St. Louis easy. They also help make St. Louis an important center for receiving and shipping goods. Why does St. Louis attract industries?

Look at the picture of the Gateway Arch. Can you tell why the Arch is a monument to the present as well as to the past importance of St. Louis? █

Cleveland, Ohio, depends a great deal on the iron and steel industry. These ships are delivering steel mill supplies. The city's skyline is seen in the background.

Cleveland, Largest City on Lake Erie

Iron ore and coal help many people make a living in the cities along Lake Erie's southern shore. The map of the North Central states on page 227 shows how close these cities are to the important coal fields of the vast Appalachian Plateau.

Cleveland is important as a manufacturing and trading center and port on Lake Erie. You have already seen that it is among the world's largest receiving ports for iron ore. The St. Lawrence Seaway also gives it a large overseas trade. Cleveland was laid out at the mouth of the Cuyahoga (kī ə hô′gə) River in 1796 by Moses Cleveland. From a trading post, it has grown to be the largest city in Ohio, and one of the largest cities in the United States.

Much of Cleveland's work is carried on in the wide, flat valley of the Cuyahoga River. Here are railroad tracks, lumber yards, power plants, blast furnaces, steel mills, and docks. Cleveland's factories make a variety of products. But iron and steel and the products made from them are the most important manufacturing done in this lake city.

More than 2 million people live in the metropolitan area around Cleveland. The city's industries and other activities provide most of these people with jobs.

Toledo, a Lake and River Port

Toledo is another important port on the southern shore of Lake Erie. It is also at the mouth of a river. Along its banks are docks, factories, and railyards.

Thousands of cars of coal come into Toledo each year. They bring coal from mines in Ohio, Kentucky, and West Virginia. At Toledo's coal docks huge machines pick up the coal cars and lift them into the air. They turn them upside down and dump the coal into the holds of waiting lake freighters. The freighters carry the coal up the lakes to Detroit, Milwaukee, Gary, Chicago, and Duluth. Toledo is a major shipper of soft coal, or lignite. Leading industries make automotive parts and glass. Oil refining and the making of food and metal products are among its other industries.

Kansas City, Two Cities on the Missouri

Kansas City, Missouri, and Kansas City, Kansas, began as river towns. Today Kansas City, Missouri, is the larger. These cities are so close together they are like one big city.

Kansas City is one of our largest livestock markets and an important meat-packing center. Good railroads make it easy to send the meat products to markets in all parts of our nation. This district is also an important grain market and one of our country's leading flour-milling centers.

There are other kinds of mills and factories in the Kansas City area. But most people earn their living doing work connected with livestock from western ranches and wheat from farms in the surrounding country.

Another trade center on the Missouri River is Jefferson City, the capital of Missouri. Jefferson City handles the products of the surrounding farms.

Minneapolis and St. Paul, Twin Cities

Minneapolis and St. Paul, Minnesota, are often called the Twin Cities. St. Paul is on the eastern bank of the Mississippi River. Minneapolis, on the western bank, is a few miles upstream from St. Paul. Barges can now go up the river right into the heart of Minneapolis. Barges carry great loads of oil, gasoline, coal, and machinery to this city. St. Paul is the capital of Minnesota. But both cities share in the trade and other business of the region around them. On the map of the North Central states on page 227 find these Mississippi River cities.

Minneapolis, now the larger of the twin cities, grew up at the Falls of St. Anthony. The falls supplied water power for the early settlers to saw logs from the nearby forests. Later wheat became important on the western plains. Then the power of the falls was used to grind grain. Flour mills were built close to the falls. Minneapolis became an important flour-milling center. Today along with Buffalo and Kansas City it is one of our nation's leading flour-milling cities.

The Minneapolis-St. Paul district has stockyards and meat-packing plants. Of the dairy products produced, butter is the most important. Farm tools are also made there.

The North Central states have fertile land, a climate good for farming, and important minerals. These states have some of the largest cities in our country. In them the products of farms, mines, and forests are sold, processed or manufactured, and shipped out. This region is one of our country's chief farming, mining, and manufacturing areas.

Do You Know?

1. What is the corn belt? Why is it a good place to grow corn?
2. Where is wheat raised?
3. What industry developed in the Great Lakes region by the time the Civil War ended?
4. What are the chief minerals of this area?
5. What are some of the largest cities in the North Central states? How many are lake and river ports?

To Help You Learn

Using New Words

bran
combine
prairie
territory
disk harrow
seed drill
linseed oil
sod

taconite
reaper
sterilize
pasteurize
processing
threshing machine
open-pit mining

The phrases below explain the words or terms listed above. Number a paper from 1 through 15. After each number write the word or term that matches the definition.

1. A machine with sharp, curved steel blades, used to break up lumps of earth
2. A machine which cuts grain and separates kernel from straw
3. To kill germs in milk by means of heat
4. The darker, outer coat of a wheat seed
5. A machine which separates kernels of grain from stalks
6. A machine used to plant wheat or other small grains
7. To kill germs
8. A product made from crushed flaxseed
9. Preparing food for marketing
10. Mining done on the surface of the earth
11. An ore-bearing rock with iron in it
12. Settled area, not yet a state, governed by Congress
13. A wide, grassy plain
14. A machine used to cut grain
15. The part of the soil containing grass and its roots

Finding the Facts

1. What twelve states are called the North Central states?
2. What is the climate of the North Central states like?
3. Why was the plan of government set up for the Northwest Territory important?
4. What was the Louisiana Purchase?
5. How did the government provide free land to settlers?
6. How has the St. Lawrence Seaway helped cities along the Great Lakes to grow?
7. Why is farming a big business in the North Central states? What do most farms in this region grow or raise?
8. What happened to the forests which the North Central states once had?
9. Below is a list of persons whom you met in Unit 7 and descriptions of these people. Match the persons with their descriptions.

    Clark   Jefferson
    McCormick   Baldwin
    Putnam

    a. I was President when the Louisiana Territory was bought by the United States.
    b. I captured the Northwest Territory from the British.

c. I invented a harvesting machine, called a reaper.

d. I helped to found the first settlement in the Northwest Territory.

e. I made the first suction milking machine.

10. What minerals are mined in this region?

11. Why are these cities important: Chicago, Cleveland, Detroit, St. Louis?

Learning from Maps

1. On the map of the United States, on pages 92–93, find the North Central states. Between what parallels of latitude do these states lie? Which states border the Great Lakes? Which border the Mississippi? The Missouri? The Ohio?

2. Use the scale of miles on the map of the North Central states on page 227 to find the distance between: (a) Cincinnati and Chicago; (b) St. Louis and Cleveland; (c) Minneapolis and Chicago; (d) Milwaukee and Kansas City.

3. On the population maps on pages 448 and 125 find the areas of greatest population in the North Central states.

4. Find the corn belt on the crop regions map (page 19), the map of the North Central states (page 227), and the corn belt map (page 244). What states are in it?

5. Use the Great Lakes map on page 258 to trace a cargo of iron ore from Duluth to Cleveland. Name the lakes, rivers, and canals through which it travels.

Using Study Skills

1. **Time Line:** Make a time line for this Unit. Put in the dates for these events: Fulton makes steamboat; railroads come into use; Congress passes the Homestead Act.

   Put in the date when each North Central state was admitted to the Union. Use the chart on page 459 to help you.

2. **Chart:** Make a chart of the North Central states like the one you made for Unit 5, page 186. Use the chart on page 459, your text, an almanac, and encyclopedias.

3. **Outline:** Make an outline of the development of wheat farming. The outline has been started for you below.

Wheat Farming Develops
   I. In early days
      A. Work done by hand
      B. Most farms small
   II. During the 1800s
      A. New and better farm machines
         1. reaper
         2.
         3.
         4.
         5.
      B. Horses pull machines
      C. Farms larger
   III. Today
      A.
      B.

4. **Diagram:** Look at the diagram on page 250. What does this diagram show? How does wheat get from the grain elevator to the mill? What does the first machine do to the wheat? What does the purifying machine do? What machine makes the flour white?

5. **Graph:** Look at the graph on page 249. What does this graph show? Which crop did the United States produce more of each year between 1880 and 1970? Did the production of corn increase or decrease between 1920 and 1930? Did the production of wheat increase or decrease between 1910 and 1920? About how many more bushels of corn were produced in 1960 than bushels of wheat?

Thinking It Through

1. Each of the events in the first list was the cause of an event in the second list. Match the causes and the results.

   Causes
   A. George Rogers Clark captured the British forts in the Ohio Valley.
   B. Congress passed the Homestead Act.
   C. The American Indians were forced to move from most of the Ohio region.
   D. President Jefferson bought the Louisiana Territory from France.
   E. The Missouri Compromise was passed by Congress.

   Results
   a. The question of slavery was settled in the Louisiana Territory.
   b. The area of the United States was doubled.
   c. The Northwest Territory became a part of the United States.
   d. Pioneers went west to settle on free land.
   e. Settlers moved into the Northwest Territory in great numbers.

2. Why are rivers an important means of transportation, even in the jet age? What kinds of goods usually go by water?

3. On what river is St. Louis situated? Why did industries like those shown in the pictures on page 261 grow up there?

4. Why did Detroit become the leading automobile city? Why do you think Kansas City became a meat-packing center? What is the leading industry in your city? Why did that industry become important?

Projects

1. Chicago is the meeting place for more lines of transportation than any other city in our country. Railroads, waterways, bus lines, and air routes serve the city. The Explorers' Committee might secure maps showing the lines of travel which make Chicago the greatest transportation center in our country.

2. Several large cities in the North Central states grew up on spots where forts or trading posts once stood. The Research Committee might find out about the early history of some of these cities. Use the encyclopedia and start with Chicago. Be sure to include St. Louis, Detroit, and Cincinnati also.

3. Draw pictures of the pioneers as they moved westward on their way to settle the Northwest Territory or of the pioneers at an activity that drew neighbors together.

4. Collect pictures of farm machines from magazines or newspapers for your scrapbook. Find out how each works.

5. Find out what articles are made or what foods are processed in your town or city. Make a list of the articles and foods.

6. The Explorers' Committee might show principal routes the pioneers used to travel west by land and by water.

7. The Reading Committee might ask the librarian to help them plan an exhibit of stories and poems of pioneer days.

8 The South Central States

Unit Preview

The four South Central states are Arkansas, Louisiana, Oklahoma, and Texas.

When the United States became independent, New Orleans and all lands west of the Mississippi were claimed by other nations. Later, in 1803, the United States purchased New Orleans and the Louisiana Territory from France.

When Mexico became independent of Spain, Texas was part of Mexico. Soon Texas became an independent nation. Nine years later, Texas became part of the Union.

Oklahoma was once known as Indian Territory. The government set aside lands there for the Indians. In 1889, the area was opened to settlers.

Most of the people who rushed to Oklahoma were looking for land to farm. Farming is still important in all the South Central states. The eastern part of this region is like the Southeast. It has the same climate and crops. Cotton, rice, and sugar are important products. In the drier western part of the South Central states cattle and sheep are raised.

But the region's greatest wealth lies under the ground. Bauxite, from which aluminum is made, and petroleum are its most important minerals. The development of these natural resources has given the South Central states many fast-growing cities. Houston is the largest city in this region.

Things to Discover

If you look carefully at the picture, map, and time line, you can answer these questions.

1. When did the United States gain New Orleans?
2. How many states are in the South Central region?
3. The picture shows the Alamo as it looks today. When was a battle fought there?
4. When did Texas become a state? How many years was this after the battle of the Alamo?
5. What body of water forms the southern border of some South Central states?
6. What country borders a state in this region?
7. What important natural resource was found in Texas in 1901?
8. When did settlers begin going to Oklahoma?

Words to Learn

You will meet these words in this unit. As you read, you will learn what they mean and how to pronounce them. The Word List will help you.

delta	mohair
derrick	raw sugar
drill	refinery
dry farming	reservation
feed lot	sulfur
flowing well	levee
gusher	mission
helium	

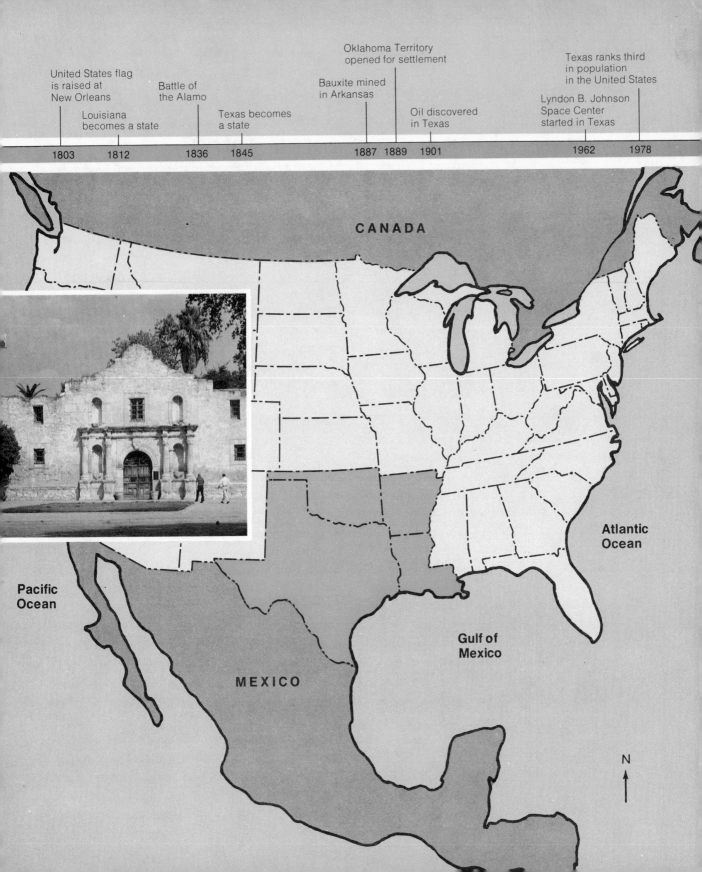

United States flag
is raised at
New Orleans

Louisiana
becomes a state

Battle of
the Alamo

Texas becomes
a state

Bauxite mined
in Arkansas

Oklahoma Territory
opened for settlement

Oil discovered
in Texas

Lyndon B. Johnson
Space Center
started in Texas

Texas ranks third
in population
in the United States

1803   1812   1836   1845   1887 1889 1901   1962   1978

CANADA

Pacific
Ocean

MEXICO

Gulf of
Mexico

Atlantic
Ocean

N

1

Geography of the South Central States

Would you like to take a jet plane and fly high above the earth? If you did, you would see that the South Central states lie about halfway between our eastern and western coasts. The South Central states are Arkansas, Louisiana, Oklahoma, and Texas. You would see from the plane that they are in the southern part of the central area of our country. For these reasons they are called the South Central states.

Surface of the Land

The region of the South Central states is a part of the great central plain of North America. Most of the land in this region has a gently rolling surface. It slopes generally toward the southeast. Look at the map of the South Central states on page 275. You can see that the rivers flow southeast. The land slopes toward the low coastal plains bordering the Gulf of Mexico.

The chief mountains in this region are the Ouachita (wäsh′ə tô′) Mountains and the Ozark (ō′zärk) Plateau, often called the Ozark Mountains. These low mountains extend from western Arkansas to eastern Oklahoma. There are also mountains in the western corner of Texas.

The Mighty Mississippi

From the plane you would see something that looks like a big tree with spreading branches. The tree trunk is really a huge river. It flows almost the whole length of our country from north to south. The river is the Mississippi, the longest river in the United States. The region it drains is called the Mississippi Valley.

You could see the Mississippi begin in northern Minnesota. From its source the Mississippi travels more than 2,000 miles (3,218 km) southward to the Gulf of Mexico. As it flows, it changes from a clear stream to a muddy one. This is because it receives dirt, or silt, from the rivers that flow into it. Gradually, too, the river slows down as it becomes broader and the land becomes more level.

You would see that the Mississippi divides into several branches near its mouth. The land the branches flow through at the mouth of the river is the Mississippi *delta* (del′tə). A delta is land built up by mud and sand brought down by a slow river. The Mississippi delta covers hundreds of square miles. See the map of the South Central states, page 275.

Flood Plains

From the plane you would also see several large rivers flowing into the Mississippi. These are the tributaries of the Mississippi River. Two of these tributaries—the Arkansas and the Red rivers—join the Mississippi in this region.

The Mississippi, Arkansas, and Red rivers have flood plains because they flow through low, flat land. A river that flows between high banks does not have flood plains. The land along such a river is higher than the water, and

THE SOUTH
CENTRAL STATES

★ State Capitals   • Other Cities

Mountains   Hills

Plateaus   Plains

Miles   0   50   100   200
Kilometers   0   80   161   322

ALABAMA

Evansville
Ohio
Wabash
Paducah
Florence
Jackson
Memphis
Meridian
Biloxi
Gulf-port
Mississippi River Delta

St. Louis
MISSOURI
TENN
MISSISSIPPI
Mobile

Jefferson City
Springfield
OZARK
Blytheville
Little Rock
HOT SPRINGS NAT'L. PARK
Jackson
Vicksburg
Baton Rouge
New Orleans
Gulf of Mexico

MISSOURI
PLATEAU
ARKANSAS
Hot Springs
Greenville
River
LOUISIANA
Mississippi

Joplin
Fort Smith
OUACHITA MOUNTAINS
Pine Bluff
El Dorado
Shreveport
Red
River
Lake Charles
Port Arthur

Arkansas
R.
Tulsa
Texarkana
Sabine
River
Beaumont
Galveston

KANSAS
Wichita
Enid
Oklahoma City
OKLAHOMA
Lawton
Wichita Falls
Dallas
Fort Worth
Waco
Austin
Houston
COASTAL
PLAIN
Corpus Christi
Brownsville

Dodge City
Amarillo
Red
River
Lubbock
Abilene
TEXAS
San Angelo
EDWARDS PLATEAU
San Antonio
Laredo
GULF

Raton
Trinidad
Clovis
Roswell
Hobbs
Pecos
NEW MEXICO
Rio
Grande
BIG BEND NAT'L. PARK
MEXICO

Alamosa
Santa Fe
ROCKY MOUNTAINS
Las Cruces
El Paso
Rio Grande

Canadian
R.
Pecos
River

© Rand McNally & Co.

90°
95°
100°
105°

35°
30°
25°

When the Mississippi River reaches its *delta* below New Orleans it divides into several branches. These narrow waterways flow through swampland into the Gulf of Mexico.

there is little danger of overflow. But these rivers have low banks and often overflow the flat land near them. For thousands of years each flood has left much rich soil on the land it covered. Today some of the richest farmland in our country is in these flood plains.

When these rivers overflow, they sometimes cause great damage. Mounds of earth, or *levees* (lev′ēz), have been built along the banks to hold back the water. The levees are made of earth strengthened by metal cables or concrete. During heavy floods people work day and night piling sandbags around the levees to strengthen them and help them hold.

Climate of the South Central States

Most of the South Central region has a mild climate. The short winters are sometimes chilly because of cold winds from the north. But in most of this region warm, moist winds blow in

from the Gulf of Mexico. The farmers usually get enough rain to grow good crops.

The Gulf Coast gets much rain and is swampy. But western Texas and Oklahoma are too far inland to get much rain from the Gulf of Mexico. See the rainfall map of North America, page 17. The winds from the Gulf usually blow toward the east and northeast. Moist winds do not reach this western area to bring it much rain. But there is enough moisture for grazing. The area west of the Pecos River receives very little rain. Crops can be raised there through irrigation.

Do You Know?

1. What four states are called the South Central states? Why?
2. What sections of the South Central states receive the most rainfall? Which receive the least rainfall?

2
Settling the South Central States

The explorers of Spain and France played important parts in the early history of what is now Louisiana and Arkansas. The flags of both countries have flown over this region.

The Spanish Explorers

De Soto was one of the most famous of the Spanish explorers. He and those with him explored parts of North America while looking for treasure. Their travels took them into the low Mississippi Valley, but they found no gold.

De Soto did find hot springs, the waters of which were said to have some healing powers. Several groups of Indians used these springs long before the Spanish arrived. Today Hot Springs is an important city in Arkansas. Each year many people visit the famous health resort there.

The French Explorers

About 140 years after De Soto's visit, the French explorer, La Salle, traveled the Mississippi River. When La Salle reached the mouth of the river, he claimed the whole Mississippi Valley for King Louis of France. It was called the Louisiana Territory.

Other French came later. They wanted furs. They found many fur-bearing animals in this region. They built trading posts and settlements there. The first trading post was Arkansas Post, near the mouth of the Arkansas River.

La Salle dreamed of making the Mississippi River Valley a French colony. He named the region Louisiana in honor of King Louis of France.

The Founding of New Orleans

Pierre d' Iberville (pē yer′ dē′ber vēl) was born in New France, as Canada was then called. From his parents, who were French, he learned to love France.

Pierre made a trip to France to see the king. He asked for permission to strengthen France's claims to the Mississippi River Valley. "To do this," he said, "we need a colony at the mouth of the Mississippi."

"You are loyal to France," the king answered. "I shall give you ships and supplies to build the settlement."

Two hundred soldiers and colonists sailed from France with Pierre and his half brother, Jean de Bienville (zhän′ də byan′vēl′).

The brothers chose a good location for a settlement. There they founded a colony. Pierre left Jean to govern the colony and then sailed back to France.

In 1718 Jean founded New Orleans, which later became the capital of the colony. He was its governor for many years.

The Founding of Little Rock

"Far to the north is a green mountain which sparkles in the sun," says an Indian to a group of French explorers. "That must be the mountain I am searching for," answers one of the explorers. He was Bernard de la Harpe. He explored part of Arkansas in a search for the green mountain. La Harpe did not discover the mountain, but he found a good place for a settlement.

During part of this journey La Harpe traveled on the Arkansas River. While on this river, he noticed a huge mass of rock rising from one of the shores. Farther on, he saw a second great rock. La Harpe called these two masses of rock Little Rock and Big Rock.

An Indian camp was near the smaller of the rocks. There La Harpe started a fur-trading post. This trading post grew into the city which today is called Little Rock.

Under Three Flags

Near the end of the French and Indian War, in 1762, France gave some of the Louisiana Territory to Spain. The territory was a gift to Spain for its help during the war. Spain held Louisiana for about 40 years. During this time, the United States had an agreement with Spain. That agreement allowed settlers near the Ohio River to send products down the Mississippi to the port of New Orleans.

In 1800 France took possession of the territory again. Now the settlers were afraid France would close the port.

President Jefferson decided to try to buy New Orleans from the French. France had been at war and needed money. The French ruler offered to sell the whole Louisiana Territory to the United States.

Louisiana, a State

So, in 1803, the United States bought the Louisiana Territory. See the map on page 91. Settlers were soon moving into the southern part of it. Just 9 years later the southeast part had enough people to become a state. Louisiana was admitted to the Union in 1812.

Arkansas, a State

Arkansas was settled more slowly. After purchasing the Louisiana Territory, the United States government sent soldiers there. The soldiers built Fort Smith in Arkansas and other forts also. These forts provided protection for the settlers.

Settlers now began to flock into Arkansas in large numbers. Most of the people who went there in the early days settled along the rivers. In 1836 Arkansas had enough people to become a state.

The French and Spanish heritage of the South Central states can be seen today. Balcony railings in New Orleans are like those in France. The Spanish built the San José *mission* near San Antonio, Texas.

Early History of Texas

The Spanish began to explore the region that is now Texas soon after Columbus discovered America. They built a few forts and *missions* (mish'ənz), or church settlements, in Texas to hold their claims to the territory.

Soon after La Salle claimed the Mississippi Valley for France, the French began to build forts along the Texas coast. The king of Spain became worried. So he sent more soldiers to the region and built more forts. The Spanish also built more missions. A few Spanish settlers followed. In this way Texas became Spanish.

Texas under Mexican Rule

After a while Spain began to have trouble with its colonies in the Americas. These colonies wanted to be independent. One of the colonies that rebelled and won its independence was Mexico. At that time Mexico included most of

what is now Texas. Very few people were living in Texas then. So the Mexican government invited Americans to go there.

The first settlers from the United States went to Texas under the leadership of Stephen Austin (ôs'tin).

Three hundred families were in the group. They arrived in 1821. Because he led the first United States settlers to Texas, Stephen Austin has sometimes been called the "Father of Texas."

People from many parts of the United States soon began arriving in Texas. Farmers from the Southeast moved to Texas to find new fields in which to grow cotton and tobacco. Cattle ranchers also drove their herds to the fresh grazing lands of Texas.

The number of settlers from the United States continued to grow. Mexico soon began to fear that it would lose Texas. So it declared that it would accept no more settlers from the

Santa Anna ordered his Mexican troops to storm the walls of the Alamo on the last day of fighting.

United States. Mexico also passed a law forbidding slavery in Texas. But the cotton planters kept the slaves they had brought to work on their new plantations.

The Texas Revolution

When General Santa Anna became the leader of Mexico, the trouble grew worse. There were a few armed fights. Then some Texans banded together. They set up their own temporary government and captured San Antonio.

Later Santa Anna marched his troops into San Antonio. They met a group of about 200 Texans who were determined to fight for their independence gathered inside the Alamo (al'ə mō). The Alamo was an old walled mission in San Antonio. Santa Anna had a large army and many cannons. He demanded that the Texans surrender. They refused.

Santa Anna's forces stormed the mission walls and forced their way inside. Within the chapel of the mission the little band of Texans fought bravely. The battle lasted 13 days. When it ended, no Texas soldiers were left alive.

When the fighting was taking place at the Alamo, Texas declared its independence from Mexico. David G. Burnet was chosen as the president of the new provisional government, and Manuel Lorenzo de Zavala (sä vä'lä) as the vice-president. Sam Houston was made commander of the Texas army.

Later, Sam Houston and a group of Texans attacked the Mexican army at San Jacinto (sän jä sēn'tō). Cries of "Remember the Alamo!" split the air as the Texans rushed into battle. They defeated Santa Anna and the Mexican army. The victory ended the war. Mexico gave up its claim to Texas, and Texas won its independence.

In 1836 the Texans set up a republic. Sam Houston was president. Their flag had one large star on a blue field and two stripes, one white and one red. Today Texas is called the Lone Star State.

Becoming a State

After Texas won freedom, many Texans wanted to join the United States. So Texas sent a request to Washington asking to become a state.

The government of Mexico did not recognize the independence of Texas. Some

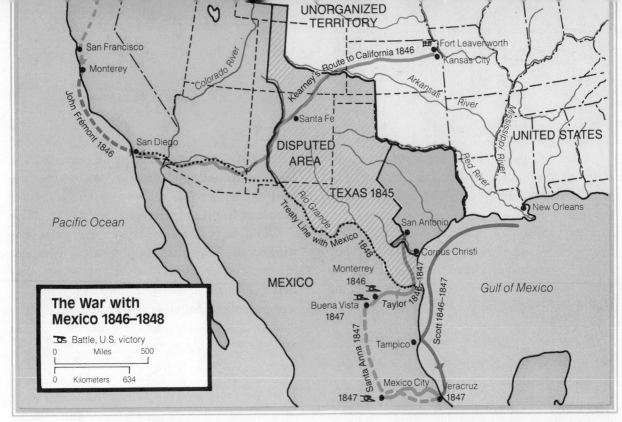

The War with
Mexico 1846–1848

⚔ Battle, U.S. victory

| 0 | Miles | 500 |
| 0 | Kilometers | 634 |

This map shows the area in which the war with Mexico was fought. Which Mexican cities were major battle sites? What river forms the border between Texas and Mexico?

Americans feared that Mexico would declare war if Congress admitted Texas.

Most northerners feared that Texas would come in as a slave state. The northerners did not want Texas to join the United States. But most of the leaders in the United States government wanted to admit Texas. They said, "A strong European country might take Texas if we do not make it part of our nation. We do not want a European power on our border." In 1845 Congress voted to make Texas a state.

War with Mexico

When the United States admitted Texas into the Union, Mexico was not pleased. A quarrel developed over boundaries between Texas and Mexico. The United States sent troops to Texas to protect Texas from Mexican soldiers. But Mexico also wanted to protect its land. A Mexican force defeated the American troops. The United States then declared war on Mexico. The United States soldiers met and defeated Santa Anna's army. The United States troops were led by General Zachary Taylor.

During this time General Winfield Scott led a group of United States soldiers across the Gulf of Mexico. One of the captains was young Robert E. Lee. They landed at Veracruz (ver′ə krōōz′) and captured it. See the map on this page. Then they marched on and captured Mexico City on September 14, 1847. That ended the war.

Under the peace treaty Mexico gave up its claim to land north of the Rio Grande. The United States paid Mexico 15 million dollars for this land.

Texas was a part of the South in the Civil War. So six flags have waved over Texas. They are the Spanish, French, and Mexican flags, the Lone Star flag, the Stars and Stripes, and the flag of the Confederacy.

Henry B. Gonzalez, Political Leader

Henry B. Gonzalez (gôn sä′lās) is a Mexican-American from San Antonio, Texas. He was born there in 1916. After college, Henry worked for a while with his father. Then he held several positions in the local government of San Antonio. Henry Gonzalez ran for the

Congressman Henry Gonzalez works in Washington, D.C., on behalf of people living in Texas.

Texas State senate in 1956. He was the first Mexican-American to serve in the state senate. In 1961 he was elected to the United States House of Representatives.

While in Congress, Henry Gonzalez has worked for laws that support small business. He has fought for civil rights protection and better education for minorities. He has also written several magazine articles about the problems of Mexican-Americans in the United States.

Early History of Oklahoma

The first explorers to reach part of what is now Oklahoma were the Spanish. They did not find gold in this region. But they did find different groups of Indians.

La Salle never explored the Oklahoma region, although he traveled down the Mississippi River. But the French claimed Oklahoma as part of the Louisiana Territory.

American Indian Reservations

During the first half of the 1800s more and more people settled in the eastern part of the United States. In doing this, they claimed more and more land that belonged to the Indians. Most of the Indians fought to keep their land. But, because the United States soldiers had superior weapons, the Indians were defeated.

The United States government attempted to provide for the Indians. It set aside for their use land in various parts of the United States. Such land set aside by the government is called a *reservation* (rez′ər vā′shən).

Thousands of people rushed to get land when the Indian Territory in Oklahoma was opened to settlers. Riders on horses were among the first to make claims.

The government passed a law that forced many Indians in the eastern United States to move to reservations in present-day Oklahoma. This region, north of Texas, became known as Indian Territory. By the late 1800s, most Indians in the United States had been forced to move to reservations west of the Mississippi River. See the map of American Indian removal on page 230.

The Oklahoma Land Rush

People asked the government to open the unsettled part of the Indian Territory to settlers. After a time the government bought from some Indians a large area in what is now Oklahoma. A great land rush took place when the government opened this land to settlers.

Settlers would get the land free. It would go to those who got there first and set out stakes to mark their claims. But everybody had to wait until noon on April 22, 1889. Let us try to imagine that we are there.

Many thousands of people have taken their places at the Kansas border. They have come in covered wagons, in carts, on horseback, and on foot. The eager pioneers have to be held back by United States troops until the hour of the opening. As the morning passes, people push their way closer to the border line.

At exactly twelve o'clock the pistol shot rings out clearly. The troops hardly have time to get out of the way. The rush of settlers into Indian Territory begins.

The people move in to stake their claims. Cities of tents appear by nightfall. The area has 50,000 people in it within 24 hours of the opening. Guthrie and Oklahoma City are suddenly cities of 10,000 people each.

Oklahoma, a State

In a short time all the free land was taken. Within a year enough people had settled in Oklahoma for it to become a territory. A few years later, in 1907, Oklahoma became a state.

Many Indians live in the South Central states today, especially in Oklahoma. The United States government is trying to improve conditions for Indians on reservations. It is also trying to help those who move to cities. The government has made laws to protect the rights of the Indians. They are now United States citizens and can live and work wherever they wish. The Indians continue to fight for their rights but the battles are now in courts of law.

Some Indians in Oklahoma continue to practice traditional crafts. Others have moved their families to cities to find work in business and industry.

Do You Know?

1. Why were Fort Smith and other forts built in Arkansas?
2. How did the location of New Orleans lead to our buying the Louisiana Territory?
3. How did the war with Mexico end?
4. Why is Texas called the Lone Star State?
5. What happened as more and more people settled in the eastern part of the United States?
6. What is a reservation?
7. How was Oklahoma settled? When did it become a state?

Before You Go On

Using New Words

levee   mission
delta   reservation

The phrases below explain the words listed above. Number a paper from 1 through 4. After each number write the word that matches the definition.

1. A church settlement built by Spaniards in the Americas
2. An area set aside by the government for the use of American Indians
3. Land built up by mud and sand brought down by a slow river
4. A bank of earth built along a river to keep it from overflowing its banks and flooding the land

Finding the Facts

1. How long is the Mississippi River? Where does it begin? Where is its mouth? What large rivers flow into it in the region of the South Central states?
2. Why do people pile sandbags around levees during heavy floods?
3. Why don't western Texas and Oklahoma get much rain from the Gulf of Mexico?
4. Who started a fur-trading post that grew into the city now called Little Rock?
5. Why did Pierre d'Iberville think it was important to found a French colony at the mouth of the Mississippi River? Who founded New Orleans in 1718?
6. What large piece of land did the United States buy from France in 1803?
7. Why did the United States government send soldiers to what is now Arkansas during the early 1800s?
8. How did the Spanish try to hold their claims to the territory that is now Texas?
9. Who led the first settlers from the United States to Texas in 1821?
10. What happened at the Alamo? What happened at San Jacinto? Who headed the Texas army and later became the president of Texas?
11. What two generals helped the United States defeat Mexico in the war that took place shortly after Texas became a state?
12. To which branch of Congress was Henry Gonzalez elected in 1961?
13. Why did the Indians in the eastern United States lose their land during the first half of the 1800s?
14. What present-day state was once known as Indian Territory?

3

Living and Working in the South Central States

Let us take a boat trip down the Mississippi River from St. Louis to New Orleans. Most travel on the Mississippi today is on barges which carry freight up and down the river. But a few river boats carry passengers.

This chart lists the major crops and livestock in the South Central states. What major crop is grown in all four states? Which states raise sheep?

Farming Products and Livestock in the South Central States

	Major Crops	Other Crops	Livestock
Arkansas	soybeans, rice, cotton	tomatoes, strawberries, wheat	chickens, hogs, cattle, turkeys
Louisiana	rice, sugarcane, soybeans, cotton, sweet potatoes	corn, hay, strawberries, melons, nuts	cattle, hogs, chickens
Oklahoma	wheat, peanuts, cotton	hay, soybeans, corn, pecans, strawberries, peaches	cattle, sheep, chickens, hogs, turkeys
Texas	cotton, rice, sorghum, wheat	barley, oats, vegetables, nuts, citrus and other fruits	cattle, sheep, hogs, chickens, goats, turkeys

Farming in the South Central States

The captain hands us a chart showing some of the farming products and livestock found in the South Central states.

The captain tells us this region has much rich farmland. Farming is one of the chief ways of earning a living in the South Central states. Some of this rich land is on the Mississippi flood plains.

Cotton, a Leading Crop

"The chief crop of the South Central states is cotton," the captain says. This region has about half the cotton land in the country. Texas is the leading cotton state in our country. Many people here make their living from cotton. See the map of climate and cotton on page 202.

The Story of Rice

Our captain tells us that another important crop of the South Central states is rice. Most of our country's rice is grown on the flood plains in Arkansas and on the coastal plain of Louisiana and Texas. Rice is a thirsty plant, and the fields must be kept under water most of the time. Low levees are built to keep the water in the fields.

Most rice is planted by low-flying airplanes which scatter the seeds onto flooded fields. Workers keep 2 to 6 inches (5 to 15 cm) of water on the rice fields. Workers also keep

Rice fields in Texas are irrigated by canals. Low *levees* help keep water on the fields. Later the rice will be stored in silos until trucks or trains carry it to market.

weeds out of the fields. The rice plants grow and cover the fields like thick grass. After a few months, the leaves begin to turn yellow. The fields are drained. It is now time to harvest the ripened grain. Most of the rice is harvested with large farm machines called combines. This machine is like the combines that reap and thresh other grains. First, the machine cuts off the stalks. Next it beats the stalks to separate the straw from the grain. The grain is then sent to mills, where it is hulled and usually polished, then packaged. New Orleans and Houston are the rice markets of the South Central states.

Other Crops

Our captain says that farmers in this region grow many other crops besides cotton and rice. Look at the chart on page 286. In addition to strawberries and tomatoes, peaches and grapes are some of the many fruits grown in Arkansas. One section of Louisiana is known for its fine strawberries. Fine citrus fruits are grown in Texas in the Rio Grande Valley. Texas is also noted for its peaches, watermelons, other fruits and vegetables, pecans, and peanuts.

Northwest Texas and western Oklahoma do not get much rain. Winter wheat is the chief crop of this area. Some farmers practice *dry farming* (drī' färm'ing). Dry farming is a way of conserving the moisture in areas where little rain falls. On these fields crops are planted every other year. The weeds are kept out so that none of the precious moisture in the soil is wasted. In this way enough moisture is stored so that a crop can be raised every 2 years.

The Story of Sugar

Do you know how much sugar you eat in a year? The average person in this country eats almost 100 pounds (45 kg) of sugar each year. Most of the sugar that we eat comes from lands outside the United States. Sugarcane needs rich, moist soil and a hot, sunny climate. The Coastal Plain and the Mississippi Flood Plain of Louisiana have such a climate. About one-fourth of the cane sugar grown in our nation is from Louisiana.

Sugarcane grows tall like corn. But unlike corn, it is not usually grown from seed. Short pieces of cane stalk are planted. Farmers use machines to plant pieces of cane stalk in furrows, or ditches, and cover them with dirt. Soon green shoots push up through the loose earth. In 7 to 22 months the stalks are 7 to 15 feet (2 to 5 m) high. They are filled with sweet juice.

When machines are used to cut the cane, the leaves and tassels are first burned off. Fire does not hurt the cane stalks because they are too full of juice to burn.

When sugarcane is cut by hand, the workers use long, sharp knives. Each knife has a long hook on the back which the worker uses to strip off the cane leaves.

The cane stalks are loaded onto trucks which take them to the sugar mill, or *refinery* (ri fī′nər ē), where raw materials are purified. The cane stalks must be taken to the refinery immediately because they dry out quickly.

The sugar refinery with its tall smokestack is one of the largest buildings in the towns of the sugar country. Here the stalks are washed as they are carried along on a moving belt. Then large rollers squeeze the sweet juice from the sugarcane. The juice is treated to purify it and cooked into a syrup. The syrup is boiled to form a brown mass of molasses and crystals. Then a machine spins most of the molasses out of the syrup. The sticky brown crystals that remain are called *raw* (rô) *sugar*. Some of this raw sugar is packaged. But most of the brown sugar is further treated to make it white. It is then shipped to all parts of the country.

Livestock in the South Central States

Some of the cattle raised by early American settlers in the South Central states were the Texas longhorns. The first settlers found these cattle roaming wild. The cattle were descended from stock brought by the Spanish explorers.

Cattle, together with hogs and other livestock, are still raised in all the South Central states. See the chart on page 286. Western Texas and Oklahoma have the largest farms, or ranches. Ranchers there travel by jeep, truck, and helicopter, as well as on horseback. Many ranchers graze their cattle on the range. After a while, the ranchers take the cattle to a *feed lot* (fēd lot). This is a pen where cattle are given special feed to fatten them for market.

Texas has more cattle, sheep, and goats than any other state. It has fine saddle horses and race horses. Texas leads in producing wool and *mohair* (mō′her′). Mohair is a special cloth made from the long, silky hair of a certain kind of goat.

The Edwards Plateau lies in southwestern Texas. See the map of the South Central states on page 275. This plateau is almost as large as the state of Pennsylvania. The chief occupation there is raising cattle, sheep, and goats.

The King Ranch, the largest in Texas, is on the Gulf Coast. It is larger than the state of Rhode Island. Many thousands of cattle and fine horses for racing are raised on this ranch.

An important new kind of cattle has been bred on the King Ranch. In long periods of hot

Modern cowhands still ride horses when they herd cattle. Today they may also use trucks and helicopters to do much of the same work on a ranch.

weather cattle become sick and die. On the low Gulf Coast there are many insects. Cattle are troubled by these insects. But the Brahman cattle of India, a country in Asia, are not bothered by heat or insects. Some of these cattle were brought from India to Texas and bred with the best Texas shorthorns. The Texas shorthorns are fine cattle for beef because they grow large and heavy.

The result of crossing the two kinds of cattle was successful. The new breed of cattle is known as the Santa Gertrudis (sant'ə ger trōōd'əs). Like the shorthorns, it is good for beef. It is not troubled by heat or insects.

Lumber, Fish, Furs

Our trip down the Mississippi River continues. As we move farther south, the trees grow thicker and thicker. The swampy delta region is covered with thick, tall grass and forests of cypress trees. Because of the warm climate and heavy rainfall, trees grow faster here than in most other parts of our country.

The captain tells us that the tall, straight cypress trees make fine lumber. Their tough wood does not rot easily. Forests cover about half the area of Louisiana and Arkansas. Eastern Texas and eastern Oklahoma also have much lumber.

We pass many small fishing boats moving up from the Gulf. The boats are filled with shrimp and oysters. The Louisiana waters supply much of the shellfish in our country. The shrimp are either canned or frozen for shipment, but the oysters are packed in ice and shipped in refrigerator cars. Probably you have eaten shrimp or oysters caught in Louisiana waters.

Trappers often take their furs to market by boat. Their catch may include mink, opossum, muskrat, and raccoon skins. These animals live in watery places. Many skins come from fur farms, where people make a living by raising the animals.

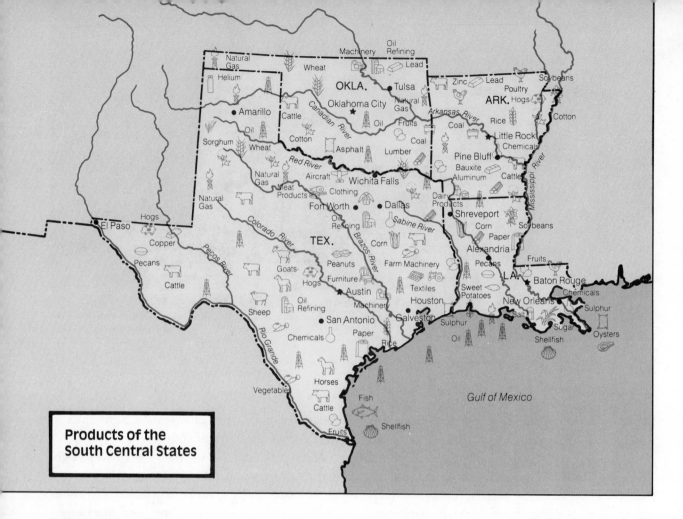

Products of the South Central States

Mining in the South Central States

Three South Central states—Texas, Louisiana, and Oklahoma—rank among the leading oil-producing states of our country. Some oil fields in this region are on land. Others are offshore in the Gulf of Mexico. Petroleum, or crude oil, is often called "black gold." Can you explain this?

The Story of Oil and Natural Gas

Can you imagine our living without the automobile and the airplane? These are only two of the machines that we probably could not use without the products of petroleum. From petroleum we get gasoline, kerosene, fuel oils, lubricating, or smoothing, oils, and many other useful products. Natural gas is often found with petroleum.

Texas and Louisiana rank among our leading states in the production of natural gas. Natural gas is a very good fuel. It leaves no dirt and is easy to use.

Petroleum is found deep down in the earth. Thousands of years ago plants and animals were buried in mud and sand. As they were pressed down under many layers of sand and rock, they decayed. This decayed matter formed oil and natural gas.

Early settlers in North America sometimes found oil while drilling, or digging, for salt. But they had no use for oil. The settlers were annoyed when they found oil instead of salt. Later it was found that kerosene, which is made from petroleum, could be burned in lamps to give light. The demand for kerosene oil began to grow.

In 1859 Edwin Drake was hired by a company in Pennsylvania to get oil by digging wells. He used a tool for boring holes, called a *drill* (dril) to dig down into the earth. The drilling was hard and slow. Then at about 70 feet (21 m), Drake struck oil. Word of Drake's success soon spread. Others began to drill for oil in many parts of the country. They found it in great amounts, first in eastern Texas, in 1901, and later in other South Central states. See the map of oil fields on page 292.

Most oil wells must be dug much deeper than 70 feet (21 m). Deep oil wells may go down many thousand feet. A few go 4 miles (6 km) into the earth. Sharp, heavy tools are used to drill the wells. Huge steel frameworks, called *derricks* (der'iks), are built to support the drilling tools. The derricks often are more than 100 feet (30 m) high.

A drill is forced down into the earth. When the drill reaches oil, the gas that is often found with the oil tries to escape to the upper air. If there is a large amount of gas to be set free, it shoots upward with great force. As it does so, it pushes the oil up too. Sometimes oil and gas shoot high in the air. Such a well is called a *gusher* (gush'ər). Gushers were allowed in the

This diagram of oil processing shows the major stages and places oil goes through on the way to market. How does it get to market after it has been processed?

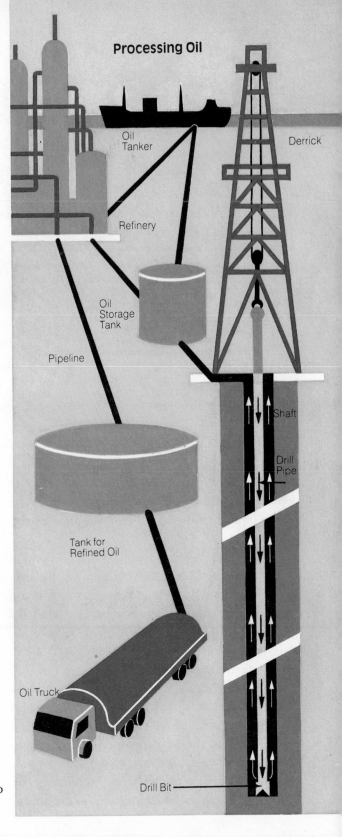

Processing Oil

Derrick

Oil Tanker

Refinery

Oil Storage Tank

Pipeline

Shaft

Drill Pipe

Tank for Refined Oil

Oil Truck

Drill Bit

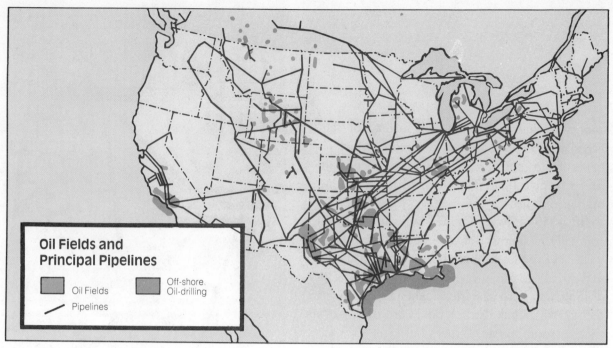

Oil Fields and Principal Pipelines

Oil Fields

Off-shore Oil-drilling

Pipelines

The major areas where oil is found are shown on the map. What states have the most oil fields? What areas of the country get oil through pipelines?

early days. Today oil workers try to prevent wasteful gushers by controlling the flow of the oil.

Usually when oil is reached, it flows in a steady stream. This is called a *flowing* (flō'ing) *well.* After a while most gushers and flowing wells stop flowing because no gas is left to push the oil up. Then the oil has to be pumped out of the well.

From the wells the oil is carried through pipes to huge storage tanks. Some oil is shipped from the storage tanks by railroad tank cars and some in boats called tankers. But in the United States most of the oil is pumped through pipelines. In any case, it goes from the storage tank to a plant called a refinery. At the refinery the oil is processed and made into useful products.

Offshore Drilling

Petroleum is sometimes found beneath the water offshore. To reach it, oil workers use drilling platforms which are towed out to sea. The legs of the platforms are lowered until they rest on the bottom. The platforms hold the derricks and drilling machinery which can drill to depths of 20,000 feet (6,000 m). The oil is pumped through underwater pipes into tankers which carry it to refineries on land.

Sometimes offshore drilling causes problems. The oil may be accidentally dumped into the water. Large tankers may collide, or an underwater pipe might leak. The oil floats on top of the water. Then it spreads out, creating a slick which pollutes the water. In 1979, an oil well blowout in the Gulf of Mexico created a slick

Oil workers on platforms drill for oil under the Gulf of Mexico. Underwater pipelines will take the oil to *refineries* on land. Piles of sulfur are loaded into railroad cars that will carry the sulfur to large chemical plants. There it will be processed into many useful products.

so large that it washed up on the shores of Texas. Many fish and shore birds were killed, and the water was unfit to use. Oil workers are trying to prevent this from happening again.

The Story of Sulfur

Much of the world's supply of *sulfur* (sul′fər) comes from the Louisiana and Texas Gulf Coast. Sulfur is a yellow mineral found deep in the ground below 500 to 1,500 feet (152 to 457 m) of gravel, sand, and clay. It lies in a hard, solid layer. For many years it could not be mined cheaply. Then Herman Frasch (hur′man fräsh), an American scientist, found a good way to mine the sulfur.

Today the sulfur is mined according to Frasch's plan. A derrick similar to that used in drilling oil wells is built. Four hollow pipes,

one inside the other, are run down to the sulfur bed. Hot water is forced down the two outside pipes. The hot water melts the sulfur, because sulfur melts at a relatively low temperature. Then air is forced through the fourth or smallest pipe. This pushes the melted, or liquid, sulfur to the surface through the third pipe. A pipeline carries away the liquid sulfur and empties it into a huge storage bin. When the sulfur cools, it hardens into a solid block. Such blocks break up easily into fine powder, which is easy to process.

Sulfur is important in the making of many things, from explosives and steel to newsprint and rayon. It is used in tanning leather, in bleaching, dyeing, and making ink and paper. Powdered sulfur is used in preparations that kill insects on plants. Sulfuric acid, used in making explosives, fertilizers, and medicines, is also made from sulfur.

Salt Quarrying

Besides petroleum and sulfur, the Gulf Coast of Louisiana yields salt. For almost 100 years, Louisiana has been a leading salt producer. The salt lies underground in thick beds of rock salt. Salt mines are like quarries under the ground. Oklahoma and Texas also produce salt.

Do you know that there are more than 1,000 uses for salt? The most common use of salt is in the kitchen and at the table to season food. But the largest amounts of salt are used in industry. Salt is used in meat-packing plants and in factories that process hides and leather. Bakers, cereal producers, and butter and cheese manufacturers use huge amounts. Farmers feed salt to livestock.

Bauxite Mining

Arkansas has some of the largest deposits of bauxite in North America. Bauxite is the ore from which aluminum is made. Bauxite, which looks like clay, is mined from open pits. The ore is washed and crushed. Then the bauxite is taken out and melted.

Aluminum is a strong, light metal which is important in the building of airplanes. Kitchen utensils are also made from aluminum.

Helium Fields

Helium (hē′lē əm) is found in Texas in large quantities. Helium is a very light gas which does not burn or explode. It is used in the blimp, which is a kind of balloon airship. A blimp is a gas bag that has no metal frame and collapses when the gas is taken out. Helium is used in rocket launchings and in some welding.

A major helium field lies near Amarillo, in the Texas Panhandle. Texas is shaped somewhat like a large pan. The "handle" of the pan is the area that extends northward from the rest of Texas. See the map of the South Central states on page 275. This field can produce helium for the United States for many years. The helium plant there is the largest in the country.

Lead and Zinc

The Ozark–Ouachita Mountains are rich in lead, zinc, coal, and other minerals. Lead and zinc are also found in Oklahoma. These two minerals are usually found and mined together. Lead is used to make water pipes, paints, bullets, and many other things. Articles made of iron and steel are coated with zinc to prevent their rusting. Zinc is also used in making refrigerators.

Chief Cities of the South Central States

The cities of this region are chiefly trade and transportation centers. In some cities, however, much manufacturing is done. The large cities are railroad and airplane centers. Some are also ports. The city of Houston is a center for our country's space program.

Cities of Louisiana

Shreveport lies on the Red River in northwestern Louisiana. It is the chief market for the gas, lumber, cotton, and oil produced in this part of the state. Shreveport has cotton mills, lumber factories, and oil refineries. But it ships most of the lumber, raw cotton, and crude oil to other parts of our country.

The capital of Louisiana is Baton Rouge (bat'ən rōōzh') a Mississippi River port. Baton Rouge is the trade and shipping center of a rich farming region. One of the largest oil refineries in the world is at Baton Rouge. Petroleum products are shipped to ports all over the world.

New Orleans is the chief trade and shipping center for the lower Mississippi Valley. It is about 100 miles (160 km) above the mouth of the river. Gulf storms seldom reach its harbor. Cotton, sugar, rice, lumber, furs, and oil are shipped from New Orleans to northern industrial cities. But some oil and sugar refining, rice milling, furniture and paper manufacturing, and shipbuilding are done in New Orleans. Early fruits and vegetables, shrimp, and oysters are shipped in refrigerated cars to large cities in other parts of our country.

Mississippi River traffic has grown in recent years. Products from the North Central states are sent down the Mississippi to New Orleans. From New Orleans they are shipped overseas by freighter.

Freighters from the Northeast bring manufactured goods to New Orleans. Vessels from Central America and South America bring coffee, bananas, lumber, and many other things. These products are sent from New Orleans to various parts of the United States and to foreign countries.

Trumpeter Louis Armstrong plays for his wife, Lucille, in their New York home. Louis was a famous jazz musician from New Orleans.

Louis Armstrong, Jazz Musician

New Orleans is the birthplace of a kind of music known as jazz. New Orleans is also the birthplace of Louis Armstrong. He was a great jazz trumpet player and singer.

Louis, also known as "Satchmo," first learned to play the cornet. He played in New Orleans and on riverboats. Then he joined a jazz band in Chicago, Illinois. Two years later, Louis joined a band in New York City. The leader of this band had Louis switch from the cornet to the trumpet. He played the trumpet from then until his death in 1971.

During his life, Louis Armstrong led both large and small bands. He began to sing in addition to playing. Soon his singing became as excellent as his trumpet playing. Louis made a large number of recordings. He performed in many European cities. He also made several films. Louis "Satchmo" Armstrong helped to make jazz an important part of American music.

295

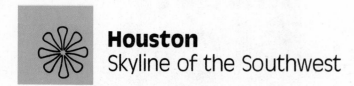

Houston
Skyline of the Southwest

In 1962, pasture land southeast of Houston, Texas, was chosen as the place to build the nation's space center. People at the space center develop and test space vehicles. Astronauts train at the space center. In the control center are people who take charge of every space flight from launch to splashdown.

Founded in 1836, Houston began as a trading center for cotton farmers and cattle ranchers. It became and still remains a leading cattle market. Then, in the early 1900s, oil was discovered in Texas. Railroad cars would not do for shipping oil. Houston needed a port for ocean tankers. Look at the map of the South Central states on page 275. Notice the channel that shows how Houston made itself a port by bringing the sea to its door.

With an ocean port, Houston's industries grew rapidly. Because oil, natural gas, and sulfur are found nearby, huge chemical factories and oil refineries have grown up. Factories also turn out farm machinery and oil-field equipment. ▪

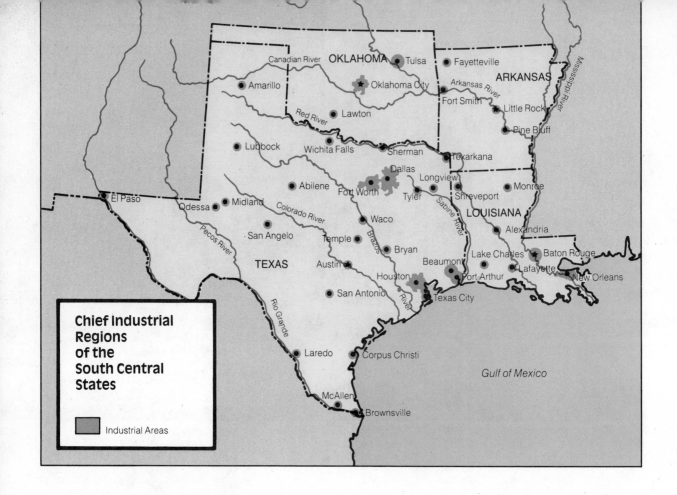

Chief Industrial
Regions
of the
South Central
States

Industrial Areas

Cities of Texas

Texas is so large that great distances separate most of its cities. However, all of the larger cities like Houston have airports. Excellent roads and highways connect cities with farming and marketing areas. Texas also has about 15,000 miles (24,140 km) of railroad.

Amarillo is the chief trade and shipping center of the Texas Panhandle. Most people in Amarillo earn a living by handling the wheat, oil, cattle, and sheep of the Panhandle area.

El Paso, in the western corner of Texas, is the main trade center of western Texas and northern Mexico. This area produces oil,

wheat, cotton, and cattle. El Paso is also a center for refining copper.

In south central Texas are the cities of San Antonio and Austin. Both were capitals of the area now known as Texas. San Antonio was the capital while the area was under Spanish and Mexican rule. After Texas won its independence, Austin became the capital. Many tourists visit these cities each year. They come to see the many historic sites. What famous mission is in San Antonio?

Austin is the trade and shipping center of a large farming and grazing region. Its industries include manufacturing brick, tile, and furniture.

San Antonio is a trade and shipping center for cotton, oil, livestock, wool, grain, vegetables, and citrus fruits. San Antonio has oil refineries, meat-packing plants, flour mills, and factories where clothing, pottery, tile, brooms, and refrigerators are manufactured.

Dallas is the headquarters for several oil firms and is a leading cotton market. Other important industries include aircraft parts, and food products, banking, insurance, and fashions center.

In early days Fort Worth was an important trading and supply center for cattle ranchers. Today it is one of the largest meat-packing cities in the South. Aircraft factories and large oil refineries are located in Fort Worth. The city is also one of the principal grain-milling centers of the South Central states. Many oil companies and insurance firms have offices in Fort Worth.

Galveston is a busy Texas port on an island off the Gulf Coast. A bridge about 3 miles (5 km) long connects Galveston with the mainland. Many people spend their vacations on the island's beaches.

Cities of Arkansas and Oklahoma

Little Rock, which is on the Arkansas River, is the capital and largest city of Arkansas. It is a trading center. It ships cotton, lumber, rice, soybeans, and minerals to other states. Some people work in factories that turn out wood products or food products. Others work in clothing or aluminum factories.

Have you ever seen a city with oil derricks? Oklahoma City, the capital and largest city of

Oil companies drill for oil wherever it may be found. These *derricks* are in front of the Oklahoma state capitol.

Oklahoma, has oil wells on front lawns, in schoolyards, and even on the state capitol grounds. This city is also a major trade and shipping center. It has one of the largest cattle stockyards in the world.

The city of Tulsa turned into a boom town with the discovery of oil beneath a cornfield. Tulsa has continued to grow. Today some of the biggest oil companies in our country are in Tulsa. This modern, bustling city is the chief trade center for northeastern Oklahoma.

Do You Know?

1. What are some of the chief crops of the South Central states?
2. What kinds of livestock are raised in the region?
3. What kinds of minerals are important in the region?

To Help You Learn

Using New Words

helium	sulfur	dry farming
drill	derrick	flowing well
gusher	refinery	reservation
mohair	levee	raw sugar
delta	feed lot	

The phrases below explain the words and terms listed above. Number a paper from 1 through 14. After each number write the word or term that matches the definition.

1. An oil well from which the oil shoots high into the air
2. A building in which raw materials are changed into finished products
3. The brown crystals that form when the juice of sugarcane is boiled and allowed to cool
4. The framework built to support the machinery needed to drill an oil well
5. A tool used to bore holes in the ground
6. Cloth made from goat hair
7. A very light gas which does not burn or explode
8. An oil well which produces oil in a steady stream without being pumped
9. A yellow mineral
10. A way of conserving moisture in dry areas by growing only one crop every 2 years on the same plot of ground
11. A pen where cattle are fed special feed to fatten them for market
12. An area set aside by the government for the use of Indians
13. Land built up by mud and sand brought down by a slow river
14. A bank of earth built along a river to keep it from overflowing its banks and flooding the land

Finding the Facts

1. What four states are called the South Central states? What is the capital city of each of these states?
2. What rivers in the South Central states have flood plains?
3. What city did Jean de Bienville found in 1718?
4. Why was the battle at San Jacinto important to Texas?
5. What caused the war between the United States and Mexico after Texas became a state? What change took place under the peace treaty after the war ended?
6. Why did the United States government set up reservations for Indians in the first half of the 1800s?
7. In what year did each of the South Central states become a state?
8. Which state is the leading cotton state in the United States?
9. What crop grown in Arkansas, Louisiana, and Texas must be kept under water most of the time?

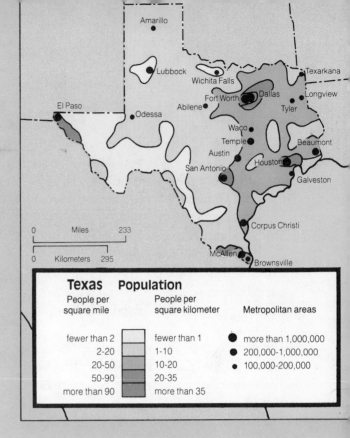

Texas Population

People per square mile		People per square kilometer	Metropolitan areas
fewer than 2		fewer than 1	● more than 1,000,000
2-20		1-10	● 200,000-1,000,000
20-50		10-20	• 100,000-200,000
50-90		20-35	
more than 90		more than 35	

10. In which South Central state is sugarcane grown?

11. When were great amounts of oil first found in Texas? What are some products made from petroleum? Why is natural gas a good fuel?

12. What are the chief uses of sulfur? Of bauxite? Of helium? Of lead? Of zinc?

13. What are the chief cities of Louisiana? What is made in these cities? Which city is the birthplace of jazz?

14. What are the chief cities of Arkansas and Oklahoma? For what industries are these cities known?

15. What are the chief cities of Texas? For what industries are these cities known?

Learning from Maps

1. On the map of the United States on pages 92 – 93 locate the four South Central states. Between what parallels of latitude do they lie? What kind of climate would you expect to find in them? Locate the capitals of these states.

2. On the same map trace the Mississippi River from its source in Minnesota down to the Gulf of Mexico. Of what states does it form the boundary? What important tributaries of the Mississippi drain the South Central states?

3. Look at the key to the map of the South Central states on page 275. What kind of land makes up most of the region? Where is the Edwards Plateau?

4. This map is a population map of Texas. It shows where many people live and where few people live in Texas. In which part of Texas do most people live?

Which city, Houston or Amarillo, has the most people living there? Which two large cities are so close that they almost look like one large city on the map?

Where is the largest area in which the fewest number of people live?

Look at the natural vegetation map of North America on page 18. What kind of natural vegetation does this area have that might explain why few people live there?

What are some of the largest cities in Texas? Look at the map of chief industrial regions of the South Central states on page 298. Which of these cities are industrial areas? Explain your findings.

5. On the map of the War with Mexico on page 281 trace the route of General Taylor. How did General Scott and his army reach Mexico City?

6. Study the products map of the South Central states on page 290. What is the most important product of this area? Which states have important fisheries? What part of the area lies in the cotton belt? See the map on page 19.

7. The map on page 292 shows the location of the oil fields in the United States. Which states have the most pipe lines carrying oil to market?

8. The map on page 455 shows cattle trails of the West about 1870. In which South Central state did the four cattle trails shown on the map begin? Trace the route of each trail.

Using Study Skills

1. **Chart:** Look at the chart on page 286. In which state are sweet potatoes a major crop? Where are peanuts a major crop? Where is sorghum a major crop? Which crop is a major one in all four states? In which state are tomatoes grown? Where are strawberries grown? What crops are raised in Texas? In which state are goats raised? Where are cattle and hogs raised? Where are chickens raised?

2. **Diagram:** Look at the diagram of processing oil on page 291. What are some of the parts of an oil drill? What happens to the oil before it reaches the refinery? What happens to the oil after it has been through the refinery?

Thinking It Through

1. When our country bought the Louisiana Territory, the land size of the United States almost doubled. The United States became the owner of New Orleans, the Mississippi River, and a large piece of land west of the Mississippi. How did this purchase help our country?

2. Parts of the South Central states are on a flood plain. What are the advantages and disadvantages of living on a flood plain?

3. Look at the photograph of the Lyndon B. Johnson Space Center, page 296. What makes the Center look like a separate city? The Center has only a few thousand employees, yet it has created tens of thousands of jobs. Why?

4. Discuss in your class what would happen to our homes, factories, and transportation if all the oil wells suddenly ran dry. Here are some points to think and read about first: What products are made from petroleum? How do we use these products? What other kinds of energy and lubrication do we have?

Projects

1. Make a model of a delta. Try to borrow a sand table and make your model in sand. Show how a river or stream deposits soil at its mouth.

2. The Research Committee should find out how the coming of the railroads and the invention of refrigerator cars helped the meat industry grow.

3. Your class might learn some songs which were sung by the cowhands in the old trail-driving days. Books which contain many of these songs are *Cowboy Songs* by John and Alan Lomax and *The American Songbag* by Carl Sandburg.

4. The Reading Committee may find books on these subjects: the settlement of Oklahoma; Texas and the war with Mexico; the Mississippi River; the Louisiana Purchase. The committee might ask the librarian to find some exciting stories about western cattle ranching in the 1860s. Read a book or story on one of these subjects and report on it to the class.

5. Many people have played an important part in the growth of the South Central states. Divide into small groups. Have each group find out about one of the following people: Davy Crockett, Juan Cortina, Barbara Jordan, Van Cliburn, Hattie Caraway, Maria Tallchief, or Stand Watie. Tell your story in the form of a play.

6. The Mississippi River and its tributaries form the largest inland waterway in the United States. Members of the Explorers' Committee might collect information about the waterway and report to the class. Let them use a map to show how barges and boats travel from New Orleans to St. Paul and Minneapolis, to Chicago, and to cities in Ohio. They should also tell what products the boats and barges carry.

7. Oklahoma, which became a state in 1907, is one of our youngest states. Find out which states of our nation are newer than Oklahoma. When were they admitted to the Union?

9 The Rocky Mountain States

Unit Preview

The Rocky Mountain states are Colorado, Montana, Wyoming, Idaho, Nevada, Utah, Arizona, and New Mexico.

Spanish explorers were the first to venture into this region. The Spanish made settlements in the southern part of this area. One of the earliest was Santa Fe. It was founded in 1610. Missions, or church settlements, were also built.

American Indian groups were living in the Southwest many years before the Spanish came. The Pueblos, Navajos, and Apaches used their skills to develop the resources they found.

The United States sent its first explorers to this region in 1806. Later, trappers and fur traders wandered throughout the area. Then wagon trains of settlers rumbled across the Rockies heading to the Far West. But few settlers came to stay in the Rocky Mountain region until after the discovery of silver and gold there.

Mining is still important in the Rockies. Besides silver and gold, copper, uranium ores, and other minerals are also mined. These minerals are important raw materials.

Farming is also important in the Rocky Mountain states, but rainfall is uncertain. Farms in some areas must be irrigated with water from dammed-up rivers. The dams are also useful for controlling the rivers and providing hydroelectric power for industry.

Things to Discover

If you look carefully at the picture, map, and time line, you can answer these questions.
1. How many states are in the Rocky Mountain region?
2. Whom did the United States send to explore this region in 1806? What famous landmark did this person discover?
3. When did Santa Fe become a capital?
4. How long after Pike's explorations was one of the main western trails opened?
5. What discovery brought a rush of settlers to the mountain country in 1859?
6. Dams have been built on many rivers in the Rocky Mountain states. The water is used for irrigation and to provide hydroelectric power. What is another way rivers are used, as shown in the picture?
7. How long after the Hoover Dam was completed was the Fort Peck Dam completed?

Words to Learn

You will meet these words in this unit. As you read, you will learn what they mean and how to pronounce them. The Word List will help you.

Continental Divide	oil shale
fleece	pueblo
geyser	ridge
hogan	shearing
international	

Coronado explores the Grand Canyon — 1540

Santa Fe made capital of New Mexico — 1610

Zebulon Pike finds Pikes Peak — 1806

Santa Fe Trail opened — 1821

Salt Lake City started by Mormons — 1847

Comstock Silver Lode opened — 1859

Yellowstone made national park — 1872

Hoover Dam completed — 1936

Fort Peck Dam completed — 1940

United States studies oil shale production — 1970s

CANADA

Atlantic Ocean

Pacific Ocean

MEXICO

N

1
Geography of the Rocky Mountain States

The plains region in the central part of our country extends westward to the Rocky Mountains. Many different plants and animals thrive in the Rockies. However, it is too cold for trees to grow on the snowy tops of these mountains.

Surface of the Land

The Rocky Mountains begin in New Mexico. They stretch north through Colorado, Utah, Wyoming, Idaho, and Montana. From there they reach on into Canada and Alaska.

East of the Rockies—in Montana, Wyoming, Colorado, and New Mexico—the Great Plains begin. The Great Plains are a part of the level or rolling region that stretches from the Rockies to the Appalachians. The map of the United States on pages 92–93 shows how wide this plains area is.

The map of the Rocky Mountain states on page 307 shows that a huge plateau lies west of the southern Rockies. A plateau is a high but rather level area. This plateau is called the Colorado Plateau. It covers much of Arizona and Utah and smaller areas of Colorado and New Mexico.

Northwest of the Colorado Plateau is a huge basin, or lower area surrounded by mountains. It is called the Great Basin. Western Utah and most of Nevada are in the Great Basin.

The Rocky Mountain region thus has a great variety of scenery. There are rugged mountains and plains, deep valleys, canyons, and rivers.

The Continental Divide

The peaks of the Rockies rise so high that they form a dividing line on the North American continent. All the rivers on one side of the *ridge* (rij), or long and narrow chain of hills or mountains, flow to the east.

On the other side of the ridge the rivers flow to the west. This ridge is called the *Continental* (kon′tə nent′ əl) *Divide.* The Continental Divide separates the rivers that flow east from those that flow west.

Four important rivers, the Arkansas, the Rio Grande, the Colorado, and the Platte, begin in the Rocky Mountains. Because of the Continental Divide, some of these rivers, such as the Arkansas, tumble down the eastern slopes of the Rockies. Then they flow eastward to the Mississippi River, southward to the Gulf of Mexico, and finally to the Atlantic Ocean. The Colorado River, however, runs down the western slopes of the Rockies to the Gulf of California, which empties into the Pacific Ocean.

Climate of the Mountain States

Moist, warm winds blow eastward from the Pacific Ocean. The winds lose much moisture as they rise to cross the mountains in the states next to the ocean. For this reason most parts of the Rocky Mountain states are very dry. Land at high altitudes thus receives more rain and snow than does lower land. The western sides of the mountains are better watered than the eastern.

CANADA

WASH.
Grand Coulee Dam
Spokane
Wenatchee
Coeur d'Alene
MT. RAINIER 14,410 FT. (4392 m)
akima
Moses Lake
Richland
Walla Walla
Lewiston
MT. HOOD 11,239 FT. (3426 m)
bia River
Pendleton
end
Baker

ORE.
Boise
Snake

GLACIER NAT'L PARK
Kalispell

MONTANA
Havre
Great Falls
Missoula
Anaconda
Butte
Helena
Bozeman
Billings
Missouri River
Glasgow
Fort Peck Dam
Yellowstone River
Glendive

YELLOWSTONE NAT'L PARK
Sheridan
Thermopolis

WYOMING
Idaho Falls
Pocatello
Twin Falls
River
Casper
Rock Springs
Laramie
Cheyenne

NORTH DAKOTA
Williston
Minot
Garrison
Garrison Dam
Dickinson
Bismarck
Missouri R.
45°

SOUTH DAKOTA
Oahe Dam
Pierre
Rapid City
BLACK HILLS

NEBR.
Scottsbluff
North Platte R.
North Platte
40°

R
O
C
K
Y

I
D
A
H
O

GREAT
Humboldt River
NEVADA
BASIN
ake
Reno
hoe
Carson City
Ely

YOSEMITE NAT'L PARK

Great Salt Lake
Logan
Ogden
Salt Lake City
Bingham Canyon
Provo
Price
WASATCH RANGE

UTAH
COLORADO
River
Cedar City

LONGS PEAK 14,255 FT. (4345 m)
Greeley
South Platte R.
Boulder
Denver

PIKES PEAK 14,110 FT. (4301 m)
Grand Junction
Colorado Springs
Pueblo
Arkansas R.

K
A
N
S
A
S

COLORADO
Alamosa
Trinidad
Durango
Raton
OKLA

MT. WHITNEY 14,495 FT. (4418 m)
DEATH VALLEY 282 Ft. (Below sea level) (−86 m)
Fresno
CALIFORNIA
SIERRA NEVADA

Lake Mead
Las Vegas
Boulder City
Hoover Dam
115°

Colorado
PLATEAU
Farmington
GRAND CANYON NAT'L PARK
Flagstaff

ARIZONA
Prescott
Gallup
Albuquerque
Santa Fe

NEW MEXICO
Amarillo
35°
Clovis

Roosevelt Lake
Roosevelt Dam
Phoenix
Globe
Roswell

Colorado
River
Gila River
Yuma

Tucson

Bisbee
Douglas

Las Cruces
El Paso
Rio Grande
Hobbs
Pecos River
Odessa

TEXAS

© Rand McNally & Co.

THE ROCKY MOUNTAIN STATES

| 50 | 100 | 200 Miles |
| 80 | 161 | 322 Kilometers |

State Capitals ☆   Other Cities ●

Mountains

Plateaus

Hills

Plains

The Rocky Mountains in Colorado have snow near their peaks even during the summer. The air is much colder at the tops of these mountains than at their bases.

In the highest ranges, rains and melting snows feed mountain streams. In some areas the people of these mountain states can use water from the rushing streams to irrigate land. The water is stored in reservoirs, or artificial lakes. From the reservoirs water is taken through canals and ditches to irrigate dry fields in the nearby area. Through irrigation the fields can produce good crops. The reservoirs also supply water for nearby cities.

The temperature of the Rocky Mountain region varies according to the altitude of the land. At lower levels much of the region has hot summers and cold winters. But the mountains stay cool even in the summer. There are stretches of hot, dry desert in parts of New Mexico, Arizona, Nevada, and Utah.

The temperature in these states also varies according to latitude. Places near Canada are much colder than are places near Mexico. The region near Mexico is usually warm all year because Mexico is closer to the equator.

Do You Know?

1. What eight states are called the Rocky Mountain states?
2. What kinds of climate do the Rocky Mountain states have?
3. How do the mountains provide water for the people who live near them?

2
Settling the Rocky Mountain States

"Far to the north are seven golden cities," said an American Indian to a group of Spanish explorers.

"I must find these golden cities," declared the Spanish adventurer Francisco Coronado. "Then I will fill Spain's treasury and win fortune for myself."

Spanish Explorations

Coronado marched north from Mexico hoping to find treasure. With him were many Spanish soldiers and a large number of American Indians. These Spaniards were the first Europeans to explore the region that is now Arizona and New Mexico.

Months of hard travel followed. Many of the Spaniards grew ill and died. Then one day Coronado saw a city in the distance which looked bright and beautiful in the sunshine. But when he finally reached it, he found that the city was a group of American Indian villages. The Spanish found plenty of food in the villages, but there was neither gold nor silver. They were greatly disappointed. Still they pushed on, searching for treasure.

Coronado and the soldiers broke up into several groups. One of these groups made a great discovery. While following the Colorado River, they came to the Grand Canyon. This is a deep, wide valley worn away by the swift waters of the Colorado River. The Spaniards were amazed by the great size and beauty of the canyon.

Coronado and the soldiers found no treasure and left no settlements in the mountain country. But they did explore and claim a large part of the area for Spain. And they discovered the Grand Canyon of the Colorado.

Southwest American Indians

American Indians were living in the southwestern part of the country long before the Spanish arrived. One of these Indian groups lived in apartment houses built close together. The

Francisco Coronado led Spaniards through large areas of the Rocky Mountain region. They saw many beautiful places in present-day New Mexico and Arizona.

309

houses were made of stone or clay and had several stories. The Spanish called such Indian villages *pueblos* (pweb′lōz).

The Pueblo Indians

The Indians living in pueblos became known as Pueblo Indians. Most of the Pueblo Indians were farmers. They grew corn, beans, and squash.

The Spanish tried to teach Christianity to the Pueblos. But the Indians wanted to keep their own religion. The Pueblos drove the Spanish away. Later the United States gained the lands on which the Pueblos lived. The government then let the Pueblos keep their old ways of life.

María Martínez, a Pueblo Indian, holds one of her famous black-on-black pots. The brilliant shine of this type of pottery is produced by firing.

Many of the Pueblo Indians of today live in pueblos in New Mexico and Arizona. Some farm. Others work in nearby cities. Still others have become well known for their art.

María Martínez, Pottery Maker

María Montoya Martínez (mär tē′näs) was born in 1887 at San Idlefonso Pueblo, New Mexico. María and her husband Julian began making black-on-black pottery in the early 1900s. This special type of pottery had been made by the Pueblo Indians a long time ago. But no one remembered how to make it. Then María and Julian made some tests and found how to make the black-on-black pottery. After Julian died in 1943, Mariá continued the work.

María used materials from the earth to make the pottery. She formed each pot by hand. The pots were perfectly shaped. Then each pot was heated a certain way to get the black finish.

Over the years the Martínez pottery became well known. María was invited to show her works at world's fairs. She was invited to the White House by four Presidents. She also received a number of awards and honors for her work. María died in 1980, but her children, grandchildren, and great-grandchildren continue to make the famous pottery.

The Navajo Indians

Another group of American Indians living in the southwest at the time the Spanish arrived were the Navajos (näv′e hōz′). They lived in houses called *hogans* (hō′gänz). The dome-shaped hogans were built of poles, tree bark, and mud.

Sand painting is one of the ceremonies of the Navajo religion. These ceremonies may be related to farming or to curing sickness and preserving health.

At first the Navajos hunted for much of their food. Then the Pueblo Indians taught them to farm. After the Spanish brought livestock to the area, many Navajos became sheep ranchers.

During the middle 1800s many settlers started ranches on Navajo lands. The Navajos fought to keep their lands. Manuelito (män wā lē′tō), a Navajo, helped lead several attacks against the settlers. Then Kit Carson and a group of United States soldiers captured thousands of Navajos. The Navajos were forced to march several hundred miles to what is now New Mexico. This march became known as the "Long Walk." In 1868 the Navajos agreed to settle on a reservation that covered parts of present-day Arizona, New Mexico, and Utah.

Today the Navajos are the largest group of American Indians in the United States. Most live in Arizona, New Mexico, and Utah. Some raise crops or tend sheep. Others own or work in businesses. Still others are craft-workers or artists.

The Apache Indians

The Apache (ə pach′ē) Indians also lived in the Southwest at the time the Spanish arrived. Some Apaches lived in thatched huts made of brush. Others lived in tepees made of animal skin.

The Apaches hunted for most of their food. They learned some farming from the Pueblo Indians, just as the Navajos had.

When the early Spanish settled on the Indian lands, the Apaches often raided them. In time other people settled on Apache lands. The Apaches, led by Cochise (kō chēz′) and Geronimo (jə rän′ ə mō′) fought to keep their lands but were defeated by United States soldiers.

This old Spanish mission, San Xavier del Bac, in Tucson, Arizona, is a reminder of the Spanish heritage of the Southwest.

The Apaches were then placed on reservations. In 1886 Geronimo led a group of Apaches from a reservation in a final attack on the soldiers. He was defeated and again placed on a reservation.

Many Apache Indians of today live in Arizona and New Mexico. Some raise sheep. Some work in the lumber or cattle business owned by Apaches.

Mission Settlements

Two priests who came to the West in early times were Father Eusebio Kino (ā oo sā′ vyō kē′nō) and Father Junipero Serra (hoo nē′pə rō ser′ə). They came to teach Christianity to the American Indians. Father Kino started a mission in 1700 in what is now Arizona. Father Serra founded at least nine missions farther west, in California. Several other church settlements were built by followers of the two priests.

For many years the West had few settlements besides missions. Let us visit one of the mission settlements in Arizona in those early days.

A Visit to a Mission

We enter this mission settlement through a gate in a thick stone wall. The wall has been built around the settlement to protect the people inside. A fort and soldiers guard the settlement.

Many American Indians are at work. Some are tanning hides. Others are making jewelry of silver set with brightly colored stones. We see a priest teaching a group how to make candles. Some are tying wicks onto a wooden rod. Others are dipping wicks into a large pot of warm animal fat. The wicks will then be hung on a frame to cool. They will be dipped again and again until enough layers of fat cover each wick to form a candle.

Clang, clang, clang! A blacksmith is working before a great fire. He is making horseshoes and wagon wheels. Farther on, we see carpenters making benches for the church and chairs and tables for their homes.

We come to a group of people working near a stone oven. They are baking loaves of wheat, corn, and barley bread. Some are kneading

312

dough on large, flat stones. Others are taking brown loaves out of the oven.

Farther along we pass a building where women are weaving cloth. Sheep are grazing in the fields of this mission settlement. From the sheep the Indians get wool for cloth. Besides sheep, this settlement has horses, cows, and oxen. The grazing lands are outside the wall.

As we leave, we see that the farmlands of this mission settlement also lie outside the stone wall. A canal has been dug from a nearby stream to irrigate these fields. Oranges, lemons, limes, and figs grow in orchards. Grains and vegetables grow in the fields.

The Santa Fe Trail

After the Louisiana Purchase in 1803, some traders from the United States began to make the long journey to Spanish settlements in Arizona and New Mexico. They traveled over a route called the Santa Fe Trail.

The city of Santa Fe was founded in 1610 as the capital of the Spanish province of New Mexico. Notice on the map of western trails on

All the routes to the West followed large rivers for part of the way. Why do you think this was so? From what city did most of the trails start? What natural barriers did settlers on the trails have to face?

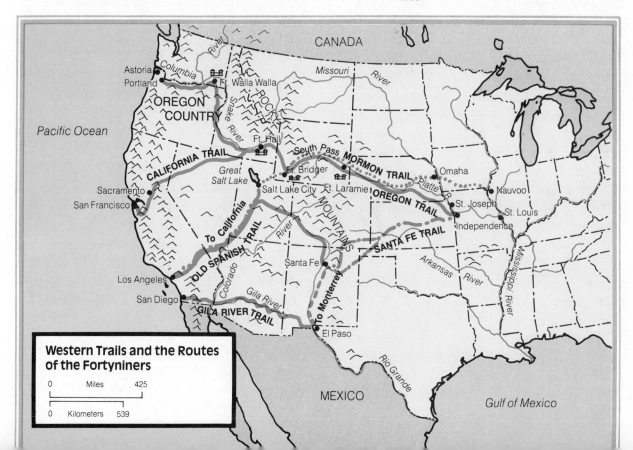

Western Trails and the Routes of the Fortyniners

| 0 | Miles | 425 |
| 0 | Kilometers | 539 |

Traders traveled on the Santa Fe Trail in covered wagons pulled by oxen. What kinds of manufactured goods do you think the traders took to Santa Fe?

page 313 that Santa Fe was the meeting point of two other trails. The Old Spanish Trail led to Los Angeles. Another trail led south along the Rio Grande to Monterrey and other Mexican cities.

In 1821, William Becknell was the first trader to use the Santa Fe Trail. After that, many traders used it to carry manufactured goods from the United States to Santa Fe. These manufactures were exchanged for the mules, furs, gold, and silver of Mexico.

The traders started from Independence, near the Missouri River. Then they journeyed southwest across the wide, flat plains to a point on the Arkansas River. Here the trail divided. The shorter, more dangerous route crossed a wide desert where there was no water for 60 miles (96 km). The longer, safer trail went through part of the Rocky Mountains. The two trails joined again before Santa Fe, New Mexico, was reached. Follow the route on the map of western trails on page 313. The trail covered almost 800 miles (1287 km). The Santa Fe Trail was once an important trade route.

Because of the dangers on this trail, traders on the Santa Fe Trail traveled in large groups. At first they used pack mules to carry the goods. Then as the trail grew wider with use, they traveled in covered wagons. Each wagon was pulled by ten oxen or mules and could carry a load of 6,000 pounds (2721 kg). A wagon train could go about 15 miles (24 km) a day along the Santa Fe Trail.

After a time stagecoaches carried passengers on their westward journeys. Then the trip from Independence, Missouri, to Santa Fe, New Mexico, took about two weeks.

The Mormons in Utah

One of the most important routes to the West was the Oregon Trail. Near that trail, in what is now Utah, is Salt Lake City. This city was built by a religious group called Mormons. These people were looking for land on which to settle.

The Mormons were searching for a place where they could worship as they wished. First they had tried to settle in Ohio. Then they moved on to Missouri and later to Illinois. But wherever they tried to settle, neighboring people objected to what the Mormons believed.

The Mormons decided that they would have to find a new region where there were no people to object to their ways of worship. So they made up their minds to move out of the United States.

Brigham Young was determined to lead his people to an area where they could worship in peace. The Mormons built a successful settlement in the desert of Utah.

Brigham Young, Mormon Leader

The leader of the Mormons in their westward travels was Brigham Young. Under his leadership about 200 Mormons started west in the winter of 1846. They traveled 1,000 miles (1,609 km) to the shore of the Great Salt Lake. This land then belonged to Mexico. No other settlers were living there. It was a very dry area where only desert shrubs grew.

The Building of Salt Lake City

All the Mormons worked together under Brigham Young's leadership to build a new settlement. They dug ditches to irrigate the land. They plowed the land and planted the crops. They built barns, houses, and a church, which they called a temple. They laid out wide, straight streets.

In their second year their crops were threatened by a huge swarm of Rocky Mountain grasshoppers. But before the grasshoppers destroyed the crops, flocks of sea gulls appeared and ate the grasshoppers. The Mormons were so grateful that they set up a statue of the sea gulls.

Within a few years several thousand other Mormons joined this settlement. Everyone worked hard. Today Salt Lake City is one of the major cities of the Rocky Mountain states.

Settlement of Nevada and Colorado

In 1848 the discovery of gold in California drew thousands of people westward. Some who reached California failed to find gold there and left. Their search for mineral treasures took them to the Rocky Mountain region.

The Comstock Lode

Ten years after the gold rush to California, a huge deposit of gold and silver was discovered in western Nevada. This mine was called the Comstock Lode. News of it brought many adventurers to Nevada.

One adventurer who went to Nevada in the days of the Comstock Lode became a well-known writer. His real name was Samuel Clemens, but he used Mark Twain as a pen name. His stories, published in a newspaper, tell us

Reaching the top of Pikes Peak is a challenge for many visitors to the Colorado Rockies. Some walk, others ride horses, and some ride a train to the top.

much about the early days in Nevada. Later Mark Twain became famous as the author of *The Adventures of Tom Sawyer* and *The Adventures of Huckleberry Finn*.

Pikes Peak or Bust

When the Comstock Lode was discovered, gold was also found in the Pikes Peak region of Colorado. Hundreds of people came to Colorado. Some traveled on foot. Some rode on horseback. Others went in covered wagons. Many covered wagons had signs reading "Pikes Peak or Bust" printed on them. When some of these wagons went home later, their covers carried the word "Busted." Today a highway and a rail-

way run to the top of Pikes Peak. Many people travel up the mountain every year to enjoy the wonderful scenery.

Becoming a Part of the United States

The map showing the growth of the United States on page 91 shows how the United States obtained the territory between the Mississippi River and the Pacific Ocean. It shows that parts of Colorado, Wyoming, and Montana lie within the region that was gained from France through the Louisiana Purchase.

Arizona, Nevada, and Utah are within the region that once belonged to Mexico. Some land that now lies within Wyoming, Colorado, and New Mexico also belonged to Mexico.

To the north was the Oregon Country, which was shared by the United States and Great Britain until 1846. After it was divided and more people settled there, new states were carved out of it. One of these was Idaho. Part of Wyoming and of Montana also belonged to the Oregon Country in the early days.

Do You Know?

1. What areas did Coronado and the Spaniards with him explore?
2. Who founded missions in Arizona?
3. Who led the Mormons in their westward travels?
4. What was the Comstock Lode?

Before You Go On

Using New Words

pueblo   Continental Divide
hogan   ridge

The phrases below explain the words or terms listed above. Number a paper from 1 through 4. After each number write the word or term that matches the definition.

1. A dome-shaped American Indian house built of poles, tree bark, and mud
2. A long, narrow chain of hills or mountains
3. A dividing ridge in the Rockies which separates the rivers flowing east from the rivers flowing west
4. An Indian village like apartment houses built of stone or clay

Finding the Facts

1. What different types of land surfaces make up the Rocky Mountain region?
2. Why don't all rivers that form in the Rocky Mountains flow in the same direction?
3. Why are most parts of the Rocky Mountain states very dry?
4. How is the temperature of the Rocky Mountain region affected by altitude and latitude?
5. What is the Grand Canyon? By whom was it discovered?
6. What three American Indian groups were living in the southwestern part of the country at the time the Spanish arrived? Which group is the largest today?
7. For what did María Martínez receive a number of awards and honors?
8. Why did Father Kino and Father Serra come to the West in early times? In which present-day state did Father Kino settle? Where did Father Serra build missions?
9. Why was the Santa Fe Trail an important route during the 1800s? How did travel on the Santa Fe Trail change as time passed?
10. Why did the Mormons journey westward? What city did they build?
11. How did the Comstock Lode help to bring settlers to Nevada?
12. What discovery brought many settlers to Colorado?
13. What foreign countries once owned parts of the region that now makes up the Rocky Mountain states? To which country did most of the land in this region once belong?

3

Living and Working in the Rocky Mountain States

Many people who live in the plains region of the mountain states earn their living by farming and livestock raising. The leading crops are wheat and cotton. Cattle and sheep feed on the tough grass that covers much of the land.

Grazing and Farming Lands

Most of the land west of the Rockies has little rain. Some regions are covered with short, coarse grass. The grasslands are used mainly for cattle and sheep grazing. Many more sheep than cattle pasture there, however. Sheep can live on less water and poorer grass than cattle can. Sheep also climb more easily and can graze on mountain slopes.

Sheep like salt in addition to the grass they eat. Sheepherders make sure salt is part of their diet. Sheep are marked so sheepherders know which sheep are theirs.

Raising Sheep

During the winter the sheep grow a thick, warm wool coat called a *fleece* (flēs). In spring the sheep are rounded up and their fleeces are clipped off. This is called *shearing* (shēr′ing) the sheep. Ranch workers bring the animals to a shearing shed. Each worker throws a sheep to the floor and holds it down. With large electric clippers the worker quickly and painlessly cuts off the sheep's coat of wool.

In the spring ranchers wait until there is no danger of a late snowfall on the mountainsides. Then the sheepherders go with the sheep to the fresh pastures. Each sheepherder must keep the flock from grazing in one place more than three days. In this way the sheep do not eat the grass so close that it will not grow again. In the late fall the sheepherders take the sheep back to the ranch for winter feeding.

Farming in the South

The dry land in Arizona and New Mexico has irrigation water for only a very small part of its area. The Elephant Butte Dam on the Rio Grande provides water for some of New Mexico's dry land. The irrigated land produces corn, wheat, and onions.

Some of the finest cotton in the world comes from Arizona. Arizona's cotton farmers get irrigation water from Roosevelt Dam, on the Salt River. Arizona is also known for its lettuce, melons, and citrus fruits. Some of these crops grow on land irrigated by water from Hoover

Dam, on the Colorado River. The reservoir made by this dam is called Lake Mead.

Lake Mead stores water to irrigate parts of Nevada as well as Arizona. Nevada is one of the driest states in the nation.

In much of Colorado the Rocky Mountains make farming difficult. Without irrigation farming would be hard in the rest of this state. Some lands are irrigated by water from streams formed by melting snow from the nearby Rocky Mountains. The farmers there grow sugar beets, potatoes, fruit, and grains.

Utah raises these crops also. It has very little rainfall except in the Wasatch Mountains, a range of the Rockies. Most farming is in the valleys near these mountains. More than 1,000,000 acres (404,854 ha) have been irrigated in Utah.

Farming in the North

Much of Montana and eastern Wyoming lies in the Great Plains. These states get very little rain except in the Rockies. Some of the land near the foot of the Rockies can be irrigated. Water from streams formed by melting snow in the Rockies irrigates ranches near these mountains.

The largest earth dam in the United States is on the Missouri River at Fort Peck, Montana. People in this plains area earn a living by raising cattle or sheep on the irrigated land.

Many sheep are also raised in the valleys on the lower slopes of the Rockies. Montana and Wyoming are among the leaders in raising sheep and in wool production.

Montana is one of our leading wheat states also. Much of the wheat is raised by dry-farming methods. Dry farming is a way of conserving moisture. It is used where there is little rain and no supply of water for irrigation. Crops are planted on part of the land during one year, while the rest of the land has no crops. This land is allowed to rest and is able to hold its moisture for the whole season. The next year crops will be planted on it, while the first area rests.

Many dams control the Missouri River. They help prevent floods in the area. Also, the dams provide water for irrigation and electricity.

The waters of the Snake River are used to irrigate much farmland in southern Idaho. This watered land grows sugar beets, wheat, fruit, and potatoes. Idaho is one of the chief potato-growing states in the United States. Idaho's vegetables are grown not only to produce food but also to produce seeds.

Mining in the Mountain States

The Rocky Mountains are rich in minerals. Gold and silver are still mined in every state in the region. Other new mineral treasures have also been found, including petroleum and uranium. The uranium mined on the Colorado Plateau is used in nuclear energy plants.

Most Rocky Mountain states produce copper. Copper is used to make water pipes, pans, faucets, and pots. It is used in telephone, telegraph, and electrical wiring. Arizona is the largest copper-producing state.

Large copper mines are also located near Bingham Canyon, Utah, and in Butte, Montana. See the map of copper deposits on page 178. The Bingham Canyon mine is a great open pit,

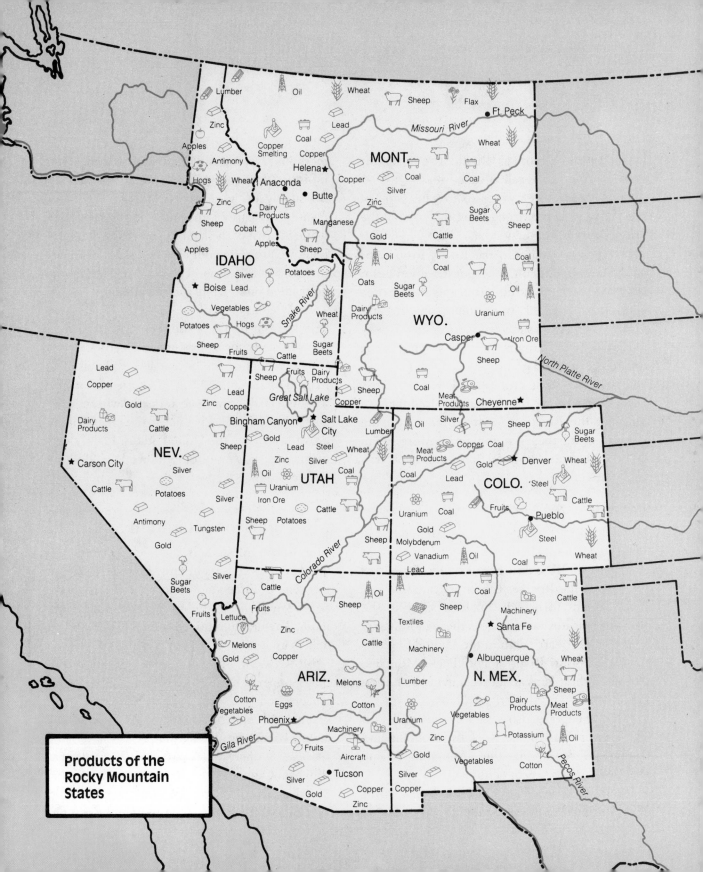

Products of the Rocky Mountain States

in which power shovels mine the copper. Under Butte, Montana, people work in tunnels to mine the copper. Above ground are huge smelters. Some of the copper is refined there. But most of the ore is sent to be smelted in Anaconda (an′ə kon′də), Montana.

Utah has coal and iron mines. Colorado, New Mexico, Montana, and Wyoming also have coal. Lead and zinc are found in Utah, Arizona, Colorado, Idaho, and Montana. See the map of lead and zinc deposits on page 255. Wyoming has much petroleum. Other states with petroleum and natural gas are Colorado, Utah, Montana, New Mexico, and Arizona.

Lumbering in the Mountain States

Lumbering is not a leading industry in the Rocky Mountain states. But Montana, Idaho, and Colorado have sawmills that produce lumber products.

Most of the wooden match sticks we use are made from Idaho white pine trees. The slopes of the Rocky Mountains in Idaho yield much of the white pine cut in the United States. White pine is a soft wood that is easy to work with. It is used for making furniture, shingles, matches, and other wood products.

Energy Sources in the Mountain States

Although the mountain states produce some petroleum and natural gas, there is a shortage of these substances. Plans are being made to use more solar, or sun, energy as a source of power. People are studying better ways of collecting and storing energy from the sun. The energy is used to heat and cool homes and other buildings. People are also studying ways of changing solar energy into electricity.

People in the mountain states and elsewhere have built houses that can be heated by solar energy. Such houses have special roofs with collectors that trap the sun's heat.

Coal is another important source of energy used in the United States. Some coal fields are in the Rocky Mountain states. Look at the map of coal deposits on page 175 to find the states where these coal fields are located.

Some people in our country think that *oil shale* (shāl), a type of rock, may be a source of oil. But the cost of making oil from oil shale is great. So oil shale has not been used much. Large amounts of oil shale can be found in Colorado, Utah, and Wyoming.

Scenic Wonders

Many tourists visit the Rocky Mountain states to enjoy their beautiful scenery. Some regions of great natural beauty have been set aside as national parks.

National Parks in the South

One of the greatest wonders of the world is the Grand Canyon in Arizona. The canyon has been carved out by waters of the Colorado River. Another national park in Arizona is the Petrified Forest. It is strewn with logs of an old woodland now turned to stone.

321

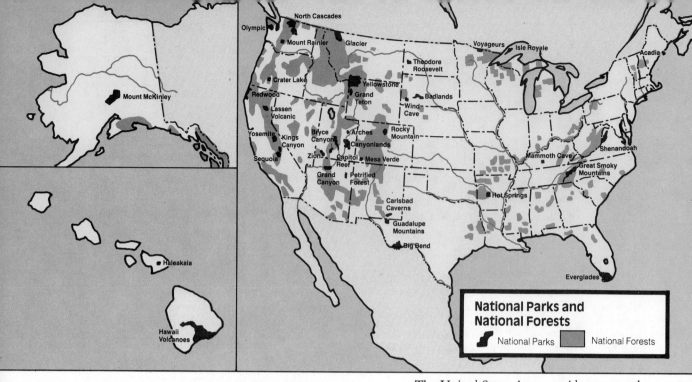

The United States has set aside many parks as places of great natural beauty. National forests are areas of timberland where wildlife is protected. Several large parks and forests are in the Rocky Mountain states.

Carlsbad Caverns National Park is in New Mexico. It is a series of huge caves with interesting rock formations.

Colorado has two national parks. Rocky Mountain National Park has many high peaks. Mesa Verde National Park is a site of Pueblo Indian cliff dwellings.

Utah has five national parks. They are Arches, Bryce Canyon, Canyonlands, Capitol Reef, and Zion. Each has interesting rock formations.

National Parks in the North

Our oldest and best-known national park is Yellowstone. Most of this park is in northwestern Wyoming, but it also reaches into Idaho and Montana. Yellowstone is one of the greatest *geyser* (gī′zər) regions in the world. A geyser is a spring which throws shafts of hot water and steam high into the air. People visiting Yellowstone are thrilled by Old Faithful, the geyser that sends water upward every 60 to 70 minutes. The park also has canyons, waterfalls, and a wide variety of plants and animals.

South of Yellowstone in Wyoming is the Grand Teton National Park. It has beautiful mountain scenery.

Another famous park in the Montana Rockies is Glacier National Park. It has many glaciers and lakes. Just north of it, Canada has made part of the Canadian Rockies into a public park. The two parks, one in Canada and one in the United States, together form a great *international* (in′tər nash′ən əl) park. "International" means belonging to, or having to do with, two or more nations.

A

B

These are some of the beautiful and unusual sites of national parks in the Rocky Mountain states: "Queen's Garden Trail" in Bryce National Park (A); clear blue lakes among jagged mountains in Glacier National Park (B); "Cliff Palace" in Mesa Verde National Park (C); the deep, long gorge of the Grand Canyon (D); and the geyser called "Old Faithful" in Yellowstone (E). Can you find these national parks on the map on page 322? Which park would you most like to visit? Why?

C

E

D

Denver
A Vital Center of Trade

In 1869 the people of Denver were worried. The first transcontinental railroad was finished. Trains could now go from coast to coast. But the railroad went through southern Wyoming. It did not go through Denver, the capital of Colorado. Denver then, as today, was important because it was a trade center. Why did people worry that Denver would become a "ghost town" after the transcontinental railroad bypassed it?

The city did not become a "ghost town." It built its own railroad line north to join the transcontinental railroad in Wyoming. Other railroads leading to Denver were built also. Today, the city is a major transportation center for the Rocky Mountain region.

Denver serves as a trade center for two regions. The city is a gateway to the Rocky Mountain region. It also serves the plains region east of the Rockies.

Many of the goods that Denver supplies to nearby areas are manufactured in other parts of the nation. However, some machinery and other goods are made in Denver's own factories.

Denver was a gateway to the mining country of the mountains before it became a plains center. The city was founded during the Pikes Peak gold rush. Then silver strikes touched off another boom.

Later the United States government built a mint in Denver for making coins. What metals are used in coins? Why was Denver a good place to build a mint?

By 1900, however, the ranches and farms of the plains were as important to Denver as the mines of the mountains. The mining booms were over. But today the mountains have given Denver another kind of boom, a tourist boom.

Look at the picture on page 308. What makes Denver a tourist center? Turn to the map of the Rocky Mountain states on page 307. What national park is located nearby? People once flocked through Denver on their way to find gold and silver in the Rockies. Even greater numbers of people go today to enjoy the region's beauty. ■

Population in the Rocky Mountain States, 1960 and 1978

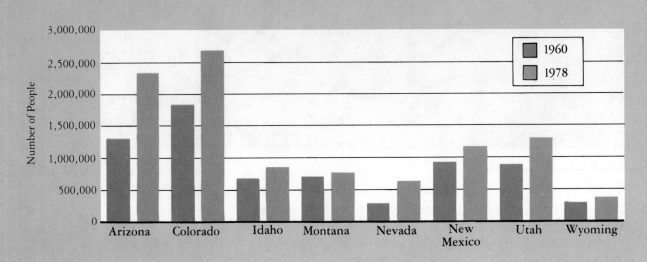

This graph shows how the population of each Rocky Mountain state grew between 1960 and 1978. Which two states grew the most between those years? Which two states grew the least?

Cities in the Mountain States

Turn to the map of the United States on pages 92–93. Notice how great an area is occupied by the Rocky Mountain states. Their area is large, but they are not densely populated. In recent years, however, their population has been growing more rapidly. As you might suppose, much growth has taken place in the cities.

The Cities of Colorado and Utah

South of Denver in Colorado is the large steel center of Pueblo. At Colorado Springs is the United States Air Force Academy. Here the Air Force trains young men and women as officers.

In Utah the capital and major city is Salt Lake City. North of this city is Ogden. It is near the meeting place of the first railroad to cross the country. Ogden is an important railroad town.

South of Salt Lake City is Provo. It lies in a valley of rich farmland. It is known as the "Steel Center of the West" because of the nearby Geneva Steel plant.

The Cities of New Mexico and Arizona

Albuquerque is the largest city in New Mexico. Because of its healthful climate Albuquerque has many hospitals and rest homes. New Mexico's second largest city is Santa Fe. Santa Fe is the capital of New Mexico and the oldest city west of the Mississippi River. Santa Fe has many reminders of its Spanish history.

In Arizona, Tucson is the trade center of the copper-mining region and of irrigated farms. Phoenix, the capital of Arizona, is the heart of a farming area irrigated by Roosevelt Dam. Yuma is another desert garden spot. Its water is piped from the Colorado River.

The Cities of Nevada and Idaho

The chief trade center in Nevada is Reno. This city handles the products of the farms and mines at the foothills of the Sierras. Near Reno is Carson City, the capital of Nevada. It was named in honor of Kit Carson. A rapidly growing city of Nevada is Las Vegas. It is not far from Hoover Dam, in the southeastern part of the state.

Boise, in southwestern Idaho, is the capital of this state and its chief city. In southeastern Idaho, Pocatello is the leading city. Both Boise and Pocatello are trade centers for farming areas irrigated by water from the Snake River.

Lewiston is the trade center for mountainous northern Idaho. It was named for the famous explorer, Meriwether Lewis. It ships lumber and minerals.

The Cities of Montana and Wyoming

The largest city in Montana is Great Falls. Butte, a copper-mining center, ranks next in size. Anaconda also produces copper. The state capital is Helena. It is a trade center for Montana's mountainous western region.

Cheyenne, in southeastern Wyoming, is the capital and largest city of this state. It is also

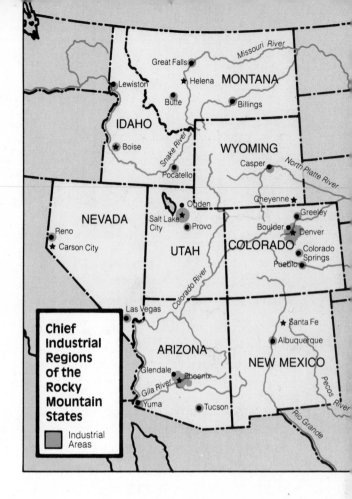

the trade center for a large grazing area. From Cheyenne, cattle are sent east to meat-packing centers. Located on the Platte River, near the center of Wyoming, is Casper. It is the trade center for this part of the state.

Do You Know?

1. Why do farmers of the mountain country practice irrigated farming?
2. What are some of the minerals found in the Rocky Mountain states?

327

To Help You Learn

Using New Words

Continental Divide	hogan
fleece	international
shearing	oil shale
geyser	pueblo

The phrases below explain the words or terms listed above. Number a paper from 1 through 8. After each number write the word or term which matches the definition.

1. Cutting off the wool of sheep
2. The thick wool of a sheep
3. Belonging to, or having to do with, two or more nations
4. A spring which throws hot water and steam high into the air
5. A type of rock that may be a source of energy
6. A dome-shaped Indian house built of poles, tree bark, and mud
7. An Indian village like apartment houses built of stone or clay
8. A ridge in the Rockies which separates rivers flowing east from rivers flowing west

Finding the Facts

1. What eight states are called the Rocky Mountain states? What is the capital city of each?
2. How was the Grand Canyon formed? What group of people discovered it?
3. How was the way of life of the Pueblo Indians in the early days different from the way of life of the Navajo Indians and the Apache Indians?
4. Who started a mission in what is now Arizona in 1700? Why did this person start a mission?
5. Why did traders use the Santa Fe Trail?
6. Who was the leader of the people who built Salt Lake City? Who were these people? Why did they go west?
7. Why did many settlers go to Nevada in the late 1850s? Why did many go to Colorado?
8. Why are so many sheep raised in the Rocky Mountain states?
9. What are three ways in which dams help the people in the Rocky Mountain states?
10. Below is a list of persons whom you met in Unit 9 and descriptions of these people. Match the people and the descriptions.

Martínez	Coronado	Young
Kino	Twain	Pike

   a. I started several missions in Arizona.
   b. I led the Mormons to Salt Lake City.
   c. I rediscovered how black-on-black pottery is made.
   d. I discovered the great mountain in Colorado now named in my honor.
   e. I wrote stories about the early days in Nevada.
   f. A group of my soldiers discovered the Grand Canyon.

11. Where is some uranium found? What is one use of uranium?

12. What are some uses of copper? Where is copper mined?

13. What national parks are found in the Rocky Mountain states? In which states are they found?

14. What is the largest city in New Mexico? In Montana?

Learning from Maps

1. On the map of the United States, on pages 92 – 93, locate the Rocky Mountain states. Find the great Rocky Mountain chain. What rivers drain the eastern slopes of these mountains? The western slopes? In what part of this region are the highest peaks? What is the Continental Divide? Where is it?

2. On the relief map on page 307 find and name the natural regions of the Rocky Mountain states. Between what parallels of latitude do these states lie? What effect do the mountains have on the climate? Look at the diagram of wind movements on page 122 before answering this.

3. Turn to the map of industrial regions, page 327. Which state has the most industry?

4. One of the most useful kinds of maps is a road map. Here is a part of a road map which shows a part of the city of Phoenix, Arizona. Phoenix is a large city. It is shown in solid yellow on the map. What smaller city is also shown?

   What kinds of roads are shown in green lines? In red lines? How are Interstate roads marked? How are U.S. roads marked? How are state roads marked?

   How can you tell from the map that Phoenix is the capital city of Arizona? How can you tell that many American Indians may have lived in the area where Phoenix is? What place does Phoenix have to help Indians?

5. Turn to the products map on page 320. What minerals are found in this region? What animals are raised? Where are sugar beets grown?

6. Look at the map of national parks and forests on page 322. What national parks are in the Rocky Mountain states? Which of the Rocky Mountain states have national forests? Why does the government set aside these large areas?

7. Study the North American maps on pages 17 – 18. Which section of the United States has the least rainfall? Which kind of natural vegetation is found in much of the Rocky Mountain states?

8. Look at the map of forest regions on page 357 to see what kinds of forests are found in the Rocky Mountain states.

State	Capital	Largest City	Dams	National Parks	Principal Products
Arizona	Phoenix Population 781,000	Phoenix Population 781,000	Hoover Roosevelt	Grand Canyon Petrified Forest	copper, cotton, fruit, lettuce
Colorado					
Idaho	Boise				wheat, copper, sheep
Montana					
Nevada					
New Mexico			Elephant Butte		
Utah	Salt Lake City				
Wyoming	Cheyenne			Grand Teton Yellowstone	

Using Study Skills

1. **Chart:** Make a chart like the one above telling some important facts about the Rocky Mountain states. Some of the information has been filled in for you. Use the maps in this unit, the Reference Tables on pages 458-461, and an almanac or encyclopedia to help you.
2. **Time Line:** The following events are not listed in the right order. Copy the statements in the right order. Use the time line on page 305 to help you.
   The founding of Salt Lake City
   The first use of the Santa Fe Trail
   The discovery of Pikes Peak
   The discovery of the Grand Canyon
   Comstock Silver Lode opened for mining

3. **Graph:** Look at the graph on page 326. Which state had the largest population in 1960? Which had the largest in 1978? Which state had the smallest population in 1960? Which had the smallest in 1978? Which state, Idaho or New Mexico, had the larger population in 1978? Which state, Nevada or Utah, had the smaller population in 1960?

   About how many more people lived in Arizona in 1978 than in 1960? Do you think that the population of the Rocky Mountain states will continue to grow? Why?

4. **Diagram:** Study the diagram of wind movements on page 122 and the map on page 307. Tell why much land in Nevada and Utah is too dry for farming without irrigation.

Thinking It Through

1. The American Indians first saw the Spanish in the 1500s. What might the way of life of the Indians have been like if they had been left alone?

2. If the pioneers of 100 years ago could see the Rocky Mountain states today, what would most attract their attention? What ways of earning a living would be familiar to the pioneers? What ways would be new and strange to their eyes?

3. Many boom towns sprang up during the gold and silver strikes in the West. But as soon as the gold or silver ran out, they became ghost towns. Why did this not happen to Denver?

4. The desire for gold and silver brought people to Colorado, Nevada, and Wyoming and helped settle these states. Later, many other minerals were discovered in the Rocky Mountain states. Among these minerals were copper, zinc, iron ore, petroleum, lead, coal, uranium, and oil shale.

   Which of these minerals are important energy sources? Why is it important that the United States has these natural resources? What other energy source holds much promise for the future?

5. Review the information about national parks on pages 321–322. How do you think areas preserved as national parks have produced an industry? Describe how this industry affects the way people make a living in communities near the parks.

6. Look at the picture on page 312. Discuss the picture, relating it to what you have read in this unit about an early mission.

7. "The wilderness shall be glad, and the desert shall blossom as the rose." These are the words of a person who lived long ago. How have these words come true in the Rocky Mountain states?

Projects

1. Collect and put on your bulletin board pictures showing some of the huge dams which provide irrigation water in the Rocky Mountain states.

2. The Research Committee might find out more about these early explorers and settlers in the Rocky Mountain states:
   Francisco Coronado   Father Eusebio Kino
   Zebulon Pike   Brigham Young
   The students could pretend to be these people as they tell their stories.

3. The Explorers' Committee should show on a map the routes these people traveled and where the first settlements were.

4. The Reading Committee will find these books interesting: *The Santa Fe Trail*, by S. H. Adams; and *Waterless Mountain*, by L. Armer. Read one of these books and report on it to the class.

10 The Pacific States

Unit Preview

Much of our country's history is a story of people moving west. Finally, they reached the Pacific. The five Pacific states are California, Oregon, Washington, Alaska, and Hawaii.

Captain Robert Gray established the United States's claim to the Pacific Coast in 1792. President Jefferson sent Lewis and Clark overland to the Pacific Coast in 1804. But American settlers were not quick to follow these explorers. The Oregon country was not settled until 1843. The first large rush of Americans to California was in 1849, when gold was discovered. In that one year, however, so many people went there that California became a state a year later.

People have not been quick, however, to move to Alaska. It is the largest state in area, but one of the smallest in population. In 1977 an 800-mile pipeline was built across Alaska to transport oil to port cities.

Alaska and Hawaii became states in 1959. Hawaii was an independent nation before that time.

To the government in Washington the Pacific region once seemed to be far away. The invention of the telegraph helped to bring the West Coast closer. A transcontinental railroad was completed in 1869. Today air travel makes Hawaii and Alaska hours, not days, away from Washington, D.C.

Things to Discover

If you look carefully at the picture, map, and time line, you can answer these questions.

1. The picture shows a scene on the Alaskan coast. What industry would make use of the boats in the harbor?
2. What form of communication began to be used in 1861?
3. Alaska and Hawaii are Pacific states, but they lie beyond the area shown on the map. How many Pacific states are shown?
4. What mineral was discovered in California in 1849?
5. When did the United States buy Alaska? How many years later did Alaska become a state?
6. What means of transportation helped people cross the mountains after 1869?

Words to Learn

You will meet these words in this unit. As you read, you will learn what they mean and how to pronounce them. The Word List will help you.

aqueduct	inlet
conveyor	Interior
current	lava
earthquake	sound
extinct	spawning
fault	trade wind
fortyniner	transcontinental
great circle route	volcano

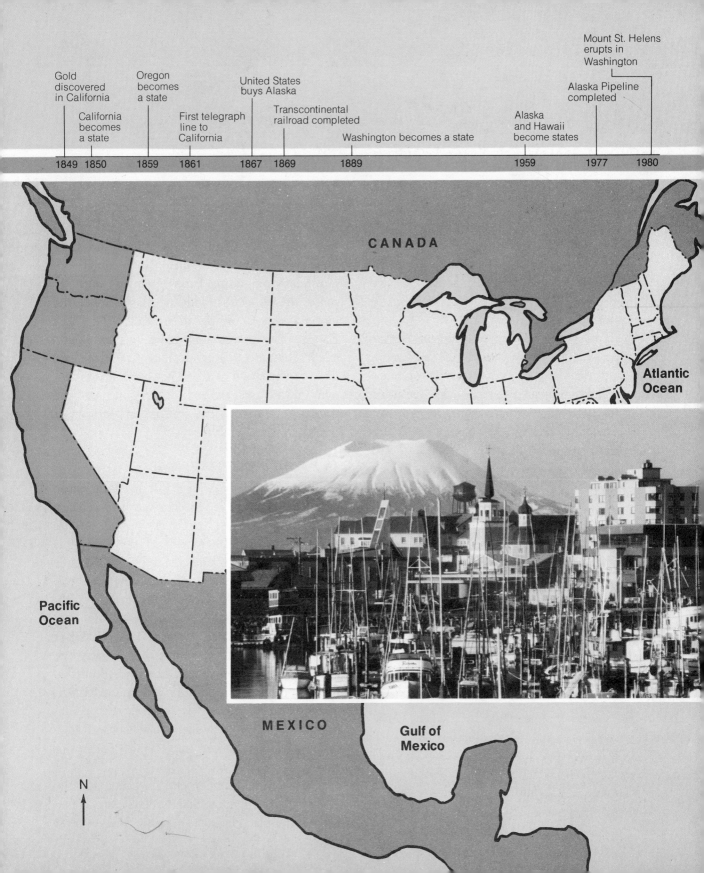

Gold discovered in California

California becomes a state

Oregon becomes a state

First telegraph line to California

United States buys Alaska

Transcontinental railroad completed

Washington becomes a state

Alaska and Hawaii become states

Alaska Pipeline completed

Mount St. Helens erupts in Washington

1849 1850   1859   1861   1867 1869   1889   1959   1977   1980

CANADA

Atlantic Ocean

Pacific Ocean

MEXICO

Gulf of Mexico

N

1
Geography of the Pacific States

The Pacific states are alike in important ways. All have coasts on the world's largest ocean. All have fine natural resources such as fertile land, minerals, and good fishing areas. All have high mountains, green valleys, sparkling lakes, and other beautiful scenery.

The five states, however, differ in certain ways. Alaska, our largest state, lies farther north and west than any other part of the United States. Hawaii is located so far south that part of it lies in the tropics. Washington, Oregon, and California, which are on the coast of the mainland, reach from Canada to Mexico. Located so far apart, the five states have a variety of climates.

In northern California sandy beaches and grasslands border the Pacific Ocean. Forests and mountains are nearby.

Surface of the Coast States

The map of Washington, Oregon, and California on page 335 shows long ranges of mountains extending from north to south. In these threee states and in Alaska also, the mountains near the ocean are called the Coast Range. The mountains lying farther inland in Washington, Oregon, and California are divided into two parts. The northern mountains, in Washington and Oregon, are the Cascade Range. To the south, in California, is the Sierra (sē er′ ə) Nevada.

In Washington and Oregon

The Coast Range is quite low in Washington and Oregon. It is broken at two places. These are at Puget (pyōō′jit) Sound, in the north, and near the mouth of the Columbia River. A *sound* (sound) is a body of water like a large bay extending into the land. See the map of Washington, Oregon, and California on page 335.

Between the Coast Range and the Cascades lies a lowland. North of the Columbia River it is called the Puget Sound Lowland. South of the Columbia it is called the Willamette Valley. This entire lowland is called the Willamette-Puget Sound Valley. The Coast Range is low enough to let rain clouds reach this valley.

To the east, between the Cascades and the Rockies, are high tablelands. They are called the Columbia Plateau and the Snake River

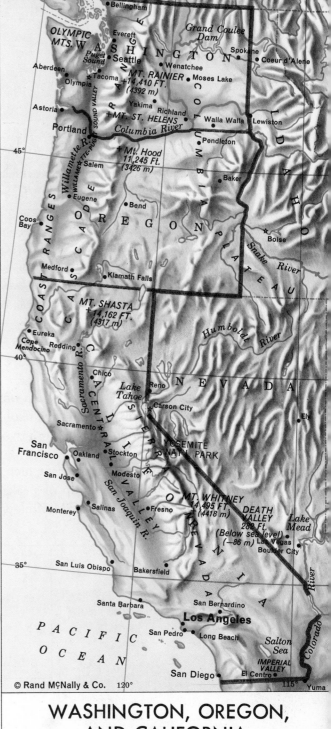

Before Mount St. Helens erupted, the mountain was 9,677 feet (2,950 meters) above sea level. It now stands at about 8,400 feet (2,560 meters). Billions of tons of matter were blown away.

Plateau. They get their names from the Columbia River and its chief tributary, the Snake River.

Mount St. Helens is in the Cascade Range. It is a *volcano* (vol kā′ nō), or opening in the earth's surface through which steam, ashes, and hot, melted rock, or *lava* (lä′və) flow. In 1980 trapped gases blew the top off Mount St. Helens and hot ashes were forced out.

In California

Low mountains make up the Coast Range of California. Between the Coast Range and the ocean there are only a very few narrow plains.

East of the Coast Range is the Central Valley of California. The Central Valley ends at the Si-

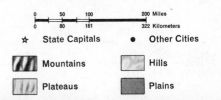

WASHINGTON, OREGON, AND CALIFORNIA

| 0 | 50 | 100 | 200 Miles |
| 0 | 80 | 161 | 322 Kilometers |

★ State Capitals   ● Other Cities

Mountains   Hills

Plateaus   Plains

335

erra Nevada, in eastern California. These mountains are higher and narrower than the Rockies. Mount Whitney, the highest mountain in California, is in the Sierra Nevada.

Sometimes *earthquakes* (urth′kwāks′) take place in California. An earthquake is a movement of a part of the earth's surface. It can be caused by a sudden shift of rock along a *fault* (fôlt) or by volcanic or other disturbances. A fault is a break in a rock mass.

What Alaska Is Like

Alaska's greatest river is the Yukon. Find it on the map of Alaska on this page. The Yukon River and its valley divide Alaska into two parts.

The region south of the river has many high, snow-capped mountains. One group of peaks makes up the Alaska Range. Mount McKinley,

the highest mountain in North America, is in the Alaska Range.

Rugged mountains also rise along the southern coast of Alaska. Narrow waterways cut into the mountainous coast. Near the shore are many rocky islands. Near the middle of the southern coast is Cook Inlet. An *inlet* (in′let′) is a narrow strip of water which reaches far inland. Just beyond Cook Inlet is the fertile Matanuska (mat ə nōō′skə) Valley.

North of the Yukon River lies another range of mountains. It is called the Brooks Range. The northern mountains gradually slope down into flat coastlands. The coastlands end at the Arctic (ärk′tik) Ocean.

Alaska also includes a long chain of islands which curve westward into the Pacific. They are the foggy, barren Aleutian (ə lōō′shən) Islands.

Alaska is becoming an important center for

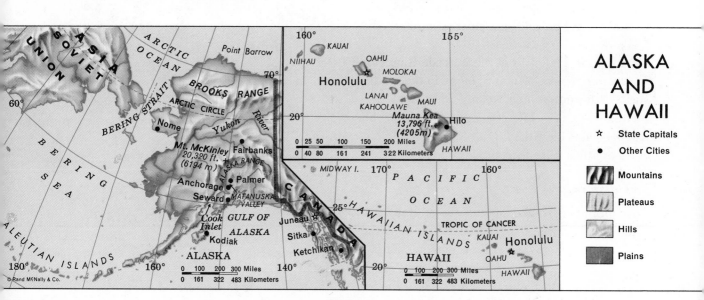

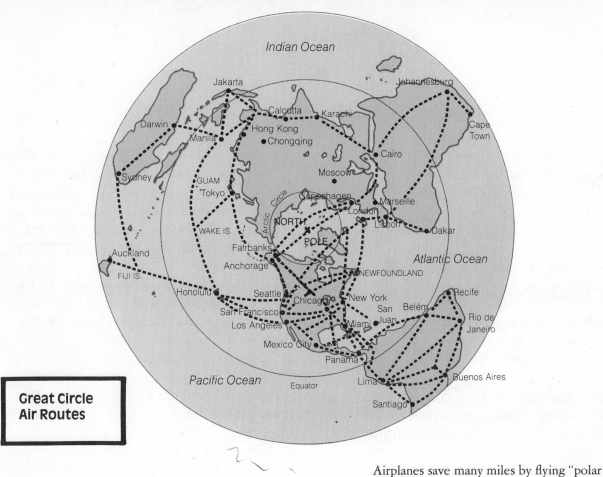

Great Circle Air Routes

Airplanes save many miles by flying "polar routes" over the top of the world. On the map find two routes from San Francisco to London. Which is shorter?

air travel. The most direct air routes from some west-coast cities to Europe or Asia are over the northern lands of North America. To prove this, use a piece of string on your classroom globe.

First, find Seattle, Washington, and Tokyo, Japan, on the globe. Next, put one end of the string on Tokyo. Now stretch it across the globe to Seattle. Be sure to place the string so that it curves around the globe at the shortest distance between these two cities. Pull the string tight. Did the route pass over some part of Alaska?

The route that you laid out on the globe is a

great circle route (rōōt). A great circle route is the most direct and the shortest route between two places on the globe. Compare it with the airplane routes on the map on this page. How many of these airplane routes pass directly over Alaska?

What Hawaii Is Like

The islands of the state of Hawaii are the tops of old volcanoes which rise above the ocean. Lava from some of these volcanoes sometimes boils up and overflows down the mountainsides.

Most of these mountainous islands have lowlands along the coast and in the river valleys. Lava which once flowed from the volcanoes has made the soil rich in important minerals. The minerals have made the soil good for growing crops.

Climate of the Pacific States

The Pacific states have a wide variety of climates. Some regions are hot and dry. Others are cooler and have much rain.

The Climate of California

Moist, warm winds from the Pacific Ocean bring the coastal area of California enough rain for farming. The rain falls during the winter season. The summers are dry.

The warm winds from the ocean give the coast mild winters and cool summers. The Central Valley has cooler winters and warmer summers. The valley also receives much less rain than the coast does. For this reason its fields need irrigation.

The western side of the Sierra Nevada receives the last of the moisture from the rain clouds that move inland from the Pacific. See the diagram showing this movement on page 122. The lands east of the mountains are dry.

The Climate of Oregon and Washington

Many people enjoy the pleasant climate of the coast of Oregon and Washington. The breezes from the Pacific keep the winters mild and the summers cool. East of the Cascades, however, the summers are hot and the winters are cold.

The coastal region has one of the heaviest rainfalls in our country. This is because the winds from the Pacific carry much moisture. The moisture is turned into rain or snow by the cold air of the mountain ranges. Winter is the wet season.

The Cascade Mountains keep the moist Pacific winds from reaching the plateaus east of this range. Most of the plateau section is too dry to farm without irrgation.

The heavy rains and melting snow from the mountains form rivers and streams in this area. Among these is the Columbia River. Water from the streams irrigates ranches near the mountains.

Many dams have been built to irrigate large areas. One is the Grand Coulee (kōō′lē) Dam, on the Columbia River. The water from this dam can irrigate more than a million acres of land. The dams also supply electric power for factories and homes.

The Climate of Alaska

Southern Alaska has a mild, rainy climate. Its summers are warm but not hot. Its winters are cool but not cold. Ships can enter the harbors of Ketchikan (kech′i kan′), Juneau (jōō′nō), and Seward (sōō′ərd) all year. These waters never freeze over.

Winds from the ocean help make the climate pleasant. On their way to Alaska they blow over a warm ocean *current* (kur′ənt). A current is a stream of water flowing through the ocean. Winds blowing toward Alaska become warm as they pass over the current. Because of this

Dog sleds have long been used to cross the snow-covered land of Arctic Alaska. Here Eskimo youths race their sleds.

current the temperature of southern Alaska almost never falls below 0°F (−18°C) in winter. The ocean winds bring heavy rainfall.

The part of Alaska through which the great Yukon River flows is often called the *Interior* (in tēr′ē ər). Interior means an area which lies inland, or away from the border and the coast. The winters of this region are long and very cold, with long nights and short days. Its summers are short and warm, with many hours of sunlight. The Yukon Valley has less rain than southern Alaska.

Arctic Alaska lies north of Interior Alaska. Its winters are long and cold. In winter the sun does not rise for days. That is because the tilt of the earth causes Arctic Alaska to be far from the sun in the winter.

The summer season in Arctic Alaska is very short. Only a foot or two (30 or 60 cm) of the frozen ground softens during the brief summer. Moss, grass, flowers, and small bushes grow in this tundra. The tundra is a treeless plain found in Arctic regions.

The Climate of Hawaii

Find Hawaii on the map of the United States, pages 92—93. Notice that the islands are north of the equator and south of the Tropic of Cancer in the low latitudes. Steady winds that blow toward the equator from the northeast, called *trade* (trād) *winds,* make the climate of Hawaii pleasant. As these winds blow over the Pacific, they gather much moisture. When they reach the islands, they rise and are cooled. They drop most of their moisture on the northeast slopes. The southwestern slopes are dry. Crops must be irrigated there. South of the equator, the trade winds also blow toward the equator, but from the southeast.

Do You Know?

1. How are the Pacific states alike? How are they different?
2. What is the surface of Alaska like?
3. Why does Hawaii have such rich soil?

339

2
Settling the Coastal States

The first European settlements on the Pacific coast were made by the Spanish in what is now California in 1769. Missionaries came and built more than 20 missions along the coast. These missions became large estates, supported by American Indian labor. There were also some small farming settlements, known as pueblos, occupied by Mexicans.

American settlers started moving to California about 1840. They sent back glowing reports of the easy life there. As more and more Americans moved to California, the Mexican government began to regard the new American settlers as a threat to its rule.

Exploring California

The United States government became interested in the region and sent John C. Frémont, a young explorer, to learn about the Far West. Frémont's guide was the famous scout and trapper, Kit Carson. He carried Frémont's messages from California to Washington, D.C.

On his last trip, Frémont went as a captain in the United States Army. He reached California just before our war with Mexico. Frémont aided a rebellion of American settlers in California against Mexican forces. Without consulting anyone, the settlers decided to set up the Republic of California.

They made a flag by painting a bear and a star on white cloth. Then they raised the "Bear Flag" over their camp. When Frémont heard

that war with Mexico had begun, he took down the Bear Flag. In its place he raised the Stars and Stripes.

As you remember, the war ended with the defeat of Mexico. Mexico lost not only Texas but also much land to the west of Texas. On the map of the growth of the United States on page 91, find the land given up by Mexico. After this war the United States stretched from the Atlantic to the Pacific.

The Rush to California

In 1848, just before the end of the war with Mexico, gold was discovered on Captain John Sutter's ranch in California. This large ranch was at the foot of the Sierra Nevada, near the present city of Sacramento. Find Sacramento on the map of California, page 335.

It was James Marshall, one of Captain Sutter's workers, who discovered the gold. He saw the shining grains while building a mill on a river that flowed through Sutter's land.

The Fortyniners

News traveled slowly in those days. Almost a year passed before the East heard of this discovery of gold in California. When the news finally reached the East, people went wild with excitement. Thousands left their homes to go to California. Since this rush began in 1849, the gold seekers were called the *fortyniners* (fôr′tē nī′nərz).

The fortyniners used three main routes to California. Some gold seekers used the all-water route. They sailed from ports on the Atlantic Coast, around South America, and north along the Pacific Coast to San Francisco. This was a long voyage.

Others went by ship to Panama. Then they traveled on foot through the hot jungles of the isthmus to the Pacific. After this they took a ship to California. Trace these two water routes on the map on page 342.

The third route was along the overland trails to California. The gold seekers faced burning

Early gold seekers shoveled earth and rocks into a trough filled with water. The water washed away the earth. Sometimes miners found gold in the rocks that were left.

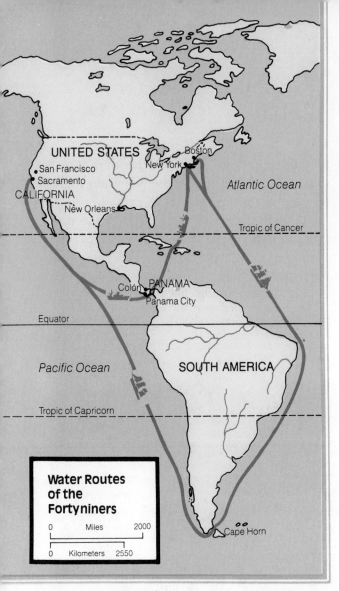

People who left their eastern homes to join the California gold rush faced a long journey. If you were a *fortyniner*, which water route would you take? Why?

deserts, snowstorms in the mountains, and American Indians who were protecting their lands.

Most land travelers to California used the Oregon Trail. See the map of western trails, page 313. The travelers started at Independence, Missouri. At Fort Hall the trail divided. The part that went southwest became known as the California Trail. Travelers to Los Angeles used the Santa Fe Trail and the Old Spanish Trail.

California Becomes a State

Gold seekers kept flocking to California. Cities were built overnight. Less than 2 years after Marshall's discovery, California had enough people to become a state. The people wrote a constitution. In this constitution they said that there was to be no slavery in California. In 1850 California joined the Union as a free state.

Connecting East and West

In the days of the gold rush it took months for mail sent from the East to reach the West. After California became a state, it was necessary to find faster and better ways to send mail. To speed up the mail, the United States government started an overland mail service.

Transcontinental Mail Service

By the new plan the mail was taken to St. Louis by train, where it was placed on stagecoaches. The coaches, carrying passengers and mail, traveled day and night. The journey from St. Louis, Missouri, to San Francisco, California, took about 25 days. This was our first *transcontinental* (trans′kon tə nent′əl) mail service. Transcontinental means across the continent.

Still mail was not fast enough for many people in the East and in California. So the pony express service was started. The pony

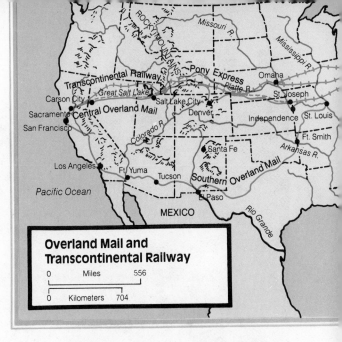

Overland Mail and Transcontinental Railway

| 0 | Miles | 556 |
| 0 | Kilometers | 704 |

express riders carried the mail from St. Joseph, Missouri, where the railroad ended, to Sacramento, California, in 10 days' time. See the Overland Mail and Transcontinental Railway map on this page. The pony express lasted for 19 months. Then a faster means of communication—the telegraph—put an end to it.

The Invention of the Telegraph

Samuel F. B. Morse invented the telegraph in 1844. The telegraph was a system of sending and receiving messages over a wire.

After working on his invention for 10 years, Morse asked Congress to help him. Congress granted Morse $30,000 to build a telegraph line to test his invention. The line stretched from Baltimore to Washington, a distance of 40 miles (64 km).

Soon telegraph lines were built all over the country. In October 1861, the first telegraph line joining California and the East replaced the pony express.

The First Transcontinental Railroad

Soon after the telegraph reached California, two railroad companies decided to extend the railroad to the west coast. Two crews of workers started laying tracks from opposite directions and worked toward each other. The workers on the Central Pacific Railroad pushed eastward from Sacramento, California. Many of these workers were Chinese. Workers on the Union Pacific Railroad worked westward from Omaha, Nebraska. Many of these workers

Between 1858 and 1869 connections between California and the East improved. Why do you think this was so important? Which of the routes shown on this map was the fastest?

were Irish. Find the routes from Sacramento and from Omaha on the map on this page.

Both crews faced great difficulties. For almost 7 years thousands of workers used axes, picks, and shovels to lay mile after mile of track. Central Pacific workers pushing eastward dug tunnels through the high Sierra Nevada. Union Pacific crews pushing westward across the plains were always in danger of attacks by Indians protecting their lands. When they reached the Rockies, they had problems like those of the Sierra Nevada workers.

On May 10, 1869, the tracks finally were joined at a point near Ogden, Utah. A large crowd of people traveled great distances to see the railroad completed.

If we could join the crowd, we might hear the crews boasting and joking. Each crew is trying to prove that it has done the best job. Then all talk stops. A Union Pacific officer and a Central Pacific officer take turns hammering

Officers from the two railroads shook hands at the place where the Union Pacific and Central Pacific lines met.

into place the last spike, a gold one. The Union Pacific locomotive and the Central Pacific locomotive draw together until they touch. The telegraph flashes the news to the whole country. Now East and West are joined by the transcontinental railroad. Westward expansion is speeded up.

Exploring Oregon and Washington

In the early days of Spanish exploration several Spanish sea captains, sailing northward, may have gone as far as Oregon. In 1579 an English sea captain, Sir Francis Drake, sailed along the coast of Oregon. About 200 years later a famous explorer, Captain Cook, did the same. Both were looking for a passage through North America from the Pacific to the Atlantic. These explorers gave England its claim to the territory.

After the War for Independence, United States ships began to sail far north on the Pacific Coast. Robert Gray, an American sea captain, was in charge of a trading vessel that was bound for China.

After he reached the Pacific, Captain Gray sailed along the coast of Oregon and Washington. He found the mouth of a broad river which emptied into the Pacific Ocean. He named this river the Columbia for his ship, the *Columbia*. Through the discovery of this river Captain Gray gave the United States a claim to the whole country drained by its waters. But many years passed before the country was explored and settled.

344

The Lewis and Clark Expedition

"The United States now owns the Louisiana Territory," said President Jefferson in 1803. "I will send people to explore the Missouri River and all the lands west of the Mississippi River."

President Jefferson chose Meriwether Lewis to lead an exploring party to the distant West. William Clark was picked as the second leader.

In the spring of 1804 Lewis and Clark with about 40 people started their journey from St. Louis, Missouri. They kept daily records of everything they saw and of what happened along the way. They took notes about the soil, plants, animals, and climate. They also drew maps of the rivers, lakes, and plains that they passed.

Late in October they reached a place in North Dakota where they set up a winter camp. During the winter they met Sacajawea (sä kä jä wē′ə), a Shoshone (shə shō′ nē) Indian, and her husband Charbonneau (shär bə nō′), a French trapper. As a child, Sacajawea had been stolen from her family and tribe and taken east. She wanted to see her old home. So Sacajawea and Charbonneau served as guides for the expedition.

In the spring the exploring party took boats to the end of the Missouri River. Then they met some Shoshone Indians. Among them was Sacajawea's brother.

Lewis and Clark were able to buy horses from the Shoshones so that they could travel across the mountains. They left their boats behind. After crossing the mountains, they came to the Snake River. They cut down trees

Sacajawea guided the Lewis and Clark Expedition through lands she knew from her childhood. A river, a peak, and a mountain pass have been named after her.

and built boats. In the boats they went down the Snake River and followed it to the Columbia River. They traveled to the mouth of the Columbia and finally reached the Pacific Ocean. Trace their route on the map, page 235.

In two and one-half years Lewis and Clark had traveled thousands of miles through unknown lands. They brought back maps and records of these lands. Although they discovered a route to the Oregon Country, it was never used as a trail to the Far West. Blackfoot Indians protecting their lands along the upper Missouri made the trail too dangerous. Years later many settlers journeyed to the Oregon country because of the reports of Lewis and Clark, but by other routes.

The Founding of Astoria

Lewis and Clark's reports of fur-bearing animals interested a New York fur trader named John Jacob Astor. Astor sent a group of trappers to the Oregon Country. Near the mouth of the Columbia River they built a trading post called Astoria. Here Indians and other trappers brought their furs to exchange for supplies.

Astoria was the first United States settlement in the Oregon Country. A few years later the Hudson's Bay Company, an English group, also built trading posts in the Oregon Country. For many years, English and American fur trappers and trading companies shared this rich land. It extended far north into Canada.

The Rendezvous System

Another businessman, Henry Ashley, also sent out trappers to bring back furs. Instead of setting up trading posts, Ashley organized the rendezvous (rän′də vōō′) system in 1826. Each year trappers went into the mountains to get furs. One year later, they carried their furs to one agreed-upon place. Meanwhile, to this place Ashley brought pack trains loaded with supplies. At these "rendezvous," usually held in Wyoming in July, the Mountain Men, as the trappers came to be called, traded their pelts for Ashley's supplies. Then the trappers went off hunting for another year. The pack trains took the furs to St. Louis.

By 1840 the fur trade was dead. The Mountain Men had disappeared or become scouts for wagon trains. Some, such as the well-known black Mountain Man James Beckwourth, discovered mountain passes that helped settlers go west.

The Oregon Trail

In 1836 two missionaries journeyed to the Oregon Country in a covered wagon. These missionaries were Marcus and Narcissa Whitman. They taught the Christian religion to the Indians there.

The Whitmans urged others to come to the Oregon Country. The settlements they helped to start there strengthened the claim of the United States to the region. The route that these early pioneers took became known as the Oregon Trail. It ended in Astoria.

The Oregon Trail was more than 2,000 miles (3,200 km) long. See the map of western trails, page 313. An exploring party sent out from Astoria was the first group to follow the whole length of the Oregon Trail. Trappers and traders used it. When settlers started moving to Oregon, the Oregon Trail was an established route to the Far West. The first large group of settlers went to Oregon in 1843. About 1,000 persons were in this group.

Each spring other groups followed. Each family had a covered wagon drawn by horse or oxen. To travel in safety families would band together. A train of 40 or 50 covered wagons would set out from Independence, Missouri, or some point on the Missouri River. They took with them some household goods, seeds, farm tools, food, and guns.

The first large wagon train to travel on the Oregon Trail is depicted on the walls of Oregon's capitol. The Cascade Mountains in the background were difficult to cross.

A scout, or guide, went with each wagon train. The scout would ride ahead on horseback to look for water and for signs of Indians. The wagons were often attacked by Indians who were fighting to keep their hunting grounds.

As the pioneers traveled westward, they had to cross hot, dusty prairies and high mountains. Snowstorms raged in the mountains. Often wagons became stuck in huge snowdrifts. At times the food and water supply ran low. Many of the pioneers became sick, and some of them died. Finally, after several months, the wagon train reached the Oregon Country.

Clipper Ships to Oregon

Some other pioneers went to the Oregon Country by ship. Starting from the East, they sailed around South America, then up the Pacific Coast to the mouth of the Columbia River. In shipyards of the East a new, faster kind of sailing ship, called a clipper ship, was developed. This fast, graceful sailing vessel had a long, slim body, high masts, and large sails.

By the 1840s many clipper ships visited the coast of the Oregon Country on their way to China. They brought manufactured goods from the eastern part of the United States. They traded the goods for shiploads of furs to be sold in China. On the return trip these clipper ships carried silks, tea, finely carved woods, and other Chinese goods. The captain of a clipper ship could always get good prices for these Chinese goods in Boston.

By the 1870s the clipper ships were replaced by steamships. But they had been useful in trade and settlement.

Government in the Oregon Country

In 1843 a large group of people from the United States came overland to the Oregon Country. They settled in the northern part of the Willamette Valley. These settlers realized they would need some kind of government.

Adopting a Democratic Plan

Let us look in upon a group as they meet to decide on the laws under which they will live.

A tall, sunburned farmer stands up. "We need laws to live by," he says. "The Pilgrims met in the cabin of the *Mayflower* to make a compact before they settled Plymouth."

Another pioneer rises to say, "Texas set up its own government for its republic. We, too, should make laws for protection and to keep peace among ourselves."

And so the meeting went. Everyone was free to speak, and the group listened to what each one had to say. After they had agreed upon the laws under which they were to live, they wrote the laws down. In this way the early settlers of Oregon learned to govern themselves.

Becoming a Part of the United States

For almost 30 years Great Britain and the United States shared the Oregon Country. But in 1846 the two countries set a boundary at the forty-ninth parallel. Great Britain kept the northern part of the region, and the United States the southern. This boundary separates Canada from our Northwest to this day. The United States and Great Britain settled their claims peacefully.

Many people went to the Northwest. Soon there were enough people for the territory to become a state. In 1859 Oregon was admitted to the Union. In 1889 Washington became a state.

American Indians in the Coastal States

In the 1860s the Modoc (mōd'äk) Indians were placed on a reservation in northern California and southern Oregon. They could barely live on the poor land. So they escaped. After 6 months of fighting, the United States soldiers forced the Modocs to give up.

Chief Joseph, a Nez Percé Leader

Joseph, a Nez Percé (nez' pərs') Indian, was born in Wallowa Valley of Oregon in about 1840. There he attended a mission school. Later, he became chief of the Nez Percé.

In 1855 the tribe agreed to live on a large reservation. The United States government promised that they could stay there. But in 1860, gold was discovered on the Indians' land. United States officials made a new treaty. It took away about three-fourths of the reservation. Chief Joseph would not accept the new treaty.

The government then ordered the Nez Percé to a reservation in Idaho. But the Nez Percé did not want to leave. Fighting broke out. Each side won some battles. But Chief Joseph knew that the Nez Percé could not defeat the soldiers. So he decided to move the Nez Percé to Canada. The Nez Percé traveled more than 1,000 miles (1,600 km).

When the Nez Percé were in Montana close to Canada, they stopped to rest. Chief Joseph thought that they were safe. But some soldiers found them. After a five-day battle, Chief Joseph decided to surrender. The Nez Percé were sent to Indian Territory, now Oklahoma. Later, Chief Joseph was sent to a reservation in Washington where he died in 1904.

Fishing Rights

Today American Indians are not forced to live on reservations. They live and work wherever they want. Some of the Indians make their living fishing salmon (sam′ən) in Puget Sound. The Indians claimed they had a right to half the salmon caught in Puget Sound. This upset other salmon fishers in the area. But in 1979 the United States Supreme Court ruled in favor of the Indians. The court stated that according to five treaties written during the 1800s, the Indians did have the right to half the salmon caught in Puget Sound.

Chief Joseph of the Nez Percé Indian tribe learned military strategy by watching United States soldiers. He was a determined leader who inspired his followers.

Do You Know?

1. By what three routes did gold seekers travel to California?
2. How was the route of Lewis and Clark on page 235 different from the route of the Oregon Trail on page 313?
3. How was the Oregon Country divided in 1846?

3

Early Days in Alaska and Hawaii

Long after the four nations of western Europe had explored and settled much of North America, another nation became interested. This nation was Russia.

Early History of Alaska

Russia was a large country. Its ruler wondered about the lands beyond the huge country. He sent Vitus Bering (bēr′ing), a Danish navigator, to find out what these lands were like.

On one of his voyages Captain Bering discovered the narrow waterway, or strait, which separates North America and Asia. The strait now bears his name. On a later voyage Bering saw the mainland of North America. This discovery, in 1741, gave Russia its claim to Alaska. Soon Russian fur traders traveled across the strait into Alaska to seek their fortunes.

Some Russians explored the North American continent as far north as the Arctic Ocean. Others made settlements or built trading posts as far south as northern California. Not long before George Washington became the President of the United States, the Russians made a permanent settlement in Alaska at Sitka (sit′kə).

As time went on, some people from the United States became interested in this far northern region. Whaling ships went to the Arctic Ocean to catch whales. Other United States vessels traded with the Russian settlements. There was talk that Russia wanted to sell Alaska. William Seward, our Secretary of State, was eager to buy this land. He thought it would become a valuable possession of the United States.

In 1867 the United States bought Alaska. We paid Russia more than 7 million dollars for this great piece of land in the northwestern corner of North America. Alaska was the first possession of the United States which was far distant from the rest of the Union. It was made a territory in 1912. In 1959 it became our forty-ninth state.

The Magic of Gold

About 30 years after we bought Alaska, gold was discovered in the Klondike region of Canada near the Alaskan boundary. Gold seekers rushed north as fast as they could. They went by dog team, on foot, or by boat on the Yukon River with their picks, shovels, and gold pans. Some became rich. Others found little gold or none. One gold seeker was Jack London, the well-known author. He found no gold, but he wrote many stories of life in the Yukon.

Settlement of Hawaii

It is believed that the first Hawaiians came from islands in the Pacific which we call Polynesia. These people sailed in giant canoes across the Pacific about 2,000 years ago. Later, a group of Polynesians from the island of

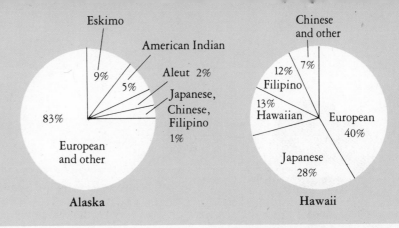

Groups of People in Alaska and Hawaii in 1980

Alaska

- Eskimo 9%
- American Indian 5%
- Aleut 2%
- Japanese, Chinese, Filipino 1%
- European and other 83%

Hawaii

- Chinese and other 7%
- Filipino 12%
- Hawaiian 13%
- European 40%
- Japanese 28%

The United States has always been the home of many different groups of people. These circle graphs show the groups that live in our newest states.

Tahiti (tə hē′tē) arrived. The Hawaiians got their food by fishing, farming, and gathering wild nuts.

Captain Cook in Hawaii

When the English explorer, Captain James Cook, arrived in Hawaii, the Hawaiians thought Cook was a god. Captain Cook was the first white explorer to discover the island. He was on his way to the Far North to look for a waterway between the Pacific and the Atlantic oceans. He stopped at the islands to get fresh food and water. The Hawaiians welcomed Captain Cook and the crew and treated them well.

On a later trip Captain Cook returned to the islands for ship repairs. This time a quarrel developed between the crew and the Hawaiians. Soon fighting broke out. In one of these fights Captain Cook was killed.

Settlers from Many Lands

As the years passed, other people came to the islands. Ships on their way to China often stopped to make repairs and to get fresh food and water. Sailors from these ships sometimes settled in Hawaii. From faraway New England missionaries came to the islands to teach the Christian religion. They opened schools, invented a way of writing the Hawaiian language, and helped the rulers of Hawaii to improve their government.

Then it was found that sugarcane grew well in the soil and climate of Hawaii. People from Europe and the United States came and laid out plantations. Workers from China, Polynesia, Japan, the Philippines, and other lands were brought to work in the cane fields. Many stayed to make their homes in Hawaii. Today people from the United States, Europe, and Asia live and work well together there.

Hawaii Under Our Flag

When Captain Cook came to Hawaii, there were many kingdoms on the islands. Each kingdom had its own ruler. Later King Kamehameha I (kə mä′ə mä′hä) became ruler of all the islands. After that, the islands were united under one ruler. Some of these rulers governed well. Others ruled poorly. After a while people grew tired of the corrupt leaders.

Lydia Liliuokalani was Hawaii's last queen. American settlers controlled much of Hawaii's wealth. Some objected to the queen's power over them and their businesses.

Lydia Liliuokalani, a Hawaiian Leader

Lydia Liliuokalani (li lē ə wō kə län′ē) was born in Honolulu in 1838. In 1891 she became queen of the Hawaiian Islands following the death of her brother the king.

During her reign, Queen Liliuokalani tried to increase her power as ruler. Many people, especially American settlers, became upset. They wanted to protect their businesses. A group of Americans, British, and Germans helped to remove the queen from office in 1893. A republic was then set up in Hawaii.

Liliuokalani spent part of her time writing books and songs. Her best-known song is

Aloha Oe (Farewell to Thee). It became the farewell song of Hawaii. Liliuokalani died in Honolulu in 1917.

Joining the United States

People from the United States who had gone to Hawaii to live wanted it to become part of our country. Leaders of the new government asked that Hawaii be made part of the United States. But the leaders of our government at first said, "No." Then the Hawaiians set themselves up as an independent republic.

Five years later Hawaii again asked to be allowed to join the United States. This time our government leaders were in favor of these islands being added to our country. In August 1898 the United States flag was raised over the Hawaiian Islands. Two years later, after a constitution had been adopted by the people of the islands, Hawaii became a territory. It remained a territory until 1959, when Congress voted to admit it to the Union.

Do You Know?

1. What did Bering find on his expedition?
2. Why did the Hawaiians welcome Captain Cook?
3. How did Alaska become a part of the United States?
4. How did Hawaii become a part of the United States?

Before You Go On

Using New Words

transcontinental   great circle route
current   fault
trade wind   lava
earthquake   inlet
forty-niner   sound
volcano   Interior

The phrases below explain the words or terms listed above. Number a paper from 1 through 12. After each number write the word or term which matches the definition.

1. A stream of water flowing through the ocean
2. An area of Alaska which lies inland, away from the border and coast
3. An opening in the earth's surface through which steam, ashes, and hot, melted rock, or lava, flow
4. A steady wind that blows toward the equator
5. A movement of a part of the earth's surface caused by a shift of rock or other disturbance
6. A narrow strip of water which reaches far inland
7. A person who went to California to seek gold
8. A break in a rock mass
9. Hot melted rock
10. Most direct and shortest route between two places on the globe
11. A body of water like a large bay, extending into the land
12. Across the continent

Finding the Facts

1. Where is the Coast Range? The Cascade Range? The Sierra Nevada?
2. Why does the temperature of southern Alaska almost never fall below zero in winter?
3. What forms the islands of Hawaii?
4. Whom did the United States government send to learn about the Far West and California?
5. What discovery on John Sutter's ranch caused people to flock to California?
6. Who invented the telegraph in 1844?
7. Who was Sacajawea?
8. What did James Beckwourth do to help settlers moving westward?
9. Where did the Oregon Trail begin? End?
10. Who tried to lead the Nez Percé Indians to safety in Canada?
11. What land did our country buy from Russia in 1867?
12. What discovery caused people to rush to Alaska in the late 1800s?
13. Who was Lydia Liliuokalani?
14. What happened to Alaska and Hawaii in 1959?

4

Living and Working in the Pacific States

California, Oregon, and Washington have thriving farms and busy industries. People who live in these states have many opportunities for making a living.

Farming in California

Fine crops are raised in the California valleys. But some places in the state lack water for farming.

Southern California

We visit Imperial Valley in southern California. This area was once a desert, but a canal was built to carry water from the Colorado River to irrigate it. Since then, this valley has become rich farmland. The Imperial Valley produces fine fruits and vegetables, cotton, sugar beets, and dairy products. The lettuce and melons you eat in winter may come from the Imperial Valley.

Oranges and lemons are grown on the lower slopes of the mountains in southern California. There they are protected from the cold air which settles on the floor of valleys. Southern California also produces olives, dates, figs, apricots, peaches, pears, almonds, and walnuts.

Field workers pick heads of lettuce and pack them in boxes. Railroad refrigerator cars carry the lettuce across the country.

The Central Valley of California

The Central Valley lies between the Sierra Nevada and the Coast Range. It is 400 miles (640 km) long and almost 50 miles (80 km) wide. Most of the Central Valley is used for farming. Because California gets its rain in winter, irrigation is needed in the valley only during the summer.

Irrigation water and electricity for the Central Valley come from dams on the Sacramento and the San Joaquin (san′ wä kēn′) rivers. The San Joaquin River flows north from the lower end of the valley. The Sacramento River flows south from the upper end of the valley. These rivers meet near the middle of the Central Valley and empty into San Francisco Bay.

The Central Valley is a fine cotton-growing area. It also produces potatoes, prunes, pears, peaches, grapes, sugar beets, tomatoes, asparagus, and grain. Some of the fruit and vegetables are shipped fresh and some are canned.

The Central Valley is famous for raisins. The land near Fresno is covered with grapevines. Raisins are sun-dried grapes. After the grapes are picked, they are placed on trays among the rows of grapevines. The grapes are dried into raisins by the hot, summer sun. This valley provides more than half the world's supply of raisins. The grapes are also used for making wine.

Coastal Valleys of California

California also has rich farmland in the valleys of the Coast Range. These valleys produce flowers, fruits, vegetables, dairy products, wheat,

Products of Washington, Oregon, and California

355

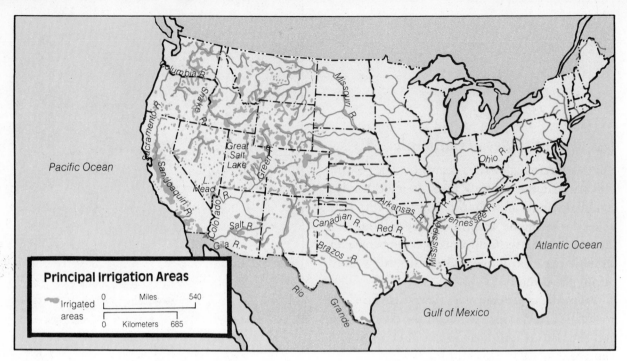

Principal Irrigation Areas

Irrigated areas

| 0 | Miles | 540 |
| 0 | Kilometers | 685 |

When dry or desert areas are irrigated they become productive farmlands. Many dams have been built on rivers in the western states to help prevent floods and to provide water for irrigation.

and poultry. One valley is famous for its fine prunes. Another is the greatest lettuce-growing area in the United States.

Manufacturing in California

Manufacturing is one of the chief industries of California. In the southern part of the state are large aircraft factories. The warm, dry climate suits this industry. It permits the flying and testing of planes in all seasons. For only about two weeks' time out of each year is the weather unfit for flying.

California also has factories that process foods, such as canned tuna, dried fruits, and frozen fruits and vegetables. There are plants that make machinery, cars, electronic equipment, rubber tires, and furniture. Shipbuilding

is another important industry. Shipyards are located along the southern coast.

Farming in Oregon and Washington

Oregon is a great producer of fruit and berries, such as apples, pears, and strawberries. Its farmers also raise wheat, livestock, and poultry.

Washington is the chief apple-growing state in our nation. Washington is also the biggest producer of raspberries and blackberries. It is an important producer of pears and peaches. The chief fruit-growing areas in Washington are in the river valleys east of the Cascades. With irrigation, farmers in this area raise fine crops of apples, pears, plums, and other fruit.

Water from the Columbia River irrigates large parts of eastern and southern Washington. In areas where there is little water, wheat is grown by dry farming.

The Willamette Valley is famous for its apples, prunes, pears, and strawberries. It is one of the leading fruit- and vegetable-canning centers in our country. The Willamette Valley also has many poultry and dairy farms.

Some farmers in the Willamette Valley produce hops. Hops are plants used in the making of beer and of certain medicines. Seeds for vegetables and flowers are also grown in this area.

Lumbering on the West Coast

The western slopes of the Sierra Nevada, in California, have thick forests of towering white and sugar pines. Gigantic redwoods grow on the

Coast Range north of San Francisco. Many people in northern California earn their living by lumbering, working in sawmills, making furniture, and manufacturing wood pulp for paper.

Oregon is the leading lumber state in the whole United States. More timber is cut in Oregon than in any other state. Oregon's northern neighbor, Washington, also produces much lumber. In the forests of Oregon and Washington the trees are large, and they grow close together. Lumber is one of the leading products shipped from Oregon and Washington. Paper mills also are found in both states.

West Coast pine forests are very valuable. The Rocky Mountain states also have vast forests, but lumber is not a large industry there. Why do you think this is so?

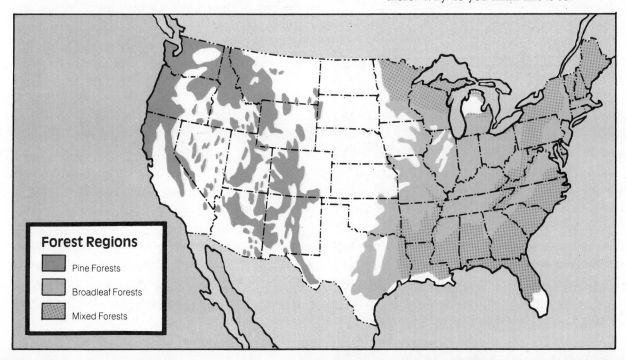

Forest Regions

- Pine Forests
- Broadleaf Forests
- Mixed Forests

Fishing on the West Coast

Many people on the California coast earn a living by fishing or canning fish. Fishing fleets set out empty from San Diego, San Pedro, and San Francisco and return filled with fish. Most of the tuna and sardines caught there are canned. But mackerel and crabs are eaten fresh.

Salmon is the most plentiful and the most valuable fish in Oregon and Washington. The people who earn a living by fishing also take halibut from the ocean and oysters from Puget Sound.

The salmon are found along the coast and in the rivers which empty into the ocean. Some of the salmon is shipped fresh in refrigerator cars to large cities throughout the country. But most of the salmon is canned. Many people work in the fish canneries.

Salmon Fishing

Each year millions of salmon swim in from the Pacific Ocean and enter the mouths of rivers there. The salmon make their way upstream, swimming against the current and leaping over waterfalls. The large dams on the Columbia River keep the salmon from swimming upstream. Fish ladders have been built to help the salmon get around these dams.

The salmon often swim hundreds of miles until they find a quiet *spawning* (spôn'ing), or nesting, place in fresh water. Here they spawn, or lay their eggs.

In 2 or 3 months the baby salmon hatch. At the end of their first year the young salmon are about 5 inches (12.7 cm) long. Soon they start to swim downstream toward the ocean. On the way many are eaten by birds or bigger fish. Some die in waters poisoned by waste materials from factories and cities. But thousands reach the ocean. The salmon spend the next 3 or 4 years in the ocean eating and growing. Then they return to spawn where they were born.

Most salmon fishing is done on the Columbia River, when the salmon begin their journey upstream. It is very easy to catch the salmon at this time. Laws now limit salmon fishing to keep too many salmon from being killed. The government has also set up places where baby salmon are hatched and taken care of.

Salmon swim up these fish ladders to their *spawning* places. Without the ladders, the fish could not get past the many dams built along the Columbia River and would die.

Mining on the West Coast

California is the chief mining state on the West Coast. It is one of our country's leading producers of petroleum and natural gas. See the map of oil fields and pipelines on page 292. Oil is found under the ocean off the coast of southern California. The lands in many parts of the Central Valley are rich in oil. California also has deposits of gold, mercury, and tungsten.

Mining is much less important in Oregon and Washington. But the two states do have some gold, silver, coal, copper, lead, iron ore, uranium, and clay.

Bridalveil Falls is one of the many breathtaking sights you can see in Yosemite National Park.

National Parks on the West Coast

Sequoia (si kwoi′ə) National Park in California is famous for its giant sequoia trees. Some of them are thousands of years old. Mount Whitney, in the Sierra Nevada, is in this park. East of Mount Whitney is the great desert known as Death Valley. This is the lowest land in the United States.

About 200 miles (320 km) east of San Francisco is Yosemite (yō sem′i tē) National Park. This beautiful park lies in the heart of the Sierra Nevada. It is noted for its waterfalls. One of these is famous for its rainbow colors. Another, which is called Bridalveil Falls, drops more than 600 feet (180 m) in a very slender column. Many tourists visit Yosemite National Park each year.

California has three other national parks. Kings Canyon National Park has many giant se-quoia trees. Lassen Volcanic National Park has lakes, hot springs, a volcano, and steep domes of lava. Redwood National Park is located along the coast of California. It has the world's tallest redwood trees.

In southwestern Oregon is Crater Lake National Park. The lake, which is round, fills the crater, or opening, in the top of a once-active volcano. In Crater Lake is a small island, supposed to be the top of a volcano which fell in when the volcano erupted.

In Washington are three national parks, Olympic, Mount Rainier, and North Cascades. Olympic National Park has rugged mountains and thick forests of Douglas fir, spruce, hemlock, and cedar. The high, snow-covered top of Mount Rainier is the most beautiful sight in Mount Rainier National Park. North Cascades National Park is a mountainous region with many glaciers and lakes.

San Francisco
City by the Bay

San Francisco was founded in 1776 by the Spanish. Today San Francisco is the chief manufacturing, trade, and shipping center in northern California. San Francisco Bay is one of the best harbors in the world. It is large, deep, and safe from storms blowing in from the Pacific Ocean. The waterfront stretches for about 15 miles (24 km) around the bay. Dozens of ships lie beside large, crowded wharves. Lumber, canned fish, fruit, vegetables, and manufactured goods are loaded on these ships. Coffee, sugar, spices, and other items are brought in from foreign ports.

Much of San Francisco was destroyed by a terrible earthquake in 1906. But the people of San Francisco were quick to rebuild their city. Today, San Francisco is one of the largest cities in the United States. Among its more than half a million people are Americans of Chinese, Japanese, Mexican, and Philippine descent.

Charming cable cars help San Franciscans up and down many of the city's steep hills. But San Francisco also has a modern transportation system, called BART, which stands for Bay Area Rapid Transit. BART connects many of the cities in the bay area. The Golden Gate Bridge is one of the world's longest suspension, or hanging, bridges. This bridge connects San Francisco, which is on a peninsula, with the north coastal counties. Another suspension bridge, the San Francisco–Oakland Bay Bridge, connects San Francisco with the cities across the Bay. ■

Chief Cities
Along the Coast

California, Oregon, and Washington have large, fast-growing cities. Each year thousands of acres of farms, gardens, and orchards are torn up. Land is needed for new homes, shopping centers, factories, streets, and freeways for the cities.

Farthest south along the coast is San Diego, one of the most rapidly growing cities in the United States. San Diego is an important port and naval base. Airplanes are also made there. Many tourists visit the city.

Los Angeles

Los Angeles is one of the three largest cities in the United States. Los Angeles is the chief industrial center of southern California. Oil refineries, automobile factories, clothing factories, and fish canneries are found there. The city is a leader in the manufacture of airplanes and equipment for space exploration. Hollywood, a part of Los Angeles, is the nation's capital for making films and television programs.

The area near Los Angeles receives little rainfall. The city had no water problem in 1781. It was only a small settlement then. But as Los Angeles grew, so did its problem of finding enough water. In 1913 the Los Angeles *Aqueduct* (ak′wə dukt) was built. An aqueduct is a pipe or channel that carries water over long distances. This pipeline brings water from the Sierra Nevada. In 1936 another aqueduct was built. The giant California Water Project began operations in 1972. It brings water from the Feather River, north of San Francisco.

The city's growth brought other problems. Los Angeles needed an ocean port for shipping its products. However, the ocean was 15 miles (24 km) away. San Pedro, a town on the coast, had a harbor. Los Angeles took in a strip of land to San Pedro and created the Port of Los Angeles. The harbor was dug out to make it wider and deeper. Then a great wall, or breakwater, was built. The breakwater was 2 miles (3.2 km) long and protected the harbor from high waves. Today the Port of Los Angeles is a busy west-coast port city.

Salem and Portland

Salem, the capital of Oregon, is located on the Willamette River. This city is about 50 miles (80 km) from the mouth of the Willamette, which flows into the Columbia. Salem is the trade and manufacturing center for the farmlands in this valley. Salem supplies lumber camps in the mountains with fruit, milk, butter, cheese, eggs, and poultry. Many people here earn their living in fruit canneries. Some people work in sawmills, where trees from the Cascade and Coast ranges are cut into lumber.

Portland is the chief trade and transportation center in Oregon. It is the gateway to the Willamette Valley and to the Pacific Ocean. When this city was founded, it lay just a few miles from the place where the Willamette River empties into the Columbia. Portland now extends all the way into the triangle of land formed by the joining of the Columbia and Willamette rivers. The Columbia River is deep enough for ocean liners to sail the more than 100 miles (160 km) from the Pacific Ocean to

Portland. Although it is quite far north, Portland's waterway does not freeze in the winter. Do you know why? See the map of North and South America on page 13.

Ocean steamships line the docks of Portland. Many carry away lumber from the Rockies, Cascades, and Coast Range. Some take away cargoes of canned salmon from the Columbia and other rivers. Other ships are loaded with grains and canned fruit from the Willamette Valley. Wheat, flour, and apples from irrigated parts of the Columbia Plateau are also shipped from Portland. Incoming ships bring farm machinery, automobiles, airplane parts, clothing, and other manufactured goods from California and the East.

Tacoma and Seattle

The cities on Puget Sound have deep, safe harbors. One of these cities is Tacoma. It is an important trade and manufacturing center. It has a huge copper refinery, large flour mills, railroad shops, machine shops, and woodwork factories. Tacoma is the chief lumber, pulp, and paper manufacturer in the Northwest.

Seattle, the leading port of the Northwest, is also on Puget Sound. Seattle started as a sawmill village at the mouth of a river which empties into Puget Sound. This village grew into a trade and shipping center for the lumber and fishing industries nearby. Then it became an important port and trade center in the days of the Alaska gold rush. Today Seattle is the chief city in Washington. It is one of the largest fur markets in this country. It also has a large aircraft industry.

363

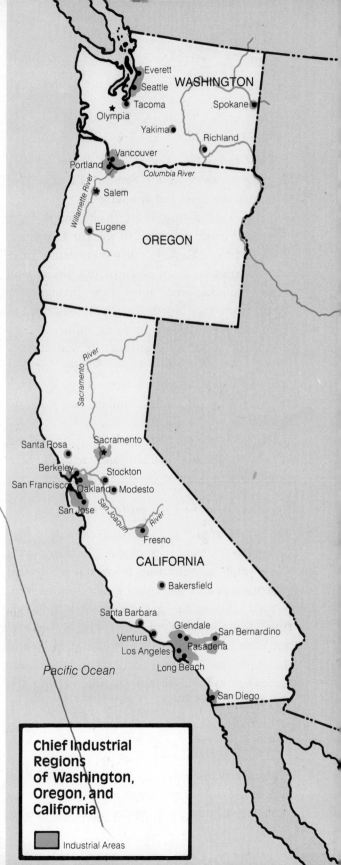

Chief Industrial Regions of Washington, Oregon, and California

Industrial Areas

The farms in the Coast Range valley produce fresh food for Seattle, Tacoma, and Olympia, the capital of Washington.

Seattle has a busy waterfront. Ships from Japan and other countries of the Far East bring many articles. Tankers carry petroleum from Los Angeles to Seattle. Farm machinery and other manufactured goods are brought by water from the Northeast. Both Seattle and Tacoma have large ship-building industries.

Lumber is a leading product in Washington. Ships carrying lumber leave Seattle for Los Angeles, South America, and Atlantic Coast cities. Seattle also ships lumber and grain to the Far East.

Railroads connect Seattle with the farmland of the Columbia Plateau and with eastern cities. Seattle is an important air center, too.

Spokane, on the Columbia Plateau

The chief trade and railroad center of the Columbia Plateau is Spokane. Railroads haul wheat and canned fruit from farms on this plateau to Seattle and other Puget Sound cities. Several important transcontinental railroads have stations in Spokane. This is because Spokane is near the only low mountain pass in the northern Rockies. Through the "Spokane Gateway" railroads run from the East to the cities on Puget Sound.

Farming in Alaska

Many Alaskans today make a living by fishing and by mining. Some trap or raise animals for their fur. Others farm or carry on lumbering.

Still others earn a living by caring for the tourists who visit Alaska each year.

The people of Alaska depend on the rest of the United States for much of their food. But farming in Alaska is growing in importance. As Alaska gains more people and new farms are started, the state will produce more and more food for its own population.

Alaska's leading farm region is the fertile Matanuska Valley, near the city of Anchorage. Cabbage, beets, lettuce, carrots, peas, and potatoes grow well in the long days of the short summers. Hay is also raised. There are many dairy farms. Farmers of this valley have good markets for their farm products. They send fresh milk and vegetables to markets in Anchorage.

The land along the Tanana River also is good for farming. Oats, barley, and spring wheat are grown there. Cabbage, peas, carrots, potatoes and other hardy vegetables are also raised. The growing season is short, but there are many hours of sunlight. In the middle of summer the sun shines more than 20 hours a day. Warm sunlight makes the crops grow fast. It makes the vegetables grow very large.

Lumbering and Mining in Alaska

Trees grow well in the mild, rainy climate of Alaska. The lower slopes of the mountains are green with thick forests of spruce and hemlock. Some lumbering is carried on, and it is becoming an important industry. As more people come to Alaska, lumbering and the making of wood pulp and paper will become even more important industries.

Mining is Alaska's most important industry. The leading mineral found there is petroleum. Oil was first produced in 1957 near Anchorage. Then, in 1968, huge quantities of oil were found in northern Alaska, between the Brooks Range and the Arctic Ocean. This region is known as the North Slope. See the map of oil fields on page 292.

Between 1974 and 1977, an 800-mile-long (1,280 km) pipeline was built across Alaska. It carries the oil from the North Slope to Valdez and other ports in the south that ships can use all year round.

Much natural gas was also discovered in the North Slope area. Many people think that even richer deposits of minerals are yet to be discovered in this northern area.

Gold, coal, copper, and uranium are also mined in Alaska, but in small quantities.

Alaska's Fishing Industry

Another important industry is fishing. Halibut, herring, cod, and king crabs are abundant in Alaskan waters. But salmon are the most important fish.

The Alaska Pipeline carries oil across the length of Alaska. The pipeline is above the ground because the earth is frozen in many parts of Alaska.

Every day boats bring their catch of salmon to canneries in Ketchikan and other cities along the coast. Much of the work at the canneries is done by machines. Machines unload the boats, placing the fish on a moving belt called a *conveyor* (kən vā′ ər). The conveyor carries the fish into a long cannery shed. Here the fish are cleaned, split open, washed and made ready for canning.

A machine cuts the fish into the right-sized pieces for each can. To make sure that each filled can is the right weight, a machine weighs the cans as they move along. Sealing machines close the cans, which are then taken to large pressure cookers. The salmon is cooked right in the cans. Later the cans are labeled and packed for shipment to all parts of the country. Salmon is Alaska's chief fish product.

Thousands of workers are needed to catch and can the salmon. Alaska does not have enough people to do all this work. So people come from Seattle and other nearby cities for the fishing season.

Government agents guard the fishing grounds by boat and by plane. They watch to see that Alaska's fishing laws are obeyed. They make sure that enough salmon reach the spawning grounds, where the baby salmon are hatched. Then there will always be a good supply of the fish.

Alaska's Fur Industry

Valuable furs have been shipped from Alaska ever since the days of the Russians. But the fur industry is no longer one of Alaska's main industries. Many people feel that it is not right to kill animals for their fur. People are worried, too, that certain kinds of animals will be completely killed off. They will become *extinct* (eks tingkt′). Extinct means no longer in existence.

The fur seals in Alaska were once in danger of becoming extinct. Find the Pribilof (prib′ə lof) Islands on the map of Alaska's products opposite. These tiny islands are the home of the fur seals. Their fine, silky furs

Products of Alaska

are used to make clothing. Every summer thousands of fur seals come to these rocky islands.

Hunters killed so many of these animals that the United States government stepped in and stopped the killing. When the main herd of seals had increased, hunters were once more allowed to kill them. But now only a certain number of seals may be killed each year.

Alaska's fur industry no longer depends on the killing of wild animals. Instead, there are fur farms where fur-bearing animals, especially mink, are raised.

Alaska's Scenic Beauty

Forest-covered slopes, snowy mountain peaks, rushing streams, waterfalls, and icy glaciers are part of Alaska's beauty. This beautiful scenery attracts thousands of visitors every year. Other visitors hunt wild game in the woods, fish in the many rivers and lakes, or camp in the mountains. Many visit Mount McKinley National Park to see Mount McKinley, with its snow-covered peak and glaciers. Taking care of tourists is an important way in which many Alaskans make their living during the summer months.

Cities in Alaska

The cities in Alaska are not as large as those in most other states. But some had a rapid growth as the oil industry developed in the 1970s.

Tourists go to Alaska by ship. Much of their journey can be made through the calm waters of the Inside Passage. Islands protect this passage from rough northern Pacific waters.

Ketchikan is the first Alaskan city reached by ships on the Inside Passage. The land is steep there. Some buildings and streets are built out over the water. In summer, the fishing boats come and go at the busy docks. Ketchikan is an important salmon-canning center. Some salmon are also frozen, smoked, or salted.

At Juneau, too, steep forest-covered mountains rise close to the coast. The city was built there because gold was discovered close by. But fishing, canning, and lumbering are the chief industries today. Juneau is the capital of Alaska. Government business gives work to many people. The city is connected by water and air with other parts of the nation.

Across the Gulf of Alaska is Seward. Find the gulf on the map of Alaska on page 336. Seward, an important port, is at the end of a railroad which runs to Fairbanks and to Anchorage.

Fairbanks is the leading city of the Interior. There is no other big town for hundreds of miles. Many people depend on Fairbanks for supplies. On its streets you see Indians, Eskimos, and military people from the large United States Air Force base at Fairbanks.

Fairbanks can be reached by airplane, train, and also by automobile. It is at the northern end of the Alaskan Highway. This highway is more than 1,500 miles (2,400 km) long. It connects Alaska with Canada. From Canada other highways go south to the rest of the United States.

Anchorage
A Modern Outpost

Getting off a plane at Anchorage's modern airport, you would hardly guess you were at a wilderness outpost. The heart of Anchorage is very modern. Yet nearby is some of the most rugged land left in the United States.

Alaska has the largest area of any state. But most of it is wild unsettled country. Only about 400,000 people live in the whole state. More than 40 percent of them live in or near Anchorage

Founded as a railroad construction camp, Anchorage today is a center for trains going into the Interior. Anchorage also has a port and major highway connections. Planes of all sizes land at Anchorage's airport, which is also an important international stopover. Why is air transportation so important to the people?

Anchorage is the main transportation center of Alaska. Why do you think Anchorage also became the main center for distributing goods? Why might it also be the natural place in Alaska for manufacturing to develop? ■

Farming in Hawaii

Hawaii, as you know, has a pleasant climate and rich soil. With these conditions, farming is one of the most important industries on the islands.

Sugarcane and pineapples are the two big money crops on the islands. The climate also favors the growing of tropical vegetable crops and coffee. Many people grow orchids and other flowers. The flowers are shipped to florists in the mainland states.

Workers harvest sugarcane with machines. You can see the color of Hawaii's rich soil where the sugarcane has been cut down.

Sugarcane, Hawaii's Largest Crop

The raising of sugarcane is a big business in Hawaii. Sugar is Hawaii's chief money crop. Most of it is grown on irrigated fields. Miles of tunnels and pipes bring water to the fields from the rainier sides of the islands. Sugar is a thirsty crop and needs much water.

It takes about 2 years for the cane to ripen. By careful planning, work on a large sugar plantation goes on all year long. Modern machinery is used to get the fields ready for planting, to plant the cane, and to harvest it.

Each plantation is like a complete town. Besides the sugar mills, there are homes, schools, churches, playgrounds, stores, and other services which the people need.

Most of the raw sugar from the sugar mills is sent to the mainland to be refined. A small part is kept in the islands.

Pineapples, Hawaii's Second Crop

Pineapples are Hawaii's second most important money crop. Like sugarcane, they grow best where it is warm all year.

As we ride through a large plantation, we smell the sweetness of the ripening pineapples. On both sides pineapple fields stretch for miles over hilly and gently sloping land. They look like a beautiful green carpet.

The rows of pineapples are planted across the slopes instead of up and down them. "Why have the pineapples been planted across the slopes?" we ask the manager.

"When we plow with the natural curve of the land, it helps to hold the soil in place. This keeps the rain from washing the soil away," the manager explains. "On steeper slopes we build terraces, or small flat hills of earth. These terraces help in holding back the water."

The manager stops the car so that we can see what a pineapple plant is like. We must be very careful not to go too close. The long leaves are like spikes and have sharp edges. For protection from the hot sun and the sharp spikes, the workers who are picking the pineapples wear dark eyeglasses and heavy gloves.

The black patches about the plants puzzle us. We look closer and see that the patches are paper! We are told that machines laid long strips of heavy paper across the fields before the pineapples were planted. The paper helps keep the soil warm and moist and prevents weeds from growing. It is left on the ground until it rots. The young pineapple plants are set out by hand through holes punched in the paper.

"About a year and a half after the pineapples are planted, the first fruit ripens," explains the manager. "We harvest the fruit chiefly in June, July, and August. But some are picked every month."

At harvest time workers put the ripe fruit on the long arm of a conveyor which reaches out across many rows of pineapple plants. A moving belt carries the pineapples to a bin on a truck. When the bin is full, the pineapples are rushed to the canneries. They are then canned, as fruit or as juice. Some are shipped as fresh fruit.

Workers harvesting pineapples need protection from the prickly fruit and the hot sun. What kinds of protective clothing do they use?

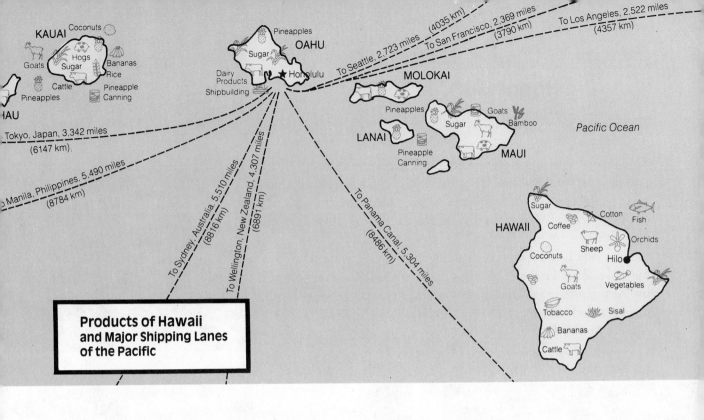

Products of Hawaii and Major Shipping Lanes of the Pacific

Hawaii's Industries

Hawaii's main industries are still based on its farm products. The processing of sugarcane and canning of pineapples are especially important. Coffee is grown and processed on the island of Hawaii. In addition, defense industries have long provided jobs. Many civilians work in or near military bases. The shipyards at Pearl Harbor employ many people.

Since Hawaii became a state, however, other industries have grown up. The construction industry has grown fast. New buildings have been built throughout the islands. Some building materials are now made in Hawaii. There are cement plants, a steel mill, and pipe manufacturing plants. An oil refinery has been built too. Hawaii's garment factories turn out popular Hawaiian shirts and dresses.

A Tourist Land

The beautiful scenery and pleasant climate of these tropical islands bring millions of visitors to Hawaii every year. Travelers enjoy the fine beaches, the mountains, and the brightly colored tropical flowers. December or June— no matter what time of the year it is—visitors are able to wear summer clothes. They can go horseback riding and play tennis or golf. They have fun at the beaches swimming, sun bathing, or riding the waves on a surf board. Some tourists like to visit the pineapple plantations and the canning factories. Others like to visit Hawaii's two national parks, Volcanoes and Haleakala (häl′ē äk′ə lä′) Crater. Taking care of tourists is a year-round business in Hawaii. Many Hawaiians earn their living that way.

Honolulu
An Island Metropolis

The ancient Hawaiians called Oahu the "Gathering Place." If you fly over the Hawaiian Islands today, you can see that Oahu is very crowded. The island's largest city, Honolulu, stretches out beneath you. Three-fourths of Hawaii's people live in or near this city.

Honolulu is the state capital and center of all government business. Pearl Harbor and other major military bases are close by. Also close by is Waikiki, the center of Hawaii's tourist business. In fact, almost all Hawaii's important business is centered in Honolulu.

One reason Oahu and especially Honolulu became the islands' gathering place is Honolulu's excellent harbor. Why is shipping vital to the island? How does Honolulu's harbor bring industry?

But the city's future growth may be limited. Most of the other islands now have deep-water harbors, too. They are also developing tourist resorts and some industries. What effect might this have on Honolulu in the future? ■

372

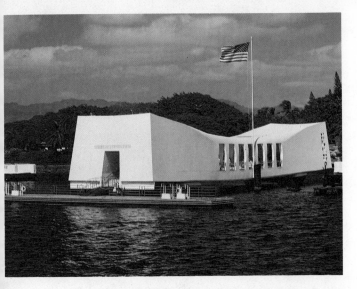

The U.S.S. *Arizona* Memorial floats on the water at Pearl Harbor. It marks the place where the ship *Arizona* sank in the 1941 bombing of the naval base.

Places where ways of travel meet and cross are often called crossroads. Hawaii is called the "Crossroads of the Pacific." Ships and planes on their way to and from Asia, Australia, and North America stop there to unload or take on mail, cargo, supplies, or passengers.

Many tourists like to visit Pearl Harbor on the island of Oahu (ō ä'hōō). It is a harbor where a very large number of United States ships are stationed. Pearl Harbor also has large airfields.

In 1941 war between Japan and the United States seemed close. But no one thought that the war would begin in Hawaii. At dawn on December 7, Japanese planes flew over Oahu, dropping bombs on the naval base and the airfields at Pearl Harbor. Many ships were sunk. Airplanes burned on the ground.

This was the beginning of World War II for the United States. The war lasted for nearly 4 years. The Hawaiian Islands were an important source of supplies in the Pacific during the war.

Because of its position on the crossroads of the Pacific, Hawaii is an outpost of defense for the United States. Pearl Harbor and other military bases on the islands are still very important.

Hawaii's location makes it important for other reasons too. It is a natural meeting place for peaceful contacts between representatives of America and Asia. The ancestors of many of Hawaii's people came from Asia.

Cities of Hawaii

Hawaii does not have many large cities. Honolulu is the largest. Hilo (hē'lō) is second in size. Hilo is on the island named Hawaii, the largest island in the group. Hawaiians call it the "Big Island." It has many sugar plantations and great cattle and sheep ranches. Hilo is the trade center and port of the "Big Island." The city is also an important tourist center.

Do You Know?

1. Where is California's Central Valley? What are some products raised there?
2. Why are there laws to regulate salmon fishing?
3. What minerals are found in Alaska?
4. What are Hawaii's most important crops?
5. Why is Hawaii important to the United States defense system?

To Help You Learn

Using New Words

volcano spawning
conveyor aqueduct
trade wind great circle route
extinct transcontinental

The phrases below explain the words or terms listed above. Number a paper from 1 through 8. After each number write the word or term which matches the definition.

1. Across the continent
2. An opening in the earth's surface through which steam, ashes, and hot, melted rock, or lava, flow
3. No longer in existence
4. Nesting place in fresh water
5. A steady wind that blows toward the equator
6. A moving belt which carries loads from one place to another
7. A pipe or channel that carries water over long distances
8. Shortest, most direct route between two places on the globe

Finding the Facts

1. What are the Pacific states? Why are these five states called the Pacific states? Which state is the largest? Which is the smallest?
2. What are the chief mountain ranges in the four coast states?
3. Where are the lowland areas in Washington and Oregon?
4. What is the highest mountain in North America? Where is it?
5. Where are the Aleutian Islands?
6. What is the climate of the five Pacific states like?
7. Who was John C. Frémont? Kit Carson? John Sutter?
8. Who were the fortyniners? By what three routes did they reach California?
9. Name three ways of sending messages that connected the East and West by the 1860s.
10. Who first discovered Alaska? From whom did we buy Alaska? When?
11. Who discovered Hawaii? When did Hawaii become part of the United States?
12. What crops are raised in California's Central Valley? In the Imperial Valley?
13. Why does southern California have so many airplane factories?
14. What is the leading lumber state in the United States?
15. Name two ways in which the Grand Coulee Dam serves the region in which it is located.
16. What fish are caught off the coasts of Oregon, Washington, and Alaska? Which kind of fish is the most valuable?
17. Why was a pipeline built across Alaska?
18. What national parks are in California?
19. What is the leading port city in the Northwest? On what body of water is it located? What are its most important industries?

20. Why is Hawaii a good place in which to grow sugarcane and pineapples?

Learning from Maps

1. Find the five Pacific states on a globe. In what direction is Alaska from Washington? Hawaii from Washington?

2. On the map of the United States on pages 92 – 93, locate the Pacific states. Why are Alaska and Hawaii shown separately from the rest of the United States?

3. Look at the map of the Lewis and Clark Expedition on page 235, and trace the route of Lewis and Clark from St. Louis to the Pacific coast. What river did they follow most of the way? By what route did they return?

4. Trace the route of the Oregon Trail on the map of western trails on page 313. Through what different kinds of land would the settlers have to travel in going from Independence, Missouri, to Portland, Oregon? The map of the United States on pages 92 – 93 will help you.

5. Study the map showing the products of the Pacific states on page 355 and answer these questions: What fruits are grown in these states? Where are the wheat lands? The lumber regions? What minerals are found in these states?

6. By using the map showing the growth of the United States on page 91, list the territories added to the United States between 1800 and 1860. Which Pacific state once belonged to Mexico?

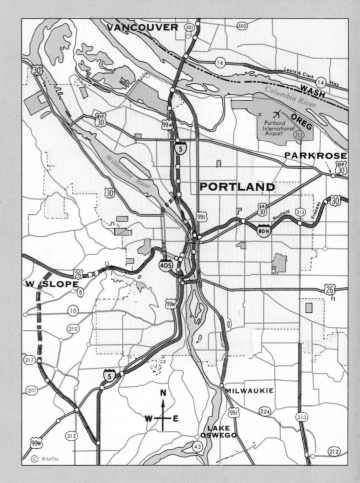

7. This road map shows the area around the city of Portland, Oregon. What roads are shown in green? What roads are shown in red? Why is State Route 14 called the Lewis and Clark Highway? What is the name of Interstate Route 80N? In which state is the city of Vancouver? What river would you cross to travel from Portland to Vancouver?

8. On the map of forest regions on page 357 locate the forest regions of Washington, Oregon, and California. What kind of forest is found in each of these states?

375

9. The elected Senators and Representatives travel to Washington to serve in the Congress. Show on a globe the shortest route Alaska's Congress members could take in traveling by airplane from Juneau to Washington, D.C.; Hawaii's Congress members from Honolulu to Washington, D.C. What large bodies of water would each group cross? What mountains would they cross? What states would they fly over?

Using Study Skills

1. **Time line:** Copy the time line on page 333. Put these other events on the time line in the right order.

   Morse invents telegraph

   Supreme Court grants fishing rights to Indians

   Bering Strait discovered

   Lewis and Clark Expedition begins

   United States and Great Britain divide Oregon Country

2. **Chart:** Make a chart of the Pacific states. List the states alphabetically beginning with Alaska. Use the chart in Unit 5 on page 186 as your model.

3. **Graph:** Look at the graphs on page 351. Which group of people made up 9% of the total population in Alaska in 1980? What percentage of the people in Alaska were American Indian in 1980? Which group of people made up the largest percentage? Which group made up the smallest percentage? Which group of people made up 40% of the total population in Hawaii in 1980? What percentage of the people in Hawaii were of Japanese ancestry? Which group was larger—those of Japanese or those of Hawaiian ancestry?

Thinking It Through

1. Early settlers in the Oregon Country had to make their own laws because they were so far away from the national government. What kind of rules did they need? How was their experience like that of the Pilgrims who drew up the Mayflower Compact? Why do all groups need rules to live happily together?

2. If gold were discovered in California today, what means of transportation would people use to reach the gold fields? Would any of these be the same as those used by people who went west in 1849?

3. When the United States bought Alaska from Russia in 1867, many Americans did not know much about the new land. They thought the purchase of Alaska was foolish and called it "Seward's Folly." What is your opinion of this purchase?

4. Most early settlers and explorers did not turn back even though they faced many hardships. Why was it so important for them to continue their journey?

5. If you had been a fortyniner, which of the three routes to California would you have preferred to take? Why? You may wish to study the map of North and South America on page 13 and the map of western trails

on page 313 before making your choice. Consider the danger, time, and cost of the route you choose.

Projects

1. Prepare an exhibit of the products of the Pacific states. Bring in sample products such as an apple, an orange, a pineapple, a can of salmon, and so on. In some cases you may have to use pictures.
2. Find a current event about one of the Pacific states and connect it with what you have learned in this unit.
3. Make a report on the Alaska Pipeline. When was it built? Why? Who built it? In what ways was it valuable? How did it affect the land around it?
4. The Research Committee might find information about Lewis and Clark's trip. Write a diary about the trip. Tell about the tribes of American Indians, the animals, and vegetation along the way.
5. The Explorers' Committee should use an outline map of the United States to show the route followed by Lewis and Clark and their exploring group in 1803–1805.
6. The Reading Committee will find these books interesting: *Narcissa Whitman, Pioneer Girl,* by Ann Warner; *Blue Willow,* by Doris Gates.

11 American Neighbors

Unit Preview

The United States has fifty states. It also has other lands. Some of these lands lie in the Atlantic Ocean. Others are in the Pacific.

To the north, the United States shares a long border with Canada. The French were the first to settle in Canada. The English came much later. The French and English went to war over North America. The war ended in favor of the English. Canada remained under English rule until 1867, when it became an independent nation.

The region south of the United States is called Latin America. Some of the countries in Latin America are clustered around the Caribbean Sea. Most of these Caribbean countries are independent nations. Some are colonies of European nations. Mexico is the Latin American country closest to the United States. The two nations share a border. In 1821 Spanish rule ended in Mexico.

Like their neighbors to the north, the countries of South America all began as colonies of European nations. Today all but one of these countries are independent. The countries of South America have important raw materials and farm products to sell to the rest of the world. All the countries want to do more than produce raw materials and farm products, however. South Americans want to develop new industries, and they have begun to do this.

Things to Discover

If you look carefully at the picture, map, and time line, you can answer these questions.

1. The picture shows the ruins of what was once a Mayan temple. The Mayas lived in Central America, the narrow strip of land between the American continents. What country is north of this region?
2. What country borders the United States on the north? On the south?
3. What ocean borders Canada on the north?
4. Which became independent first, Mexico, Cuba, or Brazil?
5. What form of government does Canada. have?

Words to Learn

You will meet these words in this unit. As you read, you will learn what they mean and how to pronounce them. The Word List will help you.

asbestos	Latin America
balsam	llano
commonwealth	mestizo
confederation	missile
Creole	pampa
ejido	Parliament
estuary	pitchblende
gaucho	province
hacienda	selva
hurricane	tungsten
latex	vulcanizing

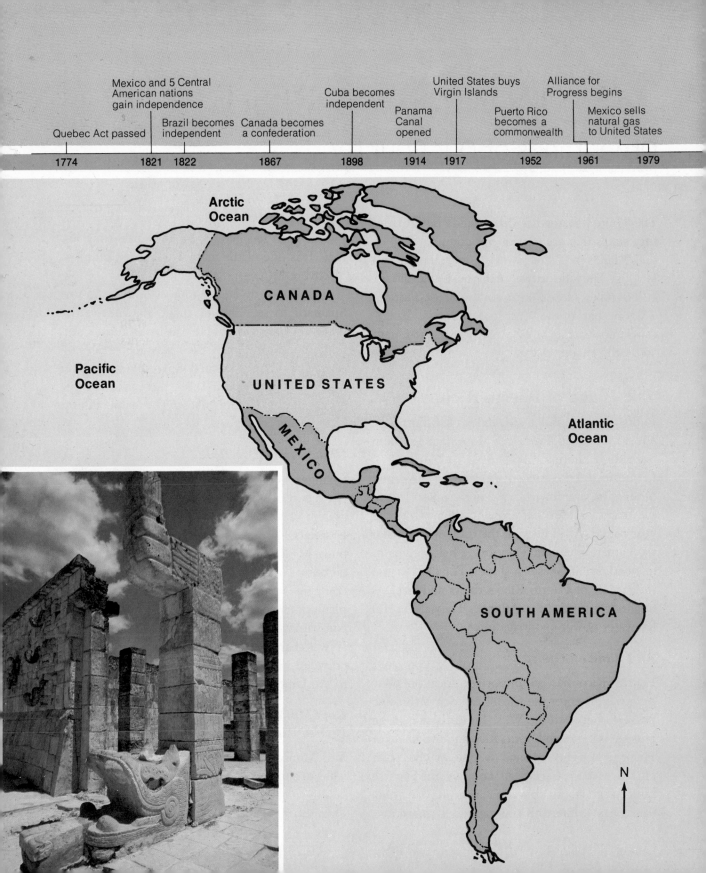

Quebec Act passed — 1774

Mexico and 5 Central American nations gain independence — 1821

Brazil becomes independent — 1822

Canada becomes a confederation — 1867

Cuba becomes independent — 1898

Panama Canal opened — 1914

United States buys Virgin Islands — 1917

Puerto Rico becomes a commonwealth — 1952

Alliance for Progress begins — 1961

Mexico sells natural gas to United States — 1979

Arctic Ocean

Pacific Ocean

Atlantic Ocean

CANADA

UNITED STATES

MEXICO

SOUTH AMERICA

N

1
Other Lands of Our Country

The United States has other lands besides the fifty states that are part of our country. Two of these lands are Puerto Rico and the Virgin Islands. They lie in the Atlantic Ocean about 1,000 miles (1,600 km) southeast of Florida. They are part of the West Indies islands. American Samoa (sə mō′ə), Midway, Wake, and Guam are in the Pacific Ocean.

The Island of Puerto Rico

Puerto Rico is about 100 miles (160 km) long and 35 miles (56 km) wide. More than 3 million people live there.

Puerto Rico is mostly a land of hills and mountains with lowlands along the coast. It is in the tropics, where the growing season lasts the year round. As in Hawaii, the trade winds make the climate pleasant. They bring heavy rains to its northern and eastern slopes. For this reason, the largest of Puerto Rico's rivers and streams flow north toward the Atlantic. They are useful for water power and irrigation.

An Island on Guard

Puerto Rico has an important location. The only way to enter the Caribbean Sea is through passages between the West Indies islands. One passage is between Puerto Rico and the island of Hispaniola. This passage is one of the chief entrances to the Caribbean. Long ago the Spanish built a great, thick-walled fort at San Juan (sän hwän′), Puerto Rico's capital, to guard it.

Under Spanish Rule

Puerto Rico has had a long and interesting history. It is one of the many lands that Columbus discovered.

Juan Ponce de León (pōns dā lā′ōn), the first Spaniard to see Florida, made the first settlement on Puerto Rico. He was its first governor. For 400 years Puerto Rico was a Spanish colony. The people learned Spanish ways. After our war with Spain in 1898, the island became a part of the United States. The name Puerto Rico means "rich port."

Under American Rule

Changes were made in Puerto Rico after it became part of the United States. A public-school system like that in our states was set up. Roads, hospitals, dams, and hydroelectric plants were built. Most of the people worked on sugar plantations or in sugar mills owned by United States companies. Much of the money made by the plantations and mills went to the United States companies. Puerto Rico received little money. It was hard to make a living on the small, crowded island. Many left Puerto Rico to come to the United States mainland.

Luis Muñoz Marin, Puerto Rican Leader

Luis Muñoz Marín (l○○ ēs′ m○○ nyōs′ mä rēn′) was born in San Juan, Puerto Rico, in 1898. His father worked for Puerto Rico in Washington, D.C. So Luis went to school in the United

States. Later, he returned to Puerto Rico. There he worked on a newspaper which his father had founded.

In 1932 Luis was elected to the Puerto Rican Senate. Six years later he started a new political party, the Popular Democratic party. In 1948 the people of Puerto Rico were allowed to elect their own governor. They chose Luis Muñoz Marín as their first governor. He remained in office until 1964 when he decided not to run again. Luis died in 1980.

For more than 8 years as Senate President and later as governor, Luis worked hard to improve living conditions in Puerto Rico. He set up a series of programs known as "Operation Bootstrap."

As part of Operation Bootstrap the government of Puerto Rico bought large plantations. It divided them into small plots of land. The plots were sold at low prices to many farmers. Ways of farming were improved and better crops raised. Government irrigation projects provided water. Still, not all Puerto Ricans could be farmers. Puerto Rico needed industries to create more jobs for its people. As part of Operation Bootstrap the government helped by encouraging investors from the United States to build factories in Puerto Rico. Each new business was helped by not having to pay taxes for 10 years. New dams and power plants provided electricity for the factories. Government schools trained workers.

Operation Bootstrap brought electricity and an improved school system to all parts of the island. Old buildings were torn down and new ones were put up. A hotel was built, the first

Luis Muñoz Marín often traveled to Washington, D.C., when he was governor of Puerto Rico. He presented the interests of the *commonwealth* to the national government.

one in Puerto Rico. Tourists were invited to enjoy the island's fine climate. Many came and soon there were many hotels.

Puerto Rico as a Commonwealth

One of Luis Muñoz Marín's proudest moments came in 1952 when the United States Congress made Puerto Rico a free *commonwealth* (kom′ən welth′). A commonwealth is a form of government much like a state. As a commonwealth, it has its own constitution. Every 4 years Puerto Ricans elect their own governor and legislature.

Puerto Ricans are citizens of the United States and are free to move here. Many of them did so during the 1950s. Then almost 500,000 Puerto Ricans migrated to the mainland.

Puerto Rico's tie with the United States is of its own choice. Some day it may join the Union as a state. Or it may become an independent nation.

San Juan
Capital and Chief Port

San Juan is the capital and largest city in Puerto Rico. It has two parts. The older part of San Juan is on an island off Puerto Rico's northern coast. Along the busy, narrow streets are houses and shops of long ago. The newer part of San Juan is on the main island. In this new part of the city, buildings are as modern as any in the world. Bridges connect the two parts of the city.

San Juan was founded by followers of Ponce de León in 1521. The Spanish built forts and walls around the city to protect its harbor. The Spanish made San Juan a seat of government.

San Juan is the chief trade, manufacturing, government, and shipping center of Puerto Rico. The city's major industries make medicines, chemicals, fertilizer, and jewelry. Many people also make a living taking care of tourists. San Juan is the main port. Most of Puerto Rico's trade is with the United States. ◼

Sugar, Tobacco, Fruit

About one-third of the people of Puerto Rico earn their living by farming. Sugar, the chief crop and leading export, is grown on the rich level coastland.

Tobacco is another important crop. It is grown on small farms in the valleys in the eastern mountain regions of this tropical island.

"I make most of my living raising and selling tobacco," a farmer says. "It keeps me busy from November, when it is planted, until March, when I harvest it. I also raise corn, beans, yams, or rice. After my tobacco is harvested, I plant other crops in the same field."

"Many things have changed in Puerto Rico since I was young," another farmer says. "Many farms now have electricity and running water. Irrigation is being used on the parts of the island where the rainfall is light."

"We grow pineapples on our farm. Some we market as fresh fruit. The rest we sell to the canneries."

Electrical power plants, like this one near San Juan, were built under Operation Bootstrap. The increased use of electricity attracted new industries to Puerto Rico.

Other crops grown in Puerto Rico are bananas, oranges, and coffee. Some farmers on the island also raise cattle, pigs, and chickens.

Puerto Rico's Industries

Many Puerto Ricans no longer depend on farming for a living. New factories have given work to thousands. They furnish many products which

Products of Puerto Rico and the Virgin Islands

once were imported. They also furnish products for export. Some of Puerto Rico's industries make chemicals, clothing, machinery, electrical equipment, food products, and petroleum products. The petroleum is imported mainly from Venezuela, a country in South America.

Tourism is another thriving industry. The island enjoys a year-round mild temperature, abundant sunshine and refreshing breezes. Visitors come to see the deep forests, the flowering trees and the mountains. They enjoy shopping in city streets that are more than 400 years old, and visiting museums, chapels, and craft shops.

United States Virgin Islands

If they could only speak, what stories the bays and inlets along the coasts of the Virgin Islands could tell! Some of these once hid pirate ships.

In 1917 the United States bought the Virgin Islands from Denmark, a country of Europe, for 25 million dollars. Their location makes these islands important. They are on ship routes to the Panama Canal. They are well located to help

The capital of the Virgin Islands is an important harbor. Charlotte Amalie Harbor overlooks a calm, clear, blue sea.

guard and defend this important canal. Prove this by the map on page 406.

Ten years after the United States bought the Virgin Islands, the islanders became United States citizens. In 1968 the islanders were given the right to elect their own governor. Three years later Melvin H. Evans took office as the first governor of the Virgin Islands. In 1979 voters in the Virgin Islands turned down a constitution that would have given them more self-government. The main reason they did so was that they feared more self-government would bring about tax increases.

Making a living on the Virgin Islands has never been easy. The soil is poor and rocky. Much of the land is hilly. Even on the flat land farmers cannot be sure of getting a good crop. Crops often fail because of dry weather.

Most Virgin Islanders make their living by raising cattle, growing cane, or taking care of tourists. Caring for tourists has become an important industry. Visitors enjoy the balmy climate, the white sandy beaches, and the beautiful tropical scenery. They like to go fishing, swimming, and sailing. Many tourist ships visit Charlotte Amalie (shär'lət ə mäl'ə) on the island of St. Thomas. This beautiful and interesting city is a free port, which means that goods can be received and shipped there without being taxed. Charlotte Amalie is built on hillsides overlooking the blue waters of its bay. It is the capital and largest town in the Virgin Islands.

Among the leading industries of the Virgin Islands are bauxite refining, petroleum refining, and cloth making.

American Samoa

The beautiful Samoa Islands are far to the south of Hawaii. Part of these islands belong to the United States. The rest is an independent nation. Our country has an important naval base in American Samoa. Ships and planes on their way to Australia and New Zealand find the islands good stopping places for supplies.

The Samoa Islands were discovered in 1722 by a Dutch explorer. In 1872 the United States Navy set up a naval base at Pago Pago (päng'ō päng'ō), the capital of American Samoa. For the first half of the 1900s the United States Navy managed the island. Then the United States government took over the management. The people of American Samoa make their own laws and elect their own governor.

Some people in American Samoa grow vegetables and fruits. Others take care of tourists, fish, and make crafts by hand. Tuna canning is another major industry of American Samoa. Much of the canned tuna is exported. Most American Samoan trade is with the United States and Japan.

Midway

Midway is an important link in the chain of our Pacific islands. For many years Midway has been a cable station. A cable is a telegraph wire which is laid under water. At the cable station on Midway messages are received and sent on to the United States and to places in Asia.

Two islands, Sand Island and Eastern Island, make up Midway. The islands are controlled by

Ships stop at Pago Pago, American Samoa, to refuel on their way across the Pacific Ocean. Passengers go ashore to enjoy good food and beautiful beaches.

the United States Navy. The Battle of Midway on June 4, 1942, marked the turning point of World War II in the Pacific. The United States defeated Japan when Japan tried to capture Midway.

Wake Island

Wake Island has been a United States possession since 1898. This tiny, lonely island is an important fueling station between Hawaii and Asia. Wake Island is also a cable station.

During World War II, Japan captured Wake Island. Japan held the island until the war ended in 1945.

Guam

Ferdinand Magellan discovered Guam in 1521 on a voyage around the world. This island was a Spanish possession until our war with Spain in 1898. Since then Guam has become one of our important air and naval bases in the Pacific.

The people of Guam are United States citizens. They make their own laws and choose their own governor.

Some people in Guam farm. They grow vegetables and fruits. They raise cattle, pigs, and chickens. Some people work on the air and naval bases. Others work in oil refineries or in factories that process food or make watches or clothing. Still others fish or take care of tourists.

For years the United States paid little attention to some of its island possessions in the Pacific. They seemed small and of little importance. But they are like steppingstones from the United States to Asia or to Australia and New Zealand. Most of our Pacific Island possessions are in the tropics, or low latitudes.

Today we realize how valuable these island possessions are. Because of their location, planes or ships can stop at these islands for supplies, fuel, or repairs. Many have submarine, air, or naval bases.

Do You Know?

1. What lands fly the United States flag in the Atlantic?
2. How did we get each of these lands?
3. What island possessions does the United States have in the Pacific?
4. In which climate belt do most of the islands lie?

2
Canada, a Northern Neighbor

Canada, our northern neighbor, is the second largest country in the world. Only the Soviet Union is larger.

Canada is made up of twelve *provinces* (prov′ins ez). In Canada a province is a region much like a state in our country. Nova Scotia (nō′və skō′shə), New Brunswick, Prince Edward Island, and Newfoundland are Canada's smallest provinces. Quebec (kwi bek′) is Canada's largest province. It is about twice the size of Texas. Quebec is often called "the cradle of Canada."

Beautiful Moraine Lake is in the Canadian Rockies. The lake was formed by a glacier. It is filled with melted mountain snow.

Geography of Canada

Although Canada is large, it is thinly populated. Much of northern Canada has thick forests and frozen lands. So most Canadians live near the southern border.

Soil and Surface

The Appalachian Highland reaches into Canada. This is a region of low hills and fertile valleys. Some of Canada's best farmlands are in the lowlands along the Great Lakes and the St. Lawrence River.

The Laurentian (lô ren′shən) Upland covers almost half of Canada. It stretches from the Atlantic Ocean to the Arctic. Long ago a glacier moved over this region. As it moved, it took soil with it. It left behind rocky hills, lakes, and swamps. The region is not good for farming. But it has thick forests, many minerals, and swift rivers which furnish water power.

A wide central plain lies between the Laurentian Upland and the Rockies in the west. This fertile plain continues northward from the United States to the Arctic. Its level surface makes it easy to use machinery and to have large farms.

The Canadian Rockies are part of a region of high, rugged mountains. West of the Rockies are the Cascade Range and the Coast Mountains. Plateaus and narrow fertile valleys lie between the coastal mountains and the Rockies.

Southeastern Quebec is part of the Appalachian Highland. Southern Quebec lies in the

CANADA

	0	100	200	400		600 Miles
	0	161	322	644		966 Kilometers

⊗ National Capitals   • Other Cities

☆ Provincial Capitals

Mountains   Hills

Plateaus   Plains

© Rand McNally & Co.

fertile St. Lawrence plain. Most of Quebec is on the Laurentian Upland.

Ontario has more people than any other province. Ontario's lowlands lie in the upper part of the St. Lawrence Valley and the plains along the Great Lakes. Find the natural regions of both provinces on the map of Canada on this page.

The provinces of Manitoba, Saskatchewan (sas kach′ ə won′), and Alberta lie between Ontario and British Columbia. They are part of the great central plain which extends northward from the United States. Its northern part

is covered with trees. Its southern part has a flat, grassy, almost treeless prairie, which gives these provinces their name. Most of the people live on this fertile grassy plain. The Laurentian Upland covers much of northern Manitoba and part of Saskatchewan. Western Alberta lies in the Rockies. Find these natural regions on the map of Canada on this page.

British Columbia is Canada's most western and most mountainous province. The towering snow-capped Rockies shut it off from the other provinces. The forest-covered Coast Ranges border its Pacific coast. Between these mountain ranges are other mountains, narrow, fertile valleys, and plateaus.

Canada's huge and valuable northland stretches west from Baffin Island and Hudson Bay to Alaska. It covers almost one-third of the country. It is divided into two territories, Yukon and Northwest Territories. See the map of Canada, page 389.

Climate

Because it lies in the high latitudes much of Canada has long cold winters. Parts of southern Canada have a climate which is much like that of northern United States. The rainfall map of North America on page 17 shows how much rainfall the different parts of Canada receive.

British Columbia has extremes of climate. Its coastal lands have mild winters and cool summers caused by winds blowing over a warm ocean current. Inland the summers are hot, the winters cold. This province receives the heaviest rainfall in Canada. The warm winds bring heavy rain to the mountains along the coast. Inland the rainfall is light. The diagram showing wind movement on page 122 will help explain Canada's rainfall.

History of Canada

Eskimos lived in the far northern part of Canada long before Europeans arrived. Today Eskimos are scattered throughout Canada. They hunt, fish, and work for mining and transportation companies.

American Indians also lived in Canada long before Europeans arrived. The Indians lived mainly in the central and southern parts of the country. Today most Indians live on reserves, or reservations, set up by the Canadian government. They fish, farm, and work for lumbering and mining companies.

This chart compares Canada and the United States in several ways. Which country has more land? Which country has a greater population?

Canada and The United States

	Population (1980 estimate)	Area	Highest Point	Lowest Point	Largest Province or State	Smallest Province or State
United States	223,240,000	3,615,122 sq. mi. (9,363,123 sq. km)	Mount McKinley in Alaska 20,320 ft. (6,194 m)	Death Valley in California 282 ft. (86 m) below sea level	Alaska 586,412 sq. mi. (1,518,800 sq. km)	Rhode Island 1,214 sq. mi. (3,144 sq. km)
Canada	23,850,000	3,851,809 sq. mi. (9,976,139 sq. km)	Mount Logan in Yukon Territory 19,520 ft. (5,950 m)	Sea level	Quebec 594,860 sq. mi. (1,540,680 sq. km)	Prince Edward Island 2,184 sq. mi. (5,657 sq. km)

French and British Claims

Canada was discovered by Europeans trying to find a sea route to Asia. In 1534 Jacques Cartier (zhäk kär tē ā′) explored the Gulf of St. Lawrence. The next year he discovered and explored the St. Lawrence River. He claimed all the land drained by this river for France.

Samuel de Champlain (sham plān′) founded Quebec in 1608. This settlement was the first permanent French colony in America. Everywhere Champlain went he claimed the land for France.

French soldiers, fur traders, and missionaries continued to explore Canada. By the year 1700 the French had a firm hold in North America.

The British also explored Canada. Because of John Cabot's voyages in 1497 and 1498, they claimed all the eastern coast of North America. See the map of explorers' routes on page 42. They built forts and trading posts. Many of these grew into towns.

Important trading posts were also built in Canada by the Hudson's Bay Company. This English company was started in 1670. It was granted the huge area of land drained by all the rivers flowing into Hudson Bay. It was given the right both to trade in this region and to govern it. Even today this company has trading posts in northern Canada.

The French and Indian War

Time after time the British and the French fought for possession of North America. Their last struggle was called the French and Indian War. The war is known as the French and Indian War because many Indians helped the French.

The British won the war. The peace treaty, made in 1763, changed the map of North America. France gave up Canada and all its lands east of the Mississippi. Great Britain now controlled a large part of North America. The map of European claims in 1763 on page 74 shows how great this territory was.

British Government in Canada

The British wondered how they could rule their former enemies. There were many more French than British in Canada at that time.

In 1774 the British government passed the Quebec Act. By this law French Canadians were allowed to speak their own language and keep their own religion. Today about three out of every ten Canadians are descended from these early French colonists. Their language and many of their ways of living are much like those of the early settlers.

Since these early days Canada has had two languages—French and English. Money, stamps, and government papers are printed in both languages. In 1976, French was made an official language in Canada, equal in importance to English.

Settlers and Explorers

While the British were trying to solve their problems in Canada, trouble arose in their other North American colonies. After the War for Independence started, about 40,000 English colonists fled to Canada. They were welcomed by the British, who were glad to have more English-speaking settlers in Canada.

New settlers also came to Canada from Great

Britain. A large group from Scotland settled in Canada. The most famous of these was Alexander Mackenzie (mə ken'zē), a Scottish fur trader, who reached the Pacific in 1793. Mackenzie was the first European to reach the Pacific by traveling across Canada. Earlier he had explored the great river in northern Canada which now bears his name.

The Plan of Union

By 1837 Canada's colonists wanted more self-government. They rebelled. This revolt was soon settled, but the British government worried about losing its Canadian colonies. Lord Durham was sent to study the problem. His report urged more freedom and self-government for the Canadian colonies. The British government decided to accept his advice.

Within the next 20 years Great Britain's Canadian colonies grew. Colonists in some provinces talked of uniting the colonies under one government. At a meeting at Quebec the leaders worked out a plan for national government. They made a plan of *confederation* (kən fed'ə rā'shən), or union, that they took back to the colonies to be discussed. Later they sent representatives to London to discuss it with the British government. The plan of confederation was approved and made a law on July 1, 1867. This law, called the British North America Act, is Canada's constitution.

The new nation was made up of just four provinces: Nova Scotia, New Brunswick, Quebec, and Ontario. Manitoba was the fifth to join. Then British Columbia was added. The government promised to build a railroad to connect this distant region with eastern Canada. This railroad is now known as the Canadian Pacific Railway. Two years later Prince Edward Island joined Canada.

The building of railroads across Canada brought many settlers to the West. After 1900 settlers poured into this region from the United States, eastern Canada, the British Isles, and other parts of Europe. Then the provinces of Saskatchewan and Alberta became part of Canada.

Newfoundland, Great Britain's oldest colony, was the last to join. Canada now has ten provinces and two territories.

Canada's Government Today

In 1931 the British government passed a law saying that Canada was a fully independent nation. Since then Canada has governed itself. It makes its own laws, settles its own problems, and coins its own money. It makes treaties with foreign countries. It has chosen to be part of the group of nations called the British Commonwealth. These nations have agreed to work together. They have special trading and defense agreements. They recognize the British queen or king as their leader.

Canadians elect their officials in much the same way we do. They have a head of government, called the Prime Minister. He is much like our President. Their *Parliament* (pär'lə mənt), which makes laws for all Canada, is like our Congress. Parliament is made up of a Senate and a House of Commons. An official, called the governor-general, appoints the members of the Senate. The senators are chosen on

In Quebec many signs in stores and on the streets appear in both French and English. Why do you think this is so?

the Prime Minister's recommendation. The people elect House of Commons members.

Canada's People

Most people in Canada are English-speaking. But 80 percent of the population of Quebec is French. They speak French and maintain French ways of living. There is a movement among the French to separate from the rest of Canada and form an independent nation. In 1980, however, people of Quebec voted to remain with Canada.

During the late 1970s many Canadians were working for passage of a bill that would give women equal rights with men. In 1976 some Indians in Canada asked the government for their own province to replace the rights they

lost long ago. Eskimos in Canada also asked for their own province. The government agreed to consider each request.

Living and Working in Canada

Canada's great natural resources make it a rich country. About one-sixth of its land is suitable for farming. Forests cover more than a third of it. It has many mineral resources. Rivers and waterfalls provide water power to make electricity. Most of Canada's industries use electric power. Ninety percent of the electricity comes from water power. Great new water-power projects are now underway.

Because Canada is so large, it has a wide variety of climates, soils, and land surfaces. People of different parts of Canada make their livings in different ways. In this section, you will read about the various regions of Canada. These are the Atlantic provinces, Quebec and Ontario, the prairie provinces, British Columbia, and the northland.

The Atlantic Provinces

Nova Scotia, New Brunswick, Prince Edward Island, and Newfoundland are the Atlantic provinces.

Many people in these provinces earn their living from the sea. The Grand Bank, one of the world's largest fishing grounds, is nearby. Find it on the map of Canada's products on page 401. Cod, haddock, halibut, herring, and mackerel are caught there. In the shallow waters near the shore, lobsters are trapped.

Some people build or repair boats. Others work in fish canneries or in quick-freezing plants. The by-products of fish provide work for others. Bones, heads, and tails are ground into meal for chickens and cattle. Oil is obtained from the livers.

Farming

Where the land is suitable, hay, oats, turnips, and potatoes are grown. These crops grow well in the cool, damp summers. Farmers also raise chickens, pigs, and keep dairy cows. Prince Edward Island and New Brunswick grow most of Canada's potatoes raised for seed. These seed potatoes are sold in Canada and other countries.

Strawberries, blueberries, apples, and other fruits are grown in the Atlantic provinces.

Fur Farming

Fur farming is now carried on throughout Canada. The first fur farm was started on Prince Edward Island.

A high fence surrounds the fox farm that we visit. Inside are pens made of strong, closely woven wire. Spring is an exciting time here. The pups, or baby foxes, are born then. The foxes are given good care. They are fed meat, fish, grass, and berries. They get fresh meat every day. Good food helps make a fine quality fur. The long, cold winters make the fur grow thick.

In December when the fur is thickest the foxes are killed and skinned. The skins are sent to Montreal, the largest fur market in Canada. Minks, raccoons, and skunks are also raised on farms for fur.

Lumbering

The forests of New Brunswick, Nova Scotia, and Newfoundland provide work for many people. Some trees are large enough to be made into boards. Others are made into wood pulp. Wood pulp is the ground-up wood from which paper is made. Rayon, plastics, and film are also wood products. Newsprint, the paper used in newspapers, and wood pulp are the most important products of Canada's mills. Canada supplies more than half the world's newsprint.

Mining and Manufacturing

Nova Scotia furnishes almost one-third of Canada's coal. Newfoundland has much iron ore.

Most of this ore is sent to Sydney near the coal fields in Nova Scotia. After it is made into iron and steel there, it is shipped to many countries. Labrador, the part of Newfoundland on the mainland, has rich deposits of iron ore. Ore from its mines is sent to mills in the United States and Canada.

Manufacturing is important in the Atlantic provinces. The factories and mills use the raw materials from the farms, the sea, the forests, and the mines. They produce wood pulp, paper, steel, butter, cheese, canned fruits, and lumber. Canned and frozen fish are also produced. Manufactured goods and processed foods are exported to the United States and many other countries.

Cities

The people of these provinces live mostly in small towns. Halifax, the capital of Nova Scotia, and St. John's, in New Brunswick, are the largest cities. Both are important seaports. When the St. Lawrence River freezes over, these ports are very busy. Their harbors remain open. Then they become the most important ports of eastern Canada. Cargo is brought to their ice-free ports and shipped inland by railroad.

Newfoundland's location is important for the air routes between North America and Europe. Planes flying the North Atlantic often stop at Gander, Newfoundland, for fuel or repair. Can you tell why?

After wood chips are washed and bleached, they go into a large tank. The tank cooks the chips in an acid mixture to make wood pulp. What happens next?

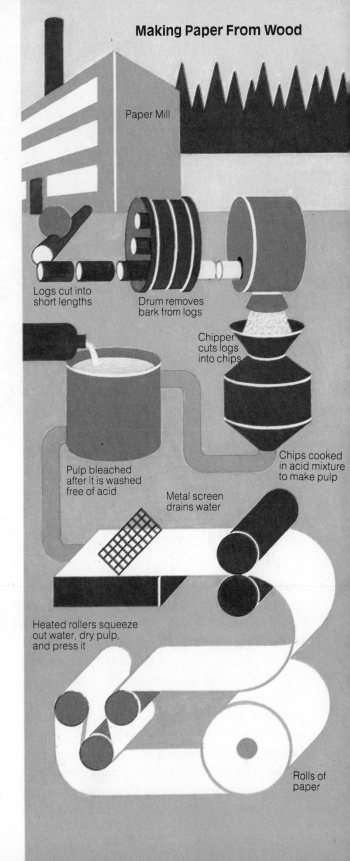

Making Paper From Wood

Paper Mill

Logs cut into short lengths

Drum removes bark from logs

Chipper cuts logs into chips

Chips cooked in acid mixture to make pulp

Pulp bleached after it is washed free of acid

Metal screen drains water

Heated rollers squeeze out water, dry pulp, and press it

Rolls of paper

Visitors to Quebec can watch the changing of the guard at the Citadel, an early British fortress. Today the Citadel is the summer home of Canada's governor-general.

Quebec and Ontario Provinces

Find the St. Lawrence River on the map of Canada on page 389. Notice the plain that lies on both sides of the river. This plain is the most important part of the province of Quebec. More people live on the St. Lawrence Plain than in any other part of the province.

The St. Lawrence Plain has rich soil and plenty of rain. Grass, hay, and potatoes grow well in its cool, moist summers. Dairy farming and the making of butter and cheese are carried on. Nearby is the Laurentian Upland. Its mines and forests furnish valuable raw materials. Its swift rivers furnish power for electricity and

help Quebec produce more water power than any other province. The St. Lawrence River is closed by ice almost five months of the year. Yet it is Canada's most important water highway. With many raw materials, much water power, and good means of transportation the St. Lawrence Plain has much industry.

The Lake Plain

Most of Ontario's people live on the plain along Lakes Ontario, Erie, and Huron. Like the St. Lawrence Plain it has farms, factories, mills, cities and towns. Of Canada's twelve largest cities, four are on this plain. They are Quebec, Montreal, Ottawa, and Toronto.

This lake plain is farther south than the St. Lawrence lowland. It has the advantage of a longer growing season. Because it is near the lakes there is not so much danger from frosts in the late spring and early fall. The northern shore of Lake Ontario is one of Canada's important fruit regions. Mixed farming is carried on and many vegetables and tobacco are raised. Dairy farms supply milk and other dairy products to nearby cities.

Ontario is Canada's chief industrial province. It produces almost all of the farm machinery, automobiles, and bicycles made in Canada. Flour, breakfast food, canned vegetables and fruits, butter, and cheese are also products of Ontario. Ontario's waterfalls and rapids and United States coal furnish power to run its manufacturing plants. The Great Lakes are a fine water highway, used by both the United States and Canada.

The Laurentian Upland

The Laurentian Upland extends across both Quebec and Ontario. Notice on the map of Canada, page 389, how much of both these provinces it covers. Only a small part of this rocky, hilly upland has soil suited to farming. The growing season is short. But hay, oats, and other hardy crops grow well there.

The Laurentian Upland also has forests and fur-bearing animals. Quebec leads Canada in the manufacturing of paper.

Valuable Minerals

There are now mining towns in the Laurentian Upland where once forests grew. Gold, silver, copper, nickel, platinum, and other minerals are the reason. Platinum is a silvery white metal which is more precious than gold. Most of the world's supply of nickel comes from Ontario.

A mineral called *asbestos* (as bes′ təs) is found in the Appalachian Highland. Since asbestos will not burn, articles made from it are said to be fireproof. Canada mines more asbestos than any other country.

Chief Cities

Quebec, a famous French city, is on the St. Lawrence lowland. This oldest city of Canada is built on two levels. Lower Town is crowded along the banks of the St. Lawrence. Here are warehouses, grain elevators, pulp mills, leather factories, stores, and docks. Many of the homes and churches are old. Upper Town is on a high cliff above the river. Many parks and historic spots are here. Quebec is the capital of Quebec Province.

Handling government business, caring for tourists, manufacturing, and shipping are ways in which people in Quebec make a living.

Ottawa (ot′ ə wə), the capital city of Canada, is also on the St. Lawrence Plain. Ottawa began as a lumber town. It is still an important center for lumber, paper, and other wood products. Since it is Canada's capital, its most important work is carrying on government business.

Toronto is Canada's second largest city and the capital of Ontario. Like Chicago, it has a good location for trade on the Great Lakes. Hamilton, near Toronto, and Windsor, near Detroit, are other important cities on the lake plain.

Montreal
An Inland Port in the Heart of Canada

Most port cities are on the seacoast. But to reach Montreal, ocean ships travel up the St. Lawrence River 1,000 miles (1,600 km) inland. Find Montreal on the maps of Canada, pages 389 and 401. Montreal is in the heart of Canada. Why is its port important to nearby regions?

Montreal is an industrial city. Port and railroad services have helped Montreal's industries grow. The city's mills and factories produce flour, clothing, iron-and-steel goods, and electrical equipment. Find Montreal again on the map. How have the streams of the Laurentian Upland helped Montreal become an industrial city?

Montreal is named after Mont Real, or Mt. Royal, a hill in the city. The French explorer Jacques Cartier named this hill when he sailed up the St. Lawrence in 1535. Montreal was as far as Cartier's ship could go. On the map of the St. Lawrence Seaway, page 160, find how far inland ocean ships go today. Why has this made Montreal's port and industries busier than ever? ■

The Prairie Provinces

The prairie provinces are Manitoba, Saskatchewan, and Alberta. The prairies are Canada's most important farming lands. Their soil is deep and fertile, but the rainfall is light. Most of it comes during the short growing season. Millions of bushels of wheat are grown on these prairies every year.

Most prairie wheat goes eastward by train to Winnipeg (win′ə peg′), in Manitoba. There it is sampled and graded. It then goes by rail to Fort William or Port Arthur, on Lake Superior. Lake freighters carry it down the Great Lakes from huge grain elevators at these twin ports.

Some of the grain goes to mills in the United States. Some goes to the Pacific port of Vancouver (van koo′vər). Most of it goes to Montreal. There it is made into flour or shipped to other countries.

Western Saskatchewan and Alberta have large sheep and cattle ranches. There is too little rain for crops, but enough for grass. This region supplies meat for Canada and some for export. In certain areas fruits, sugar beets, and other crops are grown by irrigation.

Mining and Lumbering

About half of Canada's coal is mined in these provinces. Most of the oil and natural gas found in Canada comes from Alberta and Saskatchewan. Copper, zinc, gold, nickel, silver, and *pitchblende* (pich′blend′) are also mined. Pitchblende is the mineral from which uranium is obtained.

Forests cover much of the Laurentian Upland in the prairie provinces. More than half of Canada's furs come from these provinces.

Chief Cities

Winnipeg is the largest city in the prairie provinces. It is Canada's third largest city and the capital of Manitoba. Much of the livestock and grain of the prairies is marketed there. Winnipeg is one of Canada's largest fur markets. It is an important railway center and manufacturer of railroad equipment.

Edmonton, the capital of Alberta, is an important airway center. The discovery of oil nearby brought many people and industries to this city. Calgary (kal′gər ē), in southern Alberta, has oil refineries and factories where foods are processed.

British Columbia

British Columbia leads all the provinces in fishing. Its most important catch is salmon from the Fraser River. Halibut, cod, and herring are also caught.

British Columbia is Canada's most important producer of lumber. Thick forests of cedar, fir, spruce, pine, and hemlock grow on the western slopes of the mountains. Many people work in the forests and in the saw, pulp, and paper mills.

Mixed farming, dairying, truck farming, and market gardening are carried on in the Fraser Valley. In the southern valleys apples, pears, peaches, and other fruits are grown by irrigation. The Peace River region grows much grain.

Mining and Manufacturing

Large deposits of gold, coal, copper, lead, zinc, and silver make mining British Columbia's sec-

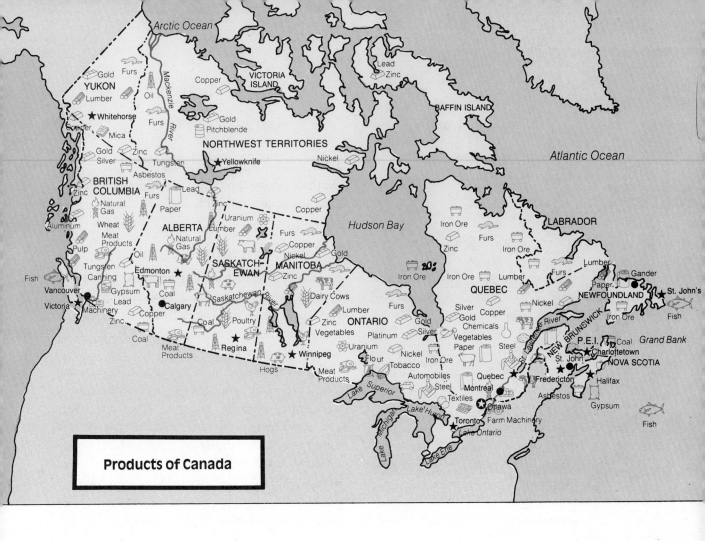

Products of Canada

Chief Cities

ond largest industry. Many people earn their living by mining, smelting, and refining these minerals.

British Columbia has abundant water power from its many rushing mountain streams. At Kitimat, aluminum is made from ore brought from South America. Electricity, produced by water power, is used to refine this aluminum.

British Columbia ranks high in manufacturing. Its industries include fish processing, pulp and paper, petroleum products, meat packing, and aluminum.

Vancouver is Canada's sixth largest city. Two railroad lines which cross Canada end there. Highway and airplane routes center on it. Vancouver's large, deep harbor is open all year round. It never freezes. Lumber, grain, newsprint, minerals, canned fish, and fruit are exported from Vancouver.

Victoria, on Vancouver Island, is the capital of British Columbia. Its mild climate, fine homes, and lovely English gardens attract thousands of tourists yearly.

401

Many people in Canada work in the lumber industry. This worker is sorting logs by kind of wood and size at the log pond of a sawmill.

Canada's Northland

Canada's northland is divided into the Yukon and Northwest Territories. Here and there is a trading post. Canada's northland has long been important for fine furs. Sometimes there is a mining town. Petroleum, gold, silver, lead, zinc, and uranium are mined there. When valuable ores are found, people settle in the northland and build towns and airfields.

Rivers and lakes are important summer highways in the Yukon and Northwest Territories. About four months each year steamers towing barges and rafts carry thousands of tons of heavy freight. Machinery, groceries, radios, and other needed supplies are taken to the towns. On their return trip they carry furs and products from the mines and oil fields.

Canada, Friendly Neighbor

Canada is rich in natural resources. It has fine forests, fertile farm lands, valuable minerals, and many lakes and rivers. It is a great trading nation and one of the important manufacturing nations of the world.

Canada is also one of the world's important food exporting countries. It produces more newsprint, asbestos, and zinc than any other country. The United States is Canada's best customer for newsprint, wood pulp, and minerals.

The United States and Canada have been friendly for a long time. The two countries worked to improve the St. Lawrence Seaway which is important to both countries.

Canada, like the United States, has set aside large areas as national parks. Banff and Jasper national parks are on the eastern slopes of the Rockies in Alberta. At these parks visitors enjoy the mountains, lakes, and forests.

Greenland and Iceland

Greenland and Iceland are Canada's island neighbors. Long before Columbus came to America, daring Norse explored and settled these islands.

Greenland

Greenland belongs to Denmark, a country of Europe, but rules itself. It is the largest island in the world. Most of its people are Eskimos.

Greenland is on a short, or great circle, route between North America and Europe. Planes flying the polar route often stop at Greenland to refuel. The United States has an air base at Thule (too′lē), on the west coast.

Greenland's weather station reports are important to the countries of northern Europe. Storms in Greenland usually mean that northern Europe will soon have the same kind of weather.

Much of Greenland is north of the Arctic Circle. Most of it is a high plateau covered with a great ice sheet. During the short summers the land along the coast is free of ice and snow. There, and on the rocky hillsides, grass and flowers grow.

Most Greenlanders make their living by fishing. Some raise sheep. Fish canneries and freezing and packing plants have been built by the Danish government.

The Republic of Iceland

Iceland lies east of Greenland about halfway between North America and Europe. Planes flying from North America to northern Europe often stop at Iceland's modern airport.

Iceland's first settlers were Norse. As the population grew, they chose a group of people, or council, to make their laws. Thus Iceland developed a system of self-government more than a thousand years ago. In 1944 Iceland became a republic.

Iceland is a land of great variety. Snow-covered peaks and icy glaciers stand side by side with hot springs, geysers, and volcanoes. Some volcanoes erupted in 1977, causing damage to a large electricity plant. The plant was rebuilt, but the volcano is still active.

The people in Iceland use their natural resources to good advantage. Pipes carry boiling water from the hot springs to heat homes and other buildings. Mountain streams and waterfalls produce electricity.

Potatoes, turnips, and hay grow well in the long, sunny days of Iceland's short summers. Sheep, cattle, and swift sturdy horses feed on the grass and hay. Cod, herring, and other kinds of fish are caught.

Iceland is a member of the North Atlantic Treaty Organization (NATO). As part of this defense system, Iceland allows the United States to maintain a naval and air base near Reykjavik (rāk′yə vēk′), the capital.

Do You Know?

1. What natural regions do Canada and the United States share? What water areas?
2. What are the chief ways that the people of Canada make a living?
3. What is the capital of Canada? Where is it located?
4. Why was July 1, 1867 an important day in Canada?
5. Why is Greenland important as a defense base and weather station?
6. How do Icelanders heat their homes?

Before You Go On

Using New Words

asbestos   province

commonwealth   Parliament

pitchblende   confederation

The phrases below explain the words listed above. Number a paper from 1 through 6. After each number write the word that matches the definition.

1. A plan for union of states or provinces
2. Mineral from which uranium is obtained
3. The body of lawmakers of Canada
4. A division of Canada somewhat like a state in our country
5. Mineral that will not burn
6. A form of government much like a state

Finding the Facts

1. Where are Puerto Rico and the Virgin Islands located?
2. What are Puerto Rico's land and climate like?
3. Who made the first settlement on Puerto Rico?
4. What changes were made in Puerto Rico after it became part of the United States?
5. Who was Puerto Rico's first governor elected by the islanders?
6. What are some crops grown in Puerto Rico?
7. What do some of Puerto Rico's industries produce?
8. How did the United States get the Virgin Islands?
9. Why is the location of the Virgin Islands important to us?
10. Why is farming difficult in the Virgin Islands?
11. What are some of the leading industries in the Virgin Islands?
12. Why is Midway important? Who controls Midway?
13. Why is Wake Island important?
14. Who discovered Guam?
15. How do people in Guam make a living?
16. How has American Samoa been managed during the 1900s?
17. How do people in American Samoa make a living?
18. How did the peace treaty of 1763 change the map of North America?
19. What was the British North America Act? When did it go into effect?
20. Name the Atlantic provinces. What are their capitals? In what ways do the people of these provinces make a living?
21. Why are Halifax and St. John's important winter ports of eastern Canada?
22. Why are forests important to Canada?
23. How has Toronto's location helped it become Canada's second largest city?
24. Name the prairie provinces. What are their capitals? In what ways do the people of these provinces make a living?
25. What makes Vancouver Canada's best Pacific port?
26. How are freight and supplies transported in the Yukon and Northwest Territories?

3

Mexico, Our Southern Border Neighbor

The region south of the United States is called *Latin* (lat'in) *America.* There Spanish, Portuguese, and French are spoken. These languages come from Latin, a language once spoken in southern Europe.

Our nearest Latin-American neighbor is Mexico. It shares an 1,800-mile (2,880-km) boundary with the United States. Mexico is larger than Texas, New Mexico, Arizona, California, and Nevada together. It has thirty-one states. It also has a federal district where Mexico City, the capital, is located. About three out of four Mexicans are *mestizos* (mes tē'zōs), or people of mixed Spanish and Indian ancestry. Most Mexicans speak Spanish and have Spanish ways and customs.

Geography of Mexico

Mexico has two coastal plains. One is along the Pacific coast. The other is along the Gulf of Mexico. Mexico shares the Gulf Coastal Plain with the United States. The map of Mexico, on page 406, shows that this eastern lowland widens out in the Yucatan (yōō kə tan') Peninsula. Note that it is wider than the western coastal lowland. Both coastal lowlands are hot. The eastern plain receives more rain.

Mexico has more highland than lowland. Ranges of high, rugged mountains rise from the lowlands along both coasts. Between these eastern and western ranges is the central plateau. This plateau is broken up into many valleys

which are separated by hills and mountains. At its southern end it is more than 1.5 miles (2.4 km) high. Because of its altitude the climate is pleasant. The northern part receives less rain than the southern section.

South of the central plateau is a region of high mountains and many volcanoes. Some of Mexico's highest mountains are in this region. They are snow-capped the year round although they are in the tropics.

Mexico has two peninsulas. The peninsula of Lower California stretches southward from our state of California. The Yucatan Peninsula stretches north and east into the Gulf of Mexico.

Because Mexico has lowlands, plateaus, and mountains, the climate patterns vary. Locate both Veracruz (ver'ə krōōs') and Mexico City on the map of Mexico on page 406. These cities are in the low latitudes. But it is more comfortable to live in Mexico City than in Veracruz. That is because Mexico City is inland and higher above sea level.

Mexico also has great differences in rainfall. Look at the rainfall map on page 17 to find the driest parts and the rainiest parts of Mexico.

History of Mexico

When the Spaniards arrived in Mexico they found the Aztecs (az'teks). The Aztecs were an Indian tribe that controlled most of central Mexico. But the Aztecs were not the first peo-

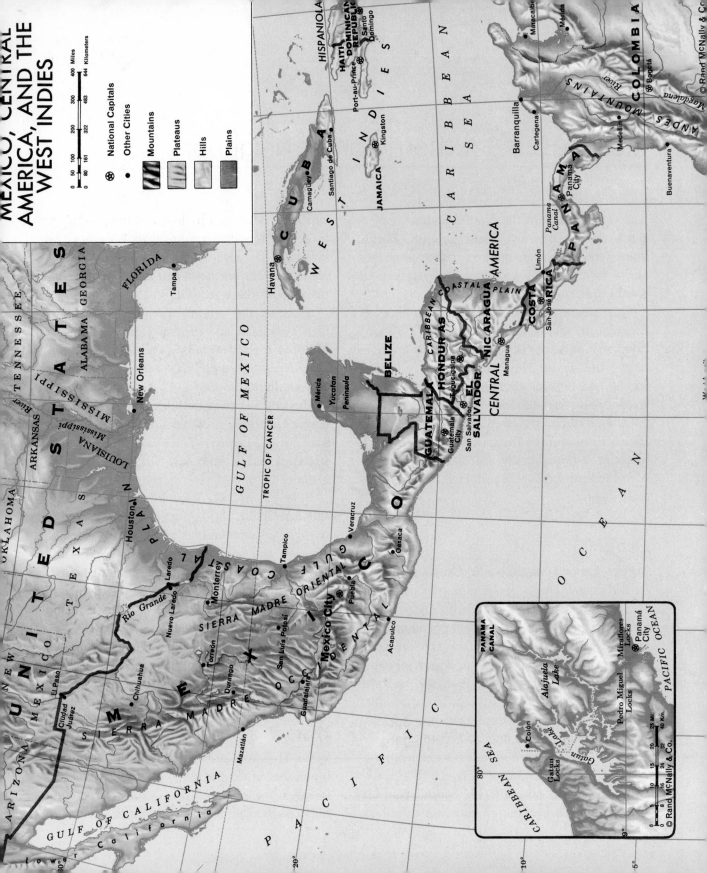

MEXICO, CENTRAL AMERICA, AND THE WEST INDIES

Legend:
⊗ National Capitals
• Other Cities

Mountains
Plateaus
Hills
Plains

0 50 100 200 300 400 Miles
0 80 161 322 483 644 Kilometers

HISPANIOLA

DOMINICAN REPUBLIC
⊗ Santo Domingo

HAITI
⊗ Port-au-Prince

WEST INDIES

CARIBBEAN SEA

COLOMBIA
⊗ Bogotá
• Medellín
• Maracaibo
• Mérida
• Barranquilla
• Cartagena
• Buenaventura

ANDES MOUNTAINS

Magdalena River

CUBA
⊗ Havana
• Camagüey
• Santiago de Cuba

JAMAICA
⊗ Kingston

FLORIDA
• Tampa

GEORGIA

ALABAMA

TENNESSEE

MISSISSIPPI
Mississippi River

ARKANSAS

LOUISIANA
• New Orleans

OKLAHOMA

UNITED STATES

TEXAS
• Houston
• Laredo
• El Paso

NEW MEXICO

ARIZONA

GULF OF MEXICO

TROPIC OF CANCER

COASTAL PLAIN

MEXICO
⊗ Mexico City
• Monterrey
• Nuevo Laredo
• Ciudad Juárez
• Chihuahua
• Torreón
• Durango
• San Luis Potosí
• Guadalajara
• Mazatlán
• Acapulco
• Puebla
• Oaxaca
• Veracruz
• Tampico
• Mérida

Rio Grande

SIERRA MADRE ORIENTAL
SIERRA MADRE OCCIDENTAL
SIERRA MADRE

Yucatán Peninsula

GULF OF CALIFORNIA
Lower California

PACIFIC OCEAN

BELIZE

GUATEMALA
⊗ Guatemala City

HONDURAS
⊗ Tegucigalpa

EL SALVADOR
⊗ San Salvador

NICARAGUA
⊗ Managua

COSTA RICA
⊗ San José
• Limón

PANAMA
⊗ Panama City

CENTRAL AMERICA

CARIBBEAN COASTAL PLAIN

Panama Canal

PANAMA CANAL (inset)

CARIBBEAN SEA

Colón

Gatún Locks

Gatún Lake

Alajuela Lake

Pedro Miguel Locks

Miraflores Locks

⊗ Panamá City

PACIFIC OCEAN

0 5 10 15 20 25 Mi.
0 8 16 24 32 40 Km.

© Rand McNally & Co.

80°

9°

10°

5°

20°

© Rand McNally & Co.

ple to live in this region. Scientists have found ruins and cave drawings painted about 1500 years before the Aztecs came to Mexico.

The Spaniards were dazzled by the wealth and great cities that the Aztecs had built. Within 3 years, the Spanish conquered the Aztecs. The Aztecs were the last in a series of great Indian civilizations in Mexico. The Spaniards forced the Indians to work in their mines or on their large farms. They took over most of the land. Only the poorer lands were left for the Indians.

The years passed. Many colonists became dissatisfied with Spanish rule. Spanish governors often treated the colonists unjustly. Colonists objected to the taxes and high prices.

Miguel Hidalgo y Costilla, Leader of Independence

Miguel Hidalgo y Costilla (mē gel′ ē däl′gō ē kōs tē′yä) was born in Guanajuato (gwän′ə wä′tō), Mexico, in 1753. He was the priest of a small Indian village. There he taught the people how to grow grapes, and how to make silk and bricks.

Father Hidalgo thought the Indians were being treated unfairly. He believed that they and other Mexicans would benefit if Mexico were free from Spain. In 1810 Father Hidalgo organized an independence movement.

Thousands joined Father Hidalgo's army. For a while they were successful against the Spanish troops. It seemed that Mexico would be freed. But then Father Hidalgo was captured and put to death in 1811.

Others took up the work of Father Hidalgo. In 1821 Mexico became independent.

Miguel Hidalgo y Costilla is called "The Father of Mexican Independence," although he did not live to see Mexico free from Spain. Monuments honoring Hidalgo are found in many Mexican cities.

After Independence

Independence brought few changes in life in Mexico. The descendants of the wealthy Spanish settlers continued to rule the country. The life of the Indians remained much the same. They toiled for the rich landowners or worked small patches of poor ground for themselves. Some people were very rich. Most were very poor.

407

On September 16 each year the people of Mexico celebrate their independence from Spain. The national cathedral in Mexico City is a center for the festivities.

"Why should we give up our large estates?" the wealthy landowners thought. Yet some leaders believed that most Mexicans would have a better life if these huge farms were broken up. They wanted the land divided among the Mexican farmers. Benito Juárez (bā nē′tō   wär′ēs), a Mexican leader, believed in this idea.

Juárez became the head of Mexico about the time Lincoln was President of the United States. Like Lincoln, Juárez wanted to help the poor people. He worked hard to weaken the power of the wealthy landowners. He wanted to give the land back to the Indians so that they could farm it for themselves. He improved methods of farming. He became one of the most honored leaders of Mexico. But he died before many of his ideas could be carried out.

After Juárez' death, the wealthy landowners continued to hold the land. Many became more powerful than ever. The Indians and mestizos remained poor farm laborers or factory workers. But other leaders, who believed as Juárez did, carried out many of his ideas.

Changing Mexico

Many changes have taken place in Mexico since Juárez' time. Most of the large estates have been broken up and the land has been divided into small and middle-sized farms. Almost half the Mexican farmers own the land that they farm. But many farmers are poor. They have not learned new farming methods. Nor is there enough good land for all.

Some farms belong to an entire village. The land of these farms has been turned over to the farming village by the government. Such land is called an *ejido* (ā hē′dō).

In some ejidos the people farm the land as one large farm. All share in the work and in the crops. In other ejidos each family is given a piece of land. These families can use the land as long as they farm it and pay taxes on it. They cannot sell it or rent it.

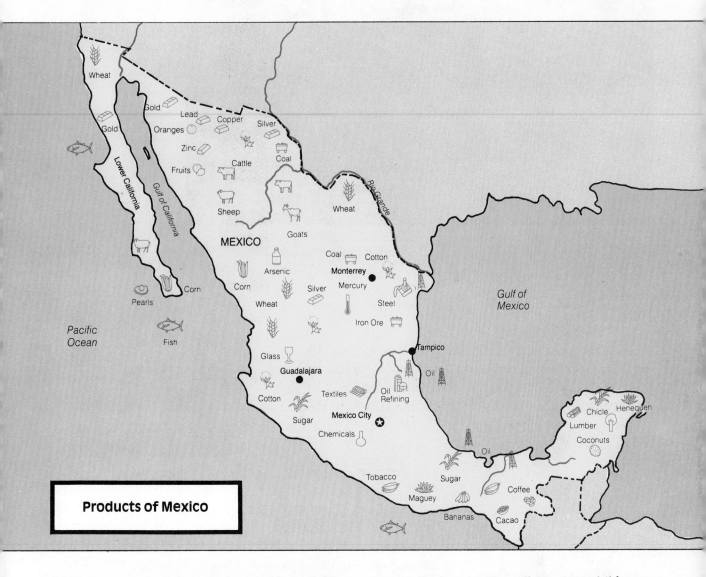

Products of Mexico

The government has tried to make available more land for farming. It has built dams and brought water to thousands of acres of dry land. It has set up a settlement plan. Farmers can become homesteaders on government land never farmed before. In 10 years, if their crops are good, they can own their home and 60 acres (24 ha) of land.

Education has greatly improved in modern Mexico. New schools have been built and new teachers have been trained. As in the United States, the law requires all Mexican children to go to school.

With new dams and hydroelectric plants, more electricity is produced. With new roads, railroads, and airports it is easier for Mexicans to travel.

Business is growing. New trades, businesses, and manufacturing have been started. In some factories, glass, cement, electrical goods, and shoes are made. There are automobile plants, tire plants, and chemical works.

Mexico City
Center of Mexican Life

Mexico City was the center of Mexican life before the Spaniards came. The city was called Tenochtitlán (tä nôch'tē tlän') It was the capital of the Aztec Empire and the hub of Aztec activities. The Spaniards destroyed Tenochtitlán, but they built their new capital on the same spot.

Mexico City continues to show the early Spanish influence. In the huge central plaza, or square, are the beautiful old Spanish buildings. The great cathedral and the National Palace are built on Aztec ruins.

But the city shows the new Mexico too. Near the central plaza are tall modern office and apartment buildings. The country's big businesses are there. Over half the nation's industrial products are now made in or near Mexico City. Many people from the villages have crowded into the city to find jobs in industry. Mexico City is Mexico's largest city. It has the country's most pleasant climate. As the center of Mexican life, Mexico City shows the old and the new Mexico. ■

410

Living and Working in Mexico

The Indians who lived in Mexico when the Spaniards came were skilled workers. They made fine pottery, beautiful blankets, and beautiful articles of gold and silver. Today many Mexicans still take pride in making articles by hand. Caring for tourists also gives work to Mexicans. Three of every five Mexicans earn their living by farming. Mining gives jobs to others. More and more Mexicans now earn their living by working in factories and offices.

Farming in Mexico

The hot, rainy Gulf coast south of Tampico is a region of thick, tropical forests. Where the forests have been cleared, tropical crops such as sugarcane and bananas are grown. Coffee is raised on the mountain slopes.

Farther south, on the Yucatan Peninsula, much of the world's henequen (hen′ə kin) is grown. Henequen is a thorny cactus plant. From its leaf fiber, twine is made.

The northern Pacific coast is desert and mountains. Irrigation brings water for corn and cotton. Along the rainy southern coast, coffee and cocoa are raised.

The central plateau is where most Mexicans live. The climate is comfortable because of the altitude. Village houses are often made of adobe (ə dō′ bē), a sun-dried clay. The chief crop is corn. It is made into thin, flat pancakes called tortillas. (tôr tē′ yas) Tortillas and beans, called frijoles, (frē hō′ lēs), are the main Mexican foods.

Minerals of Mexico

Mexico has large deposits of silver, gold, copper, lead, zinc, and petroleum. Vast new deposits of oil and gas have been found recently in Mexico. In 1979 the leaders of Mexico agreed to sell natural gas to the United States. In the same year, an oil well in the southern part of the Gulf of Mexico had a blowout. It caused one of the worst oil spills in the world. Some of the oil spread to the coast of Texas.

Mexico's Cities

Monterrey (mon tər rā′), in the northeast, is Mexico's most important city for heavy industry. Because of its steel mills, Monterrey is often called the Pittsburgh of Mexico. Both coal and iron are nearby. Railroads and roads pass through the city.

Guadalajara (gwäd′ əl ə här′ ə), Mexico's second largest city, is a manufacturing, farming, and cattle center. It is famous for its handmade glass and fine pottery.

Do You Know?

1. Where are Mexico's two coastal plains?
2. What language do most Mexicans speak?
3. What minerals are found in Mexico?
4. Who was Father Hidalgo? What did he do in 1810?
5. What did Benito Juárez want to do with the estates of wealthy landowners?

411

4

Central American and Caribbean Countries

The land between Mexico and South America is called Central America. In Central America are Guatemala (gwä′təmä′lə), El Salvador (el′ sal′vədôr), Costa Rica (kōs′tə rē′kə), Honduras (hon door′əs), Nicaragua (nik′ə räg′wə), Panama (pan′ə mä), and Belize (be lēz′). Find them on the map of Central America on page 406. American Indians, mestizos, blacks, and people of Spanish-speaking descent make up most of the population.

The West Indies are a chain of thousands of islands stretching in a curve from Florida to northern South America. They separate the Atlantic Ocean from the Caribbean Sea. Most of them are the remains of volcanoes that erupted a long time ago. Some are too small for people to live on.

Cuba (kyoo′bə), Haiti (hā′tē), the Dominican (də min′ i kən) Republic, Jamaica (jə mā′kə), Trinidad (trin′ə dad′) and Tobago (tə bā′gō), the Bahamas, (bə hä′məz), and Barbados (bär bā′dōz) are among the populated islands. Most of the population is made up of blacks, mestizos, Indians, and people of Spanish, French, British, and Dutch ancestry.

Geography

The Central American countries all lie in the low latitudes. They share three natural regions—the Pacific Coastal Plain, the central highlands, and the Caribbean Coastal Plain. The mountains of the central highland have many active volcanoes.

Between the mountains lie valleys and plateaus. This region has a pleasant climate because it is high above sea level. Thick forests of tropical trees and plants grow in the hot, rainy Caribbean lowland. The Pacific coast has grasslands and forests. Rainfall is not so heavy there.

The West Indies lie in the tropics or low latitudes. Their climate is warm all through the year. Even the highest lands are not cool enough for frost. Crops can be grown there the year round. Often two or three crops are grown in a year.

The Pan American Highway connects Mexico, Central America, and South America. This area of the highway is in Costa Rica, just west of San José.

Ruins of a Mayan city can be seen at Chichén Itzá in Mexico. Temple walls and carvings in stone used in the service of the Mayan gods still stand.

Steady northeast trade winds help make the climate mild. They bring much rain. The northeastern slopes of the mountains have more rain than the southwestern slopes. Severe tropical storms, called *hurricanes* (hur′ə kānz′), can cause damage. During August, September, and October, these hurricanes sweep across the West Indies and even reach the United States. Their strong winds and heavy rainfall often destroy everything in their path.

The West Indies are important because they are on the sea routes to the Gulf of Mexico, Central America, and the Panama Canal. The location of the West Indies also makes them important in trade. Their tropical crops are sent to countries where such crops are scarce.

History of Central America

Indians had lived in Central America long before the Spanish came. The Mayas (mī′yəz) were farmers. They were also great builders. They built large cities and beautiful stone temples in Honduras, Guatemala, and Mexico. The Mayas knew much about the stars and the movement of heavenly bodies. They created a calendar. They could write numbers up to a million and also had a form of picture writing. But the Spaniards conquered the Mayas.

After 300 years of Spanish rule, Guatemala, El Salvador, Costa Rica, Honduras, and Nicaragua declared their independence on September 15, 1821. At first these new countries were not sure what they wanted to do. When Mexico became free, they joined it. Then they broke away from Mexico and joined together as the United Provinces of Central America. This union did not last either. By the middle 1800s they were again independent countries.

On the eastern coast of the Yucatan Peninsula is Belize (formerly British Honduras). Belize remains a dependency of Great Britain. Thus Belize is the only country in Central America still controlled by a foreign nation.

A steamship moves through the Panama Canal. There are locks in the canal which allow ships to be raised or lowered from one level to another.

Panama's History

North America is joined to South America by an isthmus. This land bridge between the two great continents is the Isthmus of Panama.

For years people talked about building a waterway through the isthmus. "Ships could take a short cut between the Atlantic and the Pacific," they said. The French were the first to try to build a waterway across the isthmus. But diseases, landslides, and floods caused the French company to fail.

After the war with Spain in 1898, the United States acquired possessions in both the Atlantic and the Pacific. The United States became interested in building a canal in order to get from one ocean to the other quickly. But Colombia, which owned Panama, refused to let the United

States build a canal. The United States helped Panama to break away from Colombia and become an independent republic in 1903.

The Republic of Panama gave the United States permission to build the waterway. Panama also gave the right to rent a strip of land 10 miles (16 km) wide across the isthmus. This was the Panama Canal Zone, for which the United States paid Panama a yearly rent until 1978.

In 1904 Colonel William Gorgas was called to the Canal Zone to wipe out the mosquitos that caused fever and other diseases. Then came the great task of digging the canal through jungles, swampland, and mountains. After 10 years the waterway was completed. The two great oceans were united in 1914.

The Panama Canal is considered important for the defense of the United States. But for years many Panamanians felt that the United States should not exercise so much power in their country. They wanted a new treaty to replace the 1903 pact.

In 1978, a new treaty was signed between the Republic of Panama and the United States that gave Panamanians control of the Canal Zone. By the year 2000, Panama will have control of the canal. However, the United States keeps the right to defend the canal's neutrality, so that it can be used by all nations.

Living and Working in Central America

Rich soil, plenty of rain, and a long growing season aid farming. Farming is the chief work of the people. Crops that grow in a temperate climate as well as tropical crops are raised because of the differences in altitude.

Most manufactured products are used where they are made. Bananas, coffee, cacao, and sugar are grown for export. Valuable woods and other tropical forest products are exported. The United States is a good customer for all these products. In exchange, we ship machinery, clothing, and foods to Central America.

Guatemala, Land of the Mayas

Guatemala has the largest population of the Central American countries. More than half its people are descendants of the ancient Mayas. They live mainly in small villages in the highlands. They weave cloth, tend sheep, or make pottery. They farm their small fields of corn and beans or work on the large plantations.

Farming is the chief work in Guatemala. Corn, beans, rice, sugar, coffee, bananas, tobacco, and cotton are raised. Coffee and bananas are important exports.

Guatemala City, the capital, is the largest city in Central America. It is the manufacturing and transportation center of Guatemala. The city is also a tourist center.

Honduras

The people of Honduras make their living from farms, mines, and forests. Bananas are the chief export crop of Honduras. They are grown along the hot and rainy Caribbean coast.

Corn is the chief food crop, but wheat, beans, and other temperate-climate crops are also grown. Cattle are raised in the highlands. Coffee is the second most important export crop.

Tegucigalpa (tä gōō′sē gäl′pä), the capital and largest city, has a pleasant climate because of its location. It is on a plateau at the foot of a mountain. Much of the city looks as it did in Spanish colonial days. Some streets are narrow and steep. But modern buildings and houses are also there. The old and the new are side by side.

Some people in Guatemala wash their clothes at a community washing area. The clothes are then spread out on the grass to dry in the sun. Other people use washing machines instead.

415

El Salvador, Pacific Land

El Salvador is the smallest and most thickly settled country of Central America. It is the only country that borders entirely on the Pacific.

Almost all the land in El Salvador is farmed even though much of it is mountainous. Coffee is the most valuable money crop. Sugar, henequen, cotton, rice, and *balsam* (bôl′səm) are also exported. Balsam is made from the sap of a tree which grows along the coast. It is used in making perfumes and some medicines. Corn, beans, and wheat are grown as food.

The government of El Salvador has helped farmers learn better ways to farm and save the soil. The government has improved the school system throughout the country.

Fine roads and railroads connect the capital, San Salvador, with other cities of the country. San Salvador is a busy modern city with parks and beautiful homes.

Nicaragua, Land of Lakes

Nicaragua has more lowland than any other country of Central America. It also has many lakes. Most of the people and most of the towns are in western Nicaragua.

Sugar, cotton, corn, and rice are grown on the lake plains in western Nicaragua. Coffee is raised in the central highlands. The fine grass on the highlands makes good pasture for cattle. Gold mining is also carried on in the highlands. Cotton, gold, coffee, and lumber are valuable exports.

Managua (mə nä′gwä), the leading city and capital, is an attractive city on the shores of a lake in western Nicaragua. It has many fine parks. Because of earthquakes which destroyed many old buildings, Managua has been rebuilt as a modern city.

Costa Rica, Panama, Belize

In Costa Rica many people, rather than just a few, own the land. Most of them are descendants of the Spanish settlers. Costa Rica's people have a share in their government.

Most Costa Ricans are farmers. On soil made rich by minerals from erupting volcanoes, they grow corn, beans, potatoes, and other temperate crops. Coffee is the leading crop and most valuable export. Bananas are also exported. San José, the capital, is a modern city.

The Panama Canal and the Canal Zone are only a small part of the Republic of Panama. The rest of the country stretches away from the Canal Zone in either direction. Farming is the chief occupation outside the Canal Zone. Corn and rice are the leading food crops grown on the small farms. Bananas and cacao are export crops grown on large plantations. Stock raising and mining are becoming important. Most of the people in cities near the Canal Zone earn their living from work connected with the canal. Panama City, the capital, is near the Pacific entrance to the canal. In its old section are colonial churches, narrow streets, and Spanish style houses. Its new section has modern houses, shops, and buildings. Because it is near the canal, it is a busy city. Much trade passes through this port and through Colón (kō lōn′), at the Atlantic entrance to the canal.

The main exports of Belize are the products

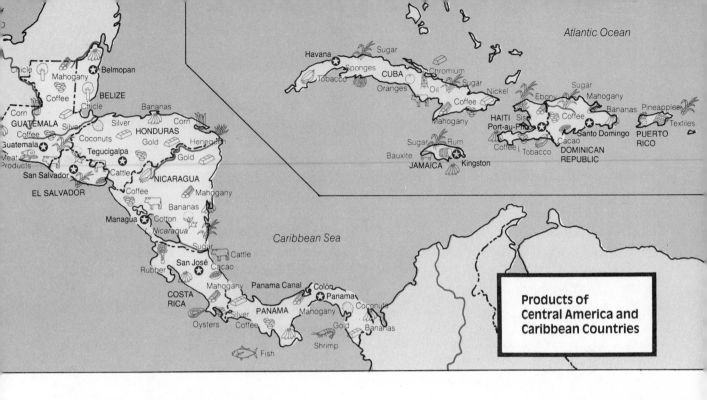

Products of
Central America and
Caribbean Countries

of its forests. Cedar, chicle (chik′əl), used for making gum, and mahogany are important exports. Mahogany is a beautiful hardwood used in making furniture. Most of the food has to be imported. Recently, bananas have become an important money crop.

History of the West Indies

The Spanish were the first Europeans to claim the West Indies. Then France, Britain, and the Netherlands began to seize some of the islands claimed by the Spanish. Denmark also took some. After a time many of the Spanish islands revolted and became independent.

Hispaniola (his′pən yō′lə) is the island where Columbus made his first settlement. Two nations, Haiti and the Dominican Republic, share the island. Hispaniola belonged to Spain for a long time. Spanish settlements were made in the eastern part of the island. Later, France gained control of the western part, now called Haiti.

Under French rule, western Hispaniola became a rich colony. Hundreds of black slaves were brought there to work on the plantations. After a while the slaves, led by Toussaint L'Ouverture (tōō san′ lōō vər tyōōr′), rebelled. The long struggle ended in independence for Haiti in 1804. Haiti was the first European colony of Latin America to become independent. The Dominican Republic gained its independence in 1844.

Jamaica, Trinidad and Tobago, Barbados, and the Bahamas are former British possessions. They now belong to the British Commonwealth. Jamaica and Trinidad and Tobago became independent in 1962, Barbados in 1966, and the Bahamas in 1973.

Other islands still belong to Great Britain, France, and the Netherlands. In 1978 Great Britain gave up control of Dominica (dō min'i kə). Martinique (mär ti nēk') and Guadeloupe (gwäd əl ōōp'), a group of islands, belong to France. The Dutch control Aruba (ə rōō'bə) and Curaçao (koor'ə sou') near the northern coast of South America.

Cuba's History

Long after Spain's other colonies had won independence, Cuba was still a Spanish possession. Many times the Cubans revolted against Spain's harsh rule.

In 1895 yet another revolution erupted. The United States became involved in the Cuban revolt when the battleship *Maine,* while lying in Havana Harbor, mysteriously blew up. The Spanish-American War lasted only a few weeks. When the war with Spain ended in 1898, the United States won control of Cuba.

The United States soon made Cuba an independent nation. But independence did not bring peace and stability to Cuba. In 1953 another revolution broke out. This one was led by

Havana, Cuba, has the largest population of all the West Indian capital cities. What are some of Havana's industries? Which capital city has the smallest population?

Countries of the West Indies

Country	Capital	Population of Capital	Some Industries and Products
Aruba and Curaçao	Willemstad	40,000	Oil refining, tourism, electronics, shipbuilding
Bahamas	Nassau	3,233	Tourism, banking, rum
Barbados	Bridgetown	8,789	Rum, molasses, tourism
Cuba	Havana	1,008,500	Textiles, wood products, cement, chemicals, cigars, sugar
Dominica	Roseau	16,800	Agriculture, tourism
Dominican Republic	Santo Domingo	673,470	Molasses, rum, cement, textiles, furniture
Guadeloupe	Basse-Terre	270,000	Agriculture
Haiti	Port-au-Prince	703,100	Rum, molasses, tourism
Jamaica	Kingston	111,879	Aluminum, rum, molasses, cigars, oil products, tourism
Martinique	Fort-de-France	60,648	Rum, tourism
Trinidad and Tobago	Port-of-Spain	250,000	Oil products, rum, cement, tourism

Fidel Castro (fē del′ käs′trō). He and his supporters kept on fighting until the dictator, Batista, went into exile.

Since 1959 Castro and his supporters have ruled Cuba. When they took over all foreign-owned businesses and properties, the United States government became concerned.

In 1960 the United States stopped buying Cuba's sugar. So Cuba began to trade with the Soviet Union and other communist countries. Then the United States broke off diplomatic relations with Cuba.

Many Cubans who did not want to live under Castro fled to the United States. These Cuban exiles tried to start a revolution against Castro. They were defeated at the Bay of Pigs.

A crisis erupted in 1962 when the United States discovered that the Soviet Union was installing *missiles* (mis′əlz) in Cuba. Missiles are weapons that are designed to be thrown or fired toward a target. The United States demanded that the missiles be removed. It set up an air and naval blockade of Cuba. After four days of tension, the Soviets agreed to remove the missiles and the crisis ended.

During the 1970s and in 1980 many Cubans fled to the United States. A large number of them settled in Florida.

Living and Working in the West Indies

Most of the people in the West Indies make their living by farming or processing farm products. Sugar cane, cacao, bananas, coffee, and pineapples are grown. Most of these tropical

Some women of Barbados and other West Indian Islands are able to carry things gracefully on their heads. This custom requires good posture and balance.

crops are raised for export to the United States and Europe. Since colonial days, more land has been used to grow money crops than to grow food crops. Much of the food used by people in the West Indies must be imported.

Many island governments now want to set up new industries to provide more jobs for their people. More people can make a living from industry than from farming.

Beautiful scenery, ocean breezes, fine beaches, warm, sunny days, and different ways of living bring thousands of tourists to these islands. The money they spend there helps many islanders earn a living.

Do You Know?

1. Where is Central America?
2. What are some exports of these countries?
3. Where are the West Indies?
4. Which islands of the West Indies are independent? Which are under foreign control?

Before You Go On

Using New Words

balsam   hurricane
ejido   missile
Latin America mestizo

The phrases below explain the words or terms listed above. Number a paper from 1 through 6. After each number write the word or term that matches the definition.

1. A person of mixed ancestry, usually Spanish or Portuguese and Indian
2. Land south of the United States, where Spanish, French, or Portuguese is spoken
3. A tropical storm with strong winds
4. Land turned over to a farming village by the government
5. The sap of a tree used in making medicines and perfumes
6. A weapon that is designed to be thrown or fired toward a target

Finding the Facts

1. Where in the Americas is Mexico?
2. Who organized a movement to set Mexico free from Spain?
3. Why is Benito Juárez remembered as one of Mexico's important leaders?
4. In what ways is the Mexican government helping its people today?
5. How do most Mexicans earn a living?
6. What countries make up Central America?
7. Where are the West Indies?
8. In what latitudes are the Central American countries and the West Indies?
9. What Central American countries declared their independence from Spain in 1821?
10. What and where is the Panama Canal?
11. How has Cuba been governed since 1898?
12. What are the chief money crops of each of the Central American countries?
13. How do most people in the West Indies make their living?

5
South America

South America is the fourth largest continent. It has thirteen countries. See the map of South America on page 422. Colombia (kə lum′bē ə) and Venezuela (ven′ə zwā′lə) are in northern South America. Colombia is as large as Texas, Oklahoma, and New Mexico put together. Venezuela is almost as large as Texas, Oklahoma, and Louisiana.

Ecuador (ek′wə dôr′), Peru (pə rōō′), and Chile (chil′ē) border the Pacific Ocean. Ecuador, the Spanish word for equator, is about as large as Colorado. Chile is a very long and narrow country.

Brazil (brə zil′), Uruguay (yoor′ə gwā′) and Argentina (är gen tē′nə) border the Atlantic Ocean. Argentina is as large as the part of our country which lies east of the Mississippi River. Uruguay is about half as large as California. Brazil, the largest South American country, is almost as large as the United States.

Guyana (gī an′ə), Suriname (soor′ə nam), and French Guiana (gē an′ə) also border the Atlantic. Bolivia (bə liv′ē ə) and Paraguay (par′ə gwā′) lie in the heart of South America. Paraguay is about the size of California.

Geography of South America

South America has a variety of land surfaces. The Andes Mountains stretch along the Pacific Ocean. They are the second highest mountains in the world. Melting snow trickles down the mountain slopes in streams used for irrigation.

Near the Atlantic coast are hills and low mountains called the Guiana and Brazilian highlands. The Guiana Highlands are shared by Venezuela, Guyana, Suriname, and French Guiana. The Brazilian Highlands stretch from northeastern Brazil almost to Uruguay.

In Bolivia the Andes Mountains divide into two chains. Between them is a high plateau. In the far south of Argentina is Patagonia (pat′ə gō′nē ə). Patagonia is a long, narrow plateau. Much of the central part, or interior, of Brazil is also plateau.

The *llanos* (lä′nōz) are grassy plains which stretch between the Andes and the Orinoco (ōr ə nō′kō) River in Venezuela. Colombia and Venezuela share the llanos. The *pampas* (pam′pəz), or treeless plains, stretch across central Argentina from the Atlantic to the Andes. North of the pampas lies the Chaco (chä′kō), a large area of grass and forests. Argentina's pampas are the flattest plains in the world. The interior of Brazil is also flat. The Atacama (ät ə käm′ə) Desert is in northern Chile. It is one of the driest deserts in the world.

Major Water Systems

The Amazon River in Brazil is the second longest river in the world. The Amazon Lowlands are drained by the Amazon River and its many tributaries. This basin includes almost half of Brazil.

The Parana (par ə nä′), the Uruguay, and the

SOUTH AMERICA

Miles					
0	100	200	400		600 Miles
0	161	322	644		966 Kilometers

⊗ National Capitals
☆ Other Capitals
• Other Cities

Mountains
Plateaus
Hills
Plains

Paraguay rivers unite to form the Plata River system. This river system is smaller than the Amazon but more important for transportation. The rivers which unite to form it empty into an *estuary* (es′chōo er′ē), or arm of the sea, called the Rio de La Plata (rē′ō dē lä plä′tə). Argentina, Uruguay, and Paraguay share the land and the rivers.

Climate

Most of South America is in the tropics. The map of South America, page 422, shows the equator passing through the northern part of the continent. Because of the varied land surfaces, South America has some of the coldest and some of the hottest places on earth. The southern part of South America is in the middle latitudes. The climate is much like that of our country. South America has great differences in rainfall. Look at the rainfall map on page 17. Find the driest and the rainiest parts of South America.

The *selvas* (sel′vəs) are the tropical rain forests of the Amazon. These deep forests have two seasons. One is a "rainy" season when it rains most of the time. The other is a "dry" season, which is not quite so rainy.

History of South America

The Incas (ing′kəz) were perhaps the greatest of the Indian civilizations in the Americas when the Spanish arrived. They lived in South America. At one time the empire stretched 2,000 miles (3,200 km) north to south along the Pacific coast of South America.

The Incas had a highly developed form of government. They were farmers and skilled builders. They built terraces so that they could farm the slopes of mountain villages, and canals to irrigate their crops. They built forts, temples, palaces, roads, and bridges. The Incas were also skilled metal workers. They had much gold and silver. But like the Aztecs and the Mayas, the Incas were conquered by the Spaniards.

For more than 300 years Spain ruled its colonies in the Americas with a firm hand. Taxes were heavy. Prices were high. Trade could be carried on only with Spain. Only Spaniards born

Large, broad-leafed plants thrive in the tropical rain forests of the Amazon. More than 80 inches (203 cm) of rain may fall there in a year.

423

in Spain could be high officers or hold the best jobs. The Spanish colonists were angry.

The Spaniards born in the Americas, who were called *Creoles* (krē'ōlz), were very unhappy. "Why are we not allowed to hold high offices?" the Creoles asked.

While Mexico and Central America were gaining their freedom, Spanish colonies in South America also were fighting for their independence. Simón Bolívar (sē mōn' bō lē'vär) led the fight for freedom in Venezuela, Colombia, Ecuador, Bolivia, and Peru. José de San Martín (hō sē' dē sän' mär tēn') was a leader in Argentina and Chile. He also helped Bolívar in Peru. Bernardo O'Higgins led the fight for freedom in Chile. He became its first president.

Bolivia was formed from part of Peru and part of Argentina. It was named for Simón Bolívar. Paraguay became independent without fighting. The Paraguayans asked their Spanish rulers to resign. The Spaniards agreed. Paraguay won its independence without war.

Brazil belonged to Portugal. The son of Portugal's king governed the colony. Brazilian colonists asked the king's son to declare Brazil an independent country and become its ruler. He agreed and in 1822 was crowned Brazil's ruler. Three years later, Uruguay, which had once been part of Brazil, declared its independence.

The English, the Dutch, and the French had settled the Guianas. Guyana (formerly British Guiana) gained independence in 1966, Suriname (Dutch Guiana) in 1975. French Guiana is the only part of South America that is not independent.

After all these countries had won their independence, they faced other problems. They fought against each other over boundaries. The citizens fought among themselves. About three out of every four persons were Indians or mestizos. Most of these people had little or no education. Powerful people, usually with the help of the army, were able to seize governments and rule as they pleased. The people suffered under these dictators. The countries remained poor.

Simón Bolívar is called "The Liberator." The United States honors people who fought for freedom in nations around the world. Bolívar's statue stands in Washington, D.C.

SIMÓN BOLÍVAR
THE LIBERATOR

Even today military governments are common in South American nations. Argentina, Brazil, Peru, Uruguay, Bolivia, and Chile all have military governments. Ecuador has often been under military control. But in 1979 voters elected a leader who did not belong to the military. Paraguay has had a series of dictators.

The governments of Colombia, Venezuela, Suriname, and Guyana are among the few democracies in South America. Guyana is a member of the British Commonwealth.

Living and Working in South America

Many people in South America make their living by farming. Some of them work in mines, in industries, or in lumbering. Still others make their living by caring for tourists.

Colombia

Most of Colombia's people live in the Andean highlands. They farm on the plateaus and in the fertile valleys. Coffee is grown on the slopes of the Andes. It is Colombia's most important money crop. Colombia is one of the world's chief coffee producers.

Colombia produces platinum, a hard metal used for jewelry and dental work. Colombia is also an important source of gold. In addition, the nation's mineral exports include silver, emeralds, and copper.

Many of Colombia's large cities are in the highlands. Medellín (med′əl ēn′) lies in a rich valley of the Andes. In its mills and factories cotton and woolen goods, shoes, soap, sugar, watches, and jewelry are manufactured. Medellín is the center of a rich farming and mining region. Gold is mined nearby. It is refined in the government mint at Medellín. Barranquilla (bär′räng kē′yä), at the mouth of the Magdalena River, is Colombia's chief port. Barranquilla is also an important air center.

West of Barranquilla is the city of Cartagena (kär′tə jē′nə). Cartagena's chief business today is oil. Petroleum is piped from oil fields more than 400 miles (640 km) away. Petroleum is Cartagena's chief export. Colombia ranks second to Venezuela in the production of oil in South America.

Bogotá (bo′gə tä′) is Colombia's capital, largest city, and the center of its art and music. It is on a high plateau in the eastern Andes Mountains. On the farms around Bogotá corn, wheat, potatoes, and barley are grown. Cattle and sheep supply food for the people of Bogotá and the coastal lowlands.

Venezuela

The Andean highlands are an important farming section of Venezuela. On the mountain slopes coffee is the chief crop. It is Venezuela's most important farm export. In the low valleys there are cacao plantations. Sugar, beans, corn, wheat, and potatoes are grown at different altitudes.

The hot, damp lowland near Lake Maracaibo (mar′ə kī′bō) brings much money to Venezuela. Oil derricks rise like a forest from the lake region. Pipelines are thick there. The most valuable product and export of Venezuela is oil.

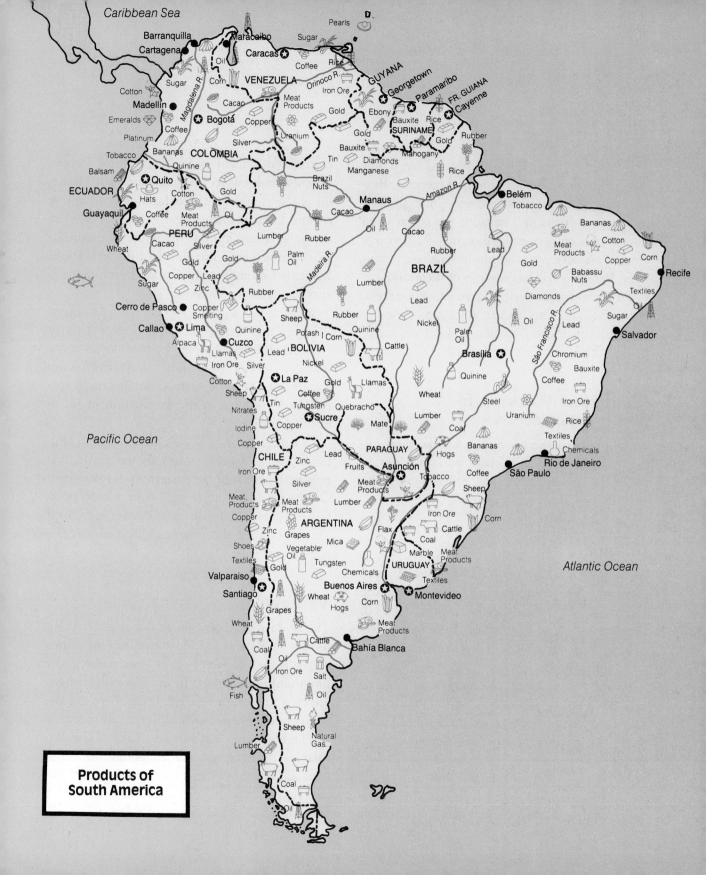

Products of South America

Venezuela ranks fifth in the world in the production of oil.

Most of the oil from these fields is sent to the Dutch-controlled islands of Aruba and Curaçao. There, it is made into gasoline and fuel oil.

Oil has made Maracaibo Venezuela's second largest city. Iron ore, sugar, and coffee as well as petroleum are exported.

Near the old colonial city of Valencia cotton is raised. The cotton is woven into cloth in the textile mills there.

Most of Venezuela's people live in the cool, comfortable Andean highlands. Caracas (kə rä′ kəs), the beautiful capital and largest city, is located in a high valley. It is an old city, yet a very modern one. La Guaira (lä gwī′ rä) is the busy seaport for Caracas.

Guyana, Suriname, French Guiana

Farming is the most important work in Guyana and Suriname. The heat and heavy rainfall produce fine tropical crops for export and for home use. Sugarcane and rice are raised along the swampy coastal plain.

The most important export is bauxite. Guyana and Suriname rank among the top six countries in the world in bauxite production. As you know, aluminum is made from this ore. Aluminum is used in making airplanes, automobiles, and trains. The United States buys much of the bauxite.

French Guiana is the smallest and the poorest of the three Guianas. Many kinds of tropical crops could be grown there. However, only a

Some of Venezuela's largest oil deposits are beneath Lake Maracaibo. Oil wells are drilled from platforms on the water. The platforms are anchored to the lake bottom.

small part of the land is used for farming. The people import much of their food. Some gold is mined.

Brazil

The people of Brazil number more than 119 million. The first Europeans to settle there were from Portugal.

Working in the Amazon Valley

In Brazil are Indians who make a living by hunting and gathering. They live in the Amazon Valley. Some gather nuts. They pick up Brazil nuts which are delicious to eat and make a fine oil for cooking. They also gather tagua (ta′ gwä) nuts which, when carved, are white and look like ivory. Other people dig the roots of the manioc (man′ ē ok′) plant. Tapioca, used in puddings, is made from the root of this plant.

Some people make a living by collecting the sap of rubber trees. Pure rubber melts in hot weather and breaks in cold weather. Few uses were found for it at first. Then a way of treat-

Some of the heavy forest growth in the Amazon Valley is being cleared to make the land suitable for farming. The cool highlands are ideal for growing coffee. Here a worker cleans coffee beans.

ing rubber with sulphur, called *vulcanizing* (vul′kə nīz′ing), was discovered. Vulcanizing keeps rubber from melting, or hardening, whatever the weather may be.

Manufacturers began to make rubber raincoats, overshoes, and other things of vulcanized rubber. Then the automobile was invented. Millions of tons of rubber were needed for tires. Workers were hired to gather *latex* (lā′teks), the sap of the rubber tree.

Then planters in Asia began to grow rubber on plantations. Asian rubber was cheaper than wild rubber from South America. Later, people learned to make synthetic rubber from gas, coal, tar, and petroleum. The United States and the rest of the world now use more synthetic rubber than natural rubber. Synthetic rubber can be produced cheaply enough to compete with natural rubber.

Brazil continues to produce natural rubber. But its rubber plantations can supply only enough rubber for the tire industry in Brazil.

Farming, Mining, Manufacturing

The northern part of the Brazilian Highlands is a great desert. In spite of the lack of water and grass, cattle and goats are raised in the northern highlands. In irrigated areas cotton, sugarcane, vegetables, and fruits grow.

Carnauba (kär nou′bə) wax and babassu (bä′bə soō′) oil are valuable products. The leaves of the carnauba palm are coated with wax. It is used in making floor and furniture polish, motion-picture films, and phonograph records. Oil from the babassu nut is used in soap, margarine, and cooking oil.

Some parts of the highlands receive heavy rains. There sugarcane, cotton, cacao, bananas, and other tropical crops are grown.

About three-fourths of the world's coffee is raised in Brazil. Most of Brazil's coffee comes from the central highlands. The coffee plant needs a cool climate, a long growing season, plenty of water while it is growing, and dry weather when it ripens.

Gold was Brazil's most important mineral product for many years. About 200 years ago diamonds were discovered in the highlands of Brazil. Most Brazilian diamonds are used for drill points and cutting tools. They are important to industry. Rich iron-ore fields lie north of Rio de Janeiro (rē ō dā jə ner′o). Most of this iron ore is exported.

Today Brazil has more factories than other South American countries. At first most of the factory products were used in Brazil. Now all kinds of goods are exported too. Automobile, steel, rubber, and meat-packing companies are found in large cities. Trained people from the United States work in these companies to help the Brazilians. Foreign aid and money have helped Brazil's industries grow.

Brazil's Cities

Manaus (mä nous′) and Belém (bə lem′) are the only large cities of the Amazon Valley. Manaus, an important river port and a market center, is inland. Belém, the chief rubber center of Brazil, is on one of the mouths of the Amazon River. It is the entrance to the Amazon Basin.

Salvador, a cacao port and railroad center, is built on two levels like many cities on Brazil's coast. Its latitude is only 12 degrees from the equator, so the heat in the lower city is almost unbearable. Most people live in the upper city, which is cooled by ocean breezes. Elevators carry them to and from work in the lower city.

Recife (rə sē′fə) is built partly on a peninsula and partly on islands. Many of its streets are canals. Recife is Brazil's chief sugar port and railroad center. It exports much cotton and tobacco. Recife's people work in cotton mills, tobacco factories, sugar refineries, on docks, and on boats. Fishing is also important.

The city of Rio de Janeiro, Brazil's old capital, is built on a bay which forms a fine harbor. In addition to being a seaport, Rio is a railway, highway, and airway center.

Because Rio de Janeiro lies between the ocean and the mountains, the city has no space to grow. Brazil's government wanted the people to move west, away from the coast. So Brazilians decided to build a new capital far inland. In 1961 government operations were moved to the new city, Brasília (brə zil′ē ə).

São Paulo
A Fast-Growing, Energetic City

São Paulo (sou pou'loo) is the largest city in Latin America. Coffee made São Paulo grow. The city spurted ahead after it became Brazil's main coffee-marketing center.

Between São Paulo and the sea are steep cliffs. The city's people overcame this barrier by hanging a railway on cables down to the port of Santos. Load after load of coffee goes down these cables. Santos is the world's busiest coffee port.

Today coffee is still São Paulo's main business. But new industries are growing. Much nearby land is now used to pasture livestock and grow cotton. What new industries do these two activities give São Paulo? Machinery and electronics equipment are made there.

To get power for new industries, São Paulo's energetic people dammed up rivers and pumped the water over mountains to make electricity. South America's first nuclear power plant was also built near São Paulo. The fast-growing city has entered the nuclear age. ■

Chile

Most Chileans make a living by farming. The most important farming region is Chile's Central Valley. On the haciendas of the Central Valley are acres and acres of winter wheat, rice, corn, rye, and barley. Beans, potatoes, and lentils are grown. Dairy cows graze in the pastures. Livestock and alfalfa to feed them are raised on the ranches. Juicy grapes hang in the vineyards. There are citrus fruit groves and orchards of apple, peach, and cherry trees.

Lumbering is important in southern Chile. The extreme southern tip is good for sheep raising.

One mineral found in Chile is nitrate of soda. Most of the nitrate is made into fertilizer. Some is used in chemicals, gunpowder, and other war materials. Iodine, used in medicine, is also made from nitrate of soda. More than half of the world's iodine comes from Chile.

Copper is now Chile's most important export product. Three important copper mines lie at the eastern edge of Atacama. One is the largest open-pit copper mine in the world.

Chile has enough coal to run its industries. Much of the coal lies below the ocean off the coast of central Chile. Tunnels where miners work, business offices, and restaurants have been built under the Pacific Ocean. Chile's growing industries need the coal from these undersea mines.

Chile's Cities

Valparaiso (val′pə rī′zō) has the best natural harbor in the country. Trade is important in Chile, and Valparaiso is its trade center. Woolen and cotton textiles and some iron-and-steel goods are manufactured. Leather, shoes, cans, wines, flour, and chemicals are made in the factories. Heavy machinery, however, must still be imported.

Santiago (san′tē ä′gō), the capital, is Chile's largest city and most important industrial center. It is the fourth largest city in South America. Its more than 3 million people work for the government and in factories, mills, stores, and offices.

Peru

Many persons in Peru make a living by farming. Sugarcane, cotton, rice, coffee, and tobacco are raised on the large haciendas of the coastal oases. Peru sells millions of pounds of raw sugar each year and even more cotton. Another important export of Peru is guano (gwä′nō). Guano is an excellent fertilizer. Guano is formed from the droppings of birds who live on the islands off the coast of Peru.

Fine cattle and horses are bred on the largest ranches of the grassy plains of Peru. Stock raising is also important on the cold northern plateau. Llamas, alpacas, and sheep grow thick coats in cold regions.

Mining is important in Peru. The land is rich in gold, silver, and other minerals. It ranks sixth in the world in lead production. Petroleum is found on the northern coastal plain. In the mountains northeast of Lima (lē′mə) are the richest copper mines in the world. Cerro de Pasco (ser′ro dā päs′kō) is the center of the copper-mining region. Cuzco (k⎯oos′kō), the old Inca capital, is the center of another mining re-

Peruvian Indians who live in cool mountain regions wear warm wool ponchos. Many of these colorful blankets are made to be sold at markets to tourists.

gion farther south. Peru is becoming a more industrial nation. A number of factories have been built in recent years. More are being built. The factories make petroleum into fuel oil, gasoline, and other products. They refine sugar. Some metal, cotton, and woolen goods are manufactured.

Peru has a large fishing industry. It ranks fourth in the world in tons of fish caught. Most of the fish are ground into meal in factories on the coast. Fish meal is used as feed for livestock.

Some manufacturing is still done by hand. Indians weave warm ponchos and other clothing from the wool of sheep, llamas, and alpacas. A poncho is a blanket with a slit in the middle so that the wearer can slip it over his or her head. Tourists buy many of these beautiful, handmade blankets.

The Spanish explorer Pizarro founded Peru's beautiful capital. Lima is the largest and most important city. Its factories, mills, and stores give work to thousands. Nearly half of its people work for the government. One of the oldest universities in the Americas is in Lima.

Lima is not on the coast. Highways connect Lima with Callao (kä yä′ ō), its port. Callao is the only seaport in Peru where ocean liners can dock. Airplanes connect Lima with Cuzco and other towns in the mountains.

Ecuador

Haciendas (hä′ sē en′ dəz), or large plantations, are found in the valleys of Ecuador. Cacao, coffee, sugar, bananas, cotton, rice, and tobacco grow on the haciendas there. Cacao beans are shipped to Europe and the United States, where they are made into chocolate. Bananas are also an important export.

The Eastern Lowland is part of the Amazon selvas. Few people live here. Two important trees grow wild in this region. Rubber is made from the sap of the rubber tree. Quinine (kwī′ nīn) comes from the bark of the cinchona tree. Quinine is a medicine used in treating malaria, a tropical disease.

Many of the people of Ecuador live in the highlands. They make a living by raising dairy cows or growing potatoes and wheat. Valuable forests of rubber trees, balsa and toquilla (tō kē′ yä) palm trees grow in the foothills. Balsa logs are lighter than cork. They are excellent for making boats, airplanes, and life rafts. Toquilla palm leaves are used to make straw hats.

432

Guayaquil (gwī′ə kēl) is Ecuador's largest and most modern city. It has an excellent natural harbor on the Guayas River.

A railroad connects the coast city of Guayaquil with Quito (kē′tō), 9,000 feet (2,700 m) above sea level. This old city, the capital of Ecuador, now has modern apartment houses, factories, stores, automobiles, and electric streetcars. Colonial buildings, people in Inca costumes, llamas, and burros are common sights. Because of its altitude, Quito is much cooler than Guayaquil.

Bolivia

About three of every four persons in Bolivia live on the plateau. They raise barley, corn, wheat, and potatoes when there is enough rain or where irrigation is possible. Potatoes are their chief crop. The main food of thousands of Indians is chuño (chōōn′yō). Chuno is made by first freezing, then drying, potatoes. Fish from the waters of Lake Titicaca adds variety to the food eaten there.

Grains, vegetables, fruit, and sugarcane thrive in the mountain valleys and on the hills of the eastern slopes. The coffee and cacao grown there are exported. This pleasant region could produce enough to feed the people of the plateau. But transportation is poor. Products must be carried across the mountains on the backs of llamas and burros. Many kinds of food would spoil before reaching the markets.

Llamas, alpacas, and sheep mean clothing, food, and transportation to the people of the plateau. Cloth is made from the wool of the sheep, llama, and alpaca. Alpaca wool brings a good price.

Minerals are Bolivia's greatest natural resource. Bolivia has more tin than any other country in the Americas. It also produces more *tungsten* (tung′stin) than any other country in South America. Tungsten is a mineral that is mixed with steel to harden it. Nine-tenths of the country's exports are minerals. Most of the tin is shipped to the United States.

Bolivia's mineral deposits lie far from the coast on the plateau. Many of the mines are 12,000 to 20,000 feet (3,600 to 6,000 m) above sea level. It is very hard and costly to take machinery up so high. Because of this, mining is not fully developed in Bolivia. Besides, few workers can mine at such high altitudes.

Bolivians weave cloth and make jewelry and pottery by hand. There is no large-scale manufacturing in Bolivia. Most manufactured goods have to be brought from other countries.

Bolivia's Capitals

Bolivia has two capital cities. One capital is La Paz (lä päs′). The other is Sucre (sōō′krə).

La Paz lies in a valley on the plateau. It is the highest capital in the world. La Paz is the largest city in Bolivia and the center of the nation's manufacturing, business, and transportation. Railways connect it with the Pacific and Atlantic coasts. Most of Bolivia's imports and exports pass through La Paz.

Sucre is a much older city. However, Sucre has poor roads and is harder to reach than La Paz. So only the Supreme Court meets there. Other government business is carried on in La Paz.

Argentina

Farming and cattle raising are the chief occupations in all parts of Argentina. One-fourth of the world's meat, one-third of the hides, and one-fifth of the wheat come from Argentina's pampas. Other money crops are corn and flax. Sugarcane, grapes, and other fruits are also grown.

Argentina's largest sheep ranches are in Patagonia. *Gauchos* (gou′chōz), or cowhands, on horseback herd the sheep. The wool and some lamb and mutton are exported.

Forests are the chief source of wealth on the northern plains. Its most valuable tree is the quebracho (kā brä′chō) tree. Quebracho wood is hard. It is used for railroad ties, paving blocks, and fence posts. Tannic acid is made from the sap of the quebracho tree. Tannic acid is used to make leather soft, firm, and strong. Leather factories of all kinds use much tannic acid.

Oil fields have been found in eastern Patagonia. The government is hoping these oil fields will help the country to pay its debts.

Argentina's Cities

Industry in Argentina is becoming more important than farming. The Plata shore between Buenos Aires and La Plata is the chief industrial region. The cities of this region are seaports, river ports, railroad, trade, and manufacturing centers. Meat packing, tanning hides and skins,

Gauchos herd sheep and cattle across the plains of Patagonia in Argentina. They do the same work as cowhands on the plains of the United States.

and milling grains are the most important industries. Most factories make goods needed in Argentina. Argentina has few minerals and not enough iron ore and coal for heavy industry such as making machinery. The people who live in the cities make a living mostly by trading with other lands.

Buenos Aires is the capital and largest city. It is also the greatest seaport and most important trading and manufacturing center in Argentina. Buenos Aires has many railroads and a livestock market. Some of the largest meat-packing houses in the world are in Buenos Aires.

Freighters sail 200 miles (320 km) up the Paraná River to Rosario, the grain port of Argentina. Rosario is also the flour-milling center of South America. The first public schools of Argentina were built in this city.

Bahía Blanca (bə hē'ə blän'kä) is the only large city of Argentina directly on the Atlantic Ocean. It handles the products of the pampas and Patagonia.

Uruguay

More than three-fourths of the land in Uruguay is used for stock and cattle raising. Cattle, sheep, pigs, horses, and mules are raised on huge ranches. There are also orchards and dairy farms. Wheat, corn, oats, and flax are grown.

Uruguay exports more beef and mutton than any South American country except Argentina. Many of its almost 3 million people work in meat-packing houses.

Uruguay has no coal, fuel oil, or iron ore, so it has few factories. Small articles for everyday use are made in these factories. Heavy machinery and other manufactured goods are imported.

A few people work in silver and copper mines. A larger number work in granite and marble quarries.

Montevideo (mon'tə vi dā'ō), the capital and largest city, has more than one million inhabitants. Montevideo is a seaport and the center of Uruguay's trade.

Paraguay

About 75 million acres (30 million ha) along the Paraguay River are just right for cotton. A bank in Asunción (ä soon syōn') furnishes farmers with free cotton seeds. These farmers supply Asunción's mills with cotton.

Quebracho trees, wild orange trees, and holly bushes grow in the forests. From the leaves of a shrub that grows wild in Paraguay a hot drink called yerba maté (yer'bə mä tā') is made. Yerba maté is often called Paraguayan tea. The bush is also grown on great plantations. Tannin from the bark of the quebracho, castor-oil beans, and leaves of the wild orange tree used for perfume are exports of Paraguay.

Asunción, the capital, is 1,000 miles (1,600 km) from the sea. Today it is the smallest of the Latin-American capitals.

Latin-American Problems and Progress

The people of Latin America face many problems. Some of these problems are geographic. Certain areas have hot, rainy, unhealthy cli-

Representatives from countries that belong to the Organization of American States meet regularly at the headquarters in Washington, D.C.

mates. Other areas are deserts. In many places, jungles and mountains make transportation difficult. Another problem is the lack of industry. But Latin Americans are making improvements. One improvement was made after World War II. This was the development of an organization called the Organization of American States, or OAS. Members of the OAS are like the members of the United Nations. They try to work out problems peacefully. The OAS supports trade, science, and education among its members.

Another improvement was the Alliance for Progress, which began in 1961. This program worked to raise living standards, increase industry, and encourage foreign trade. Members of the Alliance were twenty-two Latin American countries and the United States. Each Latin-American member decided what it could do for itself, and what help it needed from others. The United States agreed to help with money.

By 1971, many changes had been made. Today, some larges estates are divided into small farms. The governments are lending people money to buy these farms. Better housing is being built. Industry is increasing. Most important, education is improving throughout Latin America.

Do You Know?

1. What countries are in South America?
2. Why were South American colonists under Spanish rule angry and unhappy?
3. What was the Alliance for Progress?

To Help You Learn

Using New Words

commonwealth   mestizo   tungsten
vulcanizing   pampa   hacienda
Parliament   llano   selva
Creole   gaucho   estuary
Latin America   latex   hurricane

The phrases below explain the words or terms listed above. Number a paper from 1 through 15. After each number write the word or term that matches the definition.

1. A cowhand of the pampas
2. An arm of the ocean which extends into the land
3. Treeless plain
4. A form of government much like a state
5. A large plantation
6. Rainy, tropical forest of the Amazon
7. A white metal used to harden steel
8. The body of lawmakers of Canada
9. Land south of the United States, where Spanish, French, or Portuguese is spoken
10. A way of treating rubber with sulfur so that it will not melt in hot weather or become stiff in cold weather
11. The sap of the tree used to make rubber
12. A person of mixed ancestry, usually Spanish or Portuguese and Indian
13. Tropical storm with strong winds
14. Grassy plain in South America
15. A Spanish person born in the Americas

Finding the Facts

1. What two islands that are part of our country lie in the Atlantic Ocean?
2. What did the United States make Puerto Rico in 1952?
3. What and where are Midway, Wake, Guam, and American Samoa?
4. What three countries are our northern neighbors?
5. What two European groups claimed land in Canada?
6. In what ways do the people of Canada make a living?
7. What country is our nearest Latin-American neighbor?
8. What is the land between Mexico and South America called?
9. What is the chain of islands stretching in a curve from Florida to northern South America called?
10. What canal joined the Atlantic Ocean and the Pacific Ocean?
11. What mountains in South America stretch along the Pacific Ocean?
12. What is the second longest river in the world?
13. Name three persons who led the fight for freedom in South America. Which countries did each person help free?
14. How was Bolivia formed?
15. How did Paraguay become independent?

16. Which South American country once belonged to Portugal?

17. What kind of government does Colombia have?

18. What kind of government is most common in South America today?

19. What is Colombia's most important money crop?

20. What is the most valuable product and export of Venezuela?

21. Which two South American countries rank among the top six in the world in the production of bauxite?

22. What are Ecuador's chief products?

23. What are Peru's chief minerals?

24. What are two important minerals of Bolivia?

25. What is Chile's most important export?

26. What are Argentina's chief seaports?

27. Why does Uruguay have few factories?

28. What is another name for "Paraguayan tea"?

29. What is raised in the Amazon Valley?

30. Where is Brazil's coffee land? What makes Brazil's climate good for coffee growing?

31. What are Brazil's chief cities?

32. What makes transportation difficult in many places of Latin America?

33. What steps are Latin-American nations taking today to develop themselves?

Learning from Maps

1. Use the map of Canada on page 389 to answer these questions: Which province has the most highland? Which has the most lowland? Which provinces and territories share the Laurentian Upland?

2. Use the scale of miles on the map of Canada on page 389 to find the distance: (a) from the city of Quebec to Vancouver; (b) from Montreal to Toronto; (c) from Winnipeg to Edmonton.

3. On the map of Mexico, Central America, and the West Indies, on page 406, locate and name the nations bordering the United States. Which countries of Central America are farthest north? Which is farthest south? Which faces only the Pacific? Which is the largest island of the West Indies?

4. Find the Central American lands on the vegetation map of North America on page 18. What kinds of vegetation do these countries have? What does the rainfall map, page 17, tell about these lands?

5. Turn to the map of South America on page 422. Locate and name the countries..Which two countries lie farthest north? What parallel of latitude is close to this northern border? Which country extends farthest south? Which country is the largest?

6. On the same map find the answers to these questions: What ocean borders South America on the east? On the west? Compare the eastern coastline with the western. Which has more and better harbors? Why? Which coastline has more mountains? Which two countries have no coastline?

7. Study the map of products of South America on page 426. Which countries have oil? Which countries have bauxite? Which country has emeralds?

Using Study Skills

1. **Time Line:** The following events are not listed in the right order. Copy the statements in the right order and place them on a time line. Check in your book for the dates.
   a. Luis Muñoz Marín elected first governor of Puerto Rico
   b. Ponce de León founds San Juan
   c. Battle of Midway marks turning point of World War II in the Pacific
   d. United States sets up naval base at Pago Pago on Samoa Islands
   e. French Quebec founded by Champlain
   f. French made an official language in Canada, equal to English
   g. Father Hidalgo organizes movement to free Mexico
   h. Panama becomes independent republic
   i. United States stops buying Cuba's sugar
   j. Brazil's capital moved to Brasília

2. **Chart:** Look at the chart comparing Canada and the United States on page 390. Which country is larger in area? Which country is larger in population? What is the highest point in Canada? In the United States? Which of these two points is higher? Which country has the lowest point? What is the largest province in Canada? What is the largest state in the United States? Which is the larger, the province or the state? Which is smaller, Prince Edward Island or Rhode Island?

3. **Graph:** What does the pictograph on this page show? What does each figure equal? Which country was estimated to have the largest population in 1980? Which country was estimated to have the smallest population in 1980? About how many people lived in Mexico in 1980? Was that more or less than the number of people estimated for Canada? Which country was estimated to have more people, Mexico or Brazil? About how many more people were estimated to live in Canada than in Cuba in 1980? About how many fewer people were estimated to live in Brazil than in the United States in 1980?

Population of Selected American Countries 1980 estimates rounded to nearest 10 million

Country	Population
United States	▰▰▰▰▰▰▰▰▰▰▰▰▰▰▰▰▰▰▰▰▰▰
Canada	▰▰
Mexico	▰▰▰▰▰▰▰
Brazil	▰▰▰▰▰▰▰▰▰▰▰▰
Cuba	▰ Each figure equals 10 million people.

4. **Diagram:** Look at the diagram showing how wood is made into paper on page 395. What is the first thing that happens to the logs in the mill? How are chips made into pulp?

Thinking it Through

1. Each numbered event was the cause of a lettered event. Match the events.
   (1) After our war with Spain in 1898, Spain gave up some of its colonies.
   (2) The United States wanted to be able to get from the Atlantic Ocean to the Pacific quickly.
   (3) San Martín drove the Spanish out of Argentina.
   (4) In 1535 a French explorer discovered and explored the St. Lawrence River.
   (5) Spain ruled its colonies with a firm hand.
   (a) The Panama Canal was built.
   (b) France claimed land in North America.
   (c) Puerto Rico, Wake, and Guam became United States possessions.
   (d) South Americans began to fight for freedom.
   (e) Argentina gained its independence.
2. Canada and the United States are close neighbors. What might happen if they did not continue to work together?
3. The wars for independence in the South American colonies were fought for many of the same reasons as the American Revolution. What were some of them?

Projects

1. The Explorers' Committee might write to one of the airlines to find the time required to fly from: New York to the Virgin Islands; Chicago to Guam; your home town to Puerto Rico.
2. Bring in samples or pictures of products from United States possessions. Make name cards for each of the possessions. Then arrange them for display.
3. Choose a committee to plan a bulletin board about Canada. Bring in pictures from newspapers and magazines, travel folders, and post cards.
4. Plan a cruise to Central America in which you stop at a principal port of each country bordering the coast. You might write to your nearest travel agency and ask for booklets which will give ideas of places to be visited.

   Use the maps in your book or wall maps in your classroom to find about how far it is from one port to the next. List something of interest to be found in or near each place you plan to stop.
5. With the help of your teacher or parents, prepare a menu for a meal typical of a Latin American nation.
6. The Reading Committee might like to find stories about the building of the Panama Canal, the way of life of the American Indians of the Amazon Valley, or how Patagonia ("Land of the Big Feet") got its name.

Learning About Maps and Globes

Maps and globes are special tools. They help us to understand our earth and the people, places, and things on it. Maps and globes are useful tools only if we know how to use them. The lessons in this section will help you improve your skills in using maps and globes. These map and globe skills will help you to better understand the world around you.

Words to Learn

You will meet these words in this unit. As you read, you will learn what they mean and how to pronounce them. The Word List will help you.

contour line
density
elevation
grid
legend
meridians of longitude
parallels of latitude
peninsula

plain
plateau
population
prime meridian
profile
projection
relief
site

1 Latitude and Longitude

How do pilots flying around the world say exactly where they are? They use the geographer's "zip code." You can learn to use it, too. You start by learning about some imaginary lines.

Look at the globe on the right. Lines called *parallels* (par'ə lelz) *of latitude* run east and west. They never meet. Like train tracks, they are always the same distance apart. Parallels of latitude are measured in degrees north and south of the equator. From the equator to each of the poles, there are 90 degrees.

North of the equator, parallels of latitude have the letter "N" in their "zip code." "N" stands for "north." South of the equator, latitudes are given the initial "S." Degrees are shown by the symbol " ° ." For example, on the map below, the first parallel shown north of the equator is at 20 degrees. It is labeled "20° N."

Parallels of Latitude

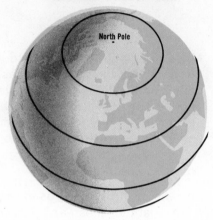

The airplanes on the maps below are flying along parallels of latitude. Are they going east and west or north and south? Find the plane flying at 40 degrees south.

Parallels of Latitude

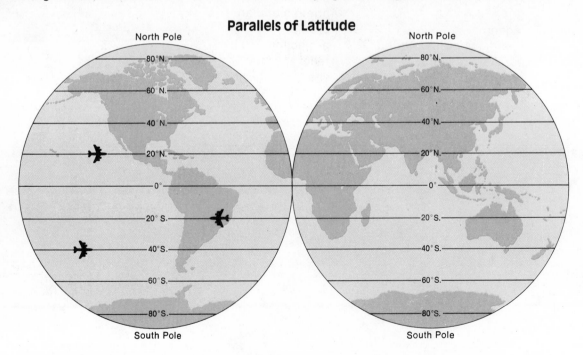

442

Meridians of Longitude

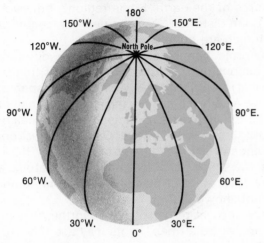

Look at the globe above. Lines called *meridians* (mə rid′ē ənz) *of longitude* connect the North and South poles. These lines, unlike parallels of latitude, eventually meet. They come together at the poles. Like the parallels, however, meridians have numbers. Those numbers measure degrees east and west. We begin counting degrees of longitude at an imaginary starting line. It runs through Greenwich, England. That line is called the *prime meridian* (prīm mə rid′ē ən). East of the prime meridian, all meridians have the letter "E" in their "zip code." It stands for "east." West of the prime meridian, all meridians are given the initial "W." For example, look at the globe. The prime meridian is at 0 degrees. The next meridian of longitude shown to the east is labeled "30° E." That is the short way of saying the line is 30 degrees east of the prime meridian.

Look at the planes on the maps below. They are flying along meridians of longitude. Are they flying east and west or north and south? Find the plane flying at 60 degrees east. Which continent will it cross? Now find the plane flying at 100 degrees west. Which continent has it already crossed?

Where is the "middle" of the United States in degrees of longitude?

Meridians of Longitude

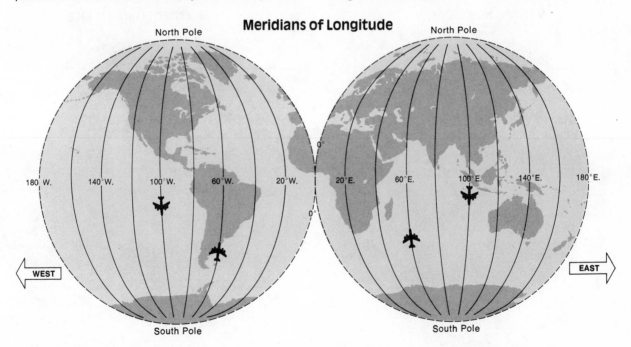

443

2 Making a Map from the Globe

Only a globe can show the true shape of the earth. That is because a globe and the earth are both round. But it is not always practical to carry a globe around. So people use maps instead. The way a mapmaker shows the round earth on a flat surface is called a *projection* (prə jek'shən). You can see four different projections on these two pages. But there are many more.

No one can make a map projection without some distortion. You can understand the problem by doing a simple experiment. Remove the peel from an orange in one big piece. Now try to lay the peel flat on a table. The only way to do it is to stretch it or tear it.

Mapmakers are faced with the same problem when they draw maps. They solve it by stretching or dividing parts of the globe. The maps shown here, for example, are fairly accurate pictures of the earth. Some regions, however, are quite distorted. Regions near the center of each map are quite accurate.

No projection is perfect. Therefore, different projections are used to show different things. Look at the map of the Western Hemisphere, below. A hemisphere, you remember, is a half of the earth. The Western Hemisphere is the half of the earth on which we live. On this projection, the equator is in the center of the map. Therefore, the shapes of places near the equator are fairly accurate. But places far from the center are not shown in their true shapes.

Now look at the map of the Northern Hemisphere, or polar map. Pilots may use this projection when flying over the North Pole. What is shown in the center of this map? Where is the equator? What parallels of latitude are shown on this map?

Western Hemisphere

Northern Hemisphere

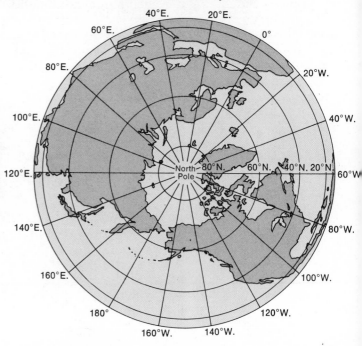

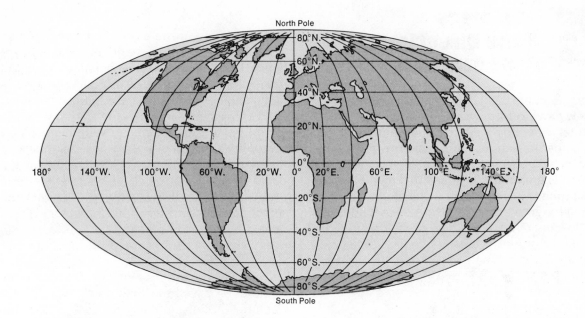

Look at the map above. It has been stretched to show all of the earth's land and water areas. It is a useful projection for showing the whole world at a glance. Again, areas close to the center of this map have accurate shapes. But all around the outer edge there is great distortion. Compare this projection with a globe. Which continents are shown closest to their true shapes? Which continents do you think are most distorted?

Below is yet another projection. Remember the orange peel? If you had pressed it flat it would have looked much like this map. This projection is useful for showing truer shapes of land areas. But the oceans have been broken, or interrupted. Would this map be a useful one for sailors? What has happened to Antarctica?

What kind of map could be drawn to show Antarctica best? Remember that Antarctica is around a pole, the South Pole.

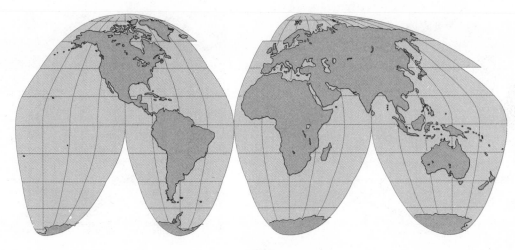

445

3 How Maps Show Directions and Locations

Imagine one small town located somewhere in the wide world. How can you find it? How can you tell where on the globe it is located? A *grid* (grid) can make your job easier. A grid is the crisscross pattern on a map made by imaginary lines. The pattern is made by meridians of longitude crossing parallels of latitude. You can see different kinds of grids on these pages.

A map grid can help you find directions as well as locations. If the meridians on a map are curved, you cannot use a compass rose. All meridians meet at the North Pole. This means that each meridian points north. Each meridian can serve as a direction pointer.

Match the grids on the left with the maps on the right. You can see that their meridians of longitude all point toward the North Pole. Where could you put arrows to show which way is north? Where are the arrows that show east and west?

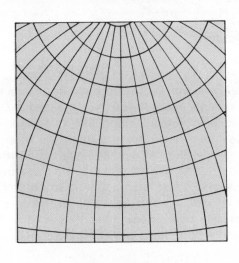

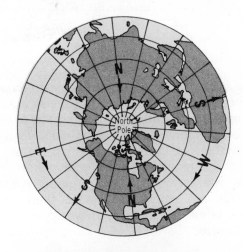

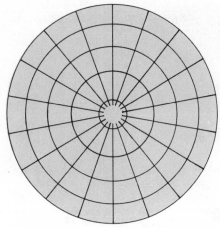

Look at the grid on the right. All of its lines are straight. The meridians of longitude appear to be parallel to each other. On a globe, however, these lines are not parallel. They meet at the North and South poles. See how distorted this map is. Land and water areas near the poles look larger than they are on a globe.

Why would anyone want a map as distorted as this? The map is useful because all directions can be shown throughout the map with one compass rose. Therefore, one compass rose shows north for every place on the map. This projection is sometimes called "the sailor's map." All lines of latitude cross all lines of longitude at right angles. Therefore, sailors can draw a straight line from where they are to where they are going. This line will show direction. Then with a compass, they can set their course.

A grid is also useful for pinpointing exactly where a place is located. Suppose you know both the degrees of latitude and the degrees of longitude of a place. You can then explain exactly where in the world that place is located.

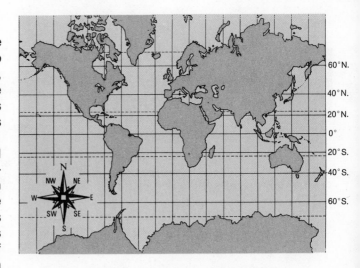

You learned that degrees of latitude and longitude are like a global zip code. The zip code helps you find and describe a location quickly.

On the map below, which letter is located at 30 degrees north latitude and 60 degrees west longitude? Which letter is located at 30 degrees south latitude and 40 degrees east longitude? Now give the locations in degrees for the two remaining letters.

Latitude and Longitude

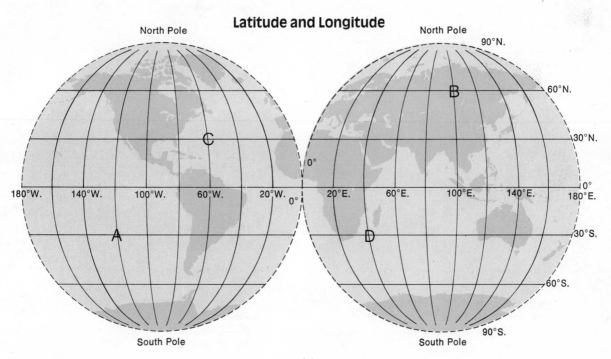

4 Using Different Kinds of Population Maps

Every 10 years, the government counts the number of people in our country. At that time, important population facts are recorded. The total number of people who live in a country is a *population* (pop'yə lā'shən).

Information about population can be shown in many ways. Graphs and tables are often used. But a special map helps people see this infor-mation at a glance. Two kinds of population maps are shown on these pages. The map below is a population dot map. A dot map shows *density* (den'sə tē), or thickness. Each dot stands for 10,000 people. In places where many people live, the dots are close together. In places where few people live, the dots are far apart. The same facts are shown differently on the large map to the right. In this case, a computer has been given population figures. It has used these figures to produce this map. You can see that the map works somewhat like a graph.

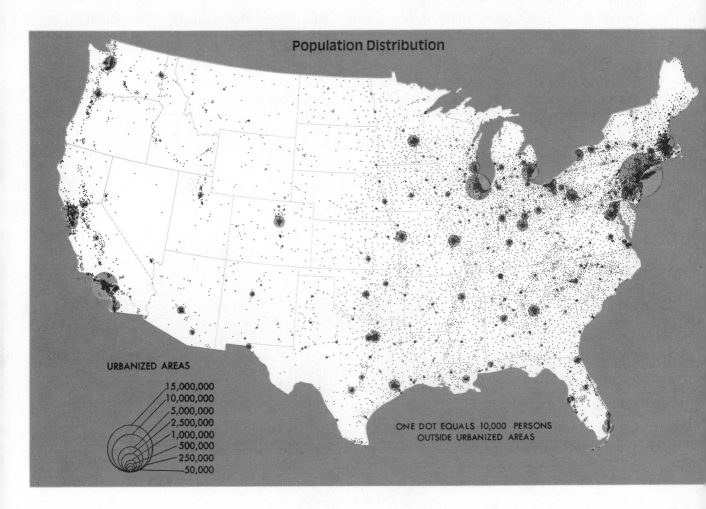

Population Distribution

URBANIZED AREAS

15,000,000
10,000,000
5,000,000
2,500,000
1,000,000
500,000
250,000
50,000

ONE DOT EQUALS 10,000 PERSONS
OUTSIDE URBANIZED AREAS

Compare the computer map with the population map in the text on page 125. How do the maps show population density in different ways? Which map shows the shape of the country more accurately? Which map, in your opinion, shows more about population density?

Identify the major population centers on the computer map. Turn to the map of the United States on pages 92–93. You can also use the dot map to help you. Which cities are shown by the three tallest "needles"? Identify other large cities in Texas, Michigan, and Pennsylvania. You can use both maps to guess where the population center of our country is located. To understand a population center, imagine a population dot map placed on top of a pin. Each

dot shows where one of the more than 220 million Americans lives. The point where the map balances on the pin will be the population center.

The population center of the United States is always changing because people move. Early in our history, people lived mainly along the eastern coast of our country. More people lived in the New England region than in the southern coastal states.

As pioneers moved west, so did the population center. During some periods, great numbers of people moved. Use the two maps on these pages to make a guess where the population center is now located.

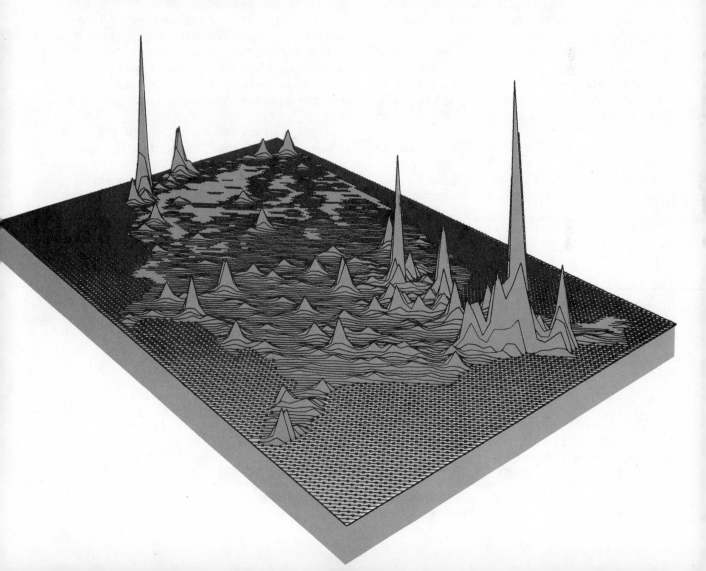

5 Understanding Contour Lines

All land surfaces are measured straight up from the level of the sea. This height above sea level is called *elevation* (el'ə vā'shən). Say that a mountain's elevation is 6,000 feet (1,800 m). That means the top of the mountain is 6,000 feet (1,800 m) higher than sea level.

Map makers have several ways of showing elevation. One way is by drawing a map with *contour* (kon'toor) *lines*. Contour means shape. A contour line connects points on a land surface that have the same elevation.

Below is a diagram of two mountains. Imagine that you can slice them into four layers. The whole surface of each layer has the same elevation. Now imagine you can take each layer out of the mountains and trace its outline on paper.

You can see that the contour lines of the map follow the same shape as the mountain. Notice that parts A, B, and C all have the same elevation. You can tell their height is the same. They are all located along the same contour line. Name two other points that have the same elevation. How can you tell their height is the same?

Another way to show height is with color. Look at the second contour map. Shades of blue have been used to show different elevations. What is the height of the land colored dark blue? Is it higher or lower than the light blue part?

The drawing on the right, above, is an elevation *profile* (prō'fīl). A profile is a side view. The mountains appear to be sliced in half to show their height. The artist has drawn and colored them to show areas above and below sea level. What is in the area below sea level?

The maps on the right show contour lines in two different regions of the United States. In the map at the left, the contour lines are drawn far apart. They show almost flat or gently rolling farmland in Iowa. In such areas, the highways and city streets can follow a rectangular pattern.

In the map on the right, contour lines are drawn close together. They show the steep, mountainous country of West Virginia. The tops of the mountains are shown by the shortest lines. Notice the ribbon-shaped roads, railroads, and towns. Why are they shaped differently from roads and towns in Iowa?

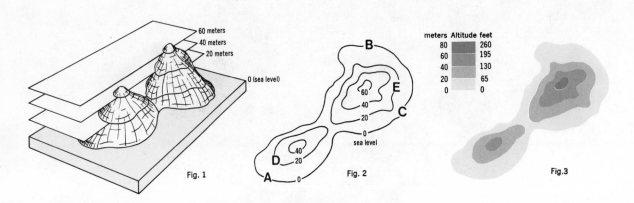

Fig. 1

Fig. 2

meters Altitude feet

meters	feet
80	260
60	195
40	130
20	65
0	0

Fig.3

ELEVATION

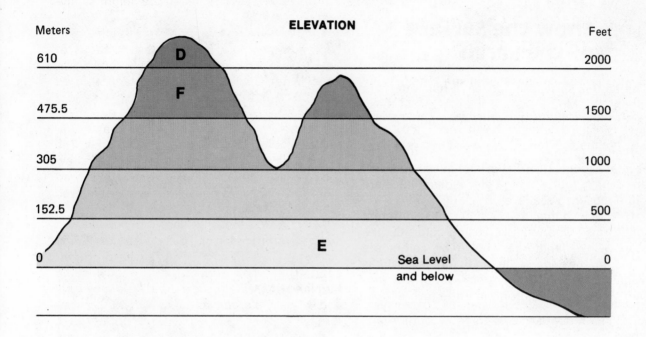

Meters		Feet
610	D F	2000
475.5		1500
305		1000
152.5		500
0	E	0
	Sea Level and below	

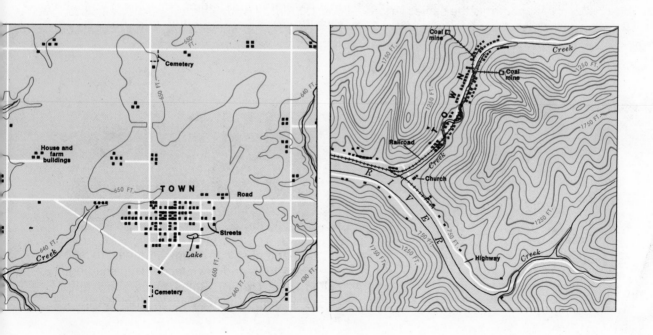

6 How Maps Show the Surface of the Earth

The earth's surface is uneven. It has four main landforms. Mountains are the highest of these landforms. Hills are lower than mountains, but have sloping sides, too.

Plains (plānz) are the earth's flatlands. *Plateaus* (pla tōz′), with flat land but steep sides, are usually found at high elevations. Plains are often closer to sea level.

How does a map maker show these different landforms? One way is by using color. On the map below, landforms shown by colors are listed in the *legend* (lej′ənd), or key. Is Las Vegas on a plain, a hill, a plateau, or a mountain? Near what landform is Butte (byōot)?

The mapmaker can draw little pictures of the landforms. Which ones do you see on this map?

The mapmaker can add color to the relief map. Color and shading together show the elevation of areas. Is Santa Fe on a plain or a plateau?

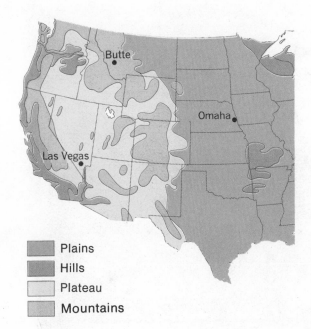

Plains
Hills
Plateau
Mountains

The mapmaker can shade in areas to show the land's high and low places. This shading is called *relief* (ri lēf′). Relief maps show differences in height. Is Kansas (written KANS. on the map) in the mountains or on the plains?

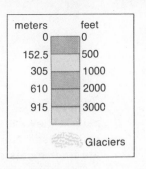

meters		feet
0		0
152.5		500
305		1000
610		2000
915		3000
		Glaciers

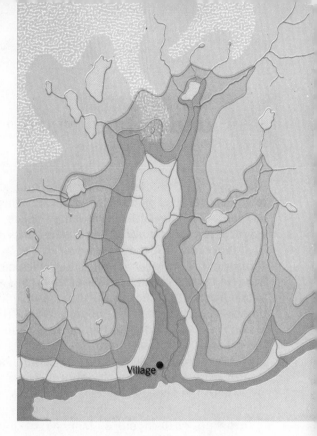

Village

A map maker can show relief with contour lines. You have already learned that contour maps show elevation. But they also tell us about the earth's natural shape. As you have read, contour means shape.

Contour lines that are close together show steep, hilly land. Contour lines that are far apart show nearly flat or gently rolling land.

The photograph below shows part of the area drawn on the contour map. Is the lake higher or lower than the village? Which contour lines show the steep mountain sides? Look at the lines that show the mountain tops. Do you think these mountain tops are pointed or fairly flat?

7 Using Maps to Understand History: Cattle Drives

American cattle drives, cowhands, and cow towns are famous all over the world. Yet few of us realize that the cattle drives lasted only a few years. They started about 1865, soon after the Civil War. By 1887, they were over.

During that period, millions of longhorn cattle were herded overland from Texas to Kansas and Missouri. The longhorns were a tough, hardy breed of cattle that had come north from Mexico. On cattle drives, the cattle grazed on the grass of the open range.

In towns such as Sedalia, Missouri, and Dodge City, Kansas, the longhorns were fattened and then loaded onto railroad cars and shipped to Chicago. From there, they were sent to growing eastern cities. Millions of immigrants, new arrivals from Europe, had increased the demand for beef.

The long "rivers" of cattle were led by hardworking cowhands. These people, some of

Transcontinental Railroads in the 1880s

---- Modern state boundaries

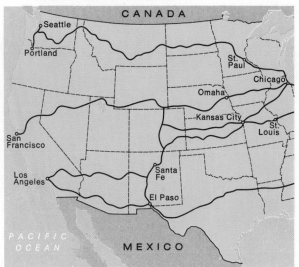

them teenagers, stopped stampedes of nervous cattle. They rounded up strays. They outwitted cattle rustlers. They slept under the stars and ate their meals beside a chuck wagon.

The chuck wagon was the kitchen of the cattle drive. But it was also a compass. Before going to sleep, the cook pointed the wagon's hitching pole toward the North Star. The next morning, it showed the cowhands the way to go.

The map shows the four main cattle trails. Use the map scale to figure some distances. Suppose you were a cowhand driving cattle from near San Antonio, Texas, to Sedalia, Missouri, over the Sedalia Trail. About how many miles (kilometers) would you have to go? Most cattle drives covered about 10 miles (16 kilometers) a day. How many days would your trip take?

Suppose you were driving cattle from San Antonio, Texas, to Dodge City, Kansas, over the Western Trail. How many days would your trip take?

Long distances, floods, and dry runs of two and three days without water were but a few of the hardships of the trail. For a few years, however, nothing stopped the cattle drives. Ranchers made quick fortunes. Cowhands got $100 for their many weeks of trouble.

Railroads were built into the cattle country. These railroads could quickly move cattle to market. Look at the map showing the western railroads. Why would cities like Kansas City, St. Louis, and Chicago become important meat packing centers?

As farmers moved west, they fenced in their lands. They did not want the herds damaging their crops. The railroads continued to move further and further west, too. As farmers and railroads moved west, the easternmost cattle drives ended. Ranchers used the westernmost trails. Which cattle trail would be the last one used? By 1887, the days of the cattle drives had passed into history. Rails, not trails, became the key to western trade with the East.

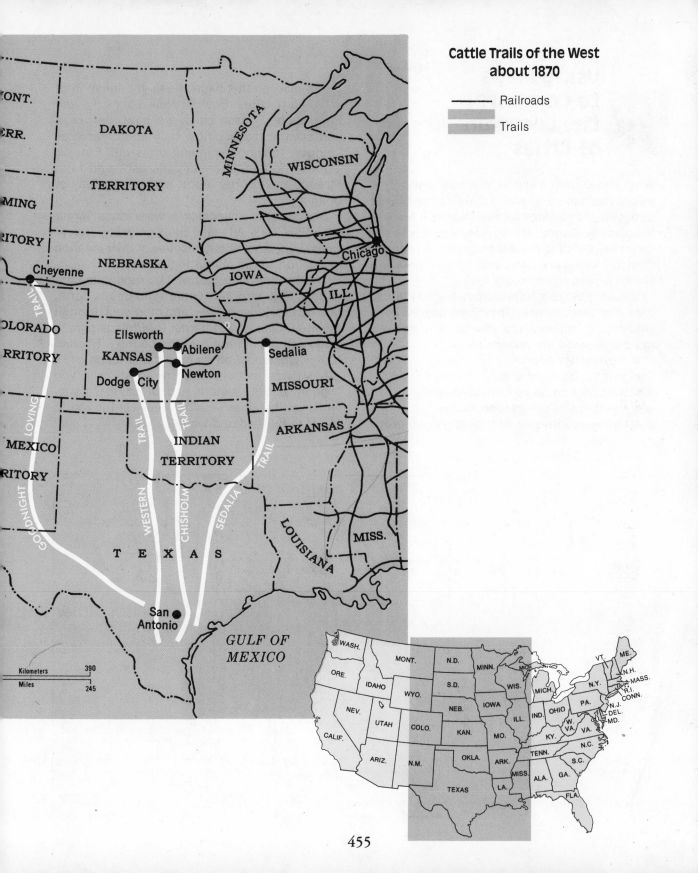

Cattle Trails of the West about 1870

— Railroads

▓ Trails

MONT.

ERR.

MING

RITORY

OLORADO

RRITORY

MEXICO

RRITORY

DAKOTA

TERRITORY

NEBRASKA

MINNESOTA

WISCONSIN

Chicago

IOWA

ILL.

Cheyenne

Ellsworth

KANSAS

Abilene

Newton

Dodge City

Sedalia

MISSOURI

ARKANSAS

GOODNIGHT LOVING TRAIL

WESTERN TRAIL

CHISHOLM TRAIL

SEDALIA TRAIL

INDIAN TERRITORY

T E X A S

LOUISIANA

MISS.

San Antonio

GULF OF MEXICO

Kilometers 390

Miles 245

WASH. MONT. N.D. MINN. VT. ME. N.H.

ORE. IDAHO S.D. WIS. MICH. N.Y. MASS. R.I. CONN.

NEV. WYO. NEB. IOWA MICH. PA. N.J. DEL. MD.

UTAH COLO. KAN. MO. ILL. IND. OHIO W.VA. VA.

CALIF. ARIZ. N.M. OKLA. ARK. TENN. KY. N.C. S.C.

TEXAS LA. MISS. ALA. GA. FLA.

Using Maps to Compare the Location of Cities

8

What if you were a settler in a new land? How would you decide where to build a town? What things would you look for in a *site* (sīt)? A site is the place where something is located. Every site has special land and water features. The sites of Boston, New York City, and Philadelphia are shown on the facing page.

The early settlers from Europe had to choose sites for their towns. They had arrived in a wilderness. Among the things the settlers looked for were the following:

- fresh water sources
- safe harbors for ships
- land that could be defended easily
- rivers for transportation routes
- fertile countryside on which to grow crops

The map on this page shows the location of three early cities: Boston, New York City, and Philadelphia. These cities are near the ocean and several rivers. Thus, they could serve as "hinges," linking the inland areas with Europe. Goods and people could pass back and forth through their ports. A port is a passageway or opening.

Boston and Philadelphia were once larger than New York. All these cities grew at different rates. This came about because of their location in relation to the rest of the country.

Look at the map below. The mountains are shown. New York City could send goods north, first up the Hudson River, and then west through the mountains. It was harder for Philadelphia to trade with inland areas of the country. Boston, too, was blocked off by mountains. Each city's growth was influenced by its location. If you lived near the western end of Lake Ontario, which of the cities would be easiest for you to travel to by road and water?

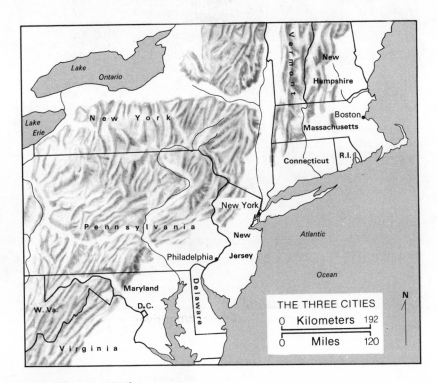

THE THREE CITIES

0 Kilometers 192

0 Miles 120

N

Boston was first settled on a small *peninsula* (pə nin′sə lə). A peninsula is land surrounded by water on three sides. The site had a good source of fresh water. Its deep harbor protected ships from the open seas. Nearby islands and peninsulas kept out the Atlantic's stormy waves. Forts could be built on these places. The narrow neck of the peninsula could also easily be defended. The town was built at the far western end of Massachusetts Bay. Later this location helped link Boston to many inland communities.

Dutch settlers bought Manhattan Island from the Delaware Indians in 1626. Today, it is the biggest and busiest port city in our country. The map shows some reasons for picking this site in the first place. Look at the land and water features. Why is New York Harbor a safe port for ships? Why did the settlers think Manhattan could be defended easily against attack?

Philadelphia was founded by William Penn. He did not try to find land that could be defended easily. He believed Philadelphia would be a city of peace. He laid down three other rules for choosing a site, however. (1) The site should be on high, dry land. Such land was considered healthier than low, swampy land. (2) The surrounding countryside should be fertile. (3) The site should have deep water nearby where ships could dock. Philadelphia, unlike Boston and New York City, was not on the coast. What river gave it a port and a route to the sea?

The Three Cities

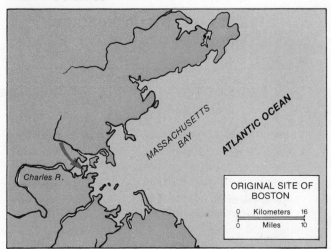

ORIGINAL SITE OF BOSTON

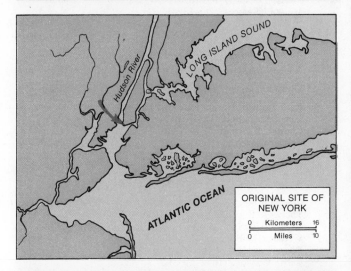

ORIGINAL SITE OF NEW YORK

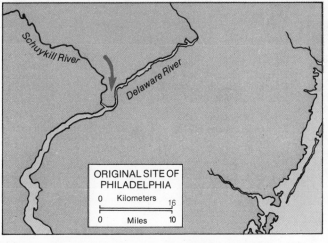

ORIGINAL SITE OF PHILADELPHIA

The Presidents of the United States

Name	Residence	Years in office	Vice-President
George Washington (1732–1799)	Virginia	1789–1797	John Adams
John Adams (1735–1826)	Massachusetts	1797–1801	Thomas Jefferson
Thomas Jefferson (1743–1826)	Virginia	1801–1809	{ Aaron Burr { George Clinton
James Madison (1751–1836)	Virginia	1809–1817	{ George Clinton { Elbridge Gerry
James Monroe (1758–1831)	Virginia	1817–1825	Daniel D. Tompkins
John Quincy Adams (1767–1848)	Massachusetts	1825–1829	John C. Calhoun
Andrew Jackson (1767–1845)	Tennessee	1829–1837	{ John C. Calhoun { Martin Van Buren
Martin Van Buren (1782–1862)	New York	1837–1841	Richard M. Johnson
William Henry Harrison (1773–1841)	Ohio	1841–1841	John Tyler
John Tyler (1790–1862)	Virginia	1841–1845	*
James K. Polk (1795–1849)	Tennessee	1845–1849	George M. Dallas
Zachary Taylor (1784–1850)	Louisiana	1849–1850	Millard Fillmore
Millard Fillmore (1800–1874)	New York	1850–1853	*
Franklin Pierce (1804–1869)	New Hampshire	1853–1857	William R. King
James Buchanan (1791–1868)	Pennsylvania	1857–1861	J. C. Breckinridge
Abraham Lincoln (1809–1865)	Illinois	1861–1865 1865–1865	{ Hannibal Hamlin { Andrew Johnson
Andrew Johnson (1808–1875)	Tennessee	1865–1869	*
Ulysses S. Grant (1822–1885)	Illinois	1869–1877	{ Schuyler Colfax { Henry Wilson
Rutherford B. Hayes (1822–1893)	Ohio	1877–1881	Wm. A. Wheeler
James A. Garfield (1831–1881)	Ohio	1881–1881	Chester A. Arthur
Chester A. Arthur (1830–1886)	New York	1881–1885	*
Grover Cleveland (1837–1908)	New York	1885–1889	Thos. A. Hendricks
Benjamin Harrison (1833–1901)	Indiana	1889–1893	Levi P. Morton
Grover Cleveland (1837–1908)	New York	1893–1897	Adlai E. Stevenson
William McKinley (1843–1901)	Ohio	1897–1901 1901–1901	{ Garret A. Hobart { Theodore Roosevelt
Theodore Roosevelt (1858–1919)	New York	1901–1905	*
Theodore Roosevelt (1858–1919)	New York	1905–1909	Charles W. Fairbanks
William Howard Taft (1857–1930)	Ohio	1909–1913	James S. Sherman
Woodrow Wilson (1856–1924)	New Jersey	1913–1921	Thomas R. Marshall
Warren G. Harding (1865–1923)	Ohio	1921–1923	Calvin Coolidge
Calvin Coolidge (1872–1933)	Massachusetts	1923–1925	*
Calvin Coolidge (1872–1933)	Massachusetts	1925–1929	Charles G. Dawes
Herbert Hoover (1874–1964)	California	1929–1933	Charles Curtis
Franklin D. Roosevelt (1882–1945)	New York	1933–1945	{ John Nance Garner { Henry A. Wallace { Harry S. Truman
Harry S. Truman (1884–1972)	Missouri	1945–1949	*
Harry S. Truman (1884–1972)	Missouri	1949–1953	Alben Barkley
Dwight D. Eisenhower (1890–1969)	New York	1953–1961	Richard M. Nixon
John F. Kennedy (1917–1963)	Massachusetts	1961–1963	Lyndon B. Johnson
Lyndon B. Johnson (1908–1973)	Texas	1963–1969	* Hubert Humphrey
Richard M. Nixon (1913–)	California	1969–1974	Spiro Agnew ** Gerald R. Ford
Gerald R. Ford (1913–)	Michigan	1974–1977	Nelson A. Rockefeller
Jimmy Carter (1924–)	Georgia	1977–1981	Walter F. Mondale
Ronald Reagan (1911–)	California	1981–	George Bush

* Succeeded from the vice-presidency on the death of the President.
** Succeeded from the vice-presidency on the resignation of the President.

The States of the United States

State	Capital	Area Sq. Mi.	Sq. Km	Population (1980)	Admitted to Union	State Flower
Alabama	Montgomery	51,609	133,667	3,890,100	1819	Camellia
Alaska	Juneau	586,412	1,518,800	400,500	1959	Forget-me-not
Arizona	Phoenix	113,909	295,023	2,717,900	1912	Saguaro cactus
Arkansas	Little Rock	53,104	137,539	2,285,500	1836	Apple blossom
California	Sacramento	158,693	411,013	23,668,600	1850	Golden poppy
Colorado	Denver	104,247	269,998	2,888,800	1876	Columbine
Connecticut	Hartford	5,009	12,973	3,107,600	1788	Mountain laurel
Delaware	Dover	2,057	5,328	595,200	1787	Peach blossom
Florida	Tallahassee	58,560	151,670	9,740,000	1845	Orange blossom
Georgia	Atlanta	58,876	152,488	5,464,300	1788	Cherokee rose
Hawaii	Honolulu	6,450	16,705	965,000	1959	Hibiscus
Idaho	Boise	83,557	216,412	943,900	1890	Lewis Mockorange
Illinois	Springfield	56,400	146,075	11,418,500	1818	Violet
Indiana	Indianapolis	36,291	93,993	5,490,200	1816	Peony
Iowa	Des Moines	56,290	145,790	2,913,400	1846	Wild rose
Kansas	Topeka	82,264	213,063	2,363,200	1861	Sunflower
Kentucky	Frankfort	40,395	104,623	3,661,400	1792	Goldenrod
Louisiana	Baton Rouge	48,523	125,674	4,204,000	1812	Magnolia
Maine	Augusta	33,215	86,026	1,124,700	1820	Pine cone
Maryland	Annapolis	10,577	27,394	4,216,400	1788	Black-eyed Susan
Massachusetts	Boston	8,257	21,386	5,737,000	1788	Arbutus
Michigan	Lansing	58,216	150,779	9,258,300	1837	Apple blossom
Minnesota	St. Paul	84,068	217,735	4,077,100	1858	Ladyslipper
Mississippi	Jackson	47,716	123,584	2,520,600	1817	Magnolia
Missouri	Jefferson City	69,686	180,486	4,917,400	1821	Hawthorn
Montana	Helena	147,138	381,086	786,700	1889	Bitterroot
Nebraska	Lincoln	77,227	200,017	1,570,000	1867	Goldenrod
Nevada	Carson City	110,540	286,297	799,200	1864	Sagebrush
New Hampshire	Concord	9,304	24,097	920,600	1788	Lilac
New Jersey	Trenton	7,836	20,295	7,364,200	1787	Violet
New Mexico	Santa Fe	121,666	315,113	1,300,000	1912	Yucca
New York	Albany	49,576	128,401	17,557,300	1788	Rose
North Carolina	Raleigh	52,586	136,197	5,874,400	1789	Dogwood
North Dakota	Bismarck	70,665	183,022	652,700	1889	Prairie Rose
Ohio	Columbus	41,222	106,764	10,797,400	1803	Scarlet carnation
Oklahoma	Oklahoma City	69,919	181,089	3,025,300	1907	Mistletoe
Oregon	Salem	96,981	251,180	2,632,700	1859	Oregon grape
Pennsylvania	Harrisburg	45,333	117,412	11,866,700	1787	Mountain laurel
Rhode Island	Providence	1,214	3,144	947,200	1790	Violet
South Carolina	Columbia	31,055	80,432	3,119,200	1788	Yellow jessamine
South Dakota	Pierre	77,047	199,551	690,200	1889	Pasque
Tennessee	Nashville	42,244	109,411	4,590,800	1796	Iris
Texas	Austin	267,338	692,402	14,228,400	1845	Bluebonnet
Utah	Salt Lake City	84,916	219,931	1,461,000	1896	Sego lily
Vermont	Montpelier	9,609	24,887	511,500	1791	Red clover
Virginia	Richmond	40,817	105,716	5,346,300	1788	Dogwood
Washington	Olympia	68,192	176,616	4,130,200	1889	Rhododendron
West Virginia	Charleston	24,282	62,628	1,949,600	1863	Rhododendron
Wisconsin	Madison	56,154	145,438	4,705,300	1848	Violet
Wyoming	Cheyenne	97,914	253,596	470,800	1890	Indian paintbrush

UNITED STATES OF AMERICA: *Area,* 3,615,122 (Sq. Mi.), 9,363,123 (Sq. Km); *Population* (1980 est.), 223,239,000
Washington, D.C., *Capital: Area,* 69 (Sq. Mi.), 176 (Sq. Km); *Population* (1980 est.), 690,000

Largest Cities in the United States

City	Population (1980 est.)	Interesting Facts and Products	City	Population (1980 est.)	Interesting Facts and Products
Akron, OH	250,000	Rubber products, paints	Honolulu,* HI	718,000	Seaport; sugar, pineapples
Albuquerque, NM	291,000	Resort; wool; rail center			
Amarillo, TX	156,000	Cattle, wheat, oil, gas	Houston, TX	1,555,000	Seaport; oil, cotton
Anaheim, CA	200,000	Canneries, fruit, wire	Huntington Beach, CA	161,000	Oil, aircraft, missiles
Anchorage, AK	210,000	Seaport; international airport; oil	Huntsville, AL	144,000	Rocket and guided-missile center
Atlanta, GA	422,000	Textiles, tobacco, fruit	Indianapolis,* IN	695,000	Engines, machinery, drugs
Austin,* TX	323,000	Cattle, oil, gas, food			
Baltimore, MD	783,000	Seaport, rail center	Jackson,* MS	191,000	Rail center, machinery
Baton Rouge, LA	220,000	Oil, chemicals	Jacksonville, FL	541,000	Ships, canned goods
Beaumont, TX	118,000	Oil, suphur, livestock, lumbering	Jersey City, NJ	232,000	Seaport; chemicals, soap
			Kansas City, KS	167,000	Stockyards, grain
Berkeley, CA	118,000	Canneries, printing, chemicals, motors	Kansas City, MO	447,000	Stockyards, grain, food
			Knoxville, TN	186,000	TVA; chemicals, textiles
Birmingham, AL	281,000	Rail center; iron, steel	Lansing,* MI	127,000	Cars, trucks, engines
Boston,* MA	562,000	Seaport; finance; wool	Las Vegas, NV	450,000	Gambling resort
Bridgeport, CT	148,000	River port; aluminum	Lexington, KY	190,000	Tobacco, race horses
Buffalo, NY	390,000	Lake port; flour, steel	Lincoln,* NB	164,000	Appliances, meat, flour
Cambridge, MA	99,000	Colleges; cameras, candy	Little Rock,* AR	145,000	Furniture, cotton
Charlotte, NC	296,000	Textiles, chemicals, food	Long Beach, CA	337,000	Seaport; resort; fish
Chattanooga, TN	165,000	Machinery, textiles, clay	Los Angeles, CA	2,950,000	Seaport; planes, movies
Chicago, IL	2,969,000	Lake port; iron, steel, livestock, machinery	Louisville, KY	323,000	River port; tobacco
			Lubbock, TX	175,000	Cotton, oil, cattle
Cincinnati, OH	403,000	Rail center; tools, meat	Macon, GA	126,100	Fruit, lumber, textiles, paper
Cleveland, OH	573,000	Lake port; iron, steel			
Colorado Springs, CO	224,000	Resort; plastics, furniture	Madison,* WI	171,000	College; dairy products
Columbus, GA	171,000	Textiles, machinery, tile	Memphis, TN	645,000	River port; cotton
Columbus,* OH	562,000	College; aircraft, food	Miami, FL	347,000	Seaport; resort; fruit
Corpus Christi, TX	224,000	Seaport; oil, gas	Milwaukee, WI	633,000	Lake port; machinery
Dallas, TX	901,450	Banking; insurance; oil	Minneapolis, MN	360,000	Rail center; flour, grain
Dayton, OH	198,000	U.S. air center; tools	Mobile, AL	203,000	Seaport; paper, ships
Denver, CO	489,000	Stockyards; U.S. mint	Montgomery,* AL	158,000	Cotton, lumber
Des Moines,* IA	202,000	Insurance; printing, meat	Nashville,* TN	440,000	Textiles, printing
			Newark, NJ	324,000	Seaport; insurance; paint
Detroit, MI	1,192,000	Lake port; cars, steel	New Haven, CT	138,000	Clocks, hardware; college
El Paso, TX	425,000	Cattle, copper, cotton	New Orleans, LA	557,000	Seaport; sugar; banking
Erie, PA	128,000	Lake port; coal, paper	Newport News, VA	142,000	Seaport; ships, sea food
Evansville, IN	134,000	Rail center; cars, tools	New York, NY	7,895,000	Seaport; banking; clothes
Flint, MI	164,000	Cars, chemicals, textiles	Norfolk, VA	278,000	Naval base; ships
Fort Lauderdale, FL	152,000	Resort; construction, machinery	Oakland, CA	332,000	Seaport; fruit
			Oklahoma City,* OK	372,000	Oil, meat, grain
Fort Wayne, IN	189,000	Equipment, trucks, wire	Omaha, NB	358,000	Livestock, frozen foods
Fort Worth, TX	420,100	Stockyards, grain, planes	Paterson, NJ	152,000	Silk machines, chemicals
Fremont, CA	120,000	Canneries, furniture	Peoria, IL	126,000	Tractors, coal, machines
Fresno, CA	201,000	Raisins, canneries, wood	Philadelphia, PA	1,680,000	Seaport; ships, textiles, U.S mint
Garden Grove, CA	121,000	Fruits, nuts, vegetables			
Gary, IN	159,000	Steel, coke, gas	Phoenix,* AZ	781,000	Resort; cattle, fruit
Glendale, CA	136,000	Planes, cement, roofing	Pittsburgh, PA	424,000	Iron, steel, glass, coal
Grand Rapids, MI	185,000	Furniture, metal products	Portland, OR	382,000	River port; lumber, grain
			Providence,* RI	162,000	Textiles, jewelry, tools
Greensboro, NC	161,000	Colleges; textiles	Raleigh,* NC	165,000	Tobacco, textiles
Hampton, VA	127,000	Building materials, metal products, fishing	Richmond,* VA	220,000	Tobacco, printing, paper
			Riverside, CA	154,000	Vegetables, fruit, aircraft
Hartford,* CT	130,000	Insurance; engines	Rochester, NY	273,000	Cameras, clothing, film
Hialeah, FL	123,000	Resort; fruit	Rockford, IL	147,000	Furniture, tools
Hollywood, FL	120,000	Resort; canneries	Sacramento,* CA	264,000	Canneries, flour, food

* Indicates that the city is the capital of the state.

460

Largest Cities in the United States *(Continued)*

City	Population (1980 est.)	Interesting Facts and Products	City	Population (1980 est.)	Interesting Facts and Products
St. Louis, MO	449,000	River port; rail center; furs, livestock, shoes	Syracuse, NY	198,000	Electronics, machinery
St. Paul,* MN	268,000	Cars, machinery, meat	Tacoma, WA	154,000	Seaport; lumber, flour, ships
St. Petersburg, FL	238,000	Resort; fish, fruit	Tampa, FL	275,000	Resort; phosphates, fruit
Salt Lake City,* UT	176,000	Copper, flour, canneries	Toledo, OH	383,000	Lake port; glass, coal
San Antonio, TX	783,000	Oil, flour, livestock	Topeka,* KA	122,000	Rail center; flour, meat
San Diego, CA	870,000	Naval base; planes, fish	Torrance, CA	136,000	Oil, steel, machinery
San Francisco, CA	574,000	Seaport; banking	Tucson, AZ	301,000	Resort; electronics
San Jose, CA	627,000	Fruit, canneries	Tulsa, OK	334,000	Oil, gas, planes
Santa Ana, CA	200,000	Fruit, cattle, vegetables	Virginia Beach, VA	236,000	Resort; farmlands
Seattle, WA	492,000	Fish, flour, planes	Warren, MI	170,000	Automotive research
Shreveport, LA	189,000	Oil, gas, cotton	Washington, D.C.	635,000	United States capital
Spokane, WA	177,000	Lumber, canneries, flour	Wichita, KS	268,000	Livestock, grain, planes
Springfield, MA	169,000	Plastics, tools, guns	Winston-Salem, NC	145,000	World's greatest tobacco center
Springfield, MO	135,000	Dairy products, poultry, flour, meat	Worcester, MA	165,000	Textile machinery, tools
Stockton, CA	132,000	Canneries, fruit, vegetables	Yonkers, NY	189,000	Elevators, textiles
			Youngstown, OH	141,000	Iron, steel, rubber

Territories and Dependencies of the United States

Name	Area Sq. Mi.	Area Sq. Km	Population (1980 est.)	Date Acquired	Name	Area Sq. Mi.	Area Sq. Km	Population (1980 est.)	Date Acquired
American Samoa	76	197	33,500	1900	Howland, Jarvis Baker Is.	3	8	(uninhabited)	1935
Canton Enderbury Is.	27	70	(uninhabited)	1939	Midway, Wake Is.	5	13	4,000	1898
Guam	212	549	94,000	1898	Puerto Rico	3,435	8,897	3,196,000	1898
					Virgin Is.	133	344	120,000	1917

The Provinces of Canada

Province	Capital	Area Sq. Mi.	Area Sq. Km	Population (1980)	Interesting Facts and Products
Alberta	Edmonton	248,800	661,185	2,053,100	National parks; grain, oil, cattle, gas
British Columbia	Victoria	359,279	948,596	2,611,700	Resort; lumber, minerals, fish
Manitoba	Winnipeg	211,775	650,087	1,026,200	Rail center; wheat, cattle, minerals, furs
New Brunswick	Fredericton	27,835	73,437	704,800	Discovered by Cartier; fish, lumber
Newfoundland	St. John's	143,045	404,517	577,400	Discovered by Cabot; lumber, fish
Nova Scotia	Halifax	20,402	55,490	851,000	Iron, steel, fish, apples, coal
Ontario	Toronto	344,092	1,068,582	8,543,300	Resort; industry, mining, dairy products
Prince Edward Is.	Charlottetown	2,184	5,657	123,900	Discovered by Cartier; fish, nickel, furs
Quebec	Quebec	594,860	1,540,680	6,288,300	Oldest province; farming, forestry
Saskatchewan	Regina	220,182	570,271	965,300	Wheat, oil, cattle, uranium
Northwest Territories		1,253,438	3,379,683	43,100	Gold, uranium, nickel, furs
Yukon Territory	White Horse	205,346	536,324	21,800	Gold, silver, furs

CANADA: *Area,* 3,851,809 (Sq. Mi.) 9,976,139 (Sq. Km); *Population* (1980 est.), 23,850,000
Capital, Ottawa, Ontario; *Largest, City,* Montreal, Quebec
Iceland: *Area,* 39,768 (Sq. Mi.), 103,000 (Sq. Km.); *Population* (1980 est.), 230,000, *Capital,* Reykjavik
Greenland: *Area,* 840,000 (Sq. Mi.), 2,175,600 (Sq. Km); *Population* (1980 est.), 50,000, *Capital,* Godthaab

Central American and Caribbean Countries

Country	Capital	Area Sq. Mi.	Sq. Km	Population (1980 est.)	Inde-pendent	Products
Bahamas	Nassau	4,404	13,935	225,000	1973	Tomatoes, lumber, fruit
Barbados	Bridgetown	166	431	250,000	1966	Sugar, molasses, rum, cotton
Belize	Belmopan	8,867	22,965	160,000	(British)	Sugarcane, citrus fruits, corn
Costa Rica	San José	19,695	50,700	2,210,000	1821	Bananas, coffee, cacao
Cuba	Havana	44,208	114,524	9,950,000	1898	Tobacco, sugar, nickel
Domínica	Roseau	300	777	85,000	1967	Bananas, oil, cacao
Dominican Republic	Santo Domingo	19,332	48,734	5,450,000	1844	Sugar, coffee, cacao
El Salvador	San Salvador	12,792	21,393	4,750,000	1821	Coffee, cotton, corn
Guadeloupe	Basse-Terre	687	1,779	325,000	(French)	Sugarcane, bananas, rum
Guatemala	Guatemala City	50,647	108,889	7,250,000	1821	Coffee, bananas, cotton
Haiti	Port-au-Prince	10,700	27,750	5,000,000	1804	Sisal, coffee, sugar
Honduras	Tegucigalpa	59,160	112,088	3,680,000	1821	Bananas, coffee, lumber
Jamaica	Kingston	4,411	10,962	2,200,000	1962	Sugar, rum, bananas, coffee
Martinique	Fort-de-France	431	1,116	330,000	(French)	Sugar, bananas, rum
Netherlands Antilles	Willemstad	817	2,124	250,000	(Dutch)	Oil
Mexico	Mexico City	758,450	1,972,547	71,900,000	1810	Cotton, petroleum, coffee, lead
Nicaragua	Managua	57,145	130,000	2,565,000	1821	Coffee, cotton, corn
Panama	Panama City	29,127	75,650	1,935,000	1903	Bananas, abacá, cacao
Trinidad and Tobago	Port-of-Spain	1,980	5,128	1,115,000	1962	Asphalt, oil, bananas, cacao

South America

Country	Capital	Area Sq. Mi.	Sq. Km	Population (1980 est.)	Inde-pendent	Products
Argentina	Buenos Aires	1,073,700	2,776,889	27,070,000	1816	Meats, wheat, wool, hides
Bolivia	La Paz; Sucre	416,040	1,098,581	5,580,000	1825	Tin, tungsten, lead, zinc
Brazil	Brasília	3,288,045	8,511,965	122,000,000	1822	Coffee, cotton, cacao, iron
Chile	Santiago	286,396	756,945	11,150,000	1810	Copper, nitrates, wheat
Colombia	Bogotá	439,553	1,138,914	27,600,000	1810	Coffee, petroleum, cattle
Ecuador	Quito	104,506	283,561	8,350,000	1822	Bananas, cacao, coffee
French Guiana	Cayenne	91,000	34,750	65,000	(French)	Rice, timber, rum
Guyana	Georgetown	83,000	215,000	860,000	1966	Bauxite, sugar, timber, rice
Paraguay	Asunción	157,047	406,572	3,055,000	1811	Lumber, tannin, livestock
Peru	Lima	482,258	1,285,216	17,770,000	1821	Cotton, sugar, lead, copper
Suriname	Paramaribo	55,400	163,265	380,000	1975	Bauxite, rice, coffee, lumber
Uruguay	Montevideo	72,173	177,508	2,900,000	1828	Wool, meat, hides
Venezuela	Caracas	352,150	912,050	13,925,000	1811	Petroleum, iron ore, coffee

The Constitution

The United States Constitution is the supreme law of our land. This document provides a plan of government for our nation. The United States has grown and changed since the Constitution was written in 1787 and ratified in 1791. The Constitution has changed too. Amendments are laws added to the Constitution. The first ten amendments are called the Bill of Rights. These amendments guarantee certain freedoms to all American citizens.

On this page you can read the introduction, or preamble, to the Constitution. The Bill of Rights is found on the next page.

The Preamble

We, the people of the United States, in order to form a more perfect Union, establish justice, insure domestic tranquility, provide for the common defense, promote the general welfare, and secure the blessings of liberty to ourselves and our posterity, do ordain and establish this Constitution for the United States of America.

The Bill of Rights

Amendment 1
Congress shall make no law respecting an establishment of religion, or prohibiting the free exercise thereof; or abridging the freedom of speech, or of the press; or the right of the people peaceably to assemble, and to petition the government for a redress of grievances.

Amendment 2
A well-regulated militia being necessary to the security of a free State, the right of the people to keep and bear arms shall not be infringed.

Amendment 3
No soldier shall, in time of peace, be quartered in any house without the consent of the owner; nor in time of war but in a manner to be prescribed by law.

Amendment 4
The right of the people to be secure in their persons, houses, papers and effects, against unreasonable searches and seizures, shall not be violated, and no warrants shall issue but upon probable cause, supported by oath or affirmation, and particularly describing the place to be searched, and the persons or things to be seized.

Amendment 5
No person shall be held to answer for a capital or otherwise infamous crime, unless on a presentment or indictment of a grand jury, except in cases arising in the land or naval forces, or in the militia, when in actual service in time of war or public danger; nor shall any person be subject for the same offense to be twice put in jeopardy of life or limb; nor shall be compelled in any criminal case to be a witness against himself, nor be deprived of life, liberty, or property, without due process of law; nor shall private property be taken for public use, without just compensation.

Amendment 6
In all criminal prosecutions the accused shall enjoy the right to a speedy and public trial, by an impartial jury of the State and district wherein the crime shall have been committed, which district shall have been previously ascertained by law, and to be informed of the nature and cause of the accusation; to be confronted with the witnesses against him; to have compulsory process for obtaining witnesses in his favor, and to have the assistance of counsel for his defense.

Amendment 7
In suits at common law, where the value in controversy shall exceed twenty dollars, the right of trial by jury shall be preserved, and no fact tried by a jury shall be otherwise reexamined in any court of the United States than according to the rules of the common law.

Amendment 8
Excessive bail shall not be required, nor excessive fines imposed, nor cruel and unusual punishments inflicted.

Amendment 9
The enumeration in the Constitution of certain rights shall not be construed to deny or disparage others retained by the people.

Amendment 10
The powers not delegated to the United States by the Constitution, nor prohibited by it to the States, are reserved to the States respectively, or to the people.

Word List

a bad	i it	oo wood	u cup	ə *stands for*	
ā cake	ī ice	o͞o food	ur turn	a *as in* ago	
ä father	j joke	oi oil	yo͞o music	e *as in* taken	
b bat	k kit	ou out	v very	i *as in* pencil	
ch chin	l lid	p pail	w wet	o *as in* lemon	
d dog	m man	r ride	wh white	u *as in* helpful	
e pet	n not	s sit	y yes		
ē me	ng sing	sh ship	z zoo		
f five	o hot	t tall	zh treasure		
g game	ō open	th thin			
h hit	ô off	th that			

A

abolitionist (ab'ə lish'ə nist): a person who believed that all slaves should be freed

act (akt): a law

altitude (al'tə to͞od'): the height of land above sea level

amendment (ə mend'mənt): a law that is added to the Constitution

anthracite (an'thrə sīt'): hard coal

aqueduct (ak'wə duct') a pipe or channel that carries water over long distances

asbestos (as bes'təs): a mineral that will not burn

assembly (ə sem'blē): a group of leaders who made laws for a colony

assembly line (ə sem'blē līn): a method of manufacturing in which each worker is responsible for adding a particular part to the product as it moves by on a belt

B

balsam (bôl'səm): the sap of a tree used in making medicine and perfume

basin (bā'sin): low region surrounded by higher lands

bauxite (bôk'sīt): the ore from which aluminum is made

bituminous (bi to͞o'mə nəs): soft coal

blockade (blo kād'): the closing of an area to prevent people or supplies from going into or out of it

boll (bōl): small seed pod of the cotton plant

boycott (boi'kot): to refuse to buy, sell, or use any goods as a protest

bran (bran): the darker, outer coat of a wheat seed

C

Cabinet (kab'ə nit): a group of persons, chosen by the President, to help with the duties of the executive branch

canal (kə nal'): a waterway built to connect two bodies of water

cannery (kan'ər ē): a factory where food is prepared and canned

capital (kap'it əl): the city where the laws for a nation or state are made

capitol (kap'it əl): the building in which lawmakers of a state or country meet

carpetbagger (kär'pit bag'ər): a Northerner who moved to the South after the Civil War

census (sen'səs): an official count of the people in a country

charter (chär'tər): a paper granting certain rights, such as permission to make settlements

citrus (sit'rəs) **fruit**: type of fruit such as oranges, lemons, and grapefruit

civil (siv'əl) **rights**: the rights of a citizen such as the right to vote

climate (klī'mit): the kind of weather a place has

coke (kōk): coal from which gas has been removed

colony (kol'ə nē): a group of settlers living in an area apart from, but under the control of, the country from which they came

combine (kom'bīn): a machine that cuts grain and separates kernel from straw

commonwealth (kom'ən welth'): a group of people making up a nation or state

communism (kom'yə niz'əm): a system of government under which all property and goods are controlled by the government

compromise (kom'prə mīz'): the settlement of a disagreement by having each side give up some part of its claims

Confederacy (kən fed'ər ə sē): the nation formed by the states that seceded from the Union

confederation (kən fed'ə rā'shən): a plan for union of states or provinces

conservation (kon'sər vā'shən): the wise use of natural resources

constitution (kon'stə tōō'shən): a group of written laws governing a nation or a state

Continental (kon'tə nent'əl) **Divide:** a dividing ridge in the Rockies, which separates the rivers flowing east from the rivers flowing west

contour (kon'toor) **line:** a line on a map connecting points of equal elevation

convention (kən ven'shən): a meeting held for a common purpose

conveyor (kən vā'ər): a moving belt which carries loads from one place to another

cotton belt: area in the South where cotton grows well

Creole (krē'ōl): a Spanish or French person born in the West Indies or Latin America

crop rotation (krop rō tā'shən): a way of building up the soil by planting different crops on the same land every 2 or 3 years

cultivator (kul'tə vā'tər): a machine used to loosen the soil and uproot weeds

current (kur'ənt): a stream of water flowing through the ocean

D

dam (dam): a wall or bank built across a river to stop the flow of water

dehydration (dē'hī drā'shən): the removal, or taking out, of water by a special process

delta (del'tə): land built up by mud and sand brought down by a slow river

democracy (di mok'rə sē): government by the people

density (den'sə tē): thickness

depression (di presh'ən): a time when there is little business and much unemployment

derrick (der'ik): the framework built to support the machinery needed to drill an oil well

dictator (dik'tā'tər): a ruler who has absolute power

disk harrow (disk har'ō): a machine with sharp, curved steel blades, used to break up lumps of earth

drill (dril): a tool used to bore holes into the earth

dry farming: a way of conserving moisture in dry areas by growing only one crop every 2 years on the same plot of ground

E

earthquake (urth'kwāk'): a movement of a part of the earth's surface caused by a shift of rock or other disturbance

ecology (ē kol'ə jē): the study of how living things relate to their natural surroundings

ejido (ə hē'dō): land turned over to a farming village by the government of Mexico

elect (i lekt'): to vote for a person for an office

electronics (i lek tron'iks): a special branch of electricity used in industry

elevation (el ə vā'shən): height above the earth's surface or above sea level

estuary (es'chōō er'ē): an arm of the ocean which extends into the land

expedition (eks'pə dish'ən): an exploring party

export (eks'pôrt): a good or product that is shipped out of a country

extinct (eks tingkt'): no longer in existence

F

fault (fôlt): a break in a rock mass

feed lot: a pen where cattle are fed special feed to fatten them for market

fleece (flēs): the thick wool of a sheep

flood (flud) **plain:** lowland that is often covered by water when rivers overflow their banks

flowing (flō'ing) **well:** an oil well which produces oil in a steady stream without being pumped

fortyniner (fôr'tē nī'nər): a person who went to California to seek gold

free enterprise (frē′ en′tər prīz′): an economic system which allows citizens to own property and businesses

free state: a state that did not permit slaves to be owned

frontier (frun tēr′): the region of a country lying along the border of an unsettled region

G

gap (gap): a narrow valley in mountains

gaucho (gou′chō): a cowhand of the pampas

geyser (gī′zər): a spring which throws hot water and steam high into the air

glacier (glā′shər): a great sheet of ice

great circle route (rōōt): most direct and shortest route between two places on the globe

grid (grid): a crisscross pattern on a map made by imaginary lines

growing season (sē′zən): the time of year when crops can be grown outdoors

gusher (gush′ər): an oil well from which the oil shoots high into the air

H

hacienda (hä′sē en′də): a large plantation

helium (hē′lē əm): a very light gas which does not burn or explode

Hispano (his pan′ō): a Spanish-speaking person

hogan (hō′gän): a dome-shaped Indian house built of poles, tree bark, and mud

House of Representatives (rep′ri zen′tə tivz): the part of Congress that has the most members

hurricane (hur′ə kān′): a tropical storm with strong winds

I

immigrant (im′ə grənt): person who moves from one land to another to make a home

import (im′pôrt): a good or product brought in from other countries

inaugurate (in ô′gyə rāt′): to put into office

indentured (in den′chərd) **servant:** a person who works a certain length of time for the person who has paid the cost of his or her passage to America

independence (in′di pen′dəns): freedom from the control of another country

indigo (in′di gō′): a plant from which a blue dye is made

industry (in′dəs trē): a word that refers to manufacturing and other businesses

inlet (in′let′): a narrow strip of water which reaches far inland

interior (in tēr′ē ər): an area which lies inland, away from the border and the coast

international (in′tər nash′ən əl): belonging to, or having to do with, two or more nations

irrigation (ir′ə gā′shən): bringing water to dry land through pipes or sprinklers

L

latex (lā′teks): the sap of the tree used to make rubber

Latin (lat′in) **America:** land south of the United States, where Spanish, French, or Portuguese is spoken

latitude (lat′ə tōod): the distance north or south of the equator

lava (lä′və): hot melted rock

legend (lej′ənd): an explanation of the symbols on a chart or map

legislature (lej′is lā′chər): a group of persons chosen to make laws

legume (leg′yōom): a vegetable, such as peas or beans, that grows in pods

levee (lev′ē): a bank of earth built along a river to keep it from overflowing its banks and flooding the land

lignite (lig′nīt): brown coal

linseed (lin′sēd′) **oil:** a product made from crushed flaxseed

llano (lä′nō): a grassy plain in South America

---

a bad, ā cake, ä father; e pet, ē me; i it, ī ice; o hot, ō open, ô off; oo wood; ōō food, oi oil, ou out; u cup, ur turn, yōō music; ə ago, taken, pencil, lemon, helpful

---

locomotive (lō′kə mō′tiv): an engine which can move on its own power

longitude (lon′jə tōōd′): distance on the earth's surface, measured in degrees east and west of the prime meridian

M

megalopolis (meg′ə lop′ə lis): a large urban area made up of a number of nearby cities

merchant marine (mur′chənt mə rēn′): the ships which carry on the trade of a nation

mestizo (mes tē′zō): a person of mixed ancestry, usually Spanish or Portuguese and Indian

migrant (mī′grənt) **worker:** a seasonal farm worker

missile (mis′əl): weapon designed to be thrown or fired toward a target

mission (mish′ən): a church settlement built by Spaniards in the Americas

mohair (mō′her′): cloth made from goat hair

money (mun′ē) **crop:** a product that is grown to be sold

mouth (mouth): the end of a river

N

natural resource (nach′ər əl rē′sôrs): material found in nature that is useful or necessary for human life

naval (nā′vəl) **stores:** turpentine, tar, and resin made from the gum of the pine tree

navigator (nav′i gā tər): a person who guides a ship

nuclear energy (nōō′klē ər en′ər jē): energy produced by splitting atoms

O

oil shale (shāl): a type of rock that may be a source of energy

open-pit mining: mining done on the surface of the earth

P

pampa (pam′pə): a treeless plain in South America

parallel of latitude (par′ə lel′ uv lat′ə tōōd): imaginary line on a map or globe measuring distance in degrees north or south of the equator

parliament (pär′lə mənt): an assembly that makes the laws of a country

pasteurize (pas′chə rīz): to kill germs in milk by means of heat

peninsula (pə nin′sə lə): a body of land surrounded almost entirely by water

phosphate (fos′fāt): a mineral needed for growth by plants and animals

piedmont (pēd′mont): an upland region between a plain and mountains

pitchblende (pich′blend′): mineral from which uranium is obtained

plain (plān): an area of level or nearly level land

plantation (plan tā′shən): a large farm on which one crop is raised

plateau (pla tō′): an area of flat land raised above the surrounding land

polar region (pō′lər rē′jən): a place in the high latitudes

pollute (pə lōōt′): to make unclean

population (pop′yə lā′shun): the total number of people living in an area

prairie (prer′ē): a grassy plain

prime meridian (prīm mə rid′ē ən): the meridian from which longitude east and west is measured

processing (pros′es ing): preparing food for marketing

profile (prō′fīl): a side view

projection (prə jek′shən): a way of showing the round earth on a flat surface

province (prov′ins): a division of Canada somewhat like a state in our country

pueblo (pweb′lō): an Indian village like apartment houses built of stone or clay

Q

quarry (kwôr′ē): an open pit from which stone is cut

R

ratify (rat′ə fī′): to approve officially

raw (rô) **sugar:** the brown crystals that form when the juice of sugarcane is boiled and allowed to cool

rayon (rā′on): a cloth that looks and feels like silk

reaper (rē′pər): a machine for cutting grain

refinery (ri fī′nər ē): a building in which raw materials are changed into finished products

relief (ri lēf′): shading, color, or lines used on a map to show the land's surfaces

representative (rep′ri zen′tə tiv): a person who acts for a group

republic (ri pub′lik): a nation in which the people govern through their chosen representatives

reservation (rez′ər vā′shən): an area set aside by the government for the use of American Indians

reservoir (rez′ər vwär′): a place like a lake, formed behind a dam, where water is stored

ridge (rij): a long and narrow chain of hills or mountains

S

secede (si sēd′): to withdraw from an organization

seed drill: a machine used to plant wheat or other small grains

segregate (seg′rə gāt′): to separate

selva (sel′və): a rainy, tropical forest of the Amazon

Senate (sen′it): the part of Congress made up of two members from each state

shaft (shaft) **mining**: a way of mining coal through a deep hole

sharecropper (sher′krop′ər): a person who works on another's farm and shares crops with the landowner

shearing (shēr′ing): cutting off the wool of sheep

site (sīt): the position or location of a town or building

slag (slag): what is left after iron is smelted

slave state: a state that allowed slaves to be used

smelt (smelt): to separate metal from ore by heating the ore

sod (sod): the part of the soil containing grass and its roots

soil erosion (i rō′zhen): the washing away of soil by heavy rains or floods

sound (sound): a body of water like a large bay, extending into the land

source (sôrs): the beginning of a river

soybean (soi′bēn): a kind of legume first brought to this country from China

spawning (spôn′ing) **place**: a fresh-water nesting place where salmon lay their eggs

spinning jenny (jen′ē): an early machine which could spin many threads at a time

sterilize (ster′ə līz): to kill germs

strip mining: a way of mining coal when it is close to the earth's surface

subtropical (sub trop′i kəl) **land**: land that lies near the tropics

suburb (sub′urb): a community close to, or on the outer edge of, a city

suffrage (suf′rij): the right to vote

sulfur (sul′fər): a yellow mineral

Supreme Court (sə prēm′ kôrt): the highest court in the United States

surplus (sur′plus′) **product**: that which is left when needs are satisfied

surrender (sə ren′dər): to give up control of

T

taconite (tak′ə nīt): a hard rock containing iron

tariff (tar′if): a tax on goods brought into a country

tax (taks): money that must be paid by people to support the government

technology (tek nol′ə jē): the use of knowledge and skills to build useful machines

temperate region (tem′pər it rē′jən): a place in the middle latitudes

tenant (ten′ənt) **farmer**: a person who pays rent for farmland either with crops or money

territory (ter′ə tôr′ē): a settled area, not yet a state, governed by Congress

textile (teks′tīl): woven cloth

threshing (thresh′ing) **machine**: a machine that separates kernels of grain from stalks

a bad, ā cake, ä father; e pet, ē me; i it, ī ice; o hot, ō open, ô off; oo wood; o̅o̅ food; oi oil, ou out; u cup, ur turn, yo̅o̅ music; ə ago, taken, pencil, lemon, helpful

tidewater region (tīd'wô'tər rē'jən): a section of the coastal plain where rivers rise and fall with the ocean tide

toll (tōl): a small sum of money paid for use of a road

tourist (toor'ist): a person who travels for pleasure

trade (trād) **wind:** a steady wind that blows toward the equator

transcontinental (trans'kon tə nent'əl): across the continent

treaty (trē'tē): an agreement between groups of people or nations

tributary (trib'yə ter'ē): a river that flows into a larger river

tropic (trop'ik): a place in the low latitudes

tundra (tun'drə): a large treeless plain

tung (tung) **oil:** oil made from the nuts of a tree brought from China

tungsten (tung'stin): a white metal used to harden steel

U

uranium (yoo rā'nē əm): a radioactive element

V

vegetation (vej'ə tā'shən): the plant life in a region

Viking (vī'king): oné of the sea rovers, often from Norway, who were among the first Europeans to find North America

volcano (vol kā'nō): an opening in the earth's surface through which steam, ashes, and lava flow

vulcanize (vul'kə nīz'): to treat rubber with sulfur so that it will not melt or become stiff

a bad, ā cake, ä father; e pet, ē me; i it, ī ice; o hot, ō open, ô off; oo wood; o͞o food, oi oil, ou out; u cup, ur turn, yo͞o music; ə ago, taken, pencil, lemon, helpful

Index

For pronunciations see guide on page 465.

472

Acknowledgments

This book was prepared and produced by Edit, Inc., Chicago.

Cover:
Milt and Joan Mann, back right, front left
Van Cleve Photography: William Means, back left; Frank H. Wood, front right

Maps:
Bielat Studios, Chris Ellithorpe, Robert Forget, Yvette Heyden, Liska and Associates, Cathy Meindl, Jeff Mellander, Jay Songero, Lowell Stumpf, George Suyeoka, John Walter & Associates
Map skills developed and produced by Educational Challenges, Inc., Alexandria, Va.

Illustrations:
Dev Appleyard, Yoshi Miyake, Tak Murakami

Photographs:
Alaska Pictorial Service: Steve McCutcheon, 368 bottom right
The American Museum of Natural History: 26, 256
Atoz/Van Cleve: Betty Crowell, 276
The Bettmann Archive Inc.: 40, 55, 63, 100, 107, 111, 112, 118, 161, 232, 233, 314, 345, 349
Black Star Publishing Co., Inc.: Ernest R. Manewal, 333; Fred Ward, 419
Brown Bros.: 135, 197, 277, 280,
California State Library, Sacramento: 341
Charleston Library Society: 68
Cities Service: 293 top
Colonial Williamsburg Foundation: 70 top and center
J. Dan Coop: 284 bottom
Corcoran Gallery: 115
Culver Pictures Inc.: 46, 66, 109 right, 113, 120, 127, 134, 143 top, 163, 198, 352
A. Devaney, Inc.: 27 left, 77, 89, 101; Dick Hanley, 148 top
Editorial Photocolor Archives: 407
Field Museum of Natural History, Chicago: Charles Knight, 23
Freeport Sulphur: 293 bottom
Georgia Historical Society: 71
Thomas Gilcrease Institute, Tulsa: 65
The Granger Collection: 315 ; 463
The Image Bank: William A. Allard, 289;

Arthur d'Arazien, 287; Ernest Braun, 359; Gerald Brimacombe, 259; Bill Carter, 264; Peter Frey, 434; Larry Dale Gordon, 388; Geoffrey Gove, 181 top left, 398; Eddie Hironaka, 323 top left, 360; Ted Horowitz, 361 left; Don Klumpp, 402; Harvey Lloyd, 51, 70 bottom, 323 top right; Richard and Mary Magruder, 385, 399 bottom; Nick Nicholson, 383; Robert Phillips, 263, 384; Jeff Smith, 166; Alvis Upitis, 148 bottom, 155; Luis Villota, 399 top right, 408
International Harvester: 237
Iowa State University Photo Service: 309,
Jerry Jacka: 310
Jeroboam Inc.: Stewart, 145
Jones and Laughlin: 179
Steve McCutcheon: 368 top and bottom left
Milt and Joan Mann: 218 top, 219 bottom, 226, 252, 260, 262, 265, 266, 273, 279 right, 297 bottom, 299, 324, 369, 370, 372 bottom left and bottom right, 373, 412, 427
Francis G. Mayer: 105
The Metropolitan Museum of Art, Gift of J. Pierpont Morgan, 1900: 33
Paintings of George Washington and Martha Washington by Gilbert Stuart. Jointly owned by the MFA, Boston and the National Portrait Gallery, Washington, D.C. 1980.1 and 1980.2. Courtesy, Museum of Fine Arts, Boston: 102
NASA: 296
New York Public Library: 38; The I. N. Phelps Stokes Collection, 240
The Oakland Museum History Department: 344 (Run of 1893, Opening of the Cherokee Strip) photographer E. R. Mosteller, courtesy Oklahoma Historical Society: 283
Oregon Department of Transportation, Salem: 347
Organization of American States: 436
J. Barry O'Rourke: 11
C. Ostman: 430 top
Painting by George W. Storm, Pennsylvania Historical and Museum Commission: 159
PFI: C. E. Rotkin, 175, 205
Photo Researchers, Inc.: Jules Bucher, 430 bottom left; Victor Englebert, 209; Jack Fields, 387; Tom Hollyman, 382 bottom; Russ Kinne, 257; Southern Living, 284 top

Photri: 75, 109 left, 125, 180, 181 top right, 182, 361 right and bottom, 399 top left, 410 center, 415, 430 bottom right; E. C. Johnson, 171; Lani, 424
Pilgrim Society: 59, 60 top
Plimoth Plantation: 60 bottom
The Rhode Island Historical Society: 61
Shostal Associates: 79; Arthur d'Arazien, 210; J. McGibbeny, 311; N. Manewal, 428 right; J. Peacock, 365
Bob and Ira Spring, 358
Tom Stack & Associates; 325 top; Stewart M. Green, 316; R. Wick, 247
Standard Oil: 414
Stock, Boston, Inc.: 170; Fredrik D. Bodin, 173; Daniel Brody, 132, 143 bottom; Gabor Demjen, 396; Owen Franken, 393, 423, 432; Raoul Hackel, 165; Ellis Herwig, 379, 413; Peter Menzel, 382 top, 410 bottom; J. Rawle, 212; John Running, 20, 189, 305; Peter Southwick, 60 center right; Cary S. Wolinsky, 181 bottom, 410 top
Taurus Photos: 297 top; K. Collidge, 323 bottom left; Vance Henry, 30; Eric Kroll, 216; Vito Palmisano, 128; L. L. T. Rhodes, 279 left; Katharine S. Thomas, 308; Ronald R. Thomas, 323 center right; R. Thompson, 323 bottom right, 325 bottom; Reggie Tucker, 318; Fred West, 243
United Nations: M. Grant, 136
United Press Int.: 139, 142, 295, 381
U.S. Capitol Historical Society: National Geographic Society, 96
United States House of Representatives: 282
United States Department of the Interior: 131
The Department of the Treasury: 162
R. Weiss, 312
Woodfin Camp & Associates: Marc and Evelynne Bernheim, 28; Dan Budnik, 147; Keith Garrett, 190; Shelly Grossman, 94; George Hall, 183, 334, 372 top; David Alan Harvey, 194; George Herban, 27 right, 339; Sylvia Johnson, 354; Loren McIntyre, 428 left; Martin Rogers, 155; Sepp Seitz, 167; Al Stephenson, 218 bottom, 219 top; William Strode, 60 center left; William S. Weems, 213; Roger Werth, 335
Yale University Art Gallery: 78, 83
Photo research by Marilyn Gartman